The publisher and the University of California Press Foundation gratefully acknowledge the generous support of the Fletcher Jones Foundation Imprint in Humanities.

Sisters in the Mirror

Sisters in the Mirror

A HISTORY OF MUSLIM WOMEN
AND THE GLOBAL POLITICS OF FEMINISM

Elora Shehabuddin

UNIVERSITY OF CALIFORNIA PRESS

University of California Press
Oakland, California

© 2021 by Elora Shehabuddin

Library of Congress Cataloging-in-Publication Data

Names: Shehabuddin, Elora, author.
Title: Sisters in the mirror : a history of Muslim women and the global politics
    of feminism / Elora Shehabuddin.
Identifiers: LCCN 2021003487 (print) | LCCN 2021003488 (ebook) |
    ISBN 9780520342514 (cloth) | ISBN 9780520974647 (epub)
Subjects: LCSH: Feminism—India—Bengal. | Muslim women—India—
    Bengal—History. | Muslim women—Political activity. | Globalization—
    Religious aspects—Islam.
Classification: LCC HQ1744.B4 S54 2021 (print) | LCC HQ1744.B4
    (ebook) | DDC 305.48/69705414—dc23
LC record available at https://lccn.loc.gov/2021003487
LC ebook record available at https://lccn.loc.gov/2021003488

Manufactured in the United States of America

30   29   28   27   26   25   24   23   22   21
10   9   8   7   6   5   4   3   2   1

For Sinan and Nur

CONTENTS

ACKNOWLEDGMENTS

I'm finishing this book several months into the COVID-19 pandemic, but, if relatively isolated and cloistered now, I've not been so over the many years I've spent on this project. I was able to research and write this book enveloped in much love, kindness, and support from many quarters.

Thank you goes to the Center for the Study of Women, Gender, and Sexuality at Rice University for providing an exciting and interdisciplinary intellectual environment: center directors Rosemary Hennessy, Susan Lurie, and Helena Michie for their steadfast support and guidance; and colleagues Elias Bongmba, Krista Comer, Jacqueline Couti, Julie Fette, Emily Houlik-Ritchey, Cymene Howe, Betty Joseph, Jeff Kripal, Moramay López Alonso, Brian Riedel, Diana Strassmann, Kamala Visweswaran, Kerry Ward, Lora Wildenthal, and Fay Yarborough for inspiration and much-needed community. Moramay and Kerry deserve special mention for companionship, good cheer, and socially distanced "study breaks" on campus during my final months of revisions. I owe special thanks to Angela Wren Wall, center coordinator, for anticipating and addressing every research and teaching need since I first arrived at Rice. My students at Rice have been a joy to teach, regularly prompting me to ask new questions of familiar materials while their varied interests have pushed me to explore new areas of research. I remain ever grateful to Laura Kang, Nancy Naples, and Robyn Wiegman for their collegiality in my first women's studies home, at the University of California, Irvine; and to Amrita Basu and Juliet Schor for setting me on this path even earlier.

The annual writing retreats sponsored by the Office of Faculty Development and the Program in Writing and Communication at Rice University helped me to start writing regularly and in a more focused way. I owe sincere thanks to Julia Amborski, Louma Ghandour, Tracy Volz, and Jennifer Wilson for all their work in organizing the retreats and writing rooms and to my fellow writers for their example and company. My WED and PMM Facebook writing groups have also been invaluable and helped me stay on track when I might have faltered. I am indebted to Nahid Shabnam Haimonty for valuable research assistance when I first started to explore the possibilities of this project. Thanks go to the fantastic staff at Fondren Library at Rice University, especially Anna Shparberg and Scott Vieira; the Wissenschaftkolleg Library in Berlin; and the Schlesinger Library at the Radcliffe Institute for helping me track down elusive books, journals, and documents.

For their generous support while I worked on this book, I am deeply grateful to Nicholas Shumway and Kathleen Canning, Rice University deans of humanities, as well as the National Endowment for Humanities. Many thanks to the Carnegie Corporation and the US Institute for Peace for their support for a very early iteration of this project. I had to change my research plans—quite drastically—in response to a war in Lebanon, a coup in Bangladesh, and the arrival of our second child, and I am grateful to both donors for their patience while I recovered my bearings.

I want to acknowledge the intellectual camaraderie I have cherished over the years through my work at the *Encyclopedia of Women and Islamic Cultures* and the Women's Studies in Religion Program at the Harvard Divinity School. Thank you, Suad Joseph, Sarah Gualtieri, Therese Saliba, and Zeina Zaatari of my EWIC family; and Ann Braude, Kecia Ali, Carol Duncan, Susannah Heschel, Sue Houchins, Laurel Thatcher Ulrich, and Tracy Wall at WSRP. Special thanks to Tracy Samperio and Gemini Wahhaj, whose editorial assistance with EWIC allowed me to carve out time to work on this book manuscript.

For long conversations and insightful comments, for conference panels, for invitations to their universities, and for their generosity with books, photographs, and sage counsel, all of which helped to shape this book, I am grateful to Leila Ahmed, Rahnuma Ahmed, Shakera Ahmed, the late Sufia Ibrahim Ahmed, Syed Refaat Ahmed, Muhammad Ahmedullah, Lila Abu-Lughod, Kamran Asdar Ali, Sonia Amin, Firdous Azim, Ayesha Banu, Maleka Begum, Tayeba Begum Lipi, Sharon Block (for introducing me to Scrivener at just the right time), Neilesh Bose, Ann Bragdon, Carl Caldwell, Elora Chowdhury, Iqbal Bahar Chowdhury, Nusrat Chowdhury, Runa Das, Sharin Elkholy, Farah Ghuznavi, Inderpal Grewal, Meghna

Guhathakurta, Shahana Hanif, Anne Hardgrove, Perween Hasan, Fayeza Hasanat, Frances Hasso, Hameeda Hossain, Naomi Hossain, Sara Hossain, Madeline Hsu, Chaumtoli Huq, Samia Huq, Shireen Huq, Iftekhar Iqbal, Rounaq Jahan, Roushan Jahan, Suad Joseph, Sultana Kamal (especially for carrying a copy of the memoirs of her mother, Sufia Kamal, from Dhaka to Berlin for me), Irshad Kamal Khan, Kishwar Kamal Khan, Naveeda Khan, Ayesha Khurshid, David Ludden, Jean Said Makdisi, Thahitun Mariam, Florence McCarthy, Gail Minault, Durba Mitra, Naeem Mohaiemen, Ali Riaz, Nayma Qayum, Uzma Quraishi, Asifa Quraishi-Landes, Seuty Sabur, Yasmin Saikia, the late Satadru Sen, Sharmila Sen, Sima Shakhsari, Nasreen Shams, Nermeen Shams, Daniel Sherman, Dina M. Siddiqi, Esha Sraboni, Robert C. Terry Jr., Stefano Tijerina, Saadia Toor, Aili Mari Tripp, Judith Tucker, Layli Uddin, and Willem van Schendel.

I am especially grateful to Samia Khatun, Gandharv Roy, Abdel Razzaq Takriti, Gemini Wahhaj, and my sisters Farhana, Sarah, and Sharmeen Shehabuddin for reading sections of the manuscript at my characteristically short notice and for their thoughtful comments.

My agent, Jeff Gerecke, was immensely enthusiastic and incredibly patient from the start—thank you for bearing with me. I am indebted to the anonymous reviewers of Oxford University Press and the University of California Press for their astute readings and fresh perspectives on the book. A big thank you goes to Rachel Fudge for her impeccable editing and for helping me cut this book down to size just when I was about to give up.

At the University of California Press, I am grateful to my editor Niels Hooper for his support and vision for this book; to Robin Manley and Madison Wetzell for their attention to detail; and to Francisco Reinking and David Peattie (of BookMatters) for overseeing the final production. Susan Silver has been a marvelous copyeditor, and the book is much better for her interventions—thank you!

Thanks go to my extended Houston family for their encouragement over the years as well as much-needed fun and sustenance: Hosam Abou-Ela, Deedee Baba, Lara Bashour, Randa Chadraoui, Dania Dandashli, Lilian Dindo, Rania El Khatib, Sarah Ellenzweig, Hana Elsahly, Rola Elserag, Fady Joudah, Mehnaaz Momen, Nidal Moukaddam, Cihan Yuksel Muslu, Caroline Quenemoen, Nahida Saker, Fidaa Shaib, Yasser Shaib, Abdel Razzaq Takriti, and Gemini Wahhaj. Thanks go to Tatiana Blanco and Nuvia Sorto in Houston, Manna Kendaya in Beirut, and Majeda Begum, Assya Khatun, Sabu Rahman, and Sabina Yasmine in Dhaka for taking meticulous care of our families and our homes, allowing us more time to devote to both work and leisure.

To my sisters Farhana, Sarah, and Sharmeen—thank you for your unconditional love and support. To my parents, K. M. and Khaleda Shehabuddin, I can only say, "Thank you for everything." This book bears the imprint of their beloved histories, epics, literatures, and music with which they surrounded us as we were growing up. I wish my father were here to hold and read this book. He asked about it every time we spoke on the phone in what would turn out to be his final months, and, while I know he has remained by my side, I've sorely missed our conversations these past six years. To my family in Beirut, Chittagong, Dhaka, Geneva, Los Angeles, and Ottawa, thank you for your love, generosity, hospitality, and stories.

Ussama Makdisi has been traveling and laughing with me for over a quarter of a century now. He read every word of this manuscript and offered valuable feedback; for that and much else, I am grateful. It is to our children, Sinan and Nur, who embody aspects of Bangladesh, Lebanon, Palestine, the United States, and so much more and are growing into beautiful, thoughtful, adventurous, and politically engaged young people, that I dedicate this book.

Parts of chapters 6, 7, and 8 appear, respectively, in "Rokeya in the World: Feminism and Islam in South Asia Today," in *Arab Feminisms: Gender and Equality in the Middle East,* edited by Jean Said Makdisi, Noha Bayumi, and Rafif Rida Sidawi, 368–76 (London: Tauris, 2014); "Feminism and Nationalism in Cold War Pakistan," *Südasien-Chronik* [South Asia chronicle], April 2014, 49–68; and "Gender and the Figure of the 'Moderate Muslim': Feminism in the 21st Century," in *The Question of Gender: Engagements with Joan W. Scott's Critical Feminism,* edited by Judith Butler and Elizabeth Weed, 102–42 (Bloomington: Indiana University Press, 2011). The Introduction uses the lyrics of a song, "Sisters Are Doing It for Themselves," words and music by Annie Lennox and David Stewart (copyright © 1985 by Universal Music Publishing International MGB Ltd., all rights administered by Universal Music—MGB Songs International; copyright secured; all rights reserved; reprinted by permission of Hal Leonard LLC).

Introduction

IN THE FALL OF 1985, the duet "Sisters Are Doing It for Themselves" hit the charts on both sides of the Atlantic with its celebration of, as legendary singers Aretha Franklin and Annie Lennox put it, "the conscious liberation of the female state." The accompanying video was remarkable in its inclusion of women of varied racial, ethnic, and national backgrounds. Through a montage of sexist images interspersed with women's accomplishments, the video reminded viewers that the struggle for women's liberation had started some time ago—and that it was far from over even as the twentieth century was drawing to a close.[1] The refrain of this feminist anthem encapsulated its boldness:

> Sisters are doing it for themselves
> Standing on their own two feet
> And ringing on their own bells
> Sisters are doing it for themselves

The single and video were released at a time marked by many accomplishments in women's rights around the world. The UN Decade for Women, which drew to a close that year, was instrumental in persuading governments to pay serious attention to women's issues in their policy making. However, as the clashes at the UN conferences for women revealed, women from countries in Asia, Africa, and Latin America and women of color in Europe and North America disagreed vehemently with the agendas and priorities of White Western women, including the latter's embrace of the notion of global sisterhood. Among the points of contention were the colonial and racist legacies and ongoing exploitative relations between and within countries and, indeed, between women. *Sisters in the Mirror* recounts the protracted history of these tensions as well as of instances of empathy, collaboration, and even solidarity—with attention to women's rights advocates in the West and the Muslim world.

Feminists around the world tell two conflicting stories about the global history and politics of feminism. One is that it originated among White women in the West, who exported it to the rest of the world, where it took on local forms. Versions of this story dominate in the West and are also repeated by opponents of feminism elsewhere who use this narrative to tarnish all feminist efforts as Western imperialist impositions. Parallel stories circulate about racial equality, human rights, LGBTQ+ rights, and so on. The other story, often told by feminists in Asia, Africa, and Latin America, is that each society has its own history of indigenous and authentic feminism; this story is strategically deployed against critics who see feminism as a Western import.

We can choose, however, to narrate a third, more historically accurate story—if we understand feminism to encompass both ideas about gender equality and social movements to enact change based on these ideas and if we keep in mind the history of unequal power relations binding different parts of the world. This third story recognizes that people around the world have long reflected on the unequal roles and opportunities of women and men in their societies. However, their ability to speak out about these injustices, put their ideas in writing, and mobilize in movements for change has necessarily been shaped by social, economic, and political factors, including histories and legacies of imperialism that have powerfully, and often painfully, connected countries in the West with those in other parts of the world.

Today many people in the West, including scholars, feminists, and politicians, regard Muslim women as polar opposites of Western women, the former supposedly deprived of all the rights and liberties that the latter are said to enjoy. Muslim women, in that sense, represent the final frontier of twenty-first-century Western feminist humanitarian activism. The third story, however, reminds us—and *Sisters in the Mirror* shows—that, first, Muslim women, like other women, have been engaged in their own struggles for generations. Second, they have done so as individuals with a variety of personal, familial, professional, national, and international concerns that are often connected to but also extend beyond their religious identity and religious practices. And they have done so as members of societies that have been (and remain) deeply enmeshed in global relationships and that, for the most part, have been at the weaker end of disparities of wealth and power, of processes of colonization as well as policies of war, structural adjustment, economic sanctions, and Western feminist outreach. Third, Muslim women and men have long constructed their own ideas about women's and men's lives in the West, with implications for how they articulate their feminist dreams for their own societies. Finally, in contrast to recent work, including my own, on Muslim women's piety, religious practice, and faith-based or Islamic activism that challenges older Western liberal feminist understandings of feminist agency, I focus here on Muslim women's secular forms of public activism and engagement with women's rights. For that reason I also do not engage with the vast scholarship on feminist approaches to religious texts and theology. As the long history of women's writings and mobilization in and across the diverse Islamic world makes clear, Muslim women are not—and never have been—defined only by their piety or their "Muslimness"; they are also defined by their circumstances, by their histories and experiences, and by the increasingly visible, if not always recognized, roles they have played in their own emancipation.

I should point out here that I use the "West" in this introduction and occasionally in the main text as a shorthand for what is today Europe and the United States. As convenient and as problematic is the term "Muslim world," which emerged in Europe in the late nineteenth century as a distinct subset of what had been known as "the East" or "the Orient" and encompasses a dizzying array of regions, cultures, languages, political structures, and, indeed, "Muslims."

In *Sisters in the Mirror,* I argue that feminist movements in the West and in Muslim societies have developed in tandem rather than in isolation, even helping to construct one another. Specifically, Western ideas about Muslim women have long shaped the history of Western feminism, and these same ideas, combined with Western political power and Muslims' ideas about Western men and women, have also influenced feminist ideas and activism in Muslim societies. This book traces the entangled histories of depictions of Muslim and Western women since the sixteenth century and of movements for women's rights in the West and the Muslim world since the late eighteenth century. I end the book in the early twenty-first century, which has seen increased Western political, social, economic, and military presence in the lands where Muslims have historically lived, but also a growing Muslim presence in Europe and North America that blurs the very distinction between "Muslim" and "Western" contexts.

This historical span highlights changes over time in the political and economic relationships between Muslim and Western societies as well as in ideas about gender equality within these societies. These larger developments prompted changes in how men and women in Muslim and Western societies have viewed men and women in the other, with implications for feminist activism in these different contexts. At the same time the ideas and political engagement of many men and women in these different societies have contributed to social, economic, and political changes. Consider the examples of nineteenth-century British women's support for the British imperial cause and late twentieth- and early twenty-first-century US feminists' support for the invasion of Afghanistan.

By reflecting on these different sites together in one frame, I challenge assumptions about inevitable civilizational antagonism between the West and the Muslim world, a notion that has become increasingly popular in recent decades, and of a lag in the emergence of feminism in the latter. While it shouldn't be controversial to insist that male bias and privilege are present in Western as well as in Muslim-majority societies, it is more difficult to show how and why efforts to improve women's lives in even these geographically distant parts of the world have long been interconnected and interdependent.

The extended history in *Sisters in the Mirror* makes clear that these larger shifts in the balance of power between the West and the Muslim world are reflected in the ways each side has articulated its ideas about women's rights as well as how it has depicted the women of the other side. For example, during the Cold War in the second half of the twentieth century, both superpowers viewed Muslim and non-Muslim women in what came to be called "Third World" countries as equally laden with the potential to be brought forward through development and modernization. In recent decades, however, Muslim women everywhere have come to occupy a category of their own, perceived as distinct from other non-Muslim impoverished women around the world by dint of their Muslimness and as oppressed not by economic conditions, authoritarian governments, war and occupation, or even general male privilege but by a uniquely oppressive, violent, irreparably backward Islam that also threatens vaguely defined Western values.

These depictions, it turns out, have served different purposes in different political contexts. Take the figure of the oppressed, enslaved Muslim woman so familiar to us in the post-9/11 era. This figure can be found as early as the late seventeenth century in the writings of Mary Astell and a century later in Mary Wollstonecraft's work. However, while the US government, with support from some US feminists, used the figure of the oppressed Muslim woman to justify the invasion and occupation of Muslim lands such as

Afghanistan, Wollstonecraft used the Muslim woman in the harem, whom she depicted as deprived of her soul and her liberties, as a foil with which to criticize Western male philosophers like Jean-Jacques Rousseau and to argue for Englishwomen's rights. Consider now the different global political contexts in which these different Western feminists invoked Muslim women. Wollstonecraft was writing when Britain, having lost its North American colonies, was just beginning its rise to imperial dominance in the East. By contrast, the United States had declared itself the lone global superpower when, in the final years of the twentieth century, the Feminist Majority Foundation began reaching out to Muslim women in Afghanistan as though the United States had already attained feminist nirvana and the time had arrived to channel feminist energies to problems elsewhere. Some US feminists also went on to support the invasions of Afghanistan and Iraq, despite the extraordinary economic and human costs of war in the countries invaded and occupied, as well as in impoverished communities and communities of color across the United States.

Woven throughout this book alongside stories of conflict are stories of encounters that led writers to pause and reconsider norms in their own society—much as one might discover imperfections when studying oneself in a mirror—including cherished ideas about women's roles and rights. Among the English and US women who, in their words and deeds, dissented from the dominant attitude of their time and society toward Muslims and Muslim women were the eighteenth-century English playwright Delarivier Manley; her contemporary, the English aristocrat Mary Montagu; the American YWCA official Ruth Woodsmall, who toured several Muslim-majority countries in the 1920s and 1950s; the American Margaret Marcus, who rejected the middle-class New York life she was born into, converted to Islam, and became Maryam Jameelah; and the American civil rights and feminist activist Angela Davis, who recognized the parallels between the racist attacks against Muslim immigrants she witnessed in 1960s Paris and the assaults on civil rights activists in the US South—and the need to forge a shared struggle against both. That these women's valiant and thoughtful efforts to challenge the dominant Western narratives of their times about Muslims generally went unheeded is testament to the enduring power of those stories.

While the Western characters in this story are from Britain and the United States, the Muslim women and men who populate this story are primarily from South Asia, home today to a greater number of Muslims than the entire Arab world. Recounting this history of Muslims and the West from the vantage point of South Asia provides an important complement to much academic and popular writing on Islam and Muslims that is overwhelmingly focused on the Arab world, Iran, and Turkey. The story of Muslims in South Asia is significant not only for the size of its population but also for its distance from the Islamic heartlands, the particular history of the spread of Islam in the region, its long history of interaction with colonial and noncolonial European powers, its religious diversity, and its strategic location in current Western security and development concerns.

Within South Asia I focus on Bengal, especially eastern Bengal. The incarnations of this region as Eastern Bengal (and Assam) and East Bengal under British rule, East Bengal and East Pakistan following the Partition of India in 1947, and finally Bangladesh since its independence in 1971 provide a necessary reminder that national borders are political creations that cannot contain the complete stories of the people who live within them. Situated on the northeastern corner of the Indian subcontinent and the northern tip of the Bay of Bengal, Bengal is a massive flat riverine delta that is topographically unlike any other part of the subcontinent. Throughout recorded history the region has both attracted and sent forth pilgrims, adventurers, and seekers of knowledge across *sat sagor ar tero nodi* (seven seas and thirteen rivers), to borrow the expression connoting vast distances in Bengali popular literature and songs. By describing encounters of Bengalis with Europeans (and eventually Americans) both before and since the period of formal British colonial rule in India, *Sisters in the Mirror* provides necessary historical perspective to the profound intellectual, economic, political, and social changes of the colonial period.

The Muslims of Bengal, despite their demographic strength, have, with notable exceptions, been neglected in histories of Indian Muslims, which largely focus on the Urdu-speaking Muslims of north India. Historians of Bengal, for their part, have focused on the mostly Hindu elite of the colonial period and Hindus more generally in other eras. By focusing on Muslims in Bengal, we can see, for example, how Muslim reformers during the British colonial period reflected on the question of women's rights not only in relation to their adjacent Hindu, Brahmo, and Christian communities (and, of course, the British colonizers) but also in relation to developments in Muslim countries such as Egypt and Turkey.

In the postpartition era, for political and nationalist reasons, historians of both Pakistan and Bangladesh have largely disregarded the history of East Pakistan. The twenty-four years of united Pakistan (1947–71), however, merit attention for the groundwork laid for future feminist, labor, political, and cultural activism in both countries. Independent Bangladesh, for its part, has dominated the field of development studies and enjoyed pride of place as a valuable laboratory for experiments in women-centered advancement, from community-based programs and population control in the early 1950s to microcredit and climate change today, but other aspects of its culture and history have received relatively less attention.

Finally, the history and geographic location of eastern Bengal allow us to further nuance the idea of the "West." The word *poshchim,* or West, evokes not only Europe and North America but also the Maghreb or North Africa, from where we get the first Western account of Bengal, that of Ibn Battuta; the Arabian Peninsula, where observant Muslims direct their prayers; the country's western wing during its Pakistan *amol* (period); and West Bengal, from which East Bengal was separated in 1905–11 and again since 1947. All of these "Western" regions retain enormous significance, not only in the lexicon but also in cultural practices, such as how women dress and, of course, foreign policy. Given space constraints, however, this book focuses primarily on the region's relations with Britain and, since World War II, the United States.

Among the women and men who traveled from Bengal to the West and used their time there to contemplate their own society were Ihtishamuddin and Mirza Abu Taleb in the eighteenth century, Syed Ameer Ali in the nineteenth century, and Shamsunnahar Mahmud in the twentieth century. Among those who didn't travel but still feature prominently in this book is Munni Begum in the court of Bengal's eighteenth-century *nawabs* (rulers), who left no archive of her own but appears in the accounts of those who met her as well as the records of the famous Hastings trial in London. Early twentieth-century Bengali writers like Rokeya Hossain and Masuda Rahman also didn't travel to distant shores themselves but read widely and reflected on the larger colonial context in which they lived and wrote on its implications for women's freedom and national sovereignty.

To compose this long history of entanglements, I sought out accounts from Bengal, Britain, and the United States that broached the subject of women's roles and rights in these societies, particularly those that approached the subject in relation to other societies. I have consulted travelogues, memoirs, novels, newspapers, and periodicals from these different eras and places, and I have interwoven research that generally has not been put in conversation across boundaries of disciplines, historical periods, or area studies. Almost all direct quotations in the book are from the period under discussion. Not surprisingly, sources are more plentiful and more easily available as we approach the twentieth century, reflecting a rise in literacy and changes in publishing technology. Also unsurprisingly, more material is available about the European and US actors in the stories I tell than about many of the South Asian ones, reflecting the greater wealth and political power of Britain and the United States vis-à-vis South Asia. Even today, because of visa and immigration restrictions alongside financial obstacles, British and US men and women have been able to travel to and write about the people of South Asia in numbers that far exceed those of South Asians traveling to Britain and the United States. Given a universal history of women's restricted access to education and the ability to leave behind their writing, I rely on the accounts of elite women for much of the time covered in this book. Where published English translations of Bengali texts are available, I have used those to encourage the general reader to consult these works for further reading. All other translations from Bengali are my own.

Not all travelers have left written accounts, but when we read the accounts of those who have, we can see that they drew on their own experiences and interests in choosing what to cover—and how. In the past, as now, insufficient funds and local norms have limited what visitors can even see—though such constraints have not always prevented writers from discussing areas of which they have no firsthand knowledge. Consider here how European men once embellished their travelogues with detailed descriptions of Eastern women's private apartments into which they almost certainly could not have gained entry. To be clear, I read these accounts to learn about the writers and how they perceive the society they're writing about rather than for information about those societies.

The pages of this book and the extensive bibliography reveal my deep debt to the immensely productive theoretical frameworks of early modern, colonial, postcolonial, and transnational feminist studies—especially critical analyses of gender, empire, and travel—and the rich histories, ethnographies, and literary studies of and across South Asia, the Arab world, Europe, and the United States. However, I've strived for a smoother text by identifying the works I've relied on only in the numerous endnotes and bibliography.

My life trajectory across many borders as well as my scholarly pursuits and teaching interests over the past two decades shape my approach to this history. I was born in what was then West Pakistan to Muslim Bengali parents from East Pakistan. While they were born in eastern Bengal in the final years of British colonial rule in India, I was born as the united Pakistan experiment was unraveling. With my parents and three younger sisters, I lived in eight countries in South Asia, western and eastern Europe, and the Arab world, traversing the unmarked but implicit border between the so-called East and West numerous times before I traveled to the United States to attend college. Along the way I acquired new friends, teachers, and languages in these different countries and learned to appreciate the diverse cultural and religious communities among which we lived. I also witnessed the effect of major political events—even if I was too young to fully grasp the significance of the early ones—on my immediate family and the populations around us, among them the Bangladesh war of independence in 1971, the start of the civil war in Lebanon in 1975, the Solidarity movement in Poland in the 1980s, the invasion of Kuwait in 1990, and the attacks of 9/11 and the ensuing occupations of Afghanistan and Iraq.

Over the years I discovered too that there are many ways of being Muslim, not only in different Muslim countries but even within my own extended family, and that there are disparate efforts in communities around the world to create a better, more just world. Imagine then my surprise and no small measure of frustration when well-meaning friends and strangers have simply assumed that my stubborn ideas about justice and equality are an outcome only of the time I've spent in the West rather than the result of my immersion in and interactions with people and cultures in all the different places where I've lived.

Sisters in the Mirror is a feminist story about how changing global and local power disparities—between Europeans and Bengalis; between Brahmos, Hindus, and Muslims within Bengal; between feminists of the Global North and South; and between Western and Muslim feminists— have shaped ideas about change in women's lives and also the strategies by which to enact change. With the lasting shift in the balance of economic, political, and military power between Muslim and Euro-American nations toward the latter since the eighteenth century, Muslim advocates for women's rights have had to define their agendas for reform in the shadow of Western imperial and economic power. Muslim women, and their Muslim male supporters and allies, have been compelled to engage, whether explicitly or implicitly, with Western representations of Muslim women as well as, more recently, the dominance of Western feminist activism. At the same time, precisely because of these same global inequalities, feminists in Europe and North America have been less directly affected by the obverse—that is, by Muslim ideas of Western women. This has meant that while White Western feminists have largely felt free to focus on what they perceive as purely women's issues, Muslim and non-Muslim feminists in colonized contexts and, today, the Global South, and feminists of color in Western contexts have had to negotiate their demands for women's rights with other forms of struggles—for national independence or against colonialism, occupation, and racism.

I was in my last year of high school when "Sisters Are Doing It for Themselves" exploded from the radios in our small dorm rooms. My parents, then in Poland, had sent me to boarding school in England because there were no English-language high schools in Warsaw at the time. The two years I spent there represent my only experience at an all-girls institution. Like my schoolmates from all parts of Britain and the world, I chafed against the many rules prohibiting "unladylike" activities, such as chewing gum or wearing trousers in public. Despite these restrictions, the song rang true to us. Our families and teachers had encouraged us to aim high, and, unlike earlier generations of women, we took for granted that all doors would be open to us as we proceeded to the university and beyond.

Today, thirty-five years after Lennox and Franklin celebrated how far women had come, developments around the world clearly demonstrate that there remains an urgent need for feminism and, most important, for discussions and alliances within and across national and other kinds of borders. The stories in this book show that no society has a monopoly on ideas about justice and fairness (in the matter of women's or any other group's rights) or, for that matter, on male bias, violence, and injustice; no community is isolated or pure; and people everywhere are enriched by open-minded encounters with people who eat, dress, and pray differently or don't pray at all. Nowhere has change in girls' and women's lives—in the form of their greater ability to determine how to live their lives—come easily. This is as true of Western societies as it is of Muslim societies. The constraints that reformers and activists have faced, however, have varied, often in significant ways, and, in the period covered in this book, these efforts have been intertwined in ways we would do well to appreciate more fully. An awareness of the long and entangled history of such movements for change in both the East and the West should lead us beyond both self-congratulation and despair. It is through struggles rooted in solidarity, understanding, and shared knowledge that we can strive most effectively for a more just world.

ONE

Muslims of the East

MUNNI BEGUM OF THE COURT OF THE NAWAB of Bengal was not physically present at the impeachment trial of Warren Hastings in London, but she quickly emerged as a pivotal figure in the seven-year-long proceedings. The trial began in 1788, some thirty years after the British East India Company had seized economic and political power in Bengal and just over a decade after the British had lost their North American colonies. Across the English Channel the simmering grievances would give way to the French Revolution the following year, and Mary Wollstonecraft's *A Vindication of the Rights of Woman,* widely regarded as the foundational text of Anglo-American feminism, would be published four years later. The ire of the prosecutors led by Edmund Burke over Hastings's interactions with Munni Begum stemmed from a longer history of ideas about Muslim women, subsumed at the time under the category "women of the East," about Bengal, India, and about the role of the British in the region. We begin with this earlier history.

EARLY ENCOUNTERS IN BENGAL

Abu Abdallah ibn Battuta was still two days from his destination when he came across four disciples of the saint whom he had traveled to Bengal to meet. He later recounted, "The Shaykh had said to the darwishes who were with him, 'The traveler from the West has come to you; go out to welcome him.' He had no knowledge whatever about me, but this had been revealed to him."[1]

This fourteenth-century traveler from the West was from the North

FIGURE 1. "Indian Harem Scene," the frontispiece to the 1929 English edition of Ibn Battuta's *Rihla (Travels in Asia and Africa)*. It is a curious choice for the first of only three images, other than maps, in the book, perhaps better explained by early twentieth-century British preoccupation with Muslim women's seclusion in South Asia than by the content of the *Rihla*.

African city of Tangier. Bengal was not part of his initial itinerary, but, like many travelers, traders, and pilgrims before and after him, Ibn Battuta found his way there. His *Rihla,* or *Book of Travels,* compiled in 1355, offers the first descriptions of the emerging Muslim presence in Bengal. Over nearly thirty years Ibn Battuta had traveled across forty-four countries and covered some seventy-three thousand miles on camel and mule as well as wagon and boat. His many marriages, divorces, and concubines during his years on the road not only let him discover the aphrodisiacal powers of coconuts, betel, and a fish called *qulb al-mas* but also afforded him a glimpse into women's lives in different societies. Unlike other Arab-Muslim male writers of the time, he broached the topics of women and sexuality and even discussed his own feelings toward women. He recalled with affection his mother, whom he had left in Tangier; wives who had refused to leave their homes to travel with him, leading to divorce; and some of the children he had left with their mothers in various places.

Although respectful of the religious communities he encountered, among them Christians, Jews, Hindus, Zoroastrians, Buddhists, and Muslims, Ibn Battuta could not conceal his distaste for certain customs and behaviors. For instance, in Amjari (today, Amjhera, Madhya Pradesh, India), the sights and sounds that accompanied the *sati* (immolation) of three "richly dressed and perfumed" widows prompted him to almost fall off his horse.[2] In the Maldives, whose "inhabitants...are all Muslims, pious and upright," he was frustrated by his inability, even as a *qadi* (judge), to push women to adopt proper attire. He also found it "a strange thing about these islands that their ruler is a woman, Khadija." He wrote appreciatively, however, of the generosity of high-ranking women such as Khatun Bayalun of the Golden Horde, who provided him with funds and protection along his travels. The *Rihla* also provides valuable accounts of Muslim women who were able to travel great distances to Mecca to perform the obligatory hajj (pilgrimage).[3]

Ibn Battuta stopped in Bengal on his way to China as envoy to the Mongol imperial court. From the port of Sudkawan (today's Chittagong or Chattogram) in southeastern Bengal, he made the monthlong journey to the northeastern area of what is now Sylhet, a good part of it by boat on the River Meghna. His main reason for the complicated detour was to receive blessings from Shah Jalal, a Sufi saint widely revered by "Muslim and infidel" alike and credited with a variety of miracles.[4]

Bengal, Ibn Battuta later recollected, was a "vast country, abounding in rice, and nowhere in the world have I seen any land where prices are lower than there." He marveled at Shah Jalal's success in spreading Islam: "It was by his labors that the people of these mountains became converted to Islam, and that was the reason for his settling amongst them."[5] The revered Shah Jalal was among the earliest of the *pirs* (spiritual leaders) believed to have brought Islam to Bengal. Over the following centuries many more such men would dramatically alter the physical and religious landscapes of eastern Bengal, known today as Bangladesh.

The "pure and good" customs of the Muslim population and "very neat and clean" attire of "the king and the chiefs" in Bengal merited approval in the travelogue of the Muslim Chinese traveler Ma Huan, who visited Bengal almost a century after Ibn Battuta, as part of the Muslim Ming admiral Zheng He's treasure fleet to the "Western Ocean."[6] The general abundance that Ma Huan, like Ibn Batutta, observed continued to attract visitors and traders to Bengal, though the arrival of Europeans over the following centuries would transform both Bengal's economy and its reputation as a land of plenty.

MUSLIMS AS THE "SECT OF THE ABOMINABLE MAFAMEDE"

Europeans first landed on South Asian shores a few decades after the Chinese treasure fleet, following Vasco da Gama's successful 1498 voyage via the Cape of Good Hope. Since only a few intrepid European travelers and missionaries had undertaken the long overland journey to India until that point, the Portuguese knew little about the people of India or even the location of the spices, silks, and jewels they sought when they embarked on their quest to enter the maritime networks of the Indian Ocean.[7] Like other travelers, the Portuguese assessed the Muslims they encountered in India in light of their prior knowledge and experience of Muslims. The extended Muslim presence on the Iberian Peninsula, the history of the Crusades, and the ongoing rivalry with Muslim Arab traders on the Indian Ocean were the primary points of reference for the Portuguese when they interacted with Muslims in this new context.

The early chronicles of the Portuguese in India reflected well the general Portuguese attitude toward Muslims. The *Book of Duarte Barbosa* (1518), for example, recounts the legend of the conversion to the "sect of the abominable Mafamede" of the first Indian Muslim, Cheraman Perumal, a seventh-century Hindu king in what is today Kerala on India's western coast.[8] A few decades later João de Barros began his history of the Portuguese in Asia rather curiously, if not entirely surprisingly, almost a millennium before Vasco da Gama set sail. It was "more or less in the year 593 of our Redemption," he explained, that the "great anti-Christ Muhammad" arose "in the land of Arabia" and, with "the fury of his steel, and the fire of his infernal sect," went on to conquer Arabia and large swaths of Asia and Africa.[9] While he acknowledged the virtues of individual Muslim rulers, his larger narrative was one of conflict between the Portuguese and the "Moors," the latter always motivated by what he referred to as "that inborn hatred which all Moors have for Christians."[10] To be clear, the economic motive—to seize dominance over the Indian Ocean trade from Arab traders and enjoy unhindered access to Asian goods—was perhaps as important as the religious animosity, if not more so, in inspiring this relatively impoverished European country's search for the sea passage to India. Later the interest in trade and the many kinds of cloth produced in Bengal would lure the Portuguese to that northeastern corner of the subcontinent over 1,500 miles from Kerala, as it later would the Dutch and the English.[11]

THE PULL OF BENGAL

Duarte Barbosa never visited Bengal himself, so he had to rely on the reports of Portuguese merchants and sailors for the Bengal section in his book. He described the elaborate attire of "respectable Moors" by which he clearly meant the wealthier Muslims—their "white cotton smocks," "silk scarves," daggers, jewelry, and turbans. "They are luxurious, eat well and spend freely, and have many other extravagancies as well." They bathed in "great tanks" by their homes; these large ponds no doubt afforded some privacy to the women of wealthier homes who were more likely to observe *purdah* (seclusion).[12] "Every one has three or four wives or as many as he can maintain. They keep them carefully shut up, and treat them very well, giving them great store of gold, silver and apparel of fine silk." Of the "lower castes of this town," he noted that "they are all well shod, some wear shoes and some sandals." He attributed the large number of Muslims to the desire among the "Heathen of these parts daily [to] become Moors to gain the favour of their rulers."[13]

Tomé Pires's *Suma Oriental* (1515) provided additional details about the significance of Bengal and Bengalis in the Indian Ocean networks of the early sixteenth century. Among the foreigners already living in Bengal, according to Pires, were a "large number of Parsees, Rumes, Turks and Arabs, and merchants from Chaul, Dabhol and Goa." The desirable products they and Bengalis carried to Malacca included some twenty types of fine cloth and "sugar preserves of various kinds in great plenty." As remarkable as the thriving trade in goods to and from Bengal was the itinerant nature of the Bengalis themselves, who "sailed four or five ships and junks to Malacca and to Pase [or Samudra-Pasai, in northern Sumatra] every year"; many even settled in these distant towns and kingdoms.[14]

In 1521 António de Brito and his brother-in-law Diogo Pereira led a formal diplomatic mission to Bengal from the Estado da Índia (State of India), which comprised a series of coastal cities and strongholds from East Africa to southern China.[15] An unnamed scribe in the delegation produced an account of the mission's adventures and interactions with the elite in Bengal. Forced to wait for weeks in Lakhnawti (Gaur) for an audience with the sultan, the members of the mission had time to go "into the town on several occasions to investigate the local customs." These male visitors wouldn't have had access to any elite women or their living quarters, so they must have drawn on a combination of fantasy and hearsay when they ventured to discuss women's lives—much like male European travelers writing about Ottoman and Mughal harems, as we shall see shortly.[16] The Portuguese visitors to Bengal reported that the sultan, Nusrat Shah of the Husain Shahi dynasty, had "two thousand five hundred wives," who lived "in special buildings within the palace, and are guarded by eunuchs whose job it is to provide them with all they need." The king, they added, also provided for his father's three thousand wives. "The great lords each have fifteen or twenty wives...who want for nothing." The envoys were struck that upon a man's death, "the Sultan inherits half his wealth and the rest goes to his [the man's] wives and children." The account also conveyed a very clear sense of what we might characterize as a "Bengal rush" among the Portuguese to win the sultan's favor and have access to the lucrative trade to and from Bengal. The Brito-Pereira delegation came across local Muslim Portuguese men deemed *arrenegados* (renegades) by the Portuguese Crown.[17]

Given its base in distant Goa, the *estado* never exerted much control over Portuguese activities in the northern or upper Bay of Bengal. As a result, Portuguese traders, missionaries, mercenaries, travelers, and pirates drawn to Bengal by tales of its rice, sugar, textiles, and riches operated relatively unhindered by *estado* officials.[18] The success of this informal arrangement

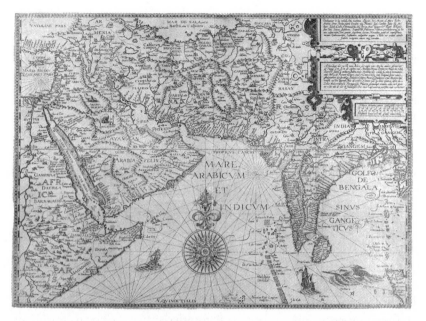

FIGURE 2. Map of Asia, by Jan Huyghen van Linschoten, 1596. Van Linschoten was a Dutch merchant and historian who worked under the Portuguese in India for several years. His publication of such maps, based on Portuguese charts he had secretly copied, would make it possible for the Dutch, French, and English to break the Portuguese monopoly in the East Indies. Beinecke Rare Book and Manuscript Library, Yale University, New Haven, CT.

was reflected in the thriving trade networks that the Portuguese of the Bay of Bengal established between Bengal, Malacca, and Macao; the enduring settlements they established in Bengal itself, despite intense competition from Arab and Persian merchants; and the importance and currency that Portuguese gained as a language.[19] Two centuries later this would prove fortuitous for Englishman Robert Clive, who was able to communicate with his Bengali mercenaries well enough in Portuguese when he set out to seize control of Bengal on behalf of the British East India Company. He never did learn any Indian languages, but he had picked up some Portuguese when he was forced ashore in Brazil for several months for ship repairs during his first passage to India to be a company clerk.[20]

After numerous failed efforts to get past the Portuguese in the Bay of Bengal, the Dutch Vereenigde Oost-Indische Compagnie (VOC; United East India Company) established factories all over Bengal starting in the 1630s. The Dutch had been drawn by Bengal's cotton textiles, raw silk, opium, sugar, and saltpeter (used to make gunpowder), which they exchanged for spices in the East Indies and for silver and copper in Japan and exported directly to Europe.[21] Their success was such that when in 1616 Sir Thomas Roe, British ambassador to the court of Mughal emperor Jahangir, inquired into the prospects of an overland trading route to Bengal, the British company factors in Surat tried to dissuade him on the grounds that "upon the sea coast, where there is any hope of benefit, the Dutch and Portingales have trade."[22] Just over a century later, however, the British would begin to surpass the other Europeans in trade in Bengal, to be followed shortly by British political dominance over Bengal and the rest of the subcontinent that would endure until the mid-twentieth century.

A DREAD OF EUROPEAN CHRISTIANS
AND THE VENERATION OF JESUS

For the South Asian Muslim communities who encountered the new arrivals from Europe starting in the early sixteenth century, their own ideas about Christians and Christianity would likely have been based on accounts of Jesus in the Quran and hadith, not Crusades fought in distant lands, and by the relatively small community of Syrian, or Thomas, Christians that dated back to the first century of the common era in southwestern India (concentrated in what is now Kerala).

Writing in the 1570s, the noted scholar Zainuddin Malabari explained that it was because the Muslims of Malabar had "sinned" and "revolted against God" that God sent "these Christian Franks—May God abandon them!" who then "tyrannized" the Muslims, "corrupted them, and practiced ignoble and infamous acts against them." Among the many Portuguese atrocities he listed were that "they decorated their own women with the jewels and the rich dresses that they had torn from the women of the Muslims." A half century earlier a poem by his grandfather had similarly described how the Portuguese had enslaved the "believers" and confined them "in narrow quarters / Like sheds for senseless sheep."[23] This fear of being captured, enslaved, and forced to convert by European Christians similarly haunted Muslims in the distant west, on the Maghrebi, or North African coast, which had seen a series of Spanish and Portuguese conquests since the early fifteenth century and long posed a substantial obstacle to Muslim and Arab travel within the "lands of the Christians."[24]

This dread of European Christians stood in sharp contrast to the reverence Muslims and the Quran accord Jesus as a prophet of Islam. Maryam, or Mary, mother of Jesus, is the only woman named in the Quran. In fact, Mary appears in the Quran more times than she does in the New Testament, and the nineteenth *sura* (chapter) of the Quran even bears her name. For her faith and obedience, she is presented in the Quran as an "example to the righteous."[25] The Mughal emperors of India, whom we will shortly meet, used the name to bestow honor on women in their family: Akbar's mother came to be known as Maryam Makani (Having the Place or Station of Mary) and Jahangir's mother as Maryam al-Zamani (Mary of the Age).[26] Moreover, women "of the Book"—that is, of the Christian and Jewish communities who had received earlier revelations from God—also appear in the Quran as "believing women" who can legitimately be taken as wives by Muslim men without any requirement that they convert to Islam. Such scriptural statements, and the fact that Muslims emerged and lived amid Christians and Jews in Arabia, meant that Christian beliefs and practices were familiar to Muslims from the earliest days of the new faith. Muslim encounters with European Christians, whether in South Asia or the Levant, followed a different trajectory.

THE MUGHALS AND THE EUROPEANS

Zahiruddin Muhammad Babur arrived in India after the Portuguese and, following his victory at Panipat, just outside Delhi, in 1526, went on to establish what became the Mughal Empire. It was not until several decades later, however, that the Mughal court would interact with the Europeans on India's western coast.

Babur's grandson Akbar was thirty years old when he met Portuguese subjects—and saw the sea—for the first time. Determined to extend his landlocked empire to the water's edge, Akbar set out to bring under Mughal control both Gujarat to the west and Bengal to the east. His conquest of Gujarat in 1572 gave Muslim pilgrims easier access to Arabia, but it also provided the Mughals with new neighbors, the Estado da Índia. In the winter of 1572–73, Akbar greeted the Portuguese missions to his court with great curiosity. As Akbar's chronicler described the *mulazamat* (interview), the emperor "made inquiries about the wonders of Portugal and the manners and customs of Europe" out of a general sense of curiosity but also as a "means of civilizing... this savage race."[27]

Tahir Muhammad, a member of Akbar's diplomatic mission to the Portuguese colony of Goa in 1579, also returned unimpressed. He noted that "the community of Franks wear very fine clothes but they are often very slovenly and pimply" and are strangely averse to using water to clean themselves but are impressive in their dexterity with firearms and bravery "on ships and in the water," if less so on land. That same year Akbar invited Portuguese Jesuit priests to his court to teach him about their religious beliefs.[28] In the coming decades the growing European presence at the Mughal court, which would soon include the English, would provide more opportunities for interaction between the Mughals and Europeans—and for reports on the women at the Mughal court.

Britain's formal relationship with the Indian subcontinent began with Queen Elizabeth I's decision to grant, on 31 December 1600, a royal charter to the "Governor and Company of Merchants of London trading to the East Indies." Although the original purpose was to facilitate the company's access to the spices of the East Indies (the Indonesian archipelago), the British East India Company's name and history would become forever intertwined instead with the Indian subcontinent. The English quickly made two discoveries that led them to turn their attention to India: access to the Spice Islands would require confronting the much better-funded Dutch, and Indian cotton textiles could be a lucrative alternative to spices.[29]

With high hopes for trade concessions and a permanent base for English traders, William Hawkins arrived in Surat on India's western coast in 1608 to negotiate a trade deal with the Mughal emperor Jahangir on behalf of the company and King James I.[30] It was not until 1613, however, that, over the strong objections of the Portuguese, Jahangir issued a royal order granting the English company permission to set up factories in India. In 1616 Sir Thomas Roe arrived at the Mughal court in Ajmer as both the British Crown's first official ambassador to India and a representative of the East India Company.[31]

Having come of age in the final years of Queen Elizabeth I's reign, Roe was familiar with the power of a female monarch, but he had perhaps not expected to find such power in an Eastern court and in a consort. The empress Nur Mahal was assuming an ever-greater role in governance, while her husband, Jahangir, indulged his various addictions and pursued interests in philosophy and the sciences.[32] Jahangir expressed concern for Roe's personal well-being following a recent illness, but Nur Mahal, by contrast, promptly turned to business matters. To confirm Roe's legitimacy she asked to see his ambassador's seal and then kept the seal in her possession overnight. Roe quickly surmised that his success depended on his engagement with the "faction" led by the "beloued queene." Nur Mahal, who appears as "Normall" and "Normahall" in Roe's letters and journal, was Jahangir's "beloued wife among foure" and "wholly gouerneth him."[33] In 1616 Jahangir ordered that her royal name be changed from Nur Mahal, "Light of the Palace," to the even grander Nur Jahan, "Light of the World."[34]

Roe's consternation notwithstanding, Nur Jahan was in good company at the Mughal court as a woman with certain forms of power and a wide range of interests, including an important economic role as consumer and trader. For example, as powerful shipowners, both Jahangir's mother, Maryam al-Zamani, and Nur Jahan were able to dictate the flow of goods within, into, and out of India. Indeed, the illegal capture of the ship *Rahimi* by the Portuguese viceroy in Goa in 1613—illegal because the ship carried the required Portuguese pass—backfired quite disastrously. The ship was carrying cargo owned by Maryam al-Zamani as well as pilgrims returning from the hajj. A furious Jahangir imposed severe sanctions on the Portuguese, thereby creating an opening for other European traders.[35] As a British company factor later put it, this "odious" deed was the "utter undoing of the Portungales" and, in another factor's words, the ship's capture led "the Great Mogul to drive the Portingals out of this place."[36]

Over time Roe came to believe that Nur Jahan was the main obstacle to his efforts to increase English trade in India, despite his attempts to bribe her.[37] This conviction no doubt explains Roe's unflattering depictions of Nur Jahan as using feminine wiles to dominate her husband: "Normahall attemptes the king with the false teares of womans bewitching flattery." Both Roe and his young chaplain, Edward Terry, recorded the execution of one of Nur Jahan's "gentellwoeman" for having kissed a eunuch, commenting not only on the "horrid" nature of the execution ordered by Jahangir but also remarking with some surprise on the woman's personal wealth. According to Roe, this "damsell yeelded in Pearle, Jewelles, and ready mony 160,000 *rupias*."[38]

Despite his detailed and ultimately productive trade negotiations with Nur Jahan, Roe never actually saw her. Highborn women of the court, he noted in his journal, relied on their servants as intermediaries in trade discussions.[39] In a letter to Thomas Smythe, the first governor of the East India Company, Roe described Nur Jahan as "more unaccessible than any goddess or mystery of heathen impiety."[40] As in the case of other European men denied entry to elite women's quarters in the East, this inaccessibility only contributed to the women's aura of mystery.

William Hawkins, who had left India by the time Roe arrived, had noted the existence of "private roomes made for [the emperor's] Queenes, most rich, where they sit and see all, but are not seene."[41] Roe described the strange sensation of being looked on by two of Jahangir's wives, "whose Curiositye made them breake litle holes in a grate of reede...to gaze on mee." He caught a glimpse and discerned that their complexion was "indifferently white," their "black hayre" was "smoothed vp," and they were bedecked in "diamondes and Pearles." They moved away from the screen when he looked up but not before he heard them being "so merry that I supposed they laughd at mee."[42]

Francisco Pelsaert, who was based at the Mughal court at Agra in 1620–27 as a Dutch company factor, described the *mahals,* or "palaces for ladies," as "adorned internally with lascivious sensuality, wanton and reckless festivity, superfluous pomp, inflated pride, and ornamental daintiness." The nobles, he continued, have "[a]s a rule...three or four wives, the daughters of worthy men, but the senior wife commands most respect." He provided an unexpectedly detailed discussion of the inner quarters, the relationship between the wives, their relationship to their husband, and the evening rituals. These "wretched women," he observed, "wear, indeed, the most expensive clothes, eat the daintiest food, and enjoy all worldly pleasures except one, and for that one they grieve, saying they would willingly give everything in exchange for a beggar's poverty." One purpose of this exposition becomes clear in his pronouncement: "The ladies of our country should be able to realise from this description the good fortune of their birth, and the extent of their freedom when compared with the position of ladies like them in other lands"—even as he conceded hastily that "this topic lies outside the scope of my task."[43] Pelsaert's book was very likely a "commercial report, drawn up for the use of the Company, not for a popular audience," but he provided a better organized and more detailed description of the women's quarters, and indeed many other aspects of life and commerce in India, than had earlier European visitors, including Roe.[44] As commander of the ill-fated *Batavia* in 1628–29, the ever-curious Pelsaert would go on to provide the first European description of a kangaroo, some 140 years before James Cook.[45]

European physicians at court who were requested to treat female patients were usually disappointed. The French physician François Bernier, who arrived in India four decades after Thomas Roe, just as Jahangir's grandson ascended to the throne, lamented in his memoirs, "It would afford me pleasure to conduct you to the Seraglio, as I have introduced you into other parts of the fortress. But who is the traveller that can describe from ocular observation the interior of that building?" He described how, on his few visits to the women's quarters to treat "a great lady so extremely ill that she could not be moved to the outward gate,...a Kachcmire shawl covered my head, hanging like a large scarf down to my feet, and an eunuch led me by the hand, as if I had been a blind man."[46] In describing his opportunity to look around the women's apartments some years later, the English physician John Fryer conceded that he was compelled to confront his preexisting notions about the proverbial harem. Fryer, who served as surgeon to the East India Company in the 1670s, expressed surprise at the fairly mundane activities he discovered the women performing in the privacy of their own space. He found them occupied with boring household tasks such as making pickles and needlework, and, no doubt to his disappointment, engaging in "no indecent decorum."[47] That Fryer could express such surprise at what he found is testament, of course, to the power of the images of the harem, or seraglio, and of Eastern women that circulated at the time, much of it based on the accounts of European travelers to the Muslim empire that lay much closer, that of the Ottomans.[48]

By this time Indian men and women had also started traveling vast distances—for example, to distant outposts of the Iberian empires and to England, as merchants, sailors, servants, captives, and wives of Englishmen—but no written accounts by these early travelers have survived, if they ever existed. Three biographies of Catarina de San Juan, often confused with *La China Poblana,* written around the time of her death in 1688, merit our attention because they offer a very different vantage point on the interconnected nature of the world of that time and on European ideas about people from elsewhere. They are also an important reminder that not all travel was undertaken voluntarily. Kidnapped from Bengal as a young child by Portuguese pirates in the first decade of the seventeenth century, she was baptized in Cochin; sold as a slave in Manila, which had been recently colonized by Spain; and shipped across the Pacific Ocean to the older colony of New Spain, or Mexico. She died in Pueblo, having lived out her final decades as a domestic servant and with a reputation as a *beata,* an extremely devout woman. Hagiographies published soon after her death claimed that she was of royal blood, the daughter of an Arab princess and the Mughal emperor himself, perhaps to make her a more acceptable object of veneration, given contemporary European elite concerns about bloodlines and purity.[49]

The most well-traveled women in India in this era were undoubtedly the elite women of the Mughal court. Although, despite their education, they left us no reports of their peregrinations, the voyages of two such women warranted mention in the chronicles of their contemporaries. One was Gulbadan Banu Begum, a poet, scholar, and the youngest daughter of Babur, the first Mughal emperor, who was in her midfifties when she traveled to Mecca for the hajj. Gulbadan and her entourage remained in the Hijaz for four hajj seasons over three and half years, but she left no account of her long voyage. Perhaps she would have set ink to paper to share her own story had she not, shortly after her return to court, accepted Akbar's request to write instead about the reigns of the first two Mughal emperors, her father, Babur, and half-brother Humayun. Gulbadan's *Humayun-nama* provides a rare and invaluable perspective on the changes in Mughal women's lives as the Central Asian House of Timur morphed into the Indian Mughal dynasty. We learn that the freedoms that Timurid women had enjoyed as members of a nomadic community gave way to new restrictions in keeping with the demands of an imperial court, to the physical separation of women in tents and in palaces. During Akbar's long reign, contemporaneous with that of Elizabeth I's, the imperial harem grew in size and political significance. In the words of Father Monserrate, a Jesuit priest based in Akbar's court for several decades, the emperor strategically used marriages "to ratify peace and to create friendly relationships with their vassal princes or neighboring monarchs."[50]

Three decades later Maryam Khan undertook the earliest documented voyage by an Indian woman to Britain. An Armenian Christian from northern India, Maryam Khan would marry two captains of the British East India Company, first William Hawkins and then Gabriel Towerson. As a ward of the Mughal royal family, she certainly would have been able to share with her husbands, and with eager readers, many sought-after details about the women's apartments in Jahangir's palaces, but what we know about her emerges primarily from the archives of company directors and officials.

Thomas Roe, for example, reported his distress over the scandal surrounding the group that accompanied Maryam Khan on her return voyage to India. Frances Webbe, an Englishwoman who had come aboard as Khan's maidservant, quickly revealed herself to be the fiancée of fellow passenger Richard Steele, also of the company, when the crew discovered she was pregnant. Roe declared, "I desier noe weomans company, but labour to leaue such incumberances behind. Beleeue mee the scandal already is not easely wiped off." He had, after all, left behind in England his own bride of just seven weeks when he set sail for India and was still trying to negotiate his place at the Mughal court. And, indeed, for many decades the company would discourage Englishwomen from traveling to India.[51]

Maryam Khan's connections at court facilitated Frances Webbe Steele's access to the women's quarters at the Mughal palace, making her, as far as we know, the first Englishwoman to gain entry and share her impressions. Steele received an invitation from the daughter of Abdur Rahim, the commander in chief of the Mughal troops, who was also a poet and translator at Jahangir's court and had been an important mentor to Nur Jahan's first husband, Ali Quli Beg. She reported on the opulence of the women's quarters, the women "of diuers Nations and complexions" present therein, and the lavishness of the gifts exchanged. We have no firsthand accounts of the travels, economic activities, and adventures of Mistress Steele in her own name; however, the English parson Samuel Purchas, who compiled several volumes of travel narratives, included among them "that which Master Steele and his wife told me of the Women of those parts." As we shall see, this silence would be broken in the late eighteenth century, when British women become increasingly prolific in sharing their observations of India and Indians in letters, journals, and books.[52] The Steeles returned to England in February 1619 with Ambassador Roe and some seventy bales of the company's first acquisition of silks from Isfahan, the capital of the Persian Safavid Empire.[53]

Maryam Khan's appearance in English records provides valuable clues as to how different English groups perceived her. In church records, for example, she appears simply as "Maria." Remarkably, her Indian origins merit no mention, perhaps nullified by her Christian birth. She appeared to have been able to interact with men and women of her equivalent class in England without difficulty, her Indianness relevant only in that it added to her allure. The correspondence of Thomas Roe and various company factors in India mentions the wife or "ladye" of Captain Towerson, who made repeated claims for maintenance after his departure for England.[54] Some fifty years after her English sojourn, Maryam Khan provided inspiration for the renowned seventeenth-century English poet and playwright John Dryden, who loosely based his play *Amboyna, or the Cruelties of the Dutch to the English Merchants* (1673) on the lives of Maryam Khan and Gabriel Towerson. Written at a time of intense hostilities between the Dutch and the English, *Amboyna* tells the story of an Indian woman, Ysabinda, who embraces Christianity out of love for an Englishman and is later raped and left to die by the Dutch.[55] This tale of an exotic noblewoman from the East who converts to Christianity out of love and leaves her own people to follow him is a familiar one, going back to eleventh-century epics such as *Song of Roland*.[56] The historical details of Maryam's story and how she was perceived by the English in her own time are significant because of the important contrast they provide to later interactions between the Indians and the English, in which notions of racial and civilizational superiority play a role, even among those of a similar class background.

THE RISE OF ISLAM IN BENGAL

Even as successive envoys of the British East India Company appeared at the Mughal court in the early seventeenth century, Emperor Jahangir was preoccupied with consolidating Mughal dominance over the distant and elusive province of Bengal. In 1612, a few years into his reign, the provincial capital shifted from Rajmahal to Dacca (today, Dhaka), and in March 1627, just months before his death, Jahangir felt sufficiently at ease with the political and economic situation in Bengal to command the then viceroy "to remit yearly from Bengal, in the shape of presents, a sum of five lakhs for the Emperor and an equal amount for the Queen-consort Nurjehan."[57] Mihr un-Nisa (Nur Jahan's birth name) had actually spent over a decade in Bengal before she married Jahangir. Legend has it that Akbar hurriedly posted her first husband, Ali Quli Beg, to Burdwan (in what is now West Bengal, India) to create as much distance as possible between Mihr un-Nisa and the future emperor Jahangir. Thus it was in Bengal that Nur Jahan began her married life, returning to the imperial court after Ali Quli's death in 1607.[58]

The Mughal rulers were concerned primarily with political control and revenue from the prosperous province of Bengal, and they were not especially invested in establishing Islam in the new territory. Yet it was under Mughal rule that this religion from the west took root in the plains of Bengal. Muslim rule in Bengal had commenced in the early thirteenth century, when the Delhi Sultanate extended its reach to the eastern delta, but control from Delhi proved short-lived and was replaced by a series of independent, Bengal-based Muslim dynasties. Even the Portuguese author Tomé Pires had noticed that "the king of Bengal is always at war with the king of Delhi."[59] Islam had been the preserve of the largely non-Bengali (mainly Turkish, Afghan, Ethiopian, and Arab) ruling and urban elite when Ibn Battuta and Ma Huan visited Bengal and the Portuguese established their first settlements. Starting in the late sixteenth century, however, Islamic ideas and practices came to be adopted by the majority of the population in eastern Bengal.

A major ecological change in the sixteenth century—a southeastward shift in the Ganges River to merge with the Padma—made the region more accessible to the Delhi-based Mughal State, while at the same time the altered flow of fresh water and fertile silt opened up new possibilities for settled agriculture and, in time, increased revenue.[60] A large number of the colonists with Mughal land grants who trekked eastward were Muslim men believed to be imbued with special religious powers, especially over nature, much like Shah Jalal, whom ibn Battuta had sought out two centuries earlier. As this new generation of holy men cleared forests and marshes to cultivate rice, they introduced Islam to the local people who gathered around the small mosques and shrines they built. Although the inhabitants of the surrounding hills and forests were generally not drawn into this process and became neither Bengali nor Muslim, Bengalis on the delta happily absorbed the new stories into their existing understandings of the history of the world.

An early example is found in *Nobi Bangsho,* a genealogy of the prophets, by the late sixteenth-century Sufi poet Syed Sultan, in which figures from Hindu tradition, such as Brahma, Rama, and Vishnu, appear as prophets alongside those of the Abrahamic faiths. Sultan presented Adam as a farmer who was trained and equipped by the angel Gabriel, and Eve as capable of making the traditional Bengali milk-sweet *sandesh* after Gabriel brought them fire. Sultan showed Eve following a beauty routine that appeared distinctly Bengali: she applied sandalwood on her skin and kohl to her eyes and wore flowers, rare elephant pearls (highly prized in Sanskrit Vaishnavi religious texts), and a vermilion dot on her forehead.[61] The very distinctly Bengali Islam reflected in such texts and traditions flourished alongside Hinduism, Buddhism, and, following the arrival of the Portuguese, Christianity. Today this distant corner of the Indian subcontinent—farther yet from the birthplace of Islam in Arabia than most of the subcontinent and in contrast to its immediately adjacent areas—is home to one of the largest Muslim communities in the world.[62] It is also where, in the mid-eighteenth century, the East India Company would first consolidate its political and military power alongside the economic privileges it already enjoyed.

The first decades of the eighteenth century saw Bengal with a prosperous economy that generated considerable revenue for government coffers, relative peace and stability, and a greater degree of independence from the Mughal court than it had enjoyed in many years. In 1700 the emperor Aurangzeb, the grandson of Jahangir and widely acknowledged as the last of the "great" Mughals, appointed Kartalab (later Murshid Quli) Khan *diwan* of Bengal, the chief Mughal representative in charge of revenue and finance in the province. Imperial control from Delhi began to wane, however, with Aurangzeb's death in 1707. A decade later, having risen to the position of the *nazim* (governor) as well as *diwan,* Quli Khan declared himself the first *nawab nazim* (prince) of Bengal, Bihar, and Orissa and moved the provincial capital from Dacca to Maksudabad, which he renamed Murshidabad.

Originally from the Deccan and a convert to Islam, Quli Khan proved a fervent champion of both Islam and his adopted home of Bengal, manifested, for example, in his decisions to blend Mughal and pre-Mughal Bengali architectural styles in the structures he had built.[63] His administrative reforms— designed to extract greater revenue for the treasury—led to changes that would prove consequential for the political, economic, and cultural landscape of Bengal for centuries. Smaller landholdings were consolidated into a few much larger parcels, creating a new landed aristocracy dominated by Hindu families whose titles as *zamindars* would become permanent under British legislation just a few decades later. Quli Khan also replaced the civil administration that had consisted of northern Indians sent by Delhi with Bengali Hindus who had mastered Persian, the language of court and government. A new class of powerful moneylenders and bankers emerged to help small zamindars pay the required revenue—and seize the property when they defaulted on their loans.[64]

The rule of Murshid Quli Khan and his successors was marked by abundance, with thriving trade in rice, cotton and silk cloth, salt, saltpeter, and other cash crops with neighboring regions and Europe.[65] Bengal was "a commercial nation of the first order," to quote the Dublin-born politician Philip Francis, who would join the newly established Supreme Council in Calcutta (today, Kolkata) in 1774 and later help build the impeachment case against Warren Hastings.[66] The Portuguese presence had diminished since a Mughal attack on the main Portuguese settlement in Hooghly (now Hugli) in 1632,

FIGURE 3. *Prince Entertained by Musicians and Dancers*, Murshidabad, ca. 1755. Fine Arts Library, Special Collections, Harvard University, Cambridge, MA.

but Armenian, Dutch, English, and French traders all maintained important settlements in Bengal and enjoyed a variety of privileges and tax exemptions. Abuse of these privileges, among other things, contributed to the escalating conflict between the English company and the nawabs. In the fierce confrontation between the company troops led by Robert Clive and the forces of the young Nawab Siraj-ad-daula in Polashi (Plassey) in 1757, the nawab was killed, propelling the company's transformation, as is often noted, from traders to rulers. With the 1765 Treaty of Allahabad, the Mughal emperor granted the British East India Company the *diwani* of Bengal (which then encompassed Bihar and Orissa)—that is, formal political control and the authority to collect land revenue—thereby cementing Bengal's role as the gateway to Britain's empire in South Asia.

The wealth enjoyed by Bengali elites and company officials did not, of course, trickle down to the larger population. The poor predictably bore the brunt of the three major famines that struck in 1769–70, 1784, and 1787. The first of these was the worst, referred to in Bengali as *chhiattorer monnontor,* the famine of '76, because it occurred in the year 1176 in the Bengali calendar, following a drought and crop failure. It is believed to have led to about ten million deaths, wiping out a third of the population of Bengal and Bihar. The catastrophe was exacerbated by the failure of the new British rulers to undertake timely famine relief efforts such as those that had existed under Mughal rule. As a result of this devastating famine, Bengal's image began to transform from one of abundance and prosperity to an enduring one of poverty, suffering, and high mortality. The British Parliament increased its oversight on the company in India, leading to the impeachment of the first governor-general, Warren Hastings.[67]

For many Bengalis the repeated Maratha (or *bargi*) invasions and the unrelenting British demands for revenue came together in a nursery rhyme that is still recited today, though with its original meaning now largely obscured:

The baby sleeps, and the countryside is at rest,
but the *bargis* have invaded our country.
The *bulbuli* birds have eaten all the rice;
how can we pay the rent?[68]

Famines dealt an additional blow to Bengali weavers already suffering under the company's new rules of trade and forms of control. Women of a variety of backgrounds, rural and urban, were skilled spinners of thread, though the quality of their thread depended on the quality of their fingers (coarse from overuse among laborers or refined among those who enjoyed greater luxuries and means). Women were also integral to the creation of the elaborate Bengali *jamdani* designs. Company officials soon recognized Bengali women's importance in the textile business. For example, John Bebb, the company's resident in Dacca, warned against any changes in how the thread was purchased: "Interfere not with the women. They are beyond the power of Government. You may confuse and harass them but you cannot improve their skill or excite their industry by regulations or by any other means than just and fair dealing in the purchase of the manufactures for which they furnish the material." On the supply side the devastating impact of the famines among female spinners led to a fall in the quantity of fine yarn and an increase in its price, further reducing the weavers' share of the price of the final cloth.[69]

MUSLIM WOMEN IN BENGAL UNDER COMPANY RULE

Conduct manuals and literary texts from eighteenth-century Bengal indicate that male Bengali writers regarded the ideal woman to be completely subservient to her husband. Syed Nuruddin and Abdullah, for example, recommended that a wife should hasten over whenever her husband called, not leave the house without his permission, and not talk back when he was angry.[70] Such guides should never be taken as an indication of what women actually did, of course. However, because in Bengal, as in other parts of the world at the time, most girls did not have access to education, we have limited access to their own thoughts and ideas about their lives and societies.

Some girls of elite families were taught to read and write at home. Others might have attended the primary schools run by the learned men of their religious communities but likely had to stop as they approached puberty. Monnuzaman Khanam, the Muslim female zamindar of Hooghly, was an advocate of girls' education and provided space in her home for girls to learn. Women poets emerged even from this small pool, such as Rahimunnesa, a late eighteenth-century Muslim poet from Chittagong. Fortunately for us, she appended an autobiographical statement to her transliteration of the medieval Bengali poet Syed Alaol's *Poddaboti* (or *Padmavati*). This brief document, written in verse, reveals how Rahimunnesa situated herself in relation to her family's history and her larger world. She wrote, for example, of her great-grandfather Jali Shah, who participated in battles against the British a few years after Plassey in an effort to regain control of Bengal.[71] Some of the most detailed information we have about an individual Muslim woman in India of that time is one who, while not born in Bengal, rose to prominence in the court of the nawabs of Bengal. Munni Begum carved out a presence for herself in the colonial archives as one of the first Indian women with whom the English directly interacted following her dramatic rise to power shortly after the East India Company seized control of Bengal in 1757.

While the young Nawab Siraj-ad-daula had his fair share of enemies, to this day Bengali children learn that it is because of the treachery of the disgruntled commander of his army, Mir Jafar, that the young nawab lost to Gen. Robert Clive of the company at the Battle of Plassey. Mir Jafar's name is still the Bengali equivalent of Judas. Following Siraj-ad-daula's defeat and death, Mir Jafar became nawab and was, by some accounts, personally escorted to the throne by Clive. Following his death eight years later, he was succeeded by his fifteen-year-old son, Najm-ud-daula—and this is where Munni Begum enters the story.

Some company councilors protested the accession almost immediately, arguing that, in accordance with the "order of succession in Europe," Mir Jafar's grandson Mir Saidu (by his eldest son, Miran) had a prior claim to the throne. The problem for many of the English was that Najm-ud-daula was the son of a concubine, Munni Begum, not of an "official" wife. It mattered not to them that Mir Jafar himself had anointed Najm-ud-daula, and there was local precedent for the son of a concubine to be recognized as a legitimate heir. Robert Clive and the company eventually settled for hand-picking Muhammad Reza Khan to serve as the *naib subah* (deputy) for the young nawab. The company severely restricted the nawab's authority by giving itself veto power over the appointment of any public servant in the government and with a stipulation that the nawab would have no military under his direct control.[72]

As the mother of the young nawab, Munni Begum assumed control of the household. Born in northern India, she had been trained as a *nautch* girl (dancer) in Delhi and had come to the court in Murshidabad with a troupe to perform at a wedding. She became part of the household of Mir Jafar, bore him two sons, Najm-ud-daulah and Saif-ud-daulah, and remained in charge of the nawab's household during her sons' all-too-brief reigns. Her wealth, power, and influence are reflected in the grand Mughal-style Chowk mosque in Murshidabad that she commissioned from 1767 to 1778, which quickly became the focal point of the town's public religious rituals. She was forced to step down in 1770, when her sons were succeeded by Mubarak-ud-daulah, the son of rival consort Babbu Begum.[73]

Munni Begum returned to power with the arrival of the first English governor-general of India, Warren Hastings, but this proved temporary.[74] In May 1775 company councilors dispatched from London relieved her of authority again, this time permanently.[75] Just a decade later, as we shall see, Munni Begum would feature prominently in the 1788–95 impeachment trial of Warren Hastings in London. Her strength of character in the nawab's court and in her dealings with the English confounded the company administration back in London, given their cherished ideas about women's frailties generally and about harems and women of the East specifically.

TWO

Soulless Seraglios in the Grievances of Englishwomen

THE SUBJECT OF WOMEN—their roles in society and the nature of liberties they might enjoy—preoccupied many thinkers of the European Enlightenment. With Europeans increasingly engaged in voyages of trade and exploration, some turned their attention to women in other parts of the world, including those of the East or "Orient," though, largely by virtue of its power as well as propinquity, the Ottoman Empire usually stood in for the East for much of the seventeenth and eighteenth centuries. Older European ideas about the East converged with Enlightenment concerns about the presence or absence of liberty and rational thought and, in time, with the realities of European assertions of imperial power and notions of intellectual and racial superiority. As English, Scottish, and French writers, among others, sought to make sense of their place on an evolutionary line of historical progress, they invoked the oppressed women of the East with increasing frequency in their discussions about women's status in their own societies, though in different ways and to different ends.

WOMEN OF THE EAST

While Thomas Roe's descriptions of his interactions with the indomitable if elusive Nur Jahan would not be published in Britain until 1899, it is unlikely that his account would have challenged the seventeenth-century English view of Muslim women as meek and subservient. This view was reinforced by successive accounts about the Near East by male travelers who claimed, rather improbably, that they had the opportunity to closely observe women of the region. Moreover, they suggested that their observations offered valuable lessons for Englishwomen.

In his 1609 account of his years as the "Preacher to the Company of English Merchants in Aleppo," for example, the English Protestant clergy William Biddulph expressed the hope that, from his book, Englishwomen might appreciate how fortunate they were compared to women elsewhere: "Here [in England] wives may learn to love their husbands, when they shall read in what slavery women live in other countries, and in what awe and subjection to their husbands, and what liberty and freedom they themselves enjoy." In his description of relations between husbands and wives under that "devilish religion" Islam, Biddulph betrayed some envy for the privileges he believed Muslim men enjoyed and extracted clear lessons for Englishwomen. A Muslim wife, he wrote, rose to greet her husband upon his return from a trip and "bows herself to her husband, and kisses his hand" and, having offered him her own seat, "stands so long as he is in presence." Such deference, Biddulph believed, was worthy of emulation: "If the like order were in England, women would be more faithful and dutiful to their husbands than many of them are."[1]

This same Biddulph would go on to play a role in shaping the British presence in India. As an East India Company factor in Ajmer and Agra, he would request the company governor in London "to send per the first ship some proper man of account to reside in Agra with the king" to better confront the competition from the Portuguese. Company and Crown responded by sending Thomas Roe as their joint envoy.[2] Descriptions of Muslim women and society by Biddulph and other travelers, such as the poet George Sandys as well as the literary works of the Spanish writer Miguel de Cervantes, informed popular stage plays like Philip Massinger's 1624 *The Renegado,* which sought to convey that the outrageous liberties available to Englishwomen could lead only to family and societal disorder and thus were neither to be admired nor encouraged. Englishwomen, instead, should emulate the perceived simplicity of women in the Near East.[3]

A corollary to the meek woman of the East, of course, was the oppressive husband. By the end of the seventeenth century, certain ideas about Muslims, specifically of the Ottoman Empire, had become sufficiently commonplace that a 1699 dictionary of slang and jargon defined Turk as "any cruel hard-hearted Man." Today's *Oxford English Dictionary* retains the historical understanding of the word as a "cruel, rigorous, or tyrannical person;

any one behaving barbarically or savagely. Also: a bad-tempered or unman-ageable person; a man who treats his wife harshly. Often (with alliterative qualification) *terrible Turk.*"[4]

Englishmen generally—and unsurprisingly—found little to criticize in Christian marriages as long as their wives remembered their proper place and avoided luxury and self-indulgence. They congratulated themselves and reminded women that they were far better lords and husbands than the men who controlled entire harems in the east.[5] Take the 1699 wedding sermon by Rev. John Sprint, published the following year as *The Bride-Woman's Counsellor.* Sprint pointed to women of the East as models for Englishwomen, much as Biddulph had almost a century earlier, and called on Englishwomen to make themselves their husbands' "help-meet" and to serve, please, and obey their men. Sprint offered the example of "Persian ladies who have the resemblance of a Foot worn on top of their Coronets" to show that the "height of their Glory, Top-Knot and all, does stoop to their Husband's feet."[6]

The most influential portrayal of the Muslim East as the mirror opposite of Europe was undoubtedly Charles de Montesquieu's 1721 *Lettres persanes (Persian Letters).* For the French philosopher the seraglio was merely the most extreme form of the many problems that plagued any despotic politi-cal regime.[7] The word *seraglio,* first used in 1581 to refer to the women's quar-ters in an aristocratic Muslim home, is believed to have emerged following the unfortunate conflation of *serai,* the Turkish word for lodging or palace, with the similar-sounding Italian word *serraglio,* which means place of con-finement, leading to the idea popular in the West over the past five centuries that Muslim women were imprisoned in their quarters.[8]

While Montesquieu intended to use his fictional world of sultans, women, and eunuchs primarily to raise questions about politics in his own society—specifically the long and absolutist reign of Louis XIV—his book also helped to solidify the image of the harem as a place of oppression, imprisonment, polygamy, and female same-sex sexual activity. Reprinted some thirty times in just a few decades, *Lettres persanes* also sharpened the contrast of Eastern women with European women, who were shown as living with liberty with their own monogamous and enlightened husbands.[9] In his 1748 book, *The Spirit of the Laws,* which would influence both the American and French Revolutions, Montesquieu further developed his views on the differences between European and Ottoman notions of government.[10] The sharp dis-tinctions he drew between the law, morality, and liberty of the former and the despotism of the latter helped to define Europe as a distinct entity with its own culture and history.[11]

The early English feminists who emerged in this period, inspired by Enlightenment debates on education and liberty, also made use of current ideas about Eastern women. In contrast to Biddulph, Sandys, and other men, the feminists used the men and women of the East not only to criticize Englishmen but to argue for more rights for themselves.

The philosopher and theologian Mary Astell, the earliest person in England to write with what we would now identify as a feminist sensibility, called for the establishment of an all-female academy that would provide women with the necessary education and community to properly develop their minds, virtue, and moral judgment. She also criticized English laws, especially those governing marriage, as clearly biased toward men. The marriages of that era, she argued, were oppressive for women, not only in terms of the social, intellectual, and economic restrictions that they imposed on women—a critique that would be familiar to late twentieth-century feminists—but also for the very real bodily danger associated with heterosexual sex, which carried the ever-present risk of pregnancy and, given the perils associated with childbearing in that era, the high probability of death. For Astell, then, true liberation for women lay in chastity, not sexuality, and in pursuits of the mind rather than those of the body. Daniel Defoe, whose success with *Robinson Crusoe* still lay ahead, was among the men who criticized Astell's plan for a women's academic institution, accusing her of seeking to revive Catholic nunneries that had been shut down in England in the 1530s.[12] Astell herself invoked the "Turk and Infidel" in an early poem when lamenting Englishwomen's exclusion from Christian missionary activity. In a later treatise Astell repeated common assumptions about Muslim women in expressing the hope that "our Christian Brethren are not of the *Turks* Opinion, That Women have no Souls."[13]

Astell's admirers included the wealthy and influential Lady Mary Wortley Montagu, who, as we shall see, would provide one of the earliest firsthand European accounts of elite Ottoman women's private quarters. In 1724 Astell wrote a preface to an early draft of her friend's *Letters,* though it doesn't appear that she used that opportunity to question her own misconceptions about women's lives there, identify connections between her desired female spaces for Englishwomen with the all-female quarters in elite Ottoman homes, or ponder anew the status of women in England.[14] Her laudatory remarks about Montagu's book stressed, however, the significance of a woman's perspective in a genre dominated by men.[15] Astell died in 1731 and did not live to see the publication of Montagu's letters in 1763. Montagu, for her part, in a letter to her daughter several decades after her sojourn in Constantinople, recalled how, as a young girl of fifteen, she had been much drawn to Mary Astell's proposal. Had she herself then been "mistress of independent fortune," she wrote, she would have founded an "English Monastery" for women and "elected" herself "Lady Abbess."[16]

Englishwomen, increasingly vocal about the state of their marriages, also invoked the tyrannous Eastern man and oppressed Eastern women, usually to urge their husbands not to be like the despots of the Orient. Lady Mary Chudleigh responded to Reverend Sprint's sermon with *The Ladies Defence,* a long poem comprising an exchange between four voices. The character Melissa takes men to task for acting like "petty Monarchs" who, "Narcissus-like," admired only their own "Perfections" and looked down on all others and, to the parson, poses the question, "Must Men command, and we alone obey?" Already married, Chudleigh urged other women to "shun that wretched state."[17] Another lament on the plight of English wives comes from Lady Sarah Cowper, who produced a 2,300-page diary of her generally unhappy marriage to Sir William Cowper. In 1701, after her overbearing husband refused to give her the key to the linen closet or to have dinner served at the hour she had suggested, she wrote that "there is not a more absolute Tyrant." Of her own overturned sense of domestic responsibilities as wife, she concluded, "The wives administer'd the affairs of the Family, but the Concubines were not to meddle with them. Surely I have been kept as a Concubine not as a Wife."[18]

One of the earliest calls by a woman for English marriage-law reform was the anonymous *Hardships of the English Laws in Relation to Wives,* published in 1735. Building on Mary Astell's work, the text's presumed author, Sarah Chapone, argued that women, married or otherwise, were entitled to true liberty, defined as freedom from domination as well as freedom to chart their own futures—and yet marriage, although an "Institution of God," was, in practice at that time, akin to slavery. While Chapone correctly lauded the greater liberal property rights that married women in Portugal enjoyed rela-

tive to wives in England, she, like her contemporaries, did not hesitate to per-
petuate common ideas about the archetypal oppression of women in the East.
She derived some comfort in her notion that women in England are at least
"treated…better here, than the Grand Seignior [sultan] treated his Slaves in
Turkey," even if her main goal was to demonstrate how low England generally ranked in such comparisons. In listing the legal disadvantages forced on
English wives—their inability to write wills, their lack of rights of property
and child custody—it did not occur to her, or to so many of her contemporaries, that Muslim women, irrespective of marital status, had enjoyed formal legal rights to contract and property since the dawn of Islam, for a thousand years already. Indeed, given the vast gap between women's legal rights
under Islamic law and their rights under Jewish and Christian law, Jewish
and Christian women under Muslim rule were known to take their cases to
Muslim courts in the hopes of receiving a more desirable hearing.[19]

In eighteenth-century Britain and the American colonies (and subsequently in the new US republic), White women were governed by British
common law and the legal doctrine of coverture, by which a woman's legal
identity was annihilated upon marriage and subsumed into or "covered" by
that of her husband. Thus, unmarried White women and widows enjoyed
legal rights to property and could enter into contracts in their own name, but
married women could not. To quote British jurist William Blackstone, who
codified English common law in 1765, "By marriage, the husband and wife
are one person in law: that is, the very being or legal existence of the woman
is suspended during the marriage, or at least is incorporated and consolidated into that of the husband."[20] A woman's "civil death" upon marriage
meant, generally speaking, that her husband gained control over any move-
able property she brought to the marriage and had ownership over any property she gained after her marriage; she had no legal rights over her children;
she could not sue or be sued or make a contract on her own. How this legal
principle was interpreted and applied varied from place to place and changed
over time, usually in light of other laws such as those governing criminal
acts, naturalization, or the poor. Still, coverture would remain on the books
in Britain, Scandinavia, and North America until legal reforms were undertaken in the late nineteenth century.[21]

Among those in England who tried to challenge prevailing ideas about
women in the Muslim East were the early eighteenth-century playwrights
Delarivier (or Delia) Manley, Catharine Trotter, and Mary Pix. Manley, for
example, saw the Ottoman seraglio not as a place marked by oppression but

rather as a place for women to gather away from men. Her 1707 play *Almyna, or The Arabian Vow,* was perhaps the earliest literary response to the first English translation of Antoine Galland's 1704 *Les mille et une nuits* (A thousand and one nights). In the play, she created space for a discussion of the oft-repeated claim that, according to Islam, women do not have souls (a proposition that, as we will see shortly, was also central to Mary Wollstonecraft's arguments against the treatment of Englishwomen by "Turks"). In her 1709 satire *The New Atalantis* about Whig society, Manley drew on her personal experience of having been tricked into a bigamous marriage to discuss polygamy as very much an English practice, rather than peculiar only to heathen Turks. Moreover, in sharp contrast to other representations of that period, she depicts Roxelana (or Hürrem), the concubine-turned-wife of Emperor Süleyman, in a historically accurate manner as a wise woman with political power and the emperor's only wife. Such references to the Ottoman Empire were made not to educate her readers about Ottoman society but rather to elucidate her points about her own society—for example, the role of polygamy in English politics.[22]

While many women writers of the eighteenth century readily conjured the men and women of the East when arguing for more and better rights for Englishwomen, few had traveled to those societies. Lady Mary Wortley Montagu (born Mary Pierrepont), who eagerly sought out and read *The New Atalantis* when it was first published, proved an important exception.[23] In August 1716 she accompanied her husband, Edward Wortley, to Istanbul to take up his post as British ambassador to the Sublime Porte (the Ottoman Empire). As was common at the time, Montagu revised and embellished her letters from her Turkey interlude to incorporate material from other letters and her diaries and, no doubt, to remove certain details; it is likely that she even created a few letters to round out the manuscript. The collection of letters was finally published in May 1763, nine months after her death.

Montagu believed that she could offer her readers new information, even as she reported that what she saw in Ottoman society generally confirmed the more realistic details, "excepting the enchantments," of Antoine Galland's vastly popular translation of the *Arabian Nights* that was already in circulation—she herself owned a twelve-volume set. After all, as a member of the diplomatic elite in Istanbul, a woman, and a mother, she was granted access to places and gatherings that few other European travelers, most of them men, had visited.[24] In her letters she pointed out that past descriptions of Turkish women's lives had often relied on scanty information and criticized them as "generally so far removed from truth and so full of absurdities, I am very well diverted with them." These earlier male authors, she continued, "never fail giving you an account of the women, which 'tis certain they never saw, and talking very wisely of the genius of the men, into whose company they are never admitted, and very often describe mosques, which they dare not peep into."[25]

In response to her friends, such as the English poet and essayist Alexander Pope and the Venetian priest and scholar Antonio Conti, whose letters were replete with examples of popular European notions about Muslim women, she attempted to correct the misconceptions that Muslim women have no souls and thus no access to a blissful afterlife. She also defended the Prophet Muhammad as a lover of the "fair sex" and too gallant a man to treat women in the barbaric manner European Christians attributed to him.[26] To her sister she suggested that Muslim women's coverings gave them an enviable degree of anonymity on the streets, an "entire Liberty of following their Inclinations without danger of Discovery."[27]

Given her own financial dependence on her husband under the rule of coverture, Montagu was particularly struck by what she perceived as elite Turkish women's greater economic rights and financial independence as well as relative ease in obtaining a divorce. As she wrote to her sister, "Neither have they much to apprehend from the resentment of their husbands, those ladies that are rich having all their money in their own hands, which they take with them upon a divorce, with an addition which he is obliged to give them." She also felt compelled to address the popular European notion of the ubiquity of polygamy. And, indeed, historical evidence suggests that the overwhelming majority of Ottoman Muslim men, much like Jewish and Christian Ottoman and European men, had only one wife. The exceptions were almost always men of immense wealth and high rank. Lady Mary's discoveries about elite Ottoman women led her to conclude dramatically, "Upon the whole, I look upon the Turkish women as the only free people in the Empire."[28]

In her oft-quoted account of her visit to the hammam (public baths) in Sofia, Montagu wrote of "majestic grace" and of the women's engagement in a variety of activities. This was very much in contrast to earlier depictions of all-women gatherings in the Muslim East by men such as Jean Dumont, Aaron Hill, Paul Rycaut, George Sandys, and Robert Withers, who, according to Montagu, invariably "lament the miserable confinement of the Turkish Ladys" and whose descriptions suggested passivity, sloth, and lasciviousness. Even her friend Pope had cited Withers in a letter to her, joking about the "land of Jealousy, where the unhappy women converse with none but Eunuchs, and where the very Cucumbers are brought to them Cutt."[29] Moreover, she insisted, those descriptions were surely inaccurate since "'tis no less than Death for a Man to be found in one of these places."[30]

Montagu, by contrast, admired the "polite" hospitality and "obliging civility" with which she was received, with "none of those disdainful smiles, or satiric whispers, that never fail in our assemblies when any body appears that is not dressed exactly in the fashion." All the women in the bathhouse were "without any distinction of rank by their dress, all being in the state of nature, that is, in plain English, stark naked.... Yet there was not the least wanton smile or immodest gesture amongst them."[31] She wistfully pointed out that the women spent about four hours a week enjoying the pleasures of the bathhouse, and this assembly served as a "coffeehouse where all the news of the town is told, scandal invented, etc." Although she recognized that women in Ottoman society did not have access to the mixed gatherings common in her circles in England, she lamented the absence of such pleasant female spaces back home, echoing Mary Astell's vision of a female academy.[32] For Montagu the elite Turkish women enjoyed a form of freedom that women back in England were still awaiting.[33]

Montagu appeared to critique the situation of Englishwomen quite pointedly—and show how she and other Englishwomen were trapped in prisons of their own—when she related the shock expressed by the women in the bathhouse at the sight of her corset: "They believed I was so locked up in that machine, that it was not in my own power to open it, which contrivance they attributed to my husband."[34] While reporting that she had remained dressed at the hammam in the midst of some two hundred "stark naked" Turkish women allowed Montagu to uphold a sense of proper English feminine modesty in front of her readers as well as her role as foreign ethnographer, her general openness allowed her to identify somewhat with those she was writing about—Turkish women—when most male writers prided themselves on their distance from and superiority to the objects of their prose.[35] Ultimately, she noted, "the Manners of Mankind do not differ so widely as our voyage Writers would make us believe."[36]

Montagu's aristocratic background undoubtedly contributed to her sense of kinship with elite Ottoman women and allowed her to regard them in some instances even as superior, as having something to teach the British regarding liberty and gender equality. In the end, however, that same upper-class identity prevented her from fully exploring the implications of her feminist impulses.[37] It would fall on Mary Wollstonecraft, born just three years before Montagu's death, to articulate English middle-class feminist ideology in the final decade of the eighteenth century, while activists would not raise the needs and concerns of working-class women until even later.

Finally, keep in mind that the larger context of the early eighteenth century would have influenced Montagu's attitude to the men and women she met: the Ottoman Empire was still a powerful force, despite recent defeats, and Britain had not yet gained valuable new colonies such as India, nor yet developed the theories of racial and civilizational superiority that would inform nineteenth-century British feminists' efforts to assist and rescue women across classes and religious communities in India, by then the jewel in the crown of the British Empire.

WOMEN AS "THERMOMETERS" OF CIVILIZATIONAL PROGRESS

Montesquieu's ideas about despotism and women in the East influenced European thinkers of the era who were trying to make sense of the diverse peoples in the "new" worlds to their west and the "old" worlds to their east. Eager to develop general laws about human societies, much as colleagues were doing in the natural sciences, some philosophers formulated what came to be called the stadial theory of history, according to which all societies pass through four progressive stages on the road to the highest level of civilization, the pinnacle represented—depending on the writer—by contemporary Britain, France, or Europe.[38] Significantly, the philosophers saw these stages as corresponding with changes in the status of women. The French philosopher Denis Diderot, for example, succinctly described women as "thermometers to register the smallest change in manners and customs."[39] The stadial approach developed by Scottish philosophers would hold great appeal for East India Company officers such as James Mill, as well as later women's rights advocates.

In the late eighteenth century, before the emergence of ostensibly scientific absolute racial hierarchies in European thought, the stadial approach to history assumed a universal human nature. To explain the differences they saw between contemporaneous societies, the Scottish philosophers looked to variations in geography and climate. Adam Ferguson, writing in 1767, suggested a link between sexual passion and warmer climates. He contrasted the "burning ardours, and the torturing jealousies of the seraglio and the haram, which have reigned so long in Asia and Africa" with the north, which was marked by a "spirit of gallantry, which employs the wit and the fancy more than the heart." His description of the "Asiatic of India" as "addicted to plea-sure" and "sunk in effeminacy" would prompt later thinkers to worry about the threat they posed to the growing British Empire, and its manners, vir-tues, and government, concerns that would become manifest in the impeach-ment trial of Warren Hastings.[40]

For John Millar, temperate climates spurred activity and industry, while tropical climates encouraged laziness and sloth.[41] Millar had studied with Adam Smith in Glasgow and is credited with the first English use in print of the word *civilization* in 1771; he was followed closely by the celebrated biog-rapher James Boswell in 1772. Millar understood the history of civilization as a "natural progress from ignorance to knowledge, and from rude to civilized manners, the several stages of which are usually accompanied with peculiar laws and customs."[42] Moreover, Millar argued, the more advanced a civili-zation, the greater the sexual modesty of its women, an argument that early feminists such as Wollstonecraft would echo a few years later.[43] The physi-cian William Alexander clarified the implications of the stadial approach for British men: unlike barbarous nations past and present that viewed women as childbearing and sexual slaves, British men, informed by enlightened chiv-alry, knew how to treat their women properly.[44] In the end, however, while many European men in the latter half of the eighteenth century were willing to celebrate women's moral and human superiority and recognize European women as the standard against which to measure civilizational progress, few were willing to consider extending to them actual political, legal, and economic rights.[45] It was into this world that Mirza Shaikh Ihtishamuddin arrived in 1766.

THE MARVELS AND WONDERS OF BRITAIN

A century and a half after Maryam Khan returned to India from England with Gabriel Towerson, and less than a decade after the Battle of Plassey, Ihtishamuddin set out for Vilayet (Europe) from Hijli, a harbor near Calcutta in Bengal. Other Indians had traveled to and from Britain before him, and, indeed, by the end of the eighteenth century, there would be about a thousand Indian women and men in Britain, mostly from Bengal, mostly Muslims, a few Catholics, and no Hindus. (Given concerns about the polluting nature of travel beyond the borders of India and over the "black waters" of the oceans, elite Hindus did not undertake travel to Europe, or at least openly write about these voyages, until the late nineteenth century.) Ihtishamuddin's trip stands out for the detailed notes he took while in England, which resulted in the earliest book-length account of an Indian's impressions of Britain and the women there, *The Wonders of Vilayet*.[46] Shortly after Ihtishamuddin's return to India, Munshi Ismail accompanied company official Claud Russell from Bengal to London and Bath, but his account of his travels was relatively brief and not published in either the original or in translation.[47]

Ihtishamuddin found that the English were already quite familiar with the sight of large numbers of Muslim "lascars [seamen] from Chittagong and Dhaka…[but] unacquainted with the clothes and manners of an Indian gentleman" such as himself.[48] Trained as a *munshi* (scholar-scribe) in the court of Bengal Nawab Mir Jafar (who had betrayed Siraj-ad-daula at Plassey and then succeeded him), he had joined the East India Company as a Persian scribe and then the court of the Mughal emperor Shah Alam II. At the Mughal court Ihtishamuddin drafted the Persian text of the 1765 Treaty of Allahabad, which consolidated Robert Clive's and the company's economic and political power in the province of Bengal-Bihar-Orissa.[49] In January 1766 he set sail for England in the company of Capt. Archibald Swinton. Their assignment, as Ihtishamuddin had understood it, was to deliver a letter from Mughal emperor Shah Alam II to King George III of Britain regarding the Allahabad treaty. After three weeks at sea, Ihtishamuddin was horrified to learn that Clive had held on to the letter, ostensibly to deliver it himself at a later date.[50]

With his diplomatic assignment derailed, Ihtishamuddin spent his time in England exploring the "streets and bazaars of the town and its environs" and observing the local people and culture. He described how the English regarded him a "great curiosity and flocked to have a look" and how he "who had gone there to enjoy a spectacle, became a spectacle" himself. He recalled that the "friendliness of the English and, more particularly, the sight of their lovely women dispelled the sorrow of solitude and cheered me greatly." At a dance party in London, Ihtishamuddin protested in vain that he knew not how to dance, and the "ladies tittered with amusement" when another guest suggested that perhaps he is "shy to dance with ladies of another race."[51]

When Ihtishamuddin resolved to return to India, his host, Captain Swinton, tried to persuade him to remain in England, proposing he take on a second and third wife, as permitted by his religion. Ihtishamuddin reported that he "began to retort in a manner consistent with my religious tenets. I said, 'I would much rather live in poverty in my own country than in affluence in yours, and to me the dusky Indian women are dearer than the fairy-faced Firinghee damsels." Insisting that he had "lived with Nawabs and the sons of emirs and shared their food and drink," and they had been quite happy to "snatch the goblet from the cup-bearer, and [guzzle] copiously," Swinton attributed Ihtishamuddin's inflexibility on matters of religious doctrine to his nonaristocratic and Bengali background. "You are a Bengali," Swinton responded, "and the Bengalis are notorious among Indians for their folly and stupidity." Ihtishamuddin countered this insult by explaining, "Among Muslims true nobility is not measured by worldly wealth but consists in acquiring knowledge, in leading an upright life and in obeying the laws of Allah and his prophet." Ihtishamuddin returned to Bengal in 1769, having been away for two years and nine months (including a "whole year aboard ship for the round trip"), and finished writing his travelogue in 1784.[52]

Ihtishamuddin marveled at the divine blessings that had brought prosperity to the British, as well as the role of education and hard work in creating their society. Perhaps unknowingly echoing British critics of Mughal luxury and waste, he reminded his readers that "worldly riches ought not to be squandered on luxurious living, on fine clothes, choice cuisine and drinks, and on collecting a bevy of singing and dancing women with whom to spend endless days and nights, as the wealthy noblemen of India are wont to do." Such practices, he warned, "would be mocked and laughed at" in Vilayet and "fill me with shame and sorrow." He contrasted too the "useless and futile labour" that the Indian gentry expended on poems "in praise of a mistress' face, or of the wine, the goblet, or a bawd" with the important and practical books that English authors write "so that mankind will benefit from their discoveries." It would appear he was quite persuaded of the validity of the new middle-class morality and austerity emerging in late eighteenth-century Britain.[53]

Yet Ihtishamuddin's open admiration for British accomplishments—or, as he put it in his title, their wonders—and his generous reading of the "customs and mores of the Firinghees" were not accompanied by a sense of inferiority as an Indian. He certainly didn't hesitate to criticize inappropriate British behavior, such as the "detestable breach of trust" by Robert Clive, who never delivered the Mughal emperor's letter. The manner in which he responded to his experiences in Britain was inevitably influenced by his own elite—if not aristocratic, as Swinton had reminded him—background. Moreover, he was writing before India had become a full-fledged colony of Britain's, even if the company had begun its political encroachments in Bengal, and before ideas about a hierarchy of civilizations had become entrenched in the West.[54] This larger context also permitted Ihtishamuddin to cast a critical eye on Indian practices, without the defensiveness that would emerge in later decades under formal colonialism.

Ihtishamuddin observed the British very much as his equals, even while recognizing important differences between them. That was why, rather than explain differences by pointing to essential, unchanging, and unchangeable civilizational peculiarities, he repeatedly attributed the differences to local circumstances or needs or, as in the case of the company's assumption of political power in Bengal, divine intervention: "*Sobhan Allah* [Glory be to God]! How ironical is fate! Those who only yesterday were supplicants for forty bighas of land are today masters of one half of India and have brought to their knees a host of proud and arrogant chieftains!"[55]

EARLY ENCOUNTERS BETWEEN ENGLISH
AND INDIAN MUSLIM WOMEN

Despite the company's early efforts to prevent Englishwomen from traveling to India and becoming "incumberances," as Thomas Roe put it following the scandal of Maryam Khan's traveling companions, the consolidation of British power in India soon enabled more Englishwomen to undertake the long voyage.[56] The earliest two accounts by Englishwomen of Muslim women in India relied on the increasingly popular epistolary form (employed by Montagu), by which writers presented their observations as letters to friends and relatives back in Britain. The genre permitted the writer to depict her observations and experiences in an intimate, leisurely, and less structured manner. Fortunately for us today, such writing also resulted in a great deal of information about the writer's priorities.[57]

As early as 1743, Jane Smart published a brief account of her visit about a year earlier with other Englishwomen to the wife of Safdar Ali Khan, nawab of Arcot in southeastern India. In her "Letter from a Lady in Madrass to Her Friends in London," Smart provided a detailed description of the "Nabob's Lady," her dress, and her many jewels: "She had many more Diamonds and

Pearls about her than would fill a Peck Measure." The Englishwomen were served tea prepared with rose water and cinnamon, and betel leaves, "which the Indians chew, of an intoxicating Nature, and very Disagreeable to the English; but we were forced to comply with that out of Compliment"; in time British rule would make such politeness vis-à-vis Indians and their customs increasingly rare. Smart also commented on the Indian women's surprise at Englishwomen's undergarments, in a scene akin to that of Lady Montagu's in the bathhouse, although that book, while circulating in certain circles in manuscript form, would not be published for another two decades: "The Nabob's Lady and her Attendants admir'd us all, but thought our Dress very odd. Two of the Lady's examin'd my Dress till they came to my Hoop-Petticoat, which they were very much astonished at....We were the first English Women they had ever seen, and I doubt not that we appeared as odd to them as they did to us." Smart ended her account by reminding her readers that, given the strict restrictions on the mobility of these elite Indian women, presumably in contrast to herself, in the end, "Their numerous Riches are all the Enjoyment they have."[58]

Montagu's *Letters* had been published by the time Jemima Kindersley set sail from England and traveled via Brazil and southern Africa to Dutch-controlled Nagapatam (today, Nagapattinam) on the southeastern coast of India in June 1765. Her husband, Nathaniel Kindersley, was an officer in the East India Company's newly reorganized Bengal Artillery. In Madras she boarded a ship to travel along the Bay of Bengal coast, arriving in Calcutta just months before Ihtishamuddin would set sail in the opposite direction. After a year in Calcutta, Kindersley traveled north to Patna, Bihar, and Allahabad.[59] Some years after her return to London in early 1769 with her young son—and after her husband's subsequent death in India—she published her own book, *Letters from the Island of Teneriffe, Brazil, the Cape of Good Hope, and the East Indies* (1777), based on her detailed notes over five years.[60] A contemporary reviewer deemed that "tho' we cannot compliment the writer with having displayed the epistolary talents of a Lady Mary Wortley Montague," the sixty-eight letters composing the book are "sensible and amusing" and "display the good sense, ingenuity, and judicious reflection of the author."[61]

Given dominant ideas about Muslims in English society, Kindersley expressed surprise that the "Mahomedans who entered Hindostan left the spirit of conversion behind them." She was struck by some elite Muslims' fondness for English ham—which they call "European mutton" in an effort to evade the law—and surmised that "Mussulmen in India are not such strict observers of their religion, as in the countries nearer the tomb of the prophet." Noting that earlier travelers had claimed that Muslims believe women have no souls "and are, by the prophet, excluded from Paradise," she clarified that those who are "learned in the Arabic language, who take their authority from the Alcoran [Quran] itself, deny this, as an absolute falsity." After all, she reported, the Prophet promised his own wives that they would have a designated place in heaven if they obeyed "his laws." In the same letter, however, she lamented what she perceived as a lack of interest in the pursuit of knowledge and rational thought: "It is not here we must look for learning and science: the wise men of the East have disappeared, I believe throughout the East, at least in Hindostan, philosophy and philosophers are no more!" Like the Scottish philosophers of that era, she attributed this to the presence of great riches, which had fostered a life of indolence and opulence, further fueled by drink, opium, and bhang, and rendered them the "prey of foreigners."[62]

Kindersley conceded that "my account of the government and people of Hindustan must appear uncharitable, or you may think, that, with the true spirit of an Englishwoman, I condemn whatever is contrary to the customs of my own country." Recognizing that she had spent a great deal of time on the "indolence and stupidity of the inhabitants of India," Kindersley resolved to devote some space to praising local production. It was by dint of "patience and neatness," she wrote, that "some of their manufactories are brought to such perfection, that Europe can boast of nothing to equal them." She was particularly impressed with muslin—"the exquisite fineness of [which] is inconceivable"—and filigree jewelry, both produced in "Dacca, in Bengal." But even while on this subject, she was unable to resist pointing out that the work takes far too long and that the artisans, who were all male, were very good at imitating and copying but lacked the ability to invent their own patterns or improve their techniques. Although she decided ultimately that "neither Mahomedans or Hindoos ever change their mode, either in dress, furniture, carriages, or any other thing: therefore invention and improvement are not part of their ideas," she was unwilling to provide a definitive answer to the "often urged" matter of "whether black people are by nature inferior in understanding to white." She preferred instead to attribute local attitudes and conditions to the larger political and economic situation in which Indians found themselves.[63]

The frontispiece of Kindersley's book was an image of "An Apartment in a Zanannah," which in its composition bore an uncanny resemblance to the frontispiece of Ibn Battuta's book, which would be published in English in 1929. Her September 1767 letter began by expressing her great excitement at finally gaining entrance to a "Mussulman's Zanannah; a favour which they are not very fond of granting to Europeans." With some approval she noted that women's dress was generally "unchangeable," unlike in Europe, and not subject to the whims of "what is called the fashion." She commented rather dispassionately on the physical restrictions on elite women's mobility and child marriage as practices that "cannot be reckoned a misfortune to these women, as they have always been accustomed to it," and "they can know little more of the world than what they see around them." The lethal possibilities of a strict system of seclusion, however, were apparent, she recognized, in the "greater violence" of fires in Patna, where homes were built of straw and the winters cold and dry and where a wealthy Muslim man's zenana (women's quarters) burned with some twenty women and children inside. "The women knew their danger, but, either dreading the jealous rage of their husbands, or the disgrace of being exposed in public, did not attempt to make their escape, and perished."[64]

In 1781 Kindersley's interest in writing about women lead her to translate Antoine Léonard Thomas's *Essai sur les femmes* (1774) into English— and also to append to it "Two Original Essays." In Kindersley's translation Thomas described Islam and Muslims as a "religion and people, who established and consecrated forever the domestic slavery of women." It was precisely to confront the "servitude of women" in the "Mahomedan religion," he explained, and "to defend the honour and rights of the weaker sex" that the men of Europe, in all their "gallantry" and "chivalry," took up arms against Saracens and Moors. Kindersley departed from Thomas in the first of her two essays, in which she drew on her observations in Indian zenanas a decade earlier to provide an informed comparison of the Dutch with the "Mahomedans in Asia." While she identified the seraglio as the "supreme delight" and a "chief amusement" of a Muslim man, she explained that the reason for keeping "beautiful and numerous women" confined and guarded was not that the Muslim man "holds them in contempt." Rather, it was because they were "his most valuable treasures." The "extreme uxoriousness" of Muslim men gave women an important "natural power over them," and it was to guard against this that the men had established so many rules governing women's conduct. By contrast, she suggested, there was less need for such regulation in Holland, where men, being "of a phlegmatic disposition, devoted

FIGURE 4. The frontispiece of Kindersley's *Letters,* 1777.

to gain, enemies of luxury, prudent, selfish, and cold in their attachments to the sex," were in "little danger" of being too kind to women or of being overwhelmed by Dutch women's "natural power." The "manners" of the two sets of women, she continued, were "no less different than the laws by which they are governed." In conclusion she observed that the Muslim wife was valued ultimately only for her beauty and the Dutch wife only for her industry and contributions to her husband's business. Thus, while the former risked losing her status as she aged and her allure dulled, the latter risked being seen only as a partner and merchant, not a woman.[65]

Elizabeth Marsh, who arrived in India after Jemima Kindersley had returned to England, merits our attention for several reasons. Her life and writings conveniently paralleled the growing shift in popular (and of course commercial) interest in Britain away from the North African coast and Ottoman Empire and in the direction of India. In addition, unlike most Englishwomen who traveled to India, Marsh was a seasoned traveler who had lived in Menorca, Gibraltar, and Morocco. Rather unusually for a British person in India at that time, she also traveled a great deal within India, overland rather than by sea, which, she pointed out with pride in her journal, was a journey that "no European lady had ever undertaken…before."[66]

Marsh was also a fairly successful published author by the time she disembarked in India. Not only was she the first woman to write about and publish on the Maghreb (North Africa), but she was also the only British woman to pen a Barbary captivity narrative in the eighteenth century. *The Female Captive,* which ostensibly drew on her own captivity in the Moroccan court of Sidi Muhammad, was published anonymously in London in May 1769. The book met a demand in the English reading public for stories about people elsewhere, and the 750 copies issued in that first and only release disappeared quickly.[67] Much as in the case of Montagu's *Letters,* published just a few years earlier, there was a particular curiosity about women's perspectives and about the hidden areas in Eastern palaces accessible only to women travelers. Unlike Montagu, Marsh was not of a wealthy, aristocratic background, so the book was also meant to serve as a crucial source of income. Perhaps for that reason it reads at times like a tell-all confession of a female captive who, while not enslaved by the sultan, was exposed to more than was considered appropriate for a young, unmarried woman and who engaged in behavior outside the bounds of propriety and decorum for her position. However, like Montagu, Marsh's direct, if brief, experience of Muslim society led her to confront prevailing notions about political rule and slavery in Muslim lands.

Her captor, Sidi Muhammad, emerges as a despot—inevitably, perhaps, since he was after all a Muslim ruler—but surprisingly also as a "tender-hearted man" and an "absolute Prince." On the subject of slavery, she was quick to explain, with some dramatic exaggeration, that "Mahometans" regard their Christian slaves "as sacred as the tombs of their saints, from the ill-usage of any but their master, the Prince."[68]

In August 1770, about a year after her book was published, Marsh set off to join her husband, James Crisp, in Madras (now Chennai in India). A few years later they moved to Bengal so that Crisp might take up a new position as salt inspector for the newly created provincial council in Dacca.[69] Warren Hastings, who had been appointed governor of Bengal by the East India Company in April 1772, had undertaken major administrative reforms such that within a year he was able to inform Sir George Colbrooke, chair of the company, that "every intermediate power is removed, and the sovereignty of this country wholly and absolutely vested in the Company."[70] Bengal, which had been the richest province in Mughal India, with its abundance of desirable commodities like cotton, salt, and rice, was now the cornerstone of the emerging British Empire in South Asia. In contrast to London but also Calcutta, the new colonial capital, Dacca, was relatively inexpensive, and Marsh was able to enjoy a life of considerable luxury and leisure there. Before long, however, she left for Madras, citing the need for ocean air to improve her health. She traveled widely for some eighteen months and began to keep a diary. And, quite remarkably, given contemporary conventions, she traveled without her husband and young child and with an unmarried man, whom she referred to as her cousin, Capt. George Smith.[71]

Indian men and women appeared infrequently in her diary, given her initial preoccupation with documenting signs of validation from Europeans she encountered. She provided few identifying details about the "palanquin boys," "slave girls," and other servants who performed various tasks for her or even about the elite Indians she met. Her diary entries, however, describe economic activities in the places she passed through, information that would prove invaluable when she and Crisp later launched new economic ventures.[72] Ultimately, in contrast to her experiences and position in North Africa some years earlier, her approach to India and Indians reflected both the changing nature of relations between Britain and India—specifically, the expanding power of the company in Bengal and elsewhere—and her own position in India as a member of the colonial elite.

Marsh's sojourn in India coincided with the Boston Tea Party, when American colonists threw British East India Company tea overboard in protest against British taxes in the absence of parliamentary representation, and in July 1776, as she was making her way back from Madras to her family in Dacca, with the American Declaration of Independence. The loss of the American colonies inspired a fresh round of literary production in Britain, with novels that sought to redeem Britain as a land of liberty. Interestingly, even this effort to respond to American accusations of British tyranny relied on popular ideas about despotism and independence as they pertained to women in the East, specifically in Bengal and the Ottoman Empire.

In Robert Bage's *Mount Henneth* (1782), for example, the Indian merchant Duverda, worried about his daughter's future "amongst the sons of slavery or rapine," begs the English soldier James Foston to take her away with him. Foston had recently saved the young woman from being raped by two Indian soldiers who had fled from the defeat at the Battle of Plassey.[73] The "fair Syrian" in Bage's 1787 novel of that name is actually a young Englishwoman, Honoria Warren, who was born in Syria when her father was there as a merchant. Saif Ebn Abu, whose father worked with Honoria's, takes her captive after she spurns his offer of marriage, to make her his principal—but not his *only*—wife. When she eventually returns to Europe, having been held captive in a series of harems, she recalls the "avarice and despotism" of the East and contrasts the "gentlemen of Europe [who] pay their court to the ladies, by a polite attention" with the "Orientals" whose looks betray the "idea of property, associated with that of the superiority of species."[74] The changing relationship between the English and North Africans is reflected too in the solicitous Lady Bembridge's interruption of Honoria's story to chide her for giving her birth date using an Islamic month when, a century earlier, Lord Oliver Cromwell had used the Islamic calendar in his correspondence with Hamet Basha.[75] Lady Bembridge tells Honoria, "Let us have Christian calculations in the future if you please; for that bear, Mahomet, with his lock-up houses for women, is my aversion....I cannot forgive him his harams."[76] A decade later, as we shall see, many of Bage's caricatures of Muslim life would reappear in Mary Wollstonecraft's *A Vindication of the Rights of Woman* and its novelistic sequel, *Maria, or The Wrongs of Woman*.[77]

THE DANGERS OF THE
"GORGEOUS EASTERN HARLOT"

Alongside literary works like Robert Bage's, the strengthening of British power in Bengal and other parts of India in the late eighteenth century prompted debates in Britain about the nature and future direction of British control of India. These debates took center stage in the impeachment trial of Warren Hastings, the first British governor-general of India. Of particular interest to us in this lengthy trial are the repeated invocations, as one caricature put it, of "begums begums begums" (term for women of families of high rank; a term of respect), referring to the inordinate attention paid to Hastings's alleged abuses of elite Indian women.[78]

The trial opened with much fanfare and hundreds of curious spectators in February 1788 in Westminster Hall in London. Few other public events had attracted such an aristocratic, fashionable, and noticeably female audience, including Queen Charlotte (consort of King George III) and her daughters. Abigail Adams, who was preparing to return to the United States, where her husband, John Adams, had hopes of a position in the new republic, reported tickets were scarce, but "as a Foreign ministers Lady I have had a Seat in the Box appropriated for them, and have had the pleasure of hearing mr Burk speak 3 hours."[79] Clearly, women and men alike were eager to witness the theatrical performances of famed orators Edmund Burke, Charles Fox, and Richard Sheridan.[80]

Hastings was charged with "high crimes and misdemeanours" for having brought the "British Name and Character" into "great Discredit, Disgrace and Dishonour." Not only had Hastings stolen and plundered in India, Burke maintained, but he had become corrupted by the East, "the chalice of the fornications of rapine, usury, and oppression which was held out by the gorgeous eastern harlot." More specifically, Hastings stood accused of having subjected elite Indian women to the "coarse male hands of the law" by dragging them to the company's courts, in violation of "all the principles of local decorum"; of having violated the zenana of the begums of Oudh (now Awadh); and of inflicting physical torture and offenses to the "honour of the whole female race" in various parts of Bengal, including Dinajpur, Rangpur, and Idrakpur—even though many of these reports had already been found to be untrue.[81] Perhaps most shocking, at least to hear the prosecution tell it, was that Hastings had invested political authority in a woman of humble background, a dancing girl who had become the wife of Mir Jafar,

FIGURE 5. "A view of the tryal of Warren Hastings Esqr. before the Court of Peers in Westminster Hall on an impeachment delivered at the Bar of the House of Lords by the Commons of Great Britain in Parliament assembled February 13, 1788." Hamilton Alexander Rosskeen Pollard, engraver, 1789, Library of Congress Prints and Photographs Division, Washington, DC.

nawab of Bengal. The woman was, of course, none other than Munni Begum, whom we met in chapter 1. For the English press and London parliamentarians, accustomed to certain ideas about the place, power, and intelligence of women in general and of nonelite women and Eastern women in particular, such a relationship was cause for both surprise and concern. For the prosecutors Hastings's decision to invest a woman, especially a low-born one, with so much power and responsibility made sense only if understood as a favor in exchange for a bribe.[82]

Hastings's reliance on a woman—especially one who "had been sold as a slave; her profession a dancer, her occupation a prostitute"—and his acceptance of gifts from her came to epitomize his misconduct in India. As evidence, the prosecution produced letters exchanged between Hastings and Munni Begum that betrayed an affectionate tone and included a discussion of the lavish presents that Munni Begum had showered on Hastings and his wife. These included furniture sets made of ivory and buffalo horn and a generous allowance of several thousand pounds for the governor-general whenever he came to Murshidabad.[83] In return, the prosecution continued, Hastings had acquiesced to Munni Begum's various requests, such as an exalted position for herself in the nawab's household and an investigation into allegations of corruption and misrule by Muhammad Reza Khan. Recall that Robert Clive had installed Reza Khan as *naib nazim* (deputy governor) of Bengal in 1765 in light of the young age of the new ruler, Mir Jafar's son with Munni Begum. Following the short reigns and early deaths of her sons, Munni Begum was removed from her position as head of the nawab's household, but she found her way back with Hastings's support.

In his efforts to govern effectively, efficiently, and pragmatically, Hastings had sought to form alliances with Indian rulers and rely on Indian intermediaries.[84] While Bahu Begum and Sadr un-Nisa Begum of Oudh, the mother and widow of Nawab Shuja ud-Daula, had wanted to withhold funds that the deceased nawab had promised the company, Munni Begum had been eager to offer sumptuous payments to Hastings in exchange for his assistance.[85] In time Hastings had come to depend on Munni Begum's counsel and support and, in a letter to her, acknowledged their shared interests and goals.[86]

Burke described as "monstrous" Hastings's very act of removing from authority Nawab Mubarak-ud-daulah's own mother (Babbu Begum), "a legitimate wife of the Nabob Jaffier Ali Khân, a woman of rank and distinction, fittest to take care of the person and interests, as far as a woman could take care of them, of her own son." Hastings deposed this woman, Burke continued, and, moreover, replaced her with a "woman in the seraglio, called Munny Begum, who was bound to the Nabob by no tie whatever of natural affection." Hastings restored Munni Begum to her former position as head of the nawab's household, "at the head of all his family and of his domestic concerns in the seraglio within doors, and at the head of the state without, together with the disposal of the whole of the revenue that was allowed him." In another impassioned speech Burke described Munni Begum as the "object of his passion and flame, to which he sacrifices as much as Antony ever did to Cleopatra." He accused Hastings of handing over to her the "administration of the civil judicature, and of the executory justice,—together with the salary which was intended for Mahomed Reza Khân."[87]

The contradictions in the prosecution's views about Indian women quickly became apparent to observers. In April 1789 the newspaper *World* noted that, while Sheridan and Burke accepted and supported the authority of the begums of Oudh, their attitude to Munni Begum was far more negative. Perhaps the prosecution was opposed not to powerful women as such but rather to the rise to power of someone of such humble origins; this would explain Burke's repeated reminders to his listeners that Munni Begum was—and thus forever remained?—a dancing girl. While the prosecutors saw the begums of Oudh as having been made to suffer by Hastings, they depicted Munni Begum as having ruined Bengal with her lowly background and uncontrolled behavior. Following Burke's repeated use of terms like the "dancing girl," "harlot," and "prostitute" to refer to Munni Begum, an anonymous report of the trial published in 1796 noted, in Hastings's defense, that the "English never knew her in any of those characters" but rather as the wife of Mir Jafar and the mother of his successor.[88] For Burke, Munni Begum was akin to the revolutionary French women who escorted Marie Antoinette from Versailles to Paris, women whom Burke would describe as "furies from hell, in the abused shape of the vilest of women" in his famous 1790 pamphlet *Reflections on the Revolution in France*. Statements like this, which reflected his support for existing social hierarchies, would provoke a prompt response from Mary Wollstonecraft in her *Vindication of the Rights of Men*.[89]

In the end Hastings was acquitted in the House of Lords, considerably impoverished but hailed the savior of British India. After all, even through the highs and lows of seven years of legal drama, there had never been any doubt about whether Britain should be in India. If anything, the trial of a high-ranking colonial official and his administration cleansed the British presence in India of corruption. This left the colonial administration free to grow in strength and, indeed, to turn its attention to reforming what it regarded as the corrupt practices of Indians that until then it had quietly ignored as local traditions. Britain was freed, in other words, to pursue its civilizing mission in India.[90]

Munni Begum continued to receive a generous monthly pension and live in style. She maintained that she was quite highly regarded by the company and, in a 1793 letter to Cornwallis—lately of the American War of Independence and by then governor-general in India—wrote about herself (in the third person): "All the English Gentlemen...regarded her as their Mother."[91] In 1803 the English noble Lord Valentia sought out a meeting with the "celebrated Munny Begum, widow of Jaffier Khan, so well known in Europe by the rhetoric of Mr. Burke."[92] A decade later Lady Maria Skinner Nugent, wife of the commander in chief of British forces in India, called on her at the nawab's palace in Murshidabad. Nugent had been curious about this nonagenarian whose "fame has been long known in England, from the trial of Mr. Hastings, and the rhetoric of Mr. Burke." Indeed, the "history of her life would include almost every event of importance, in the east, connected with British dominion, for nearly a century past." In the end Nugent was disappointed to find, like Lord Valentia, "no remains of the beauty and elegance, once said to be hers," though "now and then she seems to rally, and a glimmering of her former energies appears."[93]

Public awareness of and interest in politics, India, and empire was such that Warren Hastings and the trial soon appeared in women's fictional writings, most immediately in Phebe Gibbes's *Hartly House, Calcutta*. Published in London under the name of the book's letter-writing protagonist, Sophia Goldborne, the book landed on Mary Wollstonecraft's desk in the summer of 1789. Wollstonecraft's generally positive review appeared in the *Analytical Review* that June, even as Sheridan was dramatically describing Hastings's misdeeds with the begums of north India and just days before the storming of the Bastille across the channel.[94]

CULTIVATING ENGLISH SOULS
AND CHRISTIAN VIRTUE

The Hastings trial was still in progress—though it had lost much of its early sensational appeal and an acquittal already appeared inevitable—when Mary Wollstonecraft began to write *A Vindication of the Rights of Woman*. She was already well known by then, having published the pamphlet *Vindication of the Rights of Men* in 1790, initially anonymously. Her *Rights of Men* was a response to Burke's *Reflections on the Revolution in France* and predated Thomas Paine's own famous response to Burke by a few months. Wollstonecraft was happy, in her own words, amid the "gleams of sunshine" and "tranquility" she experienced in the study of her spacious new home in Bloomsbury, less than two miles from the Hastings trial in Westminster Hall, and she was able to complete the new 450-page manuscript in just six weeks.[95]

Published in 1792 in London, Paris, Lyon, Boston, and Philadelphia, *Rights of Woman* secured Wollstonecraft's place as the most famous women's rights advocate of the Anglo-American Enlightenment. Over a century later British feminist Rachel (or Ray) Strachey would describe the book as "the text of the movement" in her 1928 account of the women's movement in Great Britain, *The Cause*.[96] Among its immediate admirers were the much-maligned US official Aaron Burr and his wife, Theodosia Prevost. Longtime advocates of women's rights, they were easily persuaded to raise and educate their daughter, also called Theodosia, in line with Wollstonecraft's principles.

In a 1793 letter to Prevost, Burr assured her that such an education would "convince the world what neither sex appear to believe—that women have souls!"[97] Burr's commitment to education for all led him to educate enslaved Black people in his household as well as his children with Mary Eugénie Beauharnais Emmons, a Bengali household servant whom he married after Prevost's death.[98]

Writing in the aftermath of the American, French, and Haitian Revolutions, Wollstonecraft was enraged by the contradictions of most male Enlightenment philosophers who wrote of natural equality and human progress even as they clearly believed in immutable hierarchies of gender, race, and culture.[99] The English historian Catharine Macaulay, who died in 1791, deserves credit for Wollstonecraft's newfound attention to gender, a debt Wollstonecraft acknowledged in *Rights of Woman* as well as in an earlier letter to Macaulay.[100] The image of soulless women in harems proved crucial to both Macaulay's and Wollstonecraft's efforts to make a case for Englishwomen's rights.

The content and purpose of women's education preoccupied Macaulay and Wollstonecraft as it had Mary Astell, and as it would feminists around the world even in the twenty-first century. Both writers argued that there were no inherent differences between the sexes, and therefore there should be no difference in the education they receive. In making this argument, they were taking on the Geneva-born Jean-Jacques Rousseau's suggestion that "the whole education of women ought to relate to men. To please men, to be useful to them, to make herself loved and honored by them, to raise them when young, to care for them when grown, to counsel them, to console them, to make their lives agreeable and sweet—these are the duties of women at all times, and these ought to be taught from childhood."[101]

For Macaulay and Wollstonecraft such an education could only produce women akin to the vapid denizens of the seraglio. As Macaulay put it, Rousseau "would have a young French woman cultivate her agreeable talents, in order to please her future husband, with as much care and assiduity as a young Circassian cultivates hers in order to fit her for the harem of an eastern bashaw." She proposed instead a curriculum for girls and boys that included physical education and a study of the classics. This, she argued, would prepare the pupil to "act a rational part in the world, and not to fill up a niche in the seraglio of a sultan."[102]

Wollstonecraft, for her part, began *Rights of Woman* by accusing male European authors of texts "on female rights and manners" of operating "in the true style of Mahometanism." She explained that by this she meant that women "are treated as a kind of subordinate being, and not a part of the human species, when improvable reason is allowed to be the dignified distinction which raises men above the brute creation, and puts a natural scepter in a feeble hand." She also demanded of Rousseau: "Why...does he say that a girl should be educated for her husband with the same care as for an eastern haram?" For Wollstonecraft sexuality, which she understood as being solely in the service of men, was the prime source of all women's oppression. While she was quite aware of the ways a woman might use her sexuality to manipulate men, she disapproved of such "artificial graces and coquetry" or, as she put it elsewhere, of woman being "made a coquetish slave in order to render her a more alluring object of desire, a *sweeter* companion to man." She ended by calling on "men of understanding" to grant Englishwomen the rights to which they were entitled, "or ye will be worse than Egyptian task-masters."[103]

The many male advocates of enlightened or modern gallantry who so irked Wollstonecraft also used European ideas about the Turkish treatment of women to support their position regarding British women. The Scottish physicians William Alexander and John Gregory made the case that the very existence of seraglios was evidence enough of how far behind on the evolutionary scale the Turks were relative to the English. For Alexander the Turks with their seraglios were the perfect contemporary example of the backward ill-treatment of women. He saw the Turks and their beliefs and customs as unchanging, indeed occupying the same place on the evolutionary ladder as ancient Greeks, who had confined women to their homes.[104]

Gallantry posed a problem for Wollstonecraft because men's "specious homage," "trivial attentions," "condescending endearment," and "hollow respect" to women allowed them to "insultingly" bolster "their own superiority." Women, in the process, came to expect "artful flattery and sexual compliments" rather than the "language of truth and soberness."[105] Instead of being offered liberty and egalitarian friendship, women were "confined... in cages like the feathered race" and were valued only for physical attributes and "negative virtues" like "patience, docility, good-humour, and flexibility, virtues incompatible with any vigorous exertion of intellect."[106] It was this state, crucially for our purposes, that she likened to the female inmates of the Turkish seraglio. In her time women in Britain were educated only to the extent that would allow them to secure a good match in marriage, a single-minded focus that made "mere animals of them.... Surely these weak beings are only fit for a seraglio!" After all, as Wollstonecraft pointed out in a later chapter,

> In a seraglio,…all these arts are necessary; the epicure must have his palate tickled, or he will sink into apathy; but have women so little ambition as to be satisfied with such a condition? Can they supinely dream life away in the lap of pleasure, or the languor of weariness, rather than assert their claim to pursue reasonable pleasures and render themselves conspicuous by practising the virtues which dignify mankind? Surely she has not an immortal soul who can loiter life away merely employed to adorn her person, that she may amuse the languid hours, and soften the care of a fellow-creature who is willing to be enlivened by her smiles and tricks, when the serious business of life is over.[107]

Wollstonecraft's ideas about the seraglio were closely linked to her position on polygamy, which would come to define the European feminist stance on the practice. She regarded it as yet another instance of the "physical degradation" of women, a direct attack on "domestic virtue," and a practice that presumed that "women must be inferior to man, and made for him."[108] Moreover, the physical confinement that she associated with the harem (and other Eastern practices such as foot binding in China) violated her belief in the importance of fresh air and exercise for girls as for boys. Her assault on the seraglio arose also from her rejection of all-female spaces. In contrast to Mary Astell and Mary Montagu, she saw no advantages to "many females being shut up together in nurseries, schools, or convents."[109]

Wollstonecraft also drew on the popular European misconception about Islamic doctrine regarding women's souls—or the lack thereof—to make her case for Englishwomen's rights. Criticizing the poet John Milton for describing women, in *Paradise Lost,* as having been "formed for softness and sweet attractiveness," Wollstonecraft concluded that such a description made sense to her only if "in the true Mahometan Strain, he meant to deprive us of souls."[110] For Wollstonecraft the seraglios of the Turks were a suitable-enough home for those who had neither souls nor rational minds and, instead, were filled with artifice, seeking only trifles and pleasantries. By contrast, Englishwomen, although currently being treated in that manner, decidedly deserved better than to be reduced to that state.

The metaphor of slavery appeared alongside the Eastern harem in Wollstonecraft's discussions of Englishwomen's status. Remarkably, *Rights of Woman* contained over eighty references to different kinds of slavery, in contrast to her *Rights of Men,* published just two years earlier, which had included only four or five.[111] In *Rights of Woman* she drew clear parallels between the hundreds of thousands of African men and women then enslaved in Europe and the Americas, women in seraglios, and white middle-class Englishwomen whose lives were devoted to serving men. No doubt on her mind when she was writing the *Rights of Woman* were the recent failure of the Abolition Bill to pass in the House of Commons in April 1791 and the revolt of enslaved men and women in the French colony of San Domingo (today's Haiti) in August 1791. Also unfolding in 1791–92 was an early phase of the English campaign against slavery, with some three hundred thousand English women, men, and children participating in the "anti-saccharite" campaign, the boycott of sugar produced with slave labor on West Indian plantations.[112] In addition, as a reviewer for the liberal periodical *Analytical Review,* Wollstonecraft had had the opportunity to read and publish on not only Catharine Macaulay's *Letters on Education* and Phoebe Gibbes's *Hartly House, Calcutta* but also *The Interesting Narrative of the Life of Olaudah Equiano,* a chronicle of colonial slavery, and John Moore's anti-slavery novel, *Zeluco.*[113]

As the ideal of middle-class womanhood diffused throughout English society, a mirror image of the Muslim woman as *the* negative ideal came into ever sharper focus. In other words, the Western woman came to be defined as possessing precisely the many traits that the Muslim woman lacked, and vice versa. The emerging cult of domesticity, which by the mid-nineteenth century would call on middle-class Englishwomen to stay at home, be virtuous and chaste, and create a home that provided her husband with a safe harbor from the troubles of the outside world, was of course meant precisely to serve the increasing demands of the country's industrial, commercial, and colonial ventures. Even as middle-class women were told that they could best serve their nation and society by staying at home—to provide unpaid household labor, bear and raise children, and produce future soldiers and workers—they were also repeatedly reminded that they were better off than non-European women.[114] While Wollstonecraft agreed with male British writers such as John Millar that the lives of Englishwomen were superior to those of their Turkish counterparts, she forcefully accused Britain's men of oppressing Englishwomen enough that they teetered on the brink of plunging to the level of harem women. In this sense she considered English husbands to be as bad as "Mahometans," and she rebuked the "husband who lords it in his little haram."[115]

Wollstonecraft's religious grounding had persuaded her of men's and women's equality under God. It had led to a desire to address the "injustice which one half of the human race are obliged to submit to" and advocate for the "improvement and emancipation of the whole sex." She clearly had faith in the power of the right education, religious beliefs, and material conditions to bring about the desired change. As long as men and women had souls, they had the potential to acquire and display reason and virtue. Her use of the abstract "woman" in her book's title would certainly suggest that she meant all women.[116] However, by accepting and repeating the idea that Muslim women do not have souls, she ultimately excluded them from her vision for all women.

In the end Wollstonecraft and other radical writers of that era did not simply condemn what they saw as the vices of Eastern life, among them debauchery, frivolity, luxury, weakness, and idleness. Rather, by juxtaposing these vices against Western reason and liberty, Wollstonecraft was in fact outlining the traits of Englishness itself: rational, virtuous, efficient, and industrious. All that she perceived as wrong in English society—the traditionally feminine ills among the aristocracy and the popular classes—she projected onto and magnified in Eastern society. The East, then, contained not only the barbarous practices of traditional societies but also the worst features of contemporary English society. Put differently, to her mind English society could not properly progress until these residual traditional elements were excised. According to Wollstonecraft, these Eastern traits within English society were most visible in the rules governing the lives of girls and women, in matters from education to marriage and finances. Although her priority was to articulate concern for Englishwomen's rights, she cemented the idea of the East not simply as different but as inferior and, hence, less worthy of esteem (though not beyond being colonized and exploited).[117]

Wollstonecraft's work inspired literary writing by other women, who also portrayed the East as the home of true despotism and downtrodden women deprived of souls. The actor Mary Darby Robinson, for example, published *A Letter to the Women of England* (1799) under the pseudonym Anne Frances Randall. Identifying herself as a disciple of Wollstonecraft's, she too called for greater attention to women's education, given women's intellectual equality to men. In a footnote she repeated what the English now considered a truism: "The Mahometans are said to be of opinion that WOMEN have no souls!" Like Wollstonecraft, her primary concern was that British men, rather than climbing the rungs of civilization, stood in danger of slipping down, given how poorly they treated women: "And I should not be surprized, if the present system of mental subordination continues to gain strength, if, in a few years, European husbands were to imitate those beyond the Ganges. There, wives are to be purchased like slaves, and every man has as many as he pleases."[118]

At the same time, as an astute observer of her society, Robinson was sufficiently moved by the plight of the lascars—East Indian sailors who had served as crew on company ships to Britain but were offloaded and left to fend for themselves on city streets—to write about them in her poem "The Lascar, in Two Parts." The very presence of lascars in Britain in the early nineteenth century was, of course, a tangible reminder of Britain's growing imperial power and presence in India. In lamenting the plight of a young lascar, a "wretched Indian slave," she critiqued her own society's ill-treatment of these workers as well as of women, much as Wollstonecraft and other writers had used Caribbean slavery as a way to discuss the injustices perpetrated against women in English society.[119]

THE "OVERBEARING INSOLENCE" OF THE ENGLISH

Two years after Wollstonecraft's untimely death following complications from childbirth, and a generation after Ihtishamuddin's visit to Britain, another illustrious traveler from Bengal arrived in London. He would soon publish a comparative assessment of women's status in England and India, largely in response to the many misconceptions he encountered regarding "Asian women" among Europeans. This visitor was Mirza Abu Taleb Khan, also known as Mirza Abu Mohammad Tabrizi Isfahani (after his father's ancestral home in Iran). Following his time in England, he would be known popularly as Mirza Abu Taleb Londoni, a direct reversal of how he had often been referred to while in London, "The Persian Prince."[120]

Born in Lucknow, Abu Taleb initially worked under the nawabs of Oudh, the same family as the famous begums of Oudh whom Hastings was accused of having harassed. On losing the court job, he moved to Calcutta to look for employment with the English, and it was to his adopted home of Calcutta and Bengal that he would repeatedly compare the places he visited.[121] When a Scottish friend, Capt. David Richardson, invited Abu Taleb to come with him to Britain, he agreed, hoping perhaps that the voyage would help him overcome the tragic death of his four-year-old son and also that he might be able to set up a Persian-language educational institute in England that would allow him to pay off his debts.[122]

Abu Taleb's account of the sea voyage included a discussion of the technology and science at work, as well as unusual social customs he observed among the "Hollander" communities in southern Africa, where they stopped en route. From Cape Town Abu Taleb traveled to Dublin, where he called on the Marquis Cornwallis, whom he had met a number of times in India and who was then lord lieutenant of Ireland. After Richardson left for London, Abu Taleb found that his English improved much more rapidly "by not having any person to interpret for me." He finally arrived in London on 21 January 1800, "being five days short of a Lunar year from the period of my leaving Calcutta."[123]

Abu Taleb spent two and a half years in England, much of it in the company of high society. Taken to be Persian royalty, he was welcomed into exclusive gatherings, including a masquerade, and attended the theater and opera. Indeed, such was his status that the recently acquitted Warren Hastings called on him—and ruined a pair of new gloves in the process by knocking on the freshly painted door of Abu Taleb's London home. Abu Taleb's social rank also facilitated several audiences with King George III, Queen Charlotte, and the Prince of Wales.[124]

Abu Taleb was fascinated by the Indian influences already visible in British culture, in plays, in architecture—he visited Charles Cockerell's Mughal-style home in Sezincote—and in the costumes at a masquerade. Yet at the same time he was exasperated by the ignorance he encountered regarding India and Islam—a complaint that South Asian visitors to the West over the following two centuries would continue to articulate—as well as the "overbearing insolence which characterizes the vulgar part of the English in their conduct to Orientals." In response to a comment from a "genteel looking man" on a London stagecoach about the "scarcity of money" in India, Abu Taleb retorted that "no country abounded with more wealth than Hindoostan, and that it was proverbial for making the fortunes of all adventurers," surely a pointed reference to the many British, most famous among them Clive and Hastings, who had enriched themselves in India. He was also "attacked on the apparent unreasonableness and childishness of some of the Mohammedan customs."[125]

In his *Travels* Abu Taleb commented at length on the ethnic divisions within Britain, specifically, English attitudes toward the Scots and Irish; the poverty of the peasantry, especially in Ireland; and the lack of religion among the working class, which he believed should be promptly treated to avoid a revolution like that in France. Across almost thirty pages he listed what he perceived as the twelve primary vices of the English; he then sought to balance this with a list of virtues that required only five pages. He summarized the stadial theory of the Scottish philosophers as arguing, basically, that "mankind has risen from the state of savages, to the exalted dignity of the great philosopher Newton."[126]

Abu Taleb also wrote with deep appreciation about both European women and wine. No doubt because he was already married and in his late forties— and, in any case, an exotic foreigner—his flirtation with Englishwomen was not seen as inappropriate by the circles in which he socialized. Similarly, he enjoyed his witty repartees with Englishwomen, but his own flirting episodes aside, he expressed his disapproval of the lack of chastity and morality in English society, particularly in comparison to Indian society.[127]

In 1802, a few weeks after Abu Taleb had left England for his long overland journey to India via France, Italy, the Ottoman Empire, and Persia, his essay "Vindication of the Liberties of Asiatic Women" appeared in the *Asiatic Annual Register.* He had written it in Persian and then supervised its translation into English by his friend and former travel companion David Richardson. In the following decades this essay would be reprinted over ten times, including in Dutch, French, and German translations. It would also be republished as an appendix to the 1810 translation of his book *Travels.* In a brief introduction the editor of the *Register* described it as a "curious article," but one worthy of interest for all the information it contained about the "Mussulmans of Hindustan and the peculiar privileges and customs of their women." The editor noted, almost as an afterthought, that Abu Taleb also shared "imperfect and curious notions...of our habits and customs," which, to a *"Hindustanee,...* from their striking contrast to his own, they must appear so singular and unaccountable." Even in later editions, however, there was little indication that Abu Taleb's commentary on Englishwomen led to any reflection among his British publishers or readers regarding the status of Englishwomen.[128]

His "Vindication," Abu Taleb explained, was a response to those who "consider their own customs the most perfect in the world...and that the women of Asia have no liberty at all, but live like slaves, without honour and authority...[when, in fact,] it is the European women who do not possess so much power." He discussed in some detail the very issues that perplexed Europeans about women in the East and "make the liberty of the Asiatic women appear less than that of the Europeans," such as purdah, polygamy, marriage, and divorce. Without denying that there existed problems in these and other areas, he highlighted their positive aspects and tried to explain why these practices persisted. He attributed the differences in cultural practices between Britain and "Asia" not to innate cultural prejudices but rather to specific needs and conditions. Thus, one reason he gave to explain why the "liberty of the Asiatic women appear[s] less than that of the Europeans" was Britain's geographic location and the relative homogeneity of its population: "In this kingdom, placed in a corner of the globe where there is no coming and going of foreigners, the intercourse of the sexes is not attended with the consequences of a corruption of manners, as in Asia, where people of various nations dwell in the same city." Demonstrating a lack of defensiveness vis-à-vis his Hindu compatriots that would become increasingly scarce in later debates within South Asia, especially regarding women, he went on to elucidate his argument by pointing out that "before the Mussulmans entered Hindustan, the women did not conceal themselves from view" and that in Hindu villages Hindu women still did not. However, in the cities, which were much more mixed, Hindu women practiced seclusion "rigidly."[129] In other words, Indian women had to practice seclusion to protect themselves from corruption by other cultures.

Similarly, he explained that European women could not be kept "in concealment" because they had to help their husbands in their business activities, while Asiatic women had no such obligations. Social and legal arrangements "wisely determined" by lawmakers helped European women maintain their chastity and follow rules even as they gave the impression that they enjoyed freedom. These included the expectation that they would be productively occupied outside the home, not interact with strangers, not walk alone on the streets, not visit bachelors—basically, that they would have no time or opportunity for improper behavior.[130] Because Englishwomen did not own property, unlike Muslim women, they were utterly dependent on their male relatives and therefore had no choice but to submit to such rules. Elite Muslim women, by contrast, did not need to go outside because they owned property and could oversee its use from within their private quarters, a space in which they also enjoyed leisure activities. In any case Muslim women were free to go out to visit friends and relatives as long as they were properly attired.[131]

While he recognized that, for the English, "liberty may be considered as the idol, or tutelary deity" and that the "common people here enjoy more freedom and equality than in any other well-regulated government in the world," he felt compelled to conclude that in comparison to European women, for whom "liberty" *(azadi)* is about being able to move freely in

FIGURE 6. *Muslim Lady Reclining* (wearing, no doubt, the famed muslin of Bengal). Francesco Renaldi, Dacca, 1789. Paul Mellon Collection, Yale Center for British Art, New Haven, CT.

public, the Muslim women of India enjoyed a more authentic liberty and power.[132] Among the examples he provided were their power "over the property and children," their say in their children's marriages, and their choice whether to assist their husbands in their business.[133] If anything, he noted, Asiatic women had too much power over their families and servants, and this was no doubt at the root of many problems in Asiatic society.[134] He expressed no desire to introduce English manners and customs into India, especially any that pertain to women, just as he had no interest in "convert[ing] the people [of England] to Mohammedanism, and to make them forsake the religion of their forefathers," as feared by the bishop he met.[135]

As he put it in the travelogue he completed soon after his return to India,

> It is evident that English women, not withstanding their apparent liberty, and the politeness and flattery with which they are addressed, are, by the wisdom of their lawgivers, confined in strict bondage; and that on the contrary, the Muslim women, who are prohibited from mixing in society, are kept

concealed behind curtains, but are allowed to walk out in veils, and go to the baths, and visit their fathers and mothers and even female acquaintances, and to sleep away from home for several nights together, are much more mistresses of their own conduct and much more liable to fall into paths of error.[136]

His attention to his message and audience is apparent if we compare the "Vindication," which he wrote for publication in England, with the travelogue meant for his fellow elite Indians. In the latter he was more sharply critical of local practices. For example, in the travelogue he harshly criticized the local practice of polygamy that in the "Vindication" he had dismissed as a fairly rare occurrence.[137]

We don't know whether Abu Taleb read Wollstonecraft's two *Vindications,* and it is indeed possible that he used the title simply because it was common for tracts in that era.[138] We do know, however, that the Wollstonecraft essays were part of public discussion at the time Abu Taleb was in England, as was her posthumously published novel *Maria, or The Wrongs of Woman.* In seeking to nuance discussions about liberty and freedom, Abu Taleb appeared to share Wollstonecraft's ideas about the distractions of politeness, flattery, and gallantry from the pursuit of true liberty for Englishwomen. In his defense of Muslim women's liberties, he anticipated the arguments of early twentieth-century Bengali Muslim feminists such as Rokeya Hossain, who was careful not to equate unveiling with freedom, as well as early twenty-first-century Muslim women around the world who have had to defend their decision to wear the hijab against those who deem it oppressive. That said, Abu Taleb did not approach this issue as a feminist. His "Vindication" did not demand rights for Indian women in the way Wollstonecraft's did for Englishwomen, but it is plausible that, having read or at least discussed Wollstonecraft's texts in his high-society gatherings, he felt compelled to respond to the image of Eastern women that was so central to Wollstonecraft's arguments about the liberty she desired for Englishwomen.

THREE

Gospel, Adventure, and Introspection in an Expanding Empire

IN THE NINETEENTH CENTURY Bengalis encountered the West primarily through the missionaries who lived and worked among them. In 1792, the same year that Mary Wollstonecraft ushered in Anglo-American feminism with her *Rights of Woman,* the British shoemaker-turned–Baptist minister William Carey launched the modern Western Christian missionary movement with his *Enquiry into the Obligations of Christians to Use Means for the Conversion of the Heathens.* Impressed with the accomplishments of the intrepid, if rapacious, European trading companies around the world, Carey called for a closer and mutually beneficial relationship between traders and preachers of the gospel. Missionaries, he argued, should emulate "English traders" who, "for the sake of gain, surmounted all those things which have generally been counted insurmountable obstacles in the way of preaching the gospel." Like the trading companies, missionaries should also form voluntary societies like his own Baptist Missionary Society to raise funds to send missionaries overseas. In turn, by spreading the gospel, missionaries could aid the colonial enterprise by making the "heathens," whose souls he recognized to be "as immortal as ours," into "useful members of society." To more effectively share the gospel, he called on missionaries to learn as much of the languages of the "natives" to "cultivate a friendship" with them.[1]

The following year Carey left for Calcutta with his wife, Dorothy; their four children; Dorothy's sister Kitty Plackett; and fellow missionary and surgeon John Thomas, whose own family had sailed ahead. This precedent would encourage future male Protestant missionaries to take along their families. Missionary wives, in time, would be joined by single women missionaries. Together they would assume responsibility for incursions into the zenanas with the goal of producing educated converts.[2]

Carey set sail for India before the British Parliament had authorized

British missionary activity in India. With commercial ventures its primary concern, the East India Company had adopted a policy of "non-interference" in local religious customs. However, since Carey and his companions had traveled aboard a Danish ship, they were permitted to disembark in Bengal, and there Carey found work managing an indigo factory. He eventually settled in the Danish enclave of Serampore (Srirampur), just northwest of Calcutta. On 10 January 1800, coincidentally just days before Abu Taleb began his long sojourn with the English, Carey and his fellow missionaries founded the Serampore Mission under the protection of the Danish king Frederick VI.[3]

Carey's *Enquiry* inspired women and men on both sides of the Atlantic to support the new missionary cause, initially with funds and then in person, though unmarried women would face resistance to their initial efforts to travel overseas. The Boston Female Society for Missionary Purposes, also established in 1800, was the first Western Christian missionary organization for women. A 1910 book celebrating the US missionary women's movement would clarify that this society was established "two months before Carey baptized his first convert in India." According to the society's early records, fundraising efforts in 1811 yielded $200, which was quickly dispatched for the "translation of the Scriptures by the Missionaries of Serampore in Bengal."[4]

The Charter Act of 1813 renewed the East India Company's charter for twenty more years but, by revoking its monopoly over trade in India, opened up the region to other British merchants and businesses. Moreover, the act removed the ban on British missionaries in India and announced Britain's responsibility, to the tune of one lakh (100,000 rupees) a year, for the education and "improvement" of Indians—at a time when there was no public provision of education in Britain. The missionary enterprise in turn helped to legitimize to many in Britain their country's imperial presence in India. In a post-Enlightenment and post–French Revolution Europe, it was necessary for Britain to demonstrate that it was not in India simply to exploit the country's economic resources but rather that it was responsible for civilizing India and its people by confronting their despotism, illiteracy, superstitions, religious practices, and, indeed, deplorable treatment of women.[5]

THE "PAGANS AND MAHOMETANS" OF INDIA

Prevented by company rules from engaging in open missionary activity during his first two decades in Bengal, Carey instead offered classes in Bengali at the Fort William College in Calcutta. The college had been established in 1800 on the model of Oxford and Cambridge by Gov.-Gen. Marquess Wellesley to train company employees so that they might be better equipped to resist the "dangerous" revolutionary ideas of the era and work "for the stability of the British power in India." Scholars at the college also revived the Asiatic Society, founded by Sir William Jones in 1784, and devoted their energies to studies on vernacular Indian languages as well as classical texts.[6]

The printing press at the Serampore Baptist Mission played a crucial role in constructing a standard literary Bengali prose, paving the way, as we shall see, for Bengali women's own publications some decades later. Equipped with a type foundry run by the Bengali Pancanan Karmakar and a printing press, the mission published a Bengali translation of the New Testament in February 1801. It was both the first translation of the text into any South Asian language and the first book of Bengali prose. In 1809 the mission started producing its own paper, and by 1832 the Serampore Mission had published and circulated 212,000 volumes in forty languages. Among these were translations of the Bible into additional languages, including Arabic, Persian, and Urdu, ostensibly for Muslims; Bengali translations of the Sanskrit Hindu epics *Ramayana* and *Mahabharata;* books on the positive aspects of Christian life; and dictionaries and books of grammar and language instruction.[7] Pressure from missionary organizations back in Britain on Serampore and other missionary presses for evidence of missionary activity contributed to the impressive number of publications over the course of the century. By midcentury missionaries also began to respond to growing curiosity among the reading public at home regarding life in the zenana, or women's quarters.[8]

Converting Muslims had not been not part of Carey's initial plans for India. In his *Enquiry* he had described India as divided equally between "Pagans and Mahometans," distinguishing the latter, as monotheists, from the "vast proportion of the sons of Adam…who yet remain in the most deplorable state of heathen darkness, without any means of knowing the true God."[9] Once in Bengal, however, Carey and his fellow missionaries inevitably sought out Muslims, though these efforts yielded few conversions.[10]

In a January 1794 journal entry, for example, Carey wrote of preaching to a largely Muslim congregation at the "Manicktullo bazaar." When the Muslim *munshi* (scholar-scribe) and others responded to the missionaries' efforts by retorting that "the Koran was sent to confirm the words of Scripture" that had become corrupted, Carey compelled them to admit that they had never read the Quran since it was in Arabic.[11] Missionary William Ward reported the furious reaction of his listeners when he described the Prophet Muhammad as a "very great sinner, and murderer and adulterer." Similarly, many of the Serampore Mission's publications seemed designed to offend rather than gently persuade local Muslims. A Persian tract titled *An Address to Mussulmuns* described Muhammad's "Creed... [as] the source of mental darkness" and Islam as a "lying religion."[12] Another publication, *Satya Dharma Nirupan* (Finding the true faith), focused on the Prophet's "licentiousness" and his relations with women, a long-standing European trope in anti-Islamic writing: "Not content with his wife and mistresses, he even took other men's wives.... He did not consider age or relationship in gratifying the cravings of the flesh. He was a notorious robber." Missionaries published not only in the more formal Sanskritized Bengali—versions of which were mocked as *sahebi bangla,* or European Bengali—but also, to reach the larger rural population, in Mussulmani Bengali, which was heavily peppered with Persian and Arabic words.[13]

REFORMING "HERETICAL WAYS"

The British missionaries proselytized, educated, and published in an Indian setting that was in a state of flux with the emergence of reform movements within and across different regions and religious communities. The Islamic reform movements that emerged in the early nineteenth century seemed unconcerned with the European presence, whether colonial or missionary, even though they developed in a political, economic, and increasingly social context informed by that presence. These reform movements also reflected the travels of Indian Muslims to and from the Arab world. Among the local practices they targeted for reform, those of women received special attention.

The Tariqah-i-Muhammadiya movement, which sought to closely follow the Prophet Muhammad's example, spread from northern India to rural western Bengal in the 1820s under Titu Mir and to southern Bengal a few years later under Inayat Ali. In Faridpur in eastern Bengal, Shariatullah spearheaded the Faraizi movement to purify Islam. In 1821 he returned from a twenty-year sojourn at al-Azhar University in Cairo and in Mecca, where he had studied Arabic literature, Islamic jurisprudence, and Sufism and encountered the emerging theological and political force of the Wahhabis. In their insistence on the need to return to early interpretations of the Quran and hadith and to purge Islamic practice of all unlawful accretions and corruptions, the Wahhabis had destroyed historical shrines in Iraq and captured the holy cities of Mecca and Medina. Inspired by this fervor, though not identifying his own movement in Bengal as Wahhabi, Shariatullah and then his son Dudu Miyan issued calls for economic justice and social equality grounded in Islamic precepts and attacked many *riwaj* (local practices) among Muslims that they believed contradicted the spirit of Quranic teachings. Even the Islamic movements' attacks on Muslim peasants' "un-Islamic" activities indicted the oppressive practices of zamindars (landowners), British indigo plantation owners, and the mostly Hindu moneylenders and landowners. The reformers denounced, for example, the special payments that the impoverished, and primarily Muslim, cultivators were required to make to Hindu zamindars on Hindu religious occasions, or *pujas*. Under Dudu Miyan the movement grew to include, by one contemporary British estimate, three hundred thousand followers and ultimately encompassed both Hindu and Muslim peasants.[14]

For these Islamic reform movements, the profound socioeconomic changes unfolding in the Bengal countryside proved of greater immediate concern than the presence of missionaries. The Industrial Revolution in Britain and the import into India of British factory-produced textiles had been pushing local spinners and weavers, Hindu and Muslim, out of the market, severely reducing their ability to meet their basic needs and effectively destroying indigenous production. These unemployed artisans turned to farming, creating further pressure on the land. The economic changes in the Bengal countryside affected women too, and often more acutely, given women's negligible economic opportunities and their complete financial dependence on male relatives. At the same time land rents continued to rise in keeping with the provisions of the 1793 Permanent Settlement of Land Revenues. Finalized under the watchful eye of Governor-General Cornwallis, this settlement replaced the oversight powers that zamindars had enjoyed under Mughal rule with essentially absolute, private, and hereditary landownership. For the British this ensured a fixed and reliable source of revenue, allowing them to turn their attention to tasks such as developing and enforcing new laws and undertaking their own reform projects.[15]

Because Muslim women participated in a variety of practices with their Hindu neighbors, they were specially targeted as sources of corruption by reformers advocating a pristine, "correct" form of Islam. Even Carey, in a January 1798 letter, had remarked that women were the "primary actors" in a particular ritual of sun worship and concluded "even Mussulmans have so far Hinduized as to join in the idolatry." In 1868 one Munshi Samiruddin lamented the "heretical ways among our people," such as the Muslim women's celebration of the Hindu *rakhi bandhan,* or brothers' day, when sisters honor their relationship to and protection by their brothers. Others criticized Muslim women's participation in Hindu celebrations like Holi and Diwali. The colonial civil servant W. W. Hunter recorded the complaints of Muslim villagers in western Bengal about a visiting reformist preacher who had forbidden the "drums and dancing girls at the marriage of our daughters." The reformers also targeted *pirs* (mystic guides; holy men) and their *dargahs,* or *mazaars* (shrines), long frequented primarily by women for solace, amulets, and advice and in hopes of saints' and holy men's intercession with God.[16] To be sure, the reformers were concerned as much with ending the economic exploitation of the poor by pirs and mullahs who made promises in exchange for payment as they were with purging local practices of what they regarded as un-Islamic accretions.[17]

Women's education and the legitimacy of congregational prayers in the context of British rule were among the unsettled doctrinal matters debated heatedly throughout Bengal. On women's education the general sense was that educated men would somehow transmit knowledge to their female relatives, and women would benefit also from *nasihat namas,* the inexpensive mass-produced religious-instruction manuals that proliferated starting in the late nineteenth century. Typically, they provided basic information about, for example, the five pillars of Islam and addressed social and religious matters such as rules governing marriage, divorce, and relations between men and women.[18] They sought to convey the author's ideas of "proper Islam" not in the Arabic and Persian that were accessible only to the learned elites but in Bengali mixed with Arabic, Hindi, Persian, and Turkish. Maulvi Maleh Muhammad's *Tanbih al-Nissa* (1875), for instance, reaffirmed male superiority quite bluntly, informing his readers that "the Lord has given man the higher status; women must follow the orders of their husbands." He dismissed women "who quarrel if their husbands take more wives" as "cantankerous" and "scoundrels." One of the most popular *nasihat namas* of the period was that by the same Munshi Samiruddin who had railed against *rakhi bandhan;* it underwent six editions between 1848 and 1880.[19]

The poet Shah Garibullah—best known for his epic love story *Yusuf-Zulekha* and *punthis* (narrative poems combining different languages) about Satya Pir and the Prophet's uncle Hamza—also wrote about women. In his poem "Imandar Nekbibir Kechcha" (The story of the pious and faithful lady), he celebrated the wifely devotion to the husband that he believed had been the norm in days past. He cited as an ideal woman in this regard Bibi (a term of respect for women, like Begum) Fatima, the daughter of the Prophet and the wife of the Prophet's cousin Ali, himself a future Sunni caliph and the first Shia imam. In another poem Garibullah chastised the modern woman as one who spoke ill of her husband in her neighbors' homes, neglected her household tasks, and complained that her husband didn't buy her jewelry. Works on Muslim women's conduct featured exemplary women from early Islamic history, such as Bibi Khadija and Bibi Fatima, as well as Sita of the Hindu epic *Ramayana* and the Sufi saint Rabia of Basra, who had renounced a traditional life to pursue her love of God.[20]

The Baul tradition of Bengal, inspired by the songs of nineteenth-century spiritual leaders like Lalan Fakir, provided an important counterpoint to the zeal of the Islamic reformist movements. Comprising both Muslim and Hindu men and women, Bauls flouted social norms about male-female interaction, female modesty, and women's role in religious rituals. Men and women, including but not exclusively married couples, wandered the countryside together and sang in public, denouncing worldly concerns, religious bigotry, and exploitation of the weak.[21]

RUDENESS AND CIVILIZATION

Despite the ferment and debates in different parts of India in the nineteenth century, the India that dominated influential European writings of the time was static, unchanging, and in urgent need of British intervention. This stood in contrast to the late eighteenth century, when Scottish Enlightenment writers had celebrated the accomplishments of ancient India (that is, India before the arrival of Muslims) in areas such as philosophy, science, and law.[22] By the early nineteenth century, the idea that India and its culture had nothing to teach the British was accompanied by the presumption that, despite the greater ease and frequency of travel between Britain and India, it was not necessary to have ever traveled to India to write about it. "James Mill, author of *History of British India*"—as his son John Stuart Mill would later introduce him in his own *Autobiography*—famously declared that his book was "of considerable utility" precisely because he had never been to India. He claimed that it was far more impartial and informative than the accounts of travelers who were inevitably distracted by details and whose "powers of observation" were, as a result, "exceedingly limited."[23] He also explained that he had deliberately relied entirely on European sources because he considered Eastern sources to be quite unreliable. As he had put it in an earlier essay in the *Edinburgh Review,* "The people of Europe can hardly form any conception of the extent to which the principle of exaggeration carries almost all the Eastern nations."[24] For us the *History of British India*'s significance lies in how Mill used it to legitimate British imperial rule in India and British projects for "civilizing" India, including in matters pertaining to its women, whom he depicted as barbarously oppressed.

James Mill (born Milne) started his *History* in 1806, just months after the birth of his eldest child, John Stuart. Two years later he met Jeremy Bentham, with whose utilitarian philosophy he would become associated.[25] He finally published his three-volume *History of British India* in 1817 and, shortly thereafter, joined the East India Company's London headquarters at India House.[26] The company had recently consolidated its hold in India following the defeat of the Marathas, much as the larger British Empire had secured its global strength following the defeat of the French at Waterloo. The book thus appeared at a fortuitous moment. It was quickly adopted as required reading for successive generations of company officials and authorities on India, with excerpts included in such texts as the *Oxford History of India* a full century later.[27]

In this massive history of India, as in an earlier essay on China, Mill drew on the Scottish Enlightenment language of stadial historical progress. He simplified the history, however, from one of several stages of progress to one of civilization and rudeness. He saw Indians and Chinese, among others, as frozen in their barbarity—most apparent in the manner in which they treat the "weaker sex"—until they could be rescued by good laws or the intervention of a more advanced society such as Britain. Acknowledging his debt to Scottish philosopher John Millar in a footnote, he asserted, "The condition of the women is one of the most remarkable circumstances in the manners of nations, and one of the most decisive criterions of the stage of society at which they have arrived. Among rude people the women are generally degraded; among civilized people, they are exalted."[28]

James Mill made it quite clear that he did not believe there was anything the reader could learn from Indians, since they were a "rude people," and his *History*—unlike all previous endeavors, he insisted—could help the British govern India that much more effectively. He summarily dismissed as ludicrous the suggestions of scholars like William Jones, founder of the Asiatic Society of Bengal, that the British work with "some of the natives themselves" to create an Indian legal code. This work was best left, Mill argued, to the "highest measure of European intelligence," not entrusted to the "unenlightened and perverted intellects of a few Indian pundits." It was, in particular, the Indians' treatment of women—"the habitual contempt which the Hindus entertain for their women"—that confined them to the lowest rungs of the civilizational scale. Unlike the earlier Scottish philosophers, Mill saw the "barbarous" treatment of women as evidence of an inherently inferior mind rather than the product of specific histories and circumstances.[29]

Mill also cast in stark opposition the differences he perceived between Hindus and Muslims. For him the Hindus were the "aboriginal inhabitants of the country" and therefore came to stand for India, for what he saw as its few accomplishments and many flaws. He deemed the "Mahomedan race," by contrast, to be "invaders; and insignificant, in point of number, compared with the first." For Mill "the Hindu, like the Eunuch, excels in the qualities of a slave," while "the Mahomedan is more manly, more vigorous. He more nearly resembles our own half-civilized ancestors... [and] still more susceptible of increased civilization, than a people in the state of the Hindus."[30]

Turning to the treatment of Muslim women specifically, Mill conceded that Islamic "rules of evidence are not inferior; in some they are preferable, to those of the European systems." He even appeared to understand the logic behind the rule that two women are the equivalent of one man when testifying in certain kinds of cases: "They have less correctness, says the law, both in observation and memory—which so long as their education is inferior will no doubt be the case." Mill subscribed too to the inaccurate views of that era regarding Islamic injunctions on women's education: "Mahomedan customs... exclude the women from the acquisition of knowledge and experience." While he might have used the word "customs" here to mean practice as opposed to doctrine, that seems highly improbable, given his general tendency to see all Indian practice as explicitly rooted in religious doctrine.[31]

While Mill regarded a society's progress to be inextricably linked to improvement in the "condition of the weaker sex... till they associate on equal terms with the men and occupy the place of voluntary and useful coadjutors," British women's rights activists of his era and the generations to follow would not depict him as a champion of women's rights in either India or Britain.[32] After all, the progress he wanted to see in the roles of women and men in India, propelled by a British colonial administration he saw as free of impropriety and corruption, was movement toward the very ideas and customs of early nineteenth-century Britain that British women's rights activists were beginning to challenge as unjust.

Indeed, in his views on women's rights and Britain's civilizing mission in India, Mill departed even from his mentor Bentham. The older man found Mill's *History* "melancholy" and "disagreeable" and described as quite "abominable" Mill's views on the intellectual and political capacity of men under forty and of women and non-Europeans, presumably of all ages.[33] Mill's arrogance and complacency regarding British women also provoked a response from the Irish economist William Thompson and activist Anna Doyle Wheeler, whose 1825 call for sexual equality, *Appeal of One Half the Human Race, Women, against the Pretensions of the Other Half, Men, to Retain Them in Political, and Thence in Civil and Domestic, Slavery,* predated John Stuart Mill's far better-known *The Subjection of Women* by four decades.

Thompson and Wheeler sought to apply the principle—originally formulated by the Scottish philosopher Francis Hutcheson a century earlier but popularized by Bentham—of the need to pursue "the greatest happiness for the greatest number" to the arena of gender relations. Although generally supportive of extended franchise, the senior Mill had excluded women from his vision of government by arguing that men could adequately represent the interests of the women in their family.[34]

This exclusion of women from democratic politics was no less than the "inroad of barbarism, under the guise of philosophy, into the nineteenth century." Given that British marriage laws were so heavily biased against women, Thompson and Wheeler questioned Britain's claim to be the "most enlightened" and civilized country in the world. Echoing Wollstonecraft, they accused Mill of having acted "in true Eastern style" in his decision to exclude women from his vision of a democratic polity.[35] Of course, as was the case with earlier generations of writers on Englishwomen's rights, they too evinced little interest in or awareness of the many more rights in marriage, divorce, and property that many Muslim women already enjoyed in that era.

A "DIABOLICAL PRACTICE"

In India, meanwhile, British colonial officials chose sati, the practice of widow immolation, as the issue through which to demonstrate their concern for Indian women. Sati was not a "Muslim issue" as such, having been historically limited to certain upper-caste Hindu communities. However, the debate over sati and the 1829 law prohibiting it in Bengal (quickly followed by bans in Madras and Bombay) would have broad significance for all Indians because of the precedent they set for discussions about and reform of other "traditional" practices pertinent to both Hindus and Muslims, such as child marriage, widow remarriage, seclusion, and polygamy.

The word *sati* refers to the ritual of widows sacrificing themselves on their husband's funeral pyre, as well as to the woman who undertakes sati. Widow immolation had become fairly rare by the late eighteenth century, but in the early nineteenth century its incidence surged among lower-caste families, primarily for economic reasons: families encouraged widowed women to immolate themselves so that they might inherit the deceased husband's property. That they would be able to bask in the glow of the status attached to having a sati in the family was certainly an important additional incentive.[36]

A decade after the publication of the *History of British India,* Lord William Bentinck, who had served as governor of Madras several years earlier, returned to India to take up his position as the new governor-general. An advocate of utilitarianism, Bentinck assumed his post with plans to streamline the colonial administration and promulgate good laws with which to govern this vast land.[37] In 1829 Bentinck's administration abolished sati. Celebrated by some as marking the beginning of the movement for Indian women's emancipation, this law has also been seen as legitimizing a colonizing state armed with a mandate to reform and modernize.[38]

Rammohan Roy is the best-known Indian critic of sati. This highly educated Bengali social reformer, newspaper editor, and educator has been called the "Father of modern India" in recognition of, to quote his tombstone in Bristol, England, "his unwearied labours to promote the social, moral and physical condition of the people of India, his earnest Endeavours to suppress idolatry and the rite of Suttee, and his constant zealous advocacy of whatever tended to advance the glory of god and the welfare of man."[39] In 1828 Roy founded the Brahmo Sabha, later renamed the Brahmo Samaj, as an intellectual alternative to the Hindu community that Roy believed needed to be purged of various social ills and traditions. The Samaj rejected polytheism and idol worship and promoted reforms, particularly pertaining to women's rights and access to education.[40]

An address presented to Bentinck in January 1830, signed by three hundred residents of Calcutta and believed to have been written by Rammohan Roy, expressed the signatories' collective gratitude to the governor-general for the "invaluable protection which your Lordship's government has recently afforded to the lives of the Hindoo female part of your subjects, and for your humane and successful exertions in rescuing us for ever, from the gross stigma hitherto attached to our character as wilful murderers of females, and zealous promoters of the practice of suicide."[41] As this statement of relief at being rescued from the stigma of sati suggests, the debate over sati ultimately was not about women themselves so much as the priorities of the different groups of men arguing for and against outlawing the practice.[42]

Under Bentinck's watch and in the following decades, the colonial administration responded to demands by Rammohan Roy and other Bengali reformers such as Ishwar Chandra Vidyasagar to enact important changes in education and social practices: it introduced Western-style education and new legislation that permitted widow remarriage and prohibited sati, female infanticide, and child marriage. In undertaking these reforms the administration's concern applied the utilitarian principle of "the greatest good of the greatest number"—but always with the British, not the Indian, population in mind.[43]

Despite Bentinck's personal reluctance, the colonial administration undertook to provide Western education in response not only to the Hindu elite's interest in English education but also to the British colonial officials' need for Indian men to assist them in their work. Thomas Babington Macaulay, then the president of the Committee of Public Instruction, announced in his 1835 "Minute on Indian Education" that the committee would deploy its funds to teach English rather than Sanskrit or Arabic and that printing books in those languages should cease. After all, as he put it infamously, he had not met a single scholar of those languages "who could deny that a single shelf of a good European library was worth the whole native literature of India and Arabia." And since the administration lacked the funds to teach everyone, the best strategy would be to target a selected few, "who may be interpreters between us and the millions whom we govern,—a class of persons Indian in blood and colour, but English in tastes, in opinions, in morals and in intellect."[44]

Macaulay, who had traveled to India in 1834 as a member of the new Indian Law Commission, also led the effort to draft a criminal code for India. In fact, he informed his sister Hannah in a letter that his "old enemy" James Mill had facilitated his appointment with the company. Macaulay completed the utilitarianism-inspired code in 1837, and it would be enacted as the Indian Penal Code of 1860, parts of which remain in effect in South

Asian countries today.[45] These include sections 144 against unlawful assembly, 295 against hurting religious sentiments, and 377 against same-sex relations and transgender people.

MISSIONARIES AND "DEGRADED" INDIAN WOMEN

The issue of sati also mobilized British women. In the months before and after the December 1829 Bengal Sati Regulation Act, for example, fifteen distinct groups of women from all over England petitioned Parliament to abolish sati. Again, their pleas stemmed not so much from a concern for Bengali women but rather from their own involvement in the evangelical missionary movement and the campaign to mobilize support to send women missionaries, especially single British women, to India.[46]

In June 1813, while James Mill was still working on his magnum opus and the British Parliament was debating the East India Company Charter Act, the recently launched *Missionary Register* published a lengthy excerpt about sati from Serampore missionary William Ward's 1811 book on India. That these particular selections were chosen to underscore the need for a stronger British evangelical presence in India is clear from the two articles that bookended the passage—"The Groans of India for Christian Teachers" and "India Eager to Receive the Scriptures." The *Register* reinforced this claim with its introduction: "Let every Christian Woman, who reads the following Statement, pity the wretched thousands of her sex who are sacrificed every year in India to a cruel superstition, and thank God for her own light and privileges, and pray and labour earnestly for the salvation of these her miserable fellow-subjects." The selection from Ward's book, "On the Burning of Women in India," ended with the editorial assurance that "we shall give some instances of this diabolical practice in future Numbers."[47]

The abolitionist William Wilberforce, who led the ultimately successful campaign to open up India to missionaries in 1813, also based his argument on the need to end the oppression of Indian women. While, like the early British feminists, male missionary leaders drew on Enlightenment philosophy and the stadial approach to history and civilization, the missionaries' idea of progress was not simply about striving toward a British way of life. Rather, they espoused a specifically Christian British form of progress, complete with emphasis on the natural distinction between male and female spheres. Missionary leaders, like other men of their time, downplayed British feminist demands for change by pointing out how much better off British women were than their heathen sisters.[48]

Despite their formal statements of concern about the dire predicament of Indian women, British missionary societies initially restricted single British women missionaries' travel to India. In 1813 an independent missionary nurse, Ann Chaffin, managed to make her way to Bengal, but two years later three single women from Bristol eager to travel to India were turned down by the Church Missionary Society, whose leadership had decided that unmarried women could go only if "accompanying or joining their brothers." William Ward of the Serampore Mission, by contrast, tried to persuade the missionary leaders in Britain to lift the restrictions on women missionaries. Given that British women had been "raised by gracious Providence to the enjoyment of so many comforts," surely it was now incumbent on the "British fair" to work for the "emancipation" of the seventy-five million benighted "females and widows of British India." He believed that by rescuing them "from ignorance," British and US women missionaries could save Indian women "from these funeral piles," referring, of course, to sati.[49] The first unmarried women missionaries from Britain and the United States started arriving in the second and third decades of the nineteenth century, with their numbers increasing quite dramatically in the second half of the century.

By mobilizing against sati and other traditions seen as inimical to women, British women developed a sense of distance from—and moral, racial, and intellectual superiority to—Indian women. As Jane Eyre remonstrated in Charlotte Brontë's eponymous 1847 novel in response to Edward Rochester's suggestion that the two would live—and die—together, "I had as good a right to die when my time came as he did; but I should bide that time, and not be hurried away in a suttee." At the same time, in repeatedly affirming their civilized, Christian, British superiority to Indian women, many British women tacitly accepted their roles in their own society. It was this strong conviction about men's and women's distinct and complementary roles that British missionaries brought to India with the aim of saving oppressed Indian women.[50]

The education of Indian women was seen as women missionaries' particular responsibility for, as missionary William Adam announced in an 1836 report on the state of education in Bengal, "there is no instruction at all" among women and girls, and "absolute and hopeless ignorance is in general their lot." Indian parents who supported girls' education generally had little interest in missionary schools, where the teachers tended to be men. Moreover, given the practice of early marriage, young girls who did attend school only did so for a few years before marriage and relocation. Many parents were completely opposed to any education out of fear that schoolbook knowledge might lead their daughters astray—that is, make them less obedient to their parents. While the wives of male missionaries were tasked with educating the actual converts produced by their husbands, many unmarried women missionaries took up the mission of zenana education. The opportunity to tutor elite women in their zenanas was particularly attractive, for it allowed them to work autonomously of the men missionaries, though seldom without the supervision of the Indian women's male relatives, who had granted them access to their homes. Although much celebrated as pioneers in the cause of Indian women's education, women missionaries' intrusion into the zenanas ultimately yielded little in terms of conversions, educational achievements, or even information about the lives of Indian women.[51]

A century later the German missiologist Julius Richter would attribute the low status of women in northern India to the "influence of Islam" and justify the continued need for women missionaries: "The women of North India are banished to their zenanas; it has been computed that of the 150 million women and girls of India, 40 million reside in the zenanas—a population greater than that of Prussia." These zenanas, he added, are "hermetically sealed against all Christian influences," to a large extent by women themselves, with "the womanhood of India...the protectress and zealous adherent of traditional heathenism."[52]

Still, inspirational stories of successful conversions were necessary to reassure funders and inspire missionaries back home, and Edward Storrow of the Calcutta Mission of the London Missionary Society provided one in his 1856 book, *The Eastern Lily Gathered: A Memoir of Bala Shoondoree Tagore*. Through his account of a young woman of the distinguished Bengali Hindu Tagore family who died just before she could be baptized, Storrow discussed the prospects of further conversions in the region. Muslims and Muslim women made only brief appearances in his account and only to underscore Muslim women's even greater misery. "Mahomedan females," he wrote in his lengthy introduction, "are in a more degraded, humiliating position, than even their Hindu sisters are. The gross sensualism which is ever allied with their creed, polygamy, and the indifference with which the marriage tie is regarded, are the cause of this."[53] This "indifference" that so bothered Storrow and other missionaries was the contractual nature of Muslim marriage—in contrast to the sacramental Christian marriage—that Muslim women aware of their legal rights have tended to regard as a boon, for it allowed easier access to dissolution, although the provision has, of course, always been easier for men to exercise.

MUSLIMS IN THE WRITING OF INDIA'S HISTORY

Efforts to legitimate Britain's presence in India not only included avowals of concern over the degraded Indian women but also entailed a very specific way of writing the history of India in which the Muslims emerged as interlopers and the source of many of India's problems. British writers like James Mill started to recount the history of India as having three parts: a distant, "ancient" Hindu past filled with great accomplishments and freedom that was destroyed by oppressive Muslim conquerors, who ushered in a dark "medieval" period, to then be saved by the enlightened and "modern" British.[54]

Women proved to be an important part of this three-part account. Bengali reformers eager to demonstrate that India was ready to become a modern nation attributed to the Muslims many of the practices that British writers regarded as responsible for India's lowly place on the civilizational ladder. In their writings elite Hindu and Brahmo male reformers not only articulated versions of the stadial theory of history and the link noted by British writers between women's status and civilization but also made a point of stressing the role of Muslim outsiders in introducing or encouraging practices deleterious to once free and strong Hindu women, such as seclusion, polygamy, sati, and *jauhar* (mass immolation undertaken by elite women to avoid capture by the enemy). For example, despite little historical evidence to support their claim, many argued that Hindus had adopted the practice of seclusion with the politically expedient objective of blending in with the Muslim ruling elite, as well as for the practical purpose of secluding Hindu women from lascivious Muslim men.[55]

Early non-Muslim Indian travelers to Britain shared many of these ideas with the locals they encountered. In a September 1831 letter to the American Transcendentalist Unitarian theologian William Ellery Channing, British poet and writer Lucy Aikin described a visit to her home by the "excellent Ram-Mohun-Roy," who had excited in her a "personal concern in a *third* quarter of the globe." He had spoken during this visit, she wrote, on "subjects more interesting to me—Hindoo laws, especially those affecting women." He had quietly established his distance from Muslims by informing her, she wrote, that "polygamy... [was] a crime... punishable by their law, except for certain causes, by a great fine; but the Mussulmans did not enforce the fine, and their example had corrupted Hindoos; they were cruel to women, the Hindoos were forbidden all cruelty." Despite his profound respect for aspects of Islamic theology and philosophy, she added, Roy had been eager to express his appreciation to the British for delivering Bengal from the tyranny of Muslim rule and for setting in place "equitable and indulgent treatment."[56] In meetings with women activists in Britain, Rammohan Roy impressed on them their responsibility to help Indian women, given their own position of privilege. He showered blessings on Bentinck for outlawing sati and persuaded Aikin of his high regard for women. She recalled, "His feeling for women in general, still more than the admiration he expressed of the mental accomplishments of English ladies, won our hearts." Quite pleased with Roy's statements, she announced, "The dominion we hold over India is perhaps the most striking circumstance of greatness belonging to our little island."[57]

The writer Toru Dutt, whose entire family (though her mother somewhat grudgingly) had converted to Christianity, similarly responded to British representations of Indians, and especially of "Hindoos," as degraded by reminding her readers that this had not always been so. As members of a wealthy Bengali family, the sisters Toru and Aru Dutt had been educated at home in their early years and then continued their training in France and England. Toru Dutt, who died at twenty-one, left behind a remarkable body of work that included novels in both French and English, poetry in English, and numerous translations. Along the way she, like Roy some decades earlier, had accepted the European notion of progress that relegated India to the category of uncivilized and its women as unfree, in distinction to England, which was civilized and its women free. She apparently also subscribed to the view that Muslims were to blame for the degradation of Hindu women. In her long poem "Savitri," the name of a paragon of both wifely devotion and wisdom in the Hindu epic *Mahabharata,* Toru Dutt harked back to the Vedic era as a golden age for female mobility and freedom, an era that was tragically cut short presumably by the arrival of Muslims and their zenanas: "In those far-off primeval days / Fair India's daughters were not pent / In closed zenanas. On her ways, / Savitri at her pleasure went / Whither she chose." She was able to go about "where she pleased / In boyish freedom." Dutt invoked the Romantic ideals of freedom and mobility to differentiate the Hindus from their oppressive Muslim invaders. It is also worth noting that the chaste, dutiful, "child-like" Savitri here was on par with the Victorian ideal of the morally upright middle-class wife who was legally—and deemed to be intellectually—inferior to her husband: even though Savitri's intelligence allows her to trick Yama, the god of death, into returning her husband to her, she is presented here as ultimately subordinate to "her future lord and guide."[58]

INDIAN WOMEN THROUGH THE EYES OF "THE WHITE SLAVES OF ENGLAND"

In the early decades of the nineteenth century, the number of British women traveling overseas and writing about their experiences was impressive enough to elicit hostility from those who regarded travel writing as a male domain. The author of an 1828 article in *Blackwood's Magazine* (published in Edinburgh) grumbled with dismissive paternalism about the "romantic female, whose eyes are confined to some half dozen drawing rooms and who sees everything through the medium of poetical fiction."[59]

Eliza Fay, Fanny Parkes, and Helen Mackenzie were among the small number of British women who made their way to India in the late eighteenth and early nineteenth century. They published their accounts before the First War of Indian Independence—or the Great Revolt of 1857, called the Great Sepoy Mutiny by the British—would transform the formal relationship between Britain and India, with colonial control over India transferred from the East India Company to the British Crown. The late nineteenth century would see an increase in traffic from Britain to India as well as a new phase in each society's ideas about itself as well as the other.

These earlier travelers are of interest to us because of their efforts to describe occasional moments of empathy and identification with Indian women and to reflect critically on women's situation in Britain rather than, as would become increasingly common, reinforce assumptions about the plight of Indian women and demonstrate complacency about their own. Thus, they provided significant counterpoints to contemporary perspectives—of the (invariably male) established authorities on India such as James Mill; other *memsahibs,* or European women in India; and feminists back in England who invoked Indian women for their own purposes without any firsthand experience of India—as well as to later British women who traveled to India in the final decades of the nineteenth century with an urgent sense of mission to save Indian women from their perceived degradation. While these women's residence in India was also intimately connected to, and made possible by, the British colonial administration, their individual backgrounds, motivations, and experiences shaped their accounts. In any case, while they occasionally appeared to question aspects of British rule in India, such rule itself was never in question.

Eliza Fay first traveled to India in 1779 because her Irish barrister husband, Anthony Fay, was to join the court in Calcutta. Their marriage ended following his various indiscretions, and she returned to England in 1782. She then undertook three more voyages to Calcutta in efforts to engage in the trade in muslins and other goods, but her business ventures failed. Inspired by writers such as Mary Wollstonecraft and Mary Wortley Montagu, "women who do honor to their sex, as literary characters," but also motivated by a need for cash, Fay decided in 1815 to publish her "original letters from India." She died alone and penniless in Bengal before the book appeared in 1817—the year that Mill's *History of British India* was published—and the proceeds from its sale went to her various creditors. The English novelist E. M. Forster discovered Fay's *Original Letters from India* while conducting research for *Passage to India* and persuaded Virginia and Leonard Woolf to republish it in 1925.[60]

Having informed her sister that she now has "full leisure to give...some account of the East Indian customs and ceremonies," Fay began with a discussion of sati, "that horrible custom of widows burning themselves with the dead bodies of their husbands." Disclosing that she herself had never witnessed such an act, nor did she know of any European who had, she dismissed prevalent explanations for sati. She could not countenance, she declared, that this practice could be attributed to Indian women's "superior tenderness and ardent attachment" toward their husbands, for surely such feelings would have pushed them instead to stay alive to cherish their husbands' memories and care for their children. She concluded, rather, that it was "entirely a political scheme intended to insure the care and good offices of wives to their husbands, who have not failed in most countries to invent sufficient number of rules to render the weaker sex totally subservient to their authority." Clearly aware that many Indian and English men held up the sati as a paragon of wifely devotion, she continued, "I cannot avoid smiling when I hear gentlemen bring forward the conduct of the Hindoo women as a test of superior character." Writing shortly after her own bitter separation from her husband, Fay refused to idealize the sati and drew readers' attention instead to women's vulnerability to and dependence on men's whims in both India and Britain. In her view it was simply the nature of the "sacrifice" that differed, depending on the custom of the community.[61]

Fanny Parkes (born Frances Susannah Archer) arrived in India in 1822, a few years after Fay's death, and lived there until 1845 (with some extended absences for sojourns in England and South Africa). There seemed to be little about India that Parkes did not like or marvel over during her long years there. In this, like Fay, she stood apart from later British visitors to India, especially those who traveled there after 1857. But she differed even from some of her contemporaries, such as the far better-known Emily Eden, the sister of Lord Auckland, governor-general of India from 1835 to 1842. While Parkes was certainly conscious of her status as a *memsahib* and the privileges this afforded her, her lower status in the colonial hierarchy as the wife of a minor official and her travels away from the centers of colonial administration help explain the openness with which she interacted with Indians and her ability to see beyond, and occasionally even question, the official rhetoric of the colonizing power. Her position and her often unconventional intuitions may also help explain why her book, an illustrated diary published in 1850 as *Wanderings of a Pilgrim in Search of the Picturesque,* had no new editions for well over a century. By comparison Emily Eden's book, *Up the Country: Letters Written to Her Sister from the Upper Provinces of India* has rarely been out of print since its publication in 1866.[62]

Parkes wrote at a time of transition, before existing English notions of Christian, racial, and cultural superiority were distilled by the emerging field of scientific racism.[63] She was "charmed with the climate" and thought the "weather was delicious." In contrast to Emily Eden, who did not study any Indian languages, and like the male British Orientalist scholars, Parkes studied Urdu; indeed, her name appears on the cover of the 1850 edition of her book in Arabic script, as does her signature on her illustrations in the book. She learned also to play the sitar and found pure pleasure, not to mention a sense of liberation from the strictures of English societal expectations, in "vagabondising in India."[64] Fanny Eden, sister of Emily Eden and the governor-general, wrote of her own displeasure at several aspects of Parkes's company and statements, among them Parkes's insistence, as she proclaimed to Eden in Benares, that she was an "independent woman."[65]

Fanny Parkes had traveled to India with her husband, Charles Crawford Parkes, then based in Calcutta as a junior member of the Bengal Civil Service.[66] Like Mary Montagu in Constantinople a century earlier, and

FIGURE 7. *Bengali Woman,* 1850. Parkes, *Wanderings of a Pilgrim.*

Jemima Kindersley in India more recently, Parkes was aware that, although many Englishmen had written about India, only Englishwomen could claim to provide real eyewitness accounts of women's lives inside the zenana. After all, "so few persons ever have an opportunity of seeing native ladies." Indeed, she admitted, it was the "perusal" of Montagu's writing that had "rendered [her] very anxious to visit a *zenana,* and to become acquainted with the ladies of the East." When published in 1850, her book's subtitle included the highly marketable enticement, *With Revelations of Life in the Zenana.*

As was the case with other British women married to colonial administrators, most of the Indians Parkes initially encountered were members of her domestic staff. It would be four years before she finally had the opportunity she sought—to peer into a zenana—through an invitation to attend a dance performance "at the house of a rich Calcutta native gentleman." No doubt, in comparison to the aristocratic Ottoman homes visited by Montagu, Parkes's first zenana was in a more modest establishment, and she reported that she was "much disappointed: the women were not ladylike." Over the following decades Parkes had numerous occasions to visit zenanas in both Hindu and Muslim homes of different classes in various parts of India, including an invitation in February 1835 to visit the home of Princess Mulka Humanee Begum, the niece of the by then much-weakened Mughal emperor and the wife of Englishman John Gardner.[67]

Parkes's extended residence in India and the diversity and number of her encounters allowed her to move beyond platitudes about the oppression of Indian women. Even as she noted the injustice of a system under which a man might have multiple wives, but a woman risked death if she took a lover; recognized the unhappiness of women such as Mulka Begum "over the confinement of the four walls"; and found "absurd" the custom of child marriage as an effort to keep women virtuous, Parkes, like Eliza Fay, did not see the situation of Indian women as unique. "It is the same all over the world," Parkes wrote. "The women, being the weaker, are the playthings, the drudges, or the victims of men; a woman is a slave from her birth; and the more I see of life, the more I pity the condition of the women."[68]

The shared plight of Indian and English women was apparent to her, for example, while on a visit to the memorials of women who had committed sati near a Hindu temple near Ghazipur: "It is very horrible to see how the weaker are imposed upon; and *it is the same all over the world,* civilized or uncivilized." In her eyes the "laws of England relative to married women, and the state of slavery to which those laws degrade them, render the lives of some few in the higher, and of thousands in the lower ranks of life, *one perpetual sati,* or burning of the heart, from which they have no refuge but the grave, or the cap of liberty, i.e. the widow's, and either is a sad consolation."[69] In invoking sati as simply a specific Indian version of women's dependence and vulnerability everywhere, Parkes, much like Fay earlier, was responding to European men who had argued that sati represented the ideal in wifely devotion. She was also responding to those European men who had used the horror of sati to remind European women that they had no need to complain since they already lived a life free of such traditions.

The sorry plight of widows in both India and Britain came up in Parkes's conversation with the widowed Baiza Bai, deposed from the throne of Gwalior by her adopted son and bereft of the English assistance she had been promised. While Baiza Bai explained the many "privations" endured by Hindu widows—no remarriage or luxurious food, nor even a bed—Parkes described how Englishwomen are often turned out of the family home after the husband's death "to make room for the heir." She later recalled, "We spoke of the severity of the laws of England with respect to married women, how completely by law they are the slaves of their husbands, and how little hope there is of redress." In fact, she continued, "You might as well 'Twist a rope of sand,' or 'Beg a husband of a widow' as urge the men to emancipate the white slaves of England."[70]

Parkes approached even the topic of polygamy with a relatively open mind. "One cannot be surprised," she wrote, "at a Musulman taking advantage of the permission given him by his lawgiver with respect to a plurality of wives." As she informed Baiza Bai, however, without apparent judgment or disdain, polygamy was not an option in England only because it was too small a country for each man to provide separate quarters for four wives—"they would be obliged to keep the women in vessels off the shore, after the fashion in which the Chinese keep their floating farmyards of ducks and geese at anchor." Similarly, when a "Mahratta lady" expressed concern that Parkes had not arranged female company for her husband who was staying behind in India while she traveled to Britain, Parkes responded "with the utmost gravity... [that] such an arrangement never occurred to me." Her companion laughed and added that, in any case, "you English ladies would only select one wife; a Mahratta would select two to remain with her husband during her absence." Parkes wrote that she then simply explained "the opinions of the English on such subjects; our ideas appeared as strange to her as hers were to me; and she expressed herself grieved that I should omit what they considered a duty."[71]

Encounters with Indian women gave Parkes a fresh perspective on customs in her own society, prompting her to reflect, for instance, on the differences between European and Indian dress. Echoing Montagu's episode at the hammam, Parkes described Indian women's surprise at her undergarments: "I could never dress myself but half a dozen were slily [sic] peeping in from every corner of the screens (pardas), and their astonishment at the number and shape of the garments worn by a European was unbounded!" Having concluded that Indian men and women "both receive the same education, and the result is similar," she reiterated Catharine Macaulay's and Mary Wollstonecraft's critiques of the European situation: "In Europe men have so greatly the advantage of women from receiving a superior education...that of course the superiority is on the male side; the women are kept under and have not fair play." She was also aware of how "odd" other English practices appeared to Indians, such as her casual interactions with unrelated men when dining or horse riding and her pleasure in solitude when sleeping or writing.[72]

Parkes even found occasion to criticize the British authorities. She observed, for example, that "the Government interferes with native superstition where rupees are in question—witness the tax they levy on pilgrims at the junction of the Ganges and Jumna. Every man, even the veriest beggar, is obliged to give one rupee for liberty to bathe at the holy spot; and if you consider that one rupee is sufficient to keep that man in comfort for one month, the tax is severe." During a visit in the company of Gov.-Gen. William Bentinck and Lady William to the Kingdom of Oudh (Awadh), which the British would annex in 1856, she remarked, "The subjects of his Majesty of Oude are by no means desirous of participating in the blessings of British rule. They are a richer, sleeker, and merrier race than the natives in the territories of the Company." In the end, however, she was clearly aware that her very presence in India—and the ease with which she was able to roam "about with a good tent and a good Arab [horse]" and write and record her impressions of India—was made possible by her own personal connections to the colonial administration.[73]

Unlike Fay and Parkes, Helen Mackenzie was an early leader in the zenana missions that targeted women living in seclusion. And, unlike most missionary women of this period, Mackenzie published an account of her experiences. She arrived in India with her husband, Brig. Colin Mackenzie of the Hyderabad Contingent, in 1847, just two years after Parkes returned to England. In keeping with the official policy of noninterference, the company army discouraged chaplains and missionaries from proselytizing to Indians in the army and allowed Muslim sepoys to continue their Sufi rituals and practices under the leadership of military *faqirs* (holy men). However, many of the chaplains and even officers, such as Colin Mackenzie, were enthusiastic evangelicals, eager to convert Hindus and Muslims to Protestant Christianity. Following the events of 1857, the zeal would increase dramatically, with the justification that the sepoys had rebelled precisely because they had not been properly civilized—that is, Christianized.[74]

Helen Mackenzie, for her part, although ultimately disappointed by the low number of conversions among Muslims, left us a valuable journal of her six years in India, including entries detailing her impressions of the zenanas of Muslim families. The family she spent the most time with was that of Muhammad Hasan Khan's. He was an army officer she met in Ludhiana, whom she described as her "husband's devoted friend and follower." Indeed, she held him in such high esteem that she admitted, "It makes one's heart ache to think that such a man as Hasan Khan should be a Muhammadan."[75]

The illness of Hasan Khan's younger wife, Leila Bibi, provided Mackenzie with the opportunity to spend a great deal of time in the couple's home. She paid Leila Bibi daily visits and tried to help her through prayer—"the only way I could take to give Him the glory of her recovery"—as well as homeopathic medicine from her own stock. She recalled her own curiosity and surprise: "You may imagine I watched Hasan Khan very closely to see how Muhammadan husbands behave. He was most attentive to his poor wife, raising her up, giving her water every few minutes, and holding her head." She was also struck by his clothing: "He was dressed exactly as the women are, i.e. with very full trousers, muslin short shirt and scull-cap."[76]

From her frequent visits to Hasan Khan's home, Mackenzie had the opportunity to observe a "good deal of 'Life in the Harem.'" She had evidence "to refute authoritatively, as I always felt inclined to do on prima facie grounds, the fine theories of Mr. Urquhart regarding the superior happiness of Muhammadan women."[77] She was referring here to the Scottish politician and diplomat David Urquhart, who, in an 1838 book following a brief sojourn in Constantinople, had declared that the "harem" was a home, a place of "security, protection, filial duties, paternal authority, love, delicacy of manners, and of intercourse." He later also popularized Turkish baths in Britain.[78]

Like Montagu, Kindersley, and Parkes, Mackenzie took pride in the privileged access she, as a woman, could provide into the goings-on of a zenana: "What *can* a man know of the matter!...Would any Musulmani woman speak freely to a Feringhi even if he did obtain speech with her....It is presumption of him ever to talk of a Musalmani's feelings: I will flap him out of the field with the end of a purdah." She concluded from her visits that the Muslim women's "secluded life" did not automatically "make them objects of pity. They are hardly more devoid of excitement than I am myself." However, while she appreciated that there might be positive aspects to life in dedicated women's quarters, she could not come to terms with the idea of multiple wives, even as she conceded that Hasan Khan's wives seemed to get along: "It is not in human nature to be content with being the fourth part of a man's wife. They are far from viewing the matter as we do.... Still, no man can love two or more women equally, and as no woman can bear that another should share her husband's affections, I plainly see there are heart-burnings innumerable, even in this family."[79]

As steadfast evangelicals, both Mackenzies refused to grant any validity to Indian religious traditions, though Helen found herself reflecting on the conduct (if not the beliefs) of fellow Christians as a result of her interactions with Indians of other faiths. She recorded one telling exchange between Hasan Khan and her husband in which the former suggested "in a soothing voice" during a Sunday morning visit, "Your religion and ours are very much the same." Colin quickly retorted, "No, there is a great deal of difference," and he insisted that Hasan Khan take home a Persian copy of the Testament and find someone to read him the Sermon on the Mount. When Hasan Khan returned a few days later, having completed this assignment, he remarked that it was "very good" but that it was clear to him that the "Sahib Log [English people] do not live according to their book. I have only seen one or two that do so." Helen Mackenzie found herself pondering, "Is it not strange that the inconsistency of nominal Christians should be so palpable to a Muhammadan, and yet that they themselves remain so blind to it?"[80]

Encounters such as these helped women like Montagu, Fay, Parkes, and Mackenzie denaturalize their own clothing, relationships, and status in society and realize the peculiarities of the conventions that governed their own lives rather than see them as natural, inevitable, or universal. This willingness to view oneself and one's own culture through the eyes of others would become increasingly scarce over the course of the nineteenth century, as an imperial—and indeed a more explicitly feminist—arrogance took its place, and British women's demands for rights became increasingly intertwined with their nation's imperial might and notions of racial superiority.

FOUR

Feminism and Empire

OVER THE COURSE OF THE NINETEENTH CENTURY, a growing, and often discordant, chorus of demands for women's rights emerged in both Britain and India. The term *feminism* finally came into circulation by the end of the century, believed to have been first used—*bien sûr*, as *féminisme*—by the French suffrage activist Hubertine Auclert in 1882. A "feminist" congress in Paris in 1892 helped to popularize the concept further, and it crossed the English Channel a few years later.[1]

In Britain, very much the dominant global power since the Battle of Waterloo in 1815, the figure of the oppressed Eastern woman continued to be invoked by women pushing for reform in their own (typically middle- or upper-middle-class) lives—for their access to higher education, employment, divorce, child custody, suffrage, and property rights—as well as by those arguing against such changes. In India, similarly, reformers and conservatives in the Hindu and Muslim communities also invoked women of the *other* community, as well as British women, to make their case for or against changes in women's legal rights. The increased traffic between India and Britain over the course of the century, facilitated by technological developments such as the steamship and political developments such as the transfer of British power in India from the British East India Company to the Crown, led to more opportunities for direct interactions between Indian and British women and men.

EARLY STRUGGLES FOR BRITISH WOMEN'S LEGAL RIGHTS

The legal inequalities between men and women in marriage and under coverture that had so distressed Mary Montagu in the early eighteenth century were still in place a century later and would be the first restrictions to be challenged with any degree of success. The fact that, following her 1840 wedding, the young Queen Victoria would be legally unlike any other married woman in Britain only further accentuated other women's lack of rights. (However, the fact that she bore nine children, despite her clear statements in letters about her desire for far fewer children, is clear evidence that she too had little say in reproductive matters.) Her unique status is highlighted in a pamphlet titled *Letter to the Queen on the State of the Monarchy by a Friend of the People.* The author was Lord Brougham, the former radical member of Parliament, and Lord Chancellor, a founder of the prestigious *Edinburgh Review* and designer of the Brougham horse carriage, which would later inspire several motor car models. Brougham wrote, "I am an experienced man, well stricken in years. I bend myself respectfully before *you,* a girl of eighteen, who, in my own or in any other family in Europe, would be treated as a child, ordered to do as was most agreeable or convenient to others— whose inclinations would never be consulted—whose opinion would never be thought of—whose consent would never be asked upon any one thing appertaining to any other human being but yourself, beyond the choice of gown or cap, nor always upon that: yet before you I humble myself."[2]

Throughout the nineteenth century the ideology of separate spheres for men and women gained new strength and purpose but also invited numerous challenges. The ideal held that the traits and roles of husband and wife were opposite and complementary: a man was to be strong, independent, out in the world, and immersed in political and market activities, while his wife would be the queen of her domestic space. She was to be both morally superior to and economically dependent on her husband and be both his subordinate and his helpmeet.[3] Renowned Victorian artist and political thinker John Ruskin perfectly articulated this ideal when he described the man as "eminently the doer, the creator, the discoverer, the defender." Woman, he recognized, must be wise, but "not that she may set herself above her husband, but that she many never fail from his side."[4]

The separate-spheres ideal was out of the reach of the many working-class families in which women, and often also children, had to work for wages to make ends meet and, of course, of women across classes who had neither a male "provider" at home nor independent wealth. Indeed, it did not even represent the realities of most middle-class lives, but it increasingly came to define middle-class identity and thus became an aspirational symbol of middle-class status. The ideology also had very clear material consequences in that it was an arrangement on which men (of the middle class or those aspiring to be seen as part of it) depended to show themselves worthy of societal respect and even bank credit. Women, at the same time, were denied access to jobs, education, and bank accounts in their own name because they were believed to be better suited to staying at home as good wives and mothers—and, hence, confirmedly unsuited to life outside the home. Many British men (and also some women) not only wholeheartedly defended these ideals in Britain but also sought to impose them throughout Britain's colonies as the markers of "civilized" society.[5]

Decades before middle-class British women started to organize in support of women's rights around the middle of the nineteenth century, they had become active in the antislavery and antisati movements, deploying strategies such as the boycott of sugar and petitions to Parliament. Their work on these moral and social campaigns legitimated their presence outside the home and gave them valuable training in political activism, while their experiences of discrimination within the movements, such as the Chartist movement of the late 1830s, propelled them, in time, into advocacy specifically for British women's rights.[6]

Discrimination against women activists within the antislavery movement became apparent at the June 1840 Anti-Slavery Convention in London, when the British organizers refused to seat the US women delegates. As a result, the first day of the convention was taken up by a debate on the subject of women's rights—conducted entirely between men. Those opposing women's inclusion invoked the ideology of separate spheres, with George Stacey of the British and Foreign Anti-Slavery Society arguing that the "custom of this country" is that "in all matters of mere business, unless females are especially associated together...they do not become a part of the working committee." Rev. Alexander Harvey of Glasgow reminded his listeners that women had their assigned place and to admit women delegates would be "in opposition to the plain teaching of the word of God." On the other side the radical solicitor William Henry Ashurst protested that it made no sense to begin a convention about the "principles of universal benevolence" by "disenfranchising one-half of creation." The formal protest, as it turned out, was drafted by missionary William Adam, who had started his career as a Baptist minister at Serampore in Bengal. His work with Rammohan Roy on the antisati campaign had introduced him to public activism for women. He had also converted to unitarianism and, with Roy and others, founded the Calcutta Unitarian Committee. The US women's suffrage leader, Elizabeth

Cady Stanton, would later recall that the treatment of women delegates at the Anti-Slavery Convention had "stung many women into new thought and action" and helped ignite "the movement for women's political equality both in England and in the United States." While Stanton perhaps overstated the causal effect, there is no doubt that the convention provided an important opportunity for conversations between US and British female abolitionists over the issue of slavery and also women's rights.[7]

The background to the 1839 Custody of Infants Act, the first piece of British legislation to pay attention to women's needs, illustrates how one resolute, if penurious, upper-middle class-woman with writing talent was able to use traditional ideas about men's protection of women and girls to effect important legal change. It also provides an important contrast with the status of contemporaneous Muslim women in India, who already enjoyed rights pertaining to divorce and child custody, under scriptural injunctions if not always in practice. For instance, the Hanafi school of classical Sunni Islamic law, historically prevalent in much of South Asia as well as in parts of the eastern Mediterranean and Central Asia, awarded a divorced mother custody of sons until the age of seven and daughters until the age of nine, even if formal guardianship always remained with the father. If the mother remarried or was found engaging in "immoral" behavior, custody immediately shifted to the father, as long as he was deemed to be a proper parent.[8]

In June 1836 George Norton's case against the then prime minister, Lord Melbourne, went to court. Norton had charged Melbourne with having had "criminal conversation"—that is, sexual relations—with his wife, Caroline Sheridan Norton. When adultery could not be proved, the case was dismissed. Caroline Norton, who had already been locked out of the home they had shared and was estranged but unable to get a divorce, lost access to their three sons.[9]

A published poet, Caroline Norton turned to writing to earn a living and try to get her children back. Her first sale was a poem about child labor in the factories. She also wrote a prose pamphlet, *The Natural Claim of a Mother to the Custody of Her Children as Affected by the Common Law Right of the Father,* by which she hoped to change the law that had brought her so much sorrow. When publisher John Murray demanded she make changes, Norton decided to publish it privately and printed five hundred copies for distribution.[10] She also had a bill presented to the House of Commons to grant judges the power to decide, in the event of divorce or separation, which parent a child should be with until the age of twelve.

The Custody of Infants Act finally passed in both Houses in the summer of 1839, modified to say that children under the age of seven could remain with their mother, with the approval of the lord chancellor and if she were "of good character." Unfortunately, by then the Norton children were in Scotland, beyond the lord chancellor's reach, while Caroline Norton remained in financial difficulties because her husband had legal right to her earnings as well as the small inheritances she had received.

British women finally received limited divorce rights through the Matrimonial Causes Act nearly twenty years later, in 1857. These rights were limited in the sense that women seeking divorce would need to prove that their husband had committed an egregious form of adultery, for instance, through bigamy or incest, while the husband need show only simple adultery on the part of his wife. Caroline Norton joined the campaign for marriage reform when, incensed by George Norton's continued rights over her finances, she publicly criticized a marriage and divorce bill proposed in 1854 by Lord Chancellor Cranworth. She argued that the bill and the discussion thus far had failed to address men's overwhelming legal and economic power over their wives: "As *her husband,* he had a right to all that is hers; as *his wife,* she has no right to anything that is his." She also pointed out the "grotesque anomaly" that this should be the case "in a country governed by a female Sovereign." The centrality of control over married women's property led women's right activists like Barbara Bodichon and the Ladies of Langham Place group to which she belonged to take up the issue, resulting in the Married Women's Property Acts of 1870 (amended 1874 and 1882), which granted women control over their own earnings.[11] Norton's struggles both inspired and infuriated later feminists because she stubbornly maintained a public commitment to "men's natural superiority over women" and dismissed as "wild and stupid theories" the ideas of "equal rights" and "equal intelligence."[12] Her efforts are better understood as demands for men to fulfill their duty to protect women than as demands for rights, the language later feminists would use.[13]

A prominent voice on behalf of women's rights, and especially women's enfranchisement, was that of John Stuart Mill. His standing as a political theorist, a politician, and, no doubt, a man, helped to popularize ideas of female equality. His book *Subjection of Women* (1869) circulated quickly and widely, in English and in translation, including outside Europe.[14] Writing during and after the 1857 Indian Revolt as well as violently suppressed uprisings in other parts of the empire, Mill was acutely aware of the British

Empire's growing power and wealth. In India, in particular, with the passing of British authority to the Crown in 1858, a mission of social reform gave way to a new sense of racist superiority and unbridgeable distance. The question now was how to regulate this perceived immutable difference between colonizer and colonized.[15]

Like his father, John Stuart Mill never traveled to India, yet his intimate and complicated relationship to the country long preceded his own influential writings on British policy in India.[16] Having sat at the same table while his father worked on his *History of India,* the younger Mill later credited the book as having "contributed largely to my education, in the best sense of the term." He also attributed his father's delay in completing that book to his having decided to impart to his eldest child the "highest order of intellectual education." In the year before the book's publication, that child "read the manuscript to [his father] while he corrected the proofs." The loyal son later recalled the "number of new ideas which I received from this remarkable book, and the impulse and stimulus as well as guidance given to my thoughts by its criticism and disquisitions on society and civilization in the Hindoo part, on institutions and the acts of governments in the English part, made my early familiarity with it eminently useful to my subsequent progress."[17]

James Mill arranged for his son to join the East India Company when he turned seventeen, and John Stuart Mill eventually inherited his father's position as chief examiner. The company job served its purpose, providing a steady income and, crucially, time for the junior Mill, having completed his "India work" by one o'clock, to entertain visitors and work on his writings. A colleague recalled how, "when particularly inspired, he used, before sitting down at his desk, not only to strip himself of his coat and waistcoat, but of his trousers; and so set to work, alternately striding up and down the room and writing at great speed." The often tedious and mundane administrative work at the company helped shape the younger Mill's views on women, India, and the British Empire. Moreover, by exposing him to the gap that often emerges between directive and implementation, the job also taught him to shun utopian schemes for societal change: "I learnt how to obtain the best I could, when I could not obtain everything." Mill's company career would be cut short by the company's dissolution following the Great Indian Revolt of 1857.[18]

In the summer of 1830, Mill met Harriet Hardy Taylor at a dinner at John and Harriet Taylor's Finsbury home. They became intellectual collaborators soon after, and also romantically involved, though they did not marry until

1851, two years after John Taylor's death. Harriet does not appear to have taken a direct interest in India herself, though she could not have helped being drawn in, given John's own engagement and decades of work at India House. In a February 1835 diary entry, she wrote of how "furious" John was at Thomas Babington Macaulay's proposal to make English the main language of instruction in India. "We agree," she continued, that education will spread and take hold and "become customary" only if taught in "native languages."[19]

In July 1851 Harriet Taylor anonymously published *The Enfranchisement of Women* in the prestigious *Westminster Review*. She began the article by sharing her excitement over recent women's rights conventions in the United States to discuss the "enfranchisement of women: their admission, in law and in fact, to equality in all rights, political, civil, and social, with the male citizens of the community." Curiously, she did not mention the earlier, smaller 1848 gathering for women's rights at Seneca Falls, but she wrote with enthusiasm about the large attendance at the Worcester, Massachusetts, meeting "of which the president was a woman, and nearly all the chief speakers were women." Indeed, she wrote, this was a "movement not merely *for* women, but *by* them."[20] Taylor's article inspired Barbara Bodichon and her fellow activists in their campaigns for legal reform. In 1868 John Stuart Mill republished it as a pamphlet for distribution by the National Union of Women's Suffrage Societies, of which he was honorary president.[21]

Mill had demonstrated his own commitment to female equality early in life. As a young man, he distributed pamphlets about contraception in working-class neighborhoods in East London. He wrote in favor of female suffrage, along with articles condemning domestic violence and the paltry sentences meted out in the few cases that did make it to court. In May 1865 his Liberal friends encouraged him to run for the parliamentary seat for the City of Westminster. Early advocates for suffrage from the Kensington Society, among them Barbara Bodichon, Isa Craig, Emily Davies, and Bessie Rayner Parkes, helped him campaign. Mill's stepdaughter and collaborator, Helen Taylor, was also a member of the feminist discussion society that met at the Kensington home of Charlotte Manning, who had lived in Calcutta and was an ardent advocate of education in India. Davies, who would later found Girton, the first Cambridge college for women (Manning would be its first mistress), confessed to some concern about Mill's chances when she learned that his opponents were describing him "as the man who wants to have girls in Parliament."[22] But, despite strong opposition, Mill won his seat and went on to advocate for female suffrage. In May 1867, during a discussion of the

FIGURE 8. "Mill's Logic; or, Franchise for Females: 'Pray Clear the Way, There, for These-a-Persons.'" *Punch,* 30 March 1867. Punch Cartoon Library/TopFoto.

Reform Bill to expand suffrage to include working-class men, he proposed, though to no avail, an amendment to replace the word "man" with "person" and thereby open the possibility of including some women (that is, the few with the right qualifications of wealth, education, and occupation) among the new voters.[23]

Mill's final publication in his lifetime, *The Subjection of Women* (1869), was passionate, straightforward, to the point, and not quite a utilitarian tract. The utilitarianism that Mill (like his father) espoused posed a problem, after all, for a campaign for gender equality, since it could as easily support gender *in*equality if women could be shown to be happy with their unequal situation.[24] In *Subjection* Mill stated firmly that the "legal subordination of one sex to the other" was "wrong...and now one of the chief hindrances to human improvement; and...ought to be replaced by a principle of perfect equality, admitting no power or privilege on the one side, nor disability on the other." For Mill, "Marriage is the only actual bondage known to our law. There remain no legal slaves, except the mistress of every house."[25] It was by concluding that we could not know what women might be able to accomplish if given the same opportunities as men that he attempted to reconcile his advocacy of female equality with utilitarianism: some Englishwomen might well have been "happy" with their current lot, but they would probably have been happier if they had the same access to education and employment that men enjoyed.[26]

WOMEN OF THE EAST IN THE FIGHT FOR BRITISH WOMEN'S RIGHTS

Campaigners for British legal reform continued to use the women of the East as a point of comparison, arguing that British women surely deserved more rights than Eastern women, given Britain's higher status as a civilized and imperial power. For example, Junius Revividus—the pen name of the locomotive engineer and political commentator William Bridges Adams (a well-kept secret that was of much consternation to John Stuart Mill until he was finally informed)—wrote in 1833 that, under British marriage laws, women were "as much slaves as the inmates of a Turkish haram."[27] While Harriet Taylor found the Adams article unoriginal in many ways, she did not dispute the contrast he drew with Eastern women. She noted in her diary that Adams's article "abounds in parallels with my own thoughts," from the argument about the need for reforms in women's education and divorce to the comparison of "English women to a Turkish harem" and the description of marriage as "merely legalized prostitution."[28]

Similarly, in his criticism of English girls' education, Mill echoed Catharine Macaulay and Mary Wollstonecraft in describing the present system as furnishing them with no "acquirements but those of an odalisque, or of a domestic servant." On marriage he recognized that the English wife had some limited powers but ultimately was no better than a "Sultan's favourite slave [who]...has slaves under her, over whom she tyrannizes." After all, he continued, "the desirable thing would be that she should neither have slaves nor be a slave." He viewed Englishwomen who quietly accepted their situation as akin to "women in the harem of an Oriental," who "do not complain of not being allowed the freedom of European women" but rather "think our women insufferably bold and unfeminine."[29]

Indian women also featured in Mill's comparisons and, interestingly enough, as positive examples in his argument for the "natural capacity of women for government." Referring to his "long knowledge of Hindoo governments" from his years at the East India Company, he presented the "entirely unexpected" fact that "if a Hindoo principality is strongly, vigilantly, and economically governed; if order is preserved without oppression; if cultivation is extending, and the people prosperous, in three cases out of four that principality is under a woman's rule." Women did not rule, of course, "by Hindoo institutions" but rather when male rulers were felled by premature death, given their lives of "inactivity and sensual excesses," and left women as regents. While offering this positive evaluation of Hindu women rulers, Mill quickly reminded his readers that "these princesses have never been seen in public, have never conversed with any man not of their own family except from behind a curtain, that they do not read, and if they did there is no book in their languages which can give them the smallest instruction on political affairs."[30] Although he had mostly Hindu women in mind, he did provide the example of a "Mahomedan" woman—"the late Sekunder Begum of Bhopal…a most energetic, prudent, and just ruler"—in an 1870 letter to Charlotte Manning.[31] Mill left it to readers to imagine what a well-educated Englishwoman might accomplish if given the same power in government as these Indian women.

The Scottish lawyer and politician John Boyd-Kinnear, who also evoked the harem and women's souls to argue for female suffrage, drew a direct link between the harem of Western imagination and the restrictions of domestic life under the ideology of separate spheres. In his 1869 piece, "The Social Position of Women," in a volume of essays titled *Woman's Work and Women's Culture,* edited by the feminist Josephine Butler, he questioned the wisdom of preventing Englishwomen from venturing into the public sphere: "Do we not in truth reduce them to the mere slaves of the harem? Do we not, like those who keep such slaves, deny in fact that they have any souls? What can they do with souls, if nature means them only to be toys of our idle hours, the adornment of our ease and wealth, to be worshipped as idols but never taken as helpmates, permitted at most to gaze from afar at the battles of life—to crown the victor with a wreath, or to shed weak tears for the dead?"[32]

Mill, for his part, reconciled his support for progressive values such as British women's rights with his defense of colonialism and, specifically, the British presence in India through his commitment to the idea of improvement and progress. Colonization made sense to him because, he explained, he took into account "its relation, not to a single country, but to the collective economical interests of the human race."[33] In 1853 he testified in the House of Lords in defense of the record in India of the East India Company, his employer of the past three decades, describing in detail the company's many accomplishments, such as roads, canals, irrigation, new educational and legal institutions, the railway and telegraph, and the abolition of "many barbarous usages of the natives," such as sati, human sacrifice, and infanticide.[34]

Given the rampant superstition and corruption that he, like his father, associated with India, the most important task facing the British colonial authorities, in his eyes, was to introduce rational, uncorrupt self-government in this distant colony.[35] After all, he noted in a January 1854 diary entry, "the English are the fittest people to rule over barbarous or semibarbarous nations like those of the East."[36] Thus, while Mill didn't attribute the "diversities of conduct and character to inherent natural differences," he did adhere to the idea of a hierarchy of civilizations and the notion that the countries lower down on this ladder needed the active intervention of superior countries like Great Britain to be prodded out of their debased state. He was clear, however, that once British men like him had judged that India had achieved the proper form of self-government, Britain should consider its job complete and leave.[37]

"MUTINY" AND MASCULINITY

In response to the Great Revolt of 1857, which the British called the Sepoy Mutiny, the British Parliament passed the Government of India Act in August 1858. The act dissolved the East India Company and vested formal political authority in the Crown. Queen Victoria announced the changes in her 1 November 1858 proclamation to the "Princes, Chiefs and People of India," including that, henceforth, Indians would be treated as British subjects—"We hold Ourselves bound to the Natives of Our Indian Territories by the same obligations of Duty which bind Us to all Our other Subjects." The proclamation also promised that the Crown, despite its own "gratitude" for the "solace" of Christianity, would "disclaim alike the Right and the Desire to impose our Convictions on any of Our Subjects." Members of all religious communities "shall alike enjoy the equal and impartial protection of the Law." The satirical magazine *Punch* had already responded with skepticism to the new parliamentary act's grand assurances to Indians. The contrast between the clothing, posture, and position of the two women in its cartoon "The Accession of the Queen of India" makes only too clear the complete and utter political and economic submission of Indians to the Crown. Charging Indians with disloyalty, in their "mutiny," to what was in fact an occupying force, the British had tried and executed countless Indians. Even the unob-

FIGURE 9. "The Accession of the Queen of India," *Punch*, 11 September 1858. Punch Cartoon Library/TopFoto.

trusive but symbolically significant (and last) Mughal emperor, Bahadur Shah, was charged with treason and, in October 1858, exiled to Rangoon, then under British control, and there he died four years later.

Another significant consequence of the Great Revolt of 1857 was the hardening of British racism toward Indians and the proliferation of lurid ideas about Indian masculinity, especially in the wake of stories, many later discredited, of atrocities perpetrated by Indian men on Englishwomen. The

British reorganized the colonial army by recruiting those Indians who had demonstrated their loyalty to the British during the rebellion, such as the Sikhs, Gurkhas, Punjabi Muslims, and Pathans, who, conveniently, fit well with the older colonial category of "martial races," though this represented a different, more pragmatic use of the word *race* than would emerge some decades later. A century before the revolt, company official Richard Orme had identified Indians from the wheat-growing regions of the subcontinent as better built and therefore more suitable for the army than the shorter men of the rice-growing regions.[38] Bengali men fell in the latter group, and Orme was unrestrained in his lack of regard for what he saw as their "general effeminacy of character" and "weaker frame and more enervated disposition than those of any other province."[39]

In 1830 Thomas Babington Macaulay, yet to compose his famous "Minute on Education," had shared his own view of "the Bengali" in an essay about Robert Clive, the victor of Plassey: "There never perhaps existed a people so thoroughly fitted by habit for a foreign yoke."[40] In contrast to the British middle-class ideal man, who was a breadwinner and protector, the British saw Indian men not only as brute oppressors of women but also, as with the Bengalis, particularly effeminate in their failure to care properly for their dependents and their own susceptibility to conquest.

Given British assumptions about profound differences between Hindus and Muslims in India, as we saw in chapter 3 with James Mill, British images of Bengali men did not typically encompass Muslim Bengali men. Also, because even by the end of the nineteenth century only a small number of Muslim Bengali men had partaken of Western education and therefore were not in colonial government service or in as regular contact with the British as were members of the educated Hindu elite of Bengal, Muslims did not represent Bengalis in British discussions. This did not mean, however, that Muslim men were not affected by these oft-repeated colonial images. In his 1895 book, *Physical Education in India,* Abdus Salam, a Muslim member of the Provincial Civil Service of India, contrasted the "physical prowess and intrepidity, the manliness and vitality, the discipline and the presence of mind which distinguished the Mussulman race from the seventh to about the end of the eighteenth century" with the "lack of physical energy which more or less characterises the Mahomedans in India" in the late nineteenth century. He chastised the Bengali Muslim intelligentsia for both "rapidly parting with our own national ways and manners" and selecting incorrectly which aspects of Western education to adopt: "Whilst the sweet guilelessness and gentle suavity of the East is absent, the genuine sturdiness and masculine straightforwardness of the West is also wanting."[41]

THE PUSH FOR FEMALE EDUCATION IN BENGAL

By the mid-nineteenth century, a few Indian men were calling for greater attention to female education, though the majority remained opposed to the idea of formal schooling because it violated elite norms of female seclusion that held across religious lines. In the 1860s, particularly among the Brahmo (the reformed Hinduism started by Rammohan Roy) and Christian communities, men began to push for reform in the practice of seclusion and for education that would sharpen women's minds. To quote Kaliprasanna Ghose Bahadur of Bikrampur, just south of Dacca, from his 1869 book *Narijati-Bishayak Prastab* (A proposal regarding women): "If murdering a woman by not giving her any food and water is considered a sin, then depriving her of all education can be regarded as a greater sin.... Like education, she has a natural right to personal liberty and freedom. Without this right, female education becomes meaningless."[42]

In February 1870 the Bengali Brahmo leader and reformer Keshab Chandra Sen traveled to England with five fellow Brahmos to, in Sen's words, "excite the interest of the English public in the political, social, and religious welfare of the men and women of India."[43] To that end Sen traveled and gave speeches all over Britain to listeners eager to learn the "best method of forwarding [Indian women's] moral and intellectual enlightenment."[44] At his meeting with Prime Minister William E. Gladstone and Queen Victoria, "his sovereign" expressed her delight over the abolition of sati and "great concern for the miserable condition of the Hindu women."[45]

At a meeting of the East India Association, Sen and Mary Carpenter, an abolitionist and social and educational reformer, spoke about the importance of zenana, or *antahpur,* education and the need for more female teachers, specifically English women teachers. Sen argued that the "root of the mischief is the want of enlightenment" and asserted the need to "raise up the spirit of Hindu women, and stimulate their curiosity, and excite their taste for nobler and higher things." However, while he was very clear about the need for education, he did not think it desirable that Indian women should fully imitate Englishwomen: "With all my respect and admiration for civilization as it prevails in England, I have always been foremost in protesting against the demoralization of India by importing English customs into it.... The growth of society must be indigenous, native, and natural." It was on the extant "noble and good" traits of Indian women that a "superstructure of reformed female Indian society" should be built. Of particular interest is the manner in which he appealed directly to those engaged in the struggle for women's rights in England: "If Englishwomen are ready to vindicate what are called women's rights in England, ... let them show that their views and sympathies are not confined within the limits of this small island."[46]

Indeed, in the second half of the nineteenth century, British feminists came to view India as a place with opportunities for public action and activism unavailable to them in Britain, a place where they could demonstrate their commitment to their nation, race, and empire—and hence the necessity and urgency of their own political enfranchisement. For example, following their success in repealing the Contagious Diseases Acts in Britain in 1886, Josephine Butler and the militant Ladies National Association for the Repeal of the Contagious Diseases Acts would turn their attention to India. In the British context Butler and the association argued that these acts, intended to regulate prostitution and curb venereal disease through compulsory medical examinations in and around military settlements, were designed to protect the wealthy male patrons (who were not tested) and penalize the women who worked as prostitutes. Butler later recalled how the "peculiar horror and audacity of this legislative movement for the creation of a slave class of women for the supposed benefit of licentious men forced women into a new position," mobilizing even those "formerly timid or bound by conventional ideas."[47]

In India the laws were designed to protect the health and well-being of British soldiers, and thus the empire itself, from the diseased clutches of lascivious and cunning Indian prostitutes. Through their efforts to help Indian women affected by these regulations, British middle-class feminists sought to demonstrate that they could in fact strengthen British imperialism by, to quote Butler, "purifying...our nation's name in distant parts of the world" and making it more ethical. Given the capacious interpretations of the word *prostitute* by colonial administrators in India, as well as a tendency to generalize across Indian women in any case, the Ladies National Association's Indian campaign served to cement ideas about Indian women's depravity and British women's superiority.[48]

Annette Akroyd was among those who heard Keshab Chandra Sen's appeal to Englishwomen. As a member of the Kensington Society, Akroyd had attended many meetings about women's education.[49] She later described Sen's lecture as having had an "electrifying effect on us Victorian ladies."[50] Despite warnings that the "great heat" of India would prove too much for a "little soft white-skinned wee woman" as herself, Akroyd enrolled in Bengali lessons and a course for governesses to prepare for her move to India. Traveling on the *Xantho* via the newly opened Suez Canal, she arrived in Calcutta in December 1872.[51] She soon found herself at odds with Sen, however, regarding her plans to help local women. For Sen women's emancipation was to be a gradual process and without the Anglicization of the curriculum or conduct. While Akroyd did not see a need to westernize Bengali women, she did believe there was room for improvement in the area of women's dress. She expressed shock at the transparency of local dress, the lack of undergarments, and the overemphasis on jewelry. Although she recognized that these might make sense in the context of seclusion, new clothing would be needed if women were to venture out into the public sphere, as she hoped to encourage them to do. The Hindu Mahila Bidyaloy (Hindu Ladies School) that Akroyd founded in November 1873 did not survive long past her marriage to Henry Beveridge, a colonial official and vocal supporter of John Stuart Mill and Harriet Taylor.[52] After their return to England and the death of two of their children, she would take up the study of Persian and Turki and produce a new translation of the *Babur-nama* and the first translation of *Humayun-nama,* written by the Mughal princess Gulbadan, whom we met in chapter 1.[53]

In 1883, while still in India, Annette Akroyd Beveridge opposed her husband and joined other British women who objected vehemently to the Ilbert Bill, which proposed to grant senior Indian judges and magistrates the power to prosecute European citizens. The political mobilization of Englishwomen in India against the Ilbert proposal was unprecedented in size and fervor. Organized into a Ladies Committee, they—along with the British urban business community and indigo and tea plantation owners and managers—referred to the vulnerability of White womanhood and argued that Indian judges would be far too lenient with Indian men charged with raping Englishwomen.

In her 6 March 1883 article in the Calcutta newspaper the *Englishman,* Beveridge made quite clear her notions of English racial superiority when she declared, "I speak the feeling of all Englishwomen in India when I say that we regard the proposal to subject us to the jurisdiction of native Judges as an insult." She even felt compelled to clarify that "it is not the pride of race which dictates this feeling which is the outcome of something far deeper—it is the price of womanhood." She rationalized the sense of insult by pointing to the "ignorant and neglected women of India [who] rise up from their enslavement in evidence against their masters." Surely, she argued, it was outrageous "to subject civilized women to the jurisdiction of men who have done little or nothing to redeem the women of their own races and whose social ideas are still on the outer verge of civilization." Though she invoked the idea of a shared womanhood, she actually underlined her notion of racial difference between English and Indian women, between "civilized" and enslaved women. Her efforts to educate Indian women or to bring to readers Gulbadan's *Humayun-nama,* a book that had, in her words, "remained, both in India and Europe, a literary *pardanishin* [one who observes purdah]," must therefore be seen as motivated by a desire to demonstrate her superiority rather than to assert solidarity with Indians.[54] For Western-educated Indians, many of whom were now in senior positions in the civil service, the organized racist and colonial mobilization against the Ilbert Bill revealed the urgent need for a national organization of Indians of all regions and religions. This paved the way for the creation, in 1885, of the Indian National Congress, which would eventually lead the movement for India's independence from the British.

THE "DISCOVERY" OF BENGALI MUSLIMS

As part of its efforts to know Indians better—to control them better and forestall future uprisings such as those of 1857—the colonial state undertook a national census in 1871–72.[55] While there had been earlier regional censuses, this represented the first effort by the British colonial authorities "to obtain for the whole of India statistics of the age, caste, religion, occupation, education, and infirmities of the population." One of the surprises to emerge was the size and nature of the Muslim presence in Bengal. The census revealed that just over 32 percent of the Bengal population was "Mahomedan" and that the 20.5 million Muslims in the province of Bengal and Assam comprised just over half the Muslim population of all of British India, making Bengali Muslims the largest group of Muslims in the country. Moreover, the vast majority of this number was concentrated in eastern Bengal, "inhabited," according to a contemporary report, "by the Bengali, living amid a network of rivers and morasses, nourished on a watery rice diet, looking weak and puny, but able to bear much exposure, timid and slothful, but sharp-witted, industrious, and fond of sedentary employment."[56] Unlike in other parts of India, the Muslim population of Bengal included a fairly small urban elite, with the majority being poor, rural, agricultural, and Bengali speaking.[57] Also, of the Muslim populations in different parts of India, the Muslim community of Bengal had the least access to the new Western educational opportunities. The contrast between the two largest religious communities in Bengal was particularly stark at the level of higher education. In 1875 only 5.4 percent of college students were Muslim, compared to 93.9 percent Hindu. The gap was larger still among those who knew English.[58]

By the late nineteenth century, even elite Bengali Muslim families found themselves relatively impoverished, uneducated, and powerless, thanks to successive colonial administrative measures over the past hundred years, such as the 1793 Permanent Settlement of Land Revenues, the Resumption Proceedings that commenced in 1828, and the replacement of Persian with English as the language of the courts in 1837.[59] Over time the Muslim aristocracy lost access to the three occupations they had once dominated: the military, revenue collection, and judicial or political employment.[60] Muslims from the middle classes, such as the rural elites, continued to attend the local religious schools, *madrasas* and *maktabs,* in large numbers, but these offered no preparation for government jobs. The poorest Muslims, the peasants, much like the poorest Hindus, could not afford any form of education, whether religious, local, or English. In the past some poor children might have attended the local *maktab* or *pathshala* (local Muslim and Hindu elementary school, respectively), with financial support from the main landowner in the area, and there learned to read and write and, in the case of Muslims, also some basic Quranic recitation. However, given growing economic woes across the classes, even these schools fell increasingly out of reach.[61]

The 1871 census, as it turned out, also provided the first official count of women in Bengal and, given the recently passed Indian Penal Code of 1860 and the Contagious Diseases Act of 1868, the category of "prostitute" emerged as particularly significant in numbers and as a topic of debate. According to the British authorities, prostitution in India was a social evil on par with sati, polygamy, infanticide, and child marriage; indeed, they saw it as connected to these other evils. In contrast to Britain, where they believed economic considerations pushed women to take up such work, in India they blamed religion and local custom for the prevalence of this social ill.

British administrators attributed the large number of Hindu prostitutes both to the strictness of Hindu regulations and to an ancient tolerance for sexual openness in religious contexts (such as in temples). Among the (overwhelmingly Hindu) Bengali civil servants recruited into the colonial state's efforts to gather detailed information on local prostitution was Bankim Chandra Chatterjee, a deputy magistrate in western Bengal who would later gain fame for his novels and the song "Bande Mataram." Chatterjee recognized that a variety of factors, including an abusive husband or the "lonely and secluded" nature of a Hindu marriage, could propel a woman into such work—as could a woman's physical needs, especially if she had "vicious tendencies" and lacked "moral restraints," to escape the "extreme vigilance" of "Hindu society."[62]

To explain the presence of Muslim prostitutes, colonial civil servants pointed to Muslim practices outside the confines of monogamous marriage. That Muslim marriage was based on a contract had, of course, long been a source of consternation for missionaries like Edward Storrow. The new concern with prostitution added new layers of impropriety to British ideas about Muslim marriages. In the words of Dacca commissioner Alexander Abercrombie, the contractual nature of marriage meant that when the husband and wife became "thoroughly tired of each another," they could separate "without difficulty and the woman is free to go nika [make a marriage contract] with another man or set up again for herself in the bazar." Many Hindu women, Abercrombie added, converted to Islam precisely to avoid the shame and censure of their own community. Babu Taraknath Mullick, deputy magistrate of Madaripur in eastern Bengal, also attributed the large number of Muslim women counted as prostitutes to the provisions for easy divorce and serial and polygamous marriages among Muslims: "The Mohamedan religion," Mullick wrote, "affords greater facilities for leading an irregular life with intercourse with prostitutes than any other religion on the face of the Globe." In the eyes of the colonial administrators, the population of "Muslim prostitutes" included the additional wives of elite Muslim men and any unmarried women in those households, as well as, of course, courtesans and *nautch* girls reminiscent of Munni Begum, whose relationship with Warren Hastings had so enraged Edmund Burke a century earlier. While, according to Mullick, a Hindu man's wives may be "scattered over different places and districts," a Muslim man's wives lived with him. This practice had the advantage of giving him oversight over them.[63] Ultimately, the colonial authorities' search for detailed knowledge about what it deemed criminal and diseased allowed it to breathe new life into the image of Muslim harems and the greater sexual appetites of both Muslim men and women that set them apart from both the British and Bengali Hindus.

MEN AND THE FIGHT FOR FEMALE ADVANCEMENT

Male Indian Muslim writers and leaders open to working with the British were generally united on the need to prioritize the education of boys and men. The famous north Indian reformer Syed Ahmed Khan, for example, explained that he had decided to cooperate with the British "not because of any love or loyalty to the British" but because of his distress over the "present state of decline" of Indian Muslims and his conviction that their "welfare" depended on the "help of the British government."[64] In 1875 he founded the Muhammadan Anglo-Oriental College in Aligarh, envisioned as a Muslim Cambridge with Urdu and English as its common languages, with the intention of producing a new Muslim male elite in India that would thrive under British colonial rule.[65]

Syed Ahmed Khan's deep admiration for the British model of education for males stood in uncomfortable contrast to his vehement opposition to British colonial schools for Muslim girls. In his book about the 1857 revolt, translated into English in 1873 as *The Causes of the Indian Revolt,* he argued that the British push for female education was one of the factors that led to the Muslim population's resentment against the British. The idea that "girls should attend, and be taught at these Schools, and leave off the habit of sitting veiled" was completely "obnoxious...to the feelings of the Hindustanees."[66] He clarified, however, that he was not opposed to the "education of Mohammedan girls," only to their attending schools outside the home. While "Mohammedan ladies of respectable families" possess a "sort of indigenous education of a moderate degree" that includes the study of Urdu, Persian, Arabic, and even enough English to be able to "read and write telegraphic messages," the main obstacle to women's education was not religion but rather poverty. However, he could not think of any measures that the government could undertake to persuade "respectable Mohammedans... to send their daughters to Government schools for education," given their general condition and quality.[67] At a Lahore conference in 1889, he warned that schools such as those in England or that the British wanted to establish for girls in India were "neither suitable to the conditions nor would there be any need for them for our women [for] thousands of years to come."[68]

In the end, "those who hold that women should be educated and civilized prior to men are greatly mistaken. The fact is, that no satisfactory education can be provided for Mohammedan females until a large number of Mohammedan males receive a sound education. The present state of education among Mohammedan females is, in my opinion, enough for domestic happiness considering the present social and economic conditions of the Mohammedans in India."[69]

Support for Muslim girls' education was no better in Bengal, from what we can gather from the report of an incident at a January 1868 meeting of the Bengal Social Science Association in Calcutta. Present at the meeting was the renowned educationist and reformer Nawab Abdul Latif of Faridpur in eastern Bengal, who had founded the Muhammadan Literary and Scientific Society in Calcutta in 1863 with the goal of fostering the greater interaction of Bengali Muslims with both Bengali Hindus and the English.[70] When the famous Bengali Hindu writer Peary Chand Mitra, who had done much to popularize more colloquial Bengali writing with novels like *Alaler Gharer Dulal* (1857), asked Latif about plans for female education in the Muslim community, Maulvi Abdul Hakim of the Calcutta Madrasa jumped in to explain that the Islamic scriptures advocated the education of boys and girls alike, but there was no question of Muslim girls imitating the girls of other communities and violating purdah to attend school outside the home. Latif's silence following Hakim's intervention has been taken as an indication of his support for Hakim's statement, both clearly aligned with Syed Ahmed Khan on this issue.[71]

In 1873 Latif helped to found Presidency College in Calcutta, a new incarnation of the Hindu College that Rammohan Roy had helped establish in 1817. Part of the rationale for the new name was that it would encourage Muslim and other non-Hindu families to send their sons there. Latif also arranged for a scholarship fund for (presumably male) Muslim students, the Mohsin Fund.[72] Present at the founding of Presidency College was the viceroy of India, Lord Northbrook, and his cousin and private secretary, Evelyn Baring, none other than the future Lord Cromer.

One of the better-documented colonial advocates of reforms ostensibly meant to help colonized women, Cromer served the British Empire in both India and Egypt. In his two-volume book, *Modern Egypt,* which he published in 1908 after returning to England following his twenty-four-year sojourn in Egypt, Cromer noted that the "first and foremost" reason why

"Islam as a social system has been a complete failure" was that "Islam keeps women in a position of marked inferiority." He perceived a vast chasm separating the practices and principles of Muslims and Christians or Europeans, particularly regarding women, and discussed at length the "consequences which result from the degradation of women in Mohammedan countries," in particular seclusion and polygamy. The arguments about the "baneful effect on Eastern society" of seclusion are "so commonplace that it is unnecessary to dwell on them," but he continued nonetheless to explain that seclusion "cramps the intellect and withers the mental development" of half the population of Muslim countries—women—and subsequently their husbands and sons too.[73] Polygamy, he pointed out, was even worse than seclusion in its impact on women and was indicative of the alien mindset of Muslims: "The monogamous Christian respects women [and] sees in the Virgin Mary an ideal of womanhood, which would be incomprehensible in a Moslem country. The Moslem, on the other hand, despises women." In the end, although he pointed to women's education as the "obvious remedy" and, in *Modern Egypt,* claimed that the British supported the Egyptian women's movement, the policies he had pursued in Egypt were far from beneficial for Egyptian women. Among other things he had raised school fees and discouraged the training of women doctors on the grounds that—notwithstanding the wishes of local women—"throughout the civilized world, attendance by medical men is still the rule."[74]

In Bengal and across India, in the closing decades of the nineteenth century and the early years of the twentieth century, a growing number of male Muslim writers advocated for female education. Well-educated women were featured in the work of Urdu writers Nazir Ahmed and Altaf Hossain Ali, Syed Ahmed Khan's disciples from Aligarh, and of the Bengali writer Mir Mosharraf Hossain. Ultimately, however, the exemplary Muslim women characters these authors created were educated to be better prepared for their lives as wife and mother, all while observing strict purdah. These ideal women, it turned out, were modeled on none other than the by-then-widowed Queen Victoria—a skilled and educated administrator but also pious, chaste, virtuous, loyal, nurturing, domestic, and decidedly asexual.[75]

By contrast, as we shall see in the next chapter, the first Muslim Bengali women writers would envision a purpose for their own education that extended beyond their household capabilities. However, even the educationists among them would confront the challenge of enticing Bengali Muslim girls out of the home to attend formal schools without violating the norms of purdah—as would many of their successors well into the twentieth century.

INDIAN WOMEN AND THE REVERSE GAZE

The late-nineteenth-century discussions about female education in India unfolded in the context of a dramatic increase in travel between India and England. Growing numbers of Indian women made the journey in the opposite direction of British women like Eliza Fay and Annette Akroyd Beveridge. Although there are no available travel accounts by Bengali Muslim women from this era—a reflection of the different nature of engagement with the British by the different religious communities of India—the observations of elite women of Bengali Hindu background offer valuable insights on how Bengali and, more broadly, Indian women of a certain class and educational status, irrespective of religious background, perceived English women and society.[76] For Indian travelers of the late nineteenth century, the women of distant lands, and of England in particular, were no longer simply to be admired—as they had been for earlier travelers such as Abu Taleb, the author of the 1802 "Vindication of the Liberties of the Asiatic Women." Rather, Englishwomen had become models to be emulated—but, ideally while still maintaining one's own culture, faith, and identity.

In the 1870s elite, educated Bengali women began to travel to England. Among them was Rajkumari Devi, who accompanied her husband, the Brahmo reformer Sasipada Banerji. The *Asiatic of London* described Devi in 1872 as the "first Hindu lady who has ever visited England."[77] Gyandanondini Debi (also written as Jnandanandini Devi) shocked many in her family and community by sailing to England in 1877 with three children to join her husband, Satyendranath Tagore, who was the first Indian officer in the Indian Civil Service, a translator of John Stuart Mill's *The Subjection of Women*, and the older brother of famed poet Rabindranath Tagore. Gyandanondini Debi is credited with helping to usher in a more "modern" way of wearing the sari, with European-inspired "blouses" and "petticoats." Neither Rajkumari Devi nor Gyandanondini Debi produced a written record of their observations of Britain or of the women's rights activism unfolding there. It would fall instead on Krishnobhabini Das to leave us the earliest detailed narrative about England by a Bengali woman, throughout which she repeatedly juxtaposed the realities of women's lives in India and in England.[78]

The eighteen-year-old Krishnobhabini Das moved to England with her husband, Debendranath Das, in September 1882. When he had returned from England five months earlier with a master's degree in mathematics from Cambridge University, his father, a prominent Calcutta lawyer, had refused to receive him in his house because, according to strict Hindu precepts, Debendranath had been "polluted" by traveling overseas. The couple decided to leave their young daughter with her grandparents out of consideration for their daughter's future acceptability in Calcutta society and left for London, where they would live for eight years. Debendranath found work training British Indian Civil Service officers headed to India, while Krishnobhabini visited libraries such as the British Museum Library, read voraciously, and, fortunately for us, wrote prolifically.

While she shared little of her daily life in England in the pages she sent to a publisher in Calcutta, Krishnobhabini was generous in her descriptions of the places she visited and her observations of English society and culture. She wanted to learn from the English but was wary of losing too much of her own culture, of becoming too English—a concern that would also plague women and men of future generations. Although from the perspective of traditional Hindus such as her father-in-law she had violated all sorts of rules by disobeying him, the head of the family, and she knew well from experience the manner in which Hindu rules and customs could be oppressive for females, she maintained great pride in her background and community. For example, she expressed dismay at the decision of the highly educated Pandita Ramabai to convert to Christianity in England, seeing it as "rejecting Hindu religion" and as an act "which ashamed all the Hindus." She also apologized for having donned "memsahib" dress but rationalized it on the grounds that she was in England "to fulfill a dream of seeing a free country" and to discover ways to help her sisters at home.[79] Despite her expressions of admiration for England, "that very small rain-encircled place" and "the land where [freedom] ... resides," she was under no illusions as to the implications for Indians of Britain's "beloved freedom." In a "Farewell" poem addressed to India— her "favourite land," that "jeweled land," and "Mother"—that she wrote as her ship was pulling out of the harbor in Bombay, she wrote with hope and excitement about going "where the goddess of independence / Resides in every house." In contrast, she noted,

Our country is bound in strong fetters
With the rope of servitude on every human neck.

With the power of independence and free life
Are the children of Britain ensconced.

With a lot of desire, I want to see
With what power Britain is so worshipped
Trampling poor India with her feet
Clutching education and civilization to her heart.[80]

In the same poem Krishnobhabini asked why Indian women should not be able to "go to that country," like the men, "to fill our hearts with the wealth of knowledge / After seeing the independent British daughter!" And, indeed, once in England she was impressed with the higher-education degrees of some of the Englishwomen she encountered. But while she seemed more open to the idea of women learning arithmetic and geography alongside needlework and music, her goals for Indian women were still the same as those expressed by Keshab Chandra Sen over a decade earlier: that they become better mothers, wives, sisters, and daughters. English wives, she pointed out, were worthy of emulation in their morality and chastity as well as in the nature of their responsibilities within the home. These ideal wives and mothers, after all, were propelling the British Empire forward, through their commitment to religion and, unlike primitive and uncivilized people, to chastity.[81]

Again echoing earlier Indian reformers, Krishnobhabini invoked the "golden era" of gender relations in India, a time when Hindu men and women alike had been respected alongside the Greeks for their love of knowledge and contributions to mathematics and science. Unlike many of her contemporaries, however, she did not attribute the end of that era to the advent of Muslim rule in India. The point, she believed, was not to dwell on the past but to recognize that, since those accomplishments had been possible before, they could be attained again: "How we can improve the present situation, and what will benefit the future, should be our constant focus."[82]

For Krishnobhabini education, and specifically English education, was integral to any efforts to move forward. Education, sports, and intellectual engagement with men in the public sphere, she pointed out, had allowed Englishwomen to grow intellectually and morally in a way that was not available to Indian women in seclusion. Citing the examples of women like Florence Nightingale and Mary Carpenter, who had done so much to help others, she urged her Indian "sisters" to "break your cages or convince your brothers to cut the shackles, which chain the Bengali women," to discover "how independent life brought happiness to Germany and France where women never shed tears of humility" and where men do not think women "are useless" or "keep them in cages of domesticity and treat them like animals." Even as she called for the freedom of Indian women from their shackles, however, she also recognized the need of freedom for the country as a whole: "England is the center for freedom, and our India is totally enslaved. I myself have observed that since I am breathing English air and living with free people, I am developing new ideas."[83] She had drawn a contrast between the "strong fetters" that bound India and the "power of independence and free life" enjoyed by the "children of Britain" even in the poem she wrote when she first set out for Britain.[84]

Krishnobhabini later described the benefits of travel: "I used to read about other countries—some independent, some under the rule of others, some democratic and some autocratic—but was unable to realize the significance of all these terms. I can now see that I used to imagine all other countries more or less like mine, because at that time, I was like a blind person to whom day and night had no difference." To the end she remained a champion of reform in women's lives in Bengal along the lines of what she had observed among women in England.[85] After her return to Calcutta in 1890, Krishnobhabini continued to speak out against the injustices to which Indian women were subject and argued for education and social activism as the strategies with which to best address discrimination against women. The colonial government banned her book in India, though it is not clear whether it was because of its feminist or nationalist outlook or, indeed, both.[86]

THAT "OLD OFT-REPEATED STORY" ABOUT MUSLIM WOMEN

In June 1891, a year after Krishnobhabini's return to India, one Annie Reichardt published an article on "Mohammedan women" in the widely circulated British monthly *Nineteenth Century*. Reichardt's accusations of Muslim women's oppression incensed the Indian jurist and writer Syed Ameer Ali, who quickly published a response in the magazine's September issue. In "The Real Status of Women in Islam," Ameer Ali articulated for his primarily British readers rebuttals to long-standing European criticisms regarding the status of Muslim women, with special attention to seclusion, marriage, polygamy, and divorce, much as Mirza Abu Taleb had been compelled to do almost a century earlier.

A member of the Urdu- and Persian-speaking elite of Bengal, Syed Ameer Ali had studied Arabic and the Quran as a young child and then moved on to the English section of the Hooghly Madrasa and Calcutta University. Upon receiving the first scholarship in Bengal for postgraduate study in Britain, the young Ameer Ali arrived in London in January 1869 after a long voyage via Suez, Marseilles, and Paris. He carried with him three letters from no less than the viceroy, Lord Mayo, himself.[87]

Shortly after his arrival he met the English suffragist Millicent Garrett Fawcett and her husband, Henry Fawcett, a professor of political economy at Cambridge and a Liberal member of Parliament, at a small dinner at their home. He later recalled of that evening, "Both husband and wife were ardent advocates of 'equal rights for women' and as my sympathies were on the same side, our friendship was not marred by the difference of opinion, much of which was prevalent at the time."[88] Millicent Fawcett had become an earnest disciple of John Stuart Mill after hearing him speak in 1865 and credited him with having ushered in an "epoch in the history of the women's movement."[89]

In his memoirs Ameer Ali described a "great meeting" about women's suffrage that he attended in early 1870 at which both Henry and Millicent Fawcett spoke. Their words "made an ineffaceable impression" on him as he came to understand the need for "substantial improvement" in English law as it pertained to women's rights regarding earnings, property, child custody, and the franchise. Indeed, he realized "how far behind Muslim law" English law had been "in all these respects" until the passing of the Married Women's Property Acts of 1870, 1874, and 1882, which finally allowed married women to keep their earnings and to inherit property—and, eventually, because they now controlled property, even to vote.[90] At that same meeting Ameer Ali met the US abolitionist and freethinker Moncure Conway and would become a regular guest at the weekly "social reunions" of Moncure's wife, Ellen, which brought together "*litterateurs, savants,* and distinguished men and women from every part of the world."[91] And thus the young Ameer Ali's social circles continued to expand, and he encountered various groups and individuals engaged in a variety of reform efforts, including in support of women's rights.[92]

Quite early in his four-year stay in London, Ameer Ali also became good friends with Adelaide Manning, an English writer and proponent of women's education in England and India. In 1871 she and her stepmother, Charlotte

Manning (of the Kensington Society), established the London branch of the National Indian Association in Aid of Social Progress in India (NIA), founded by Mary Carpenter in Bristol a year earlier.[93] Following Carpenter's death in 1877, Adelaide Manning moved the NIA's national headquarters to her home in Maida Vale in London and served as its general secretary for the following three decades.[94] In a December 1878 letter to the *Times*, she explained that "one of the aims" of the organization was "to promote female education in that country [India]," and she welcomed any contributions for the "Indian Girls' Scholarship Fund or for the general objects of the National Indian Association."[95]

The NIA remained a major resource for Indian students in Britain until World War I. Its monthly journal *Indian Magazine and Review*, which Manning edited, provided an important forum for debates among Indians and Britons, in India and in Britain, regarding social reform in colonial India and women's education specifically.[96] The NIA soirees that Manning organized regularly brought together Indians and Britons both to spread knowledge and to help the Indian students socialize with locals and adjust to their new environment. For instance, as part of its concern with Indian students' acclimatization to life in Britain, the NIA was prepared to advise them on matters of clothing. Concurrently with dress-reform initiatives in India, the NIA strongly encouraged Indian students (mostly male in this period) to dress in European clothing, with the exception of special occasions, such as an audience with Queen Victoria, when "native costume" was preferred.[97]

When barely twenty years old, Ameer Ali became a member of the NIA's council.[98] Manning provided Ameer Ali his first public venue in which to articulate his views on Muslim women's rights and education in a lecture to the London NIA on "The Mahommedans of India." This lecture (and its later iterations and published versions) gave Ameer Ali an opportunity to respond to British, Brahmo, and Hindu charges regarding the backwardness of Indian Muslims, the oppression of Muslim women, and the alleged role played by Muslim rule in India in instituting the practice of seclusion among Hindu women. He insisted that "women among the Mohammedans possess exactly the same privileges and rights as the men" and dismissed long-standing English caricatures of Muslim women as being "no better than slaves" and at the mercy of a moody and irrational "master of the house."[99]

In a lecture in 1871, Ameer Ali felt particularly compelled to respond directly to a recent speech, also sponsored by the NIA, by the Brahmo reformer Sasipada Banerji, then in England at the invitation of his mentor, Mary Carpenter.[100] Banerji, widely recognized for having undertaken the earliest labor-welfare efforts anywhere in India and for his attention to female education, fell in line with other Brahmos of his era in attributing the practice of seclusion among Hindu women to oppressive Muslim influence.[101] In addition, in keeping with recent British histories of India, he credited the British with having saved the Hindus from Muslim oppression. As he put it in a speech that was covered in the *Birmingham Morning News* in August 1871: "Brighter days…came, when, under the Providence of God, the sceptre of the mighty Mohammedan Empire passed to the English people. This was nothing less than an indication that God wished the English people would help the Hindu nation to rise in the scale of nations."[102]

In his 1871 NIA lecture, as in many other lectures and articles, Ameer Ali objected to Muslims being given the "questionable honour of introducing what you call the Zenana system in India." He himself was in favor of modesty and privacy but distinguished between veiling and "utter seclusion."[103] In response to British ideas about the generally oppressed and unhappy Muslim woman, he compared the state of elite and nonelite women in India with their counterparts in England: "A Mahomedan wife among the lower classes is, from what I have seen and heard in England, decidedly not less happy than a married woman among the lower classes of the English. Among the upper classes, the ladies, though they do not possess the luxuries of Paris and London, certainly do not lead the life you mark out for them in your imagination. They rule despotically within their own homes."[104]

Twenty years later Ameer Ali published his response to Annie Reichardt's scurrilous attack on Islam. He objected to the idea that the Prophet of Islam "ever intended his recommendation should assume its present inelastic form or that he ever allowed or enjoined the seclusion of women." Such measures, after all, would have been "wholly opposed to the spirit of his reforms." He encouraged Reichardt and other readers to "recognise that the crimes or follies committed by Moslems may spring from other causes than religion" and that political and socioeconomic conditions may better explain the status of women in not only Muslim countries but also many Christian countries. Indeed, he argued, it was "culture and progress in material development and humanitarian science [that] called into existence that unwritten code of honour which is now in force among the really civilized communities of the West." Until these changes, he continued, "the lot of Christian women was by no means so enviable as Mrs. Reichardt would fain make us believe." For him the "backwardness [of Muslim women] is not due to the Koranic teachings, but to the general extinction among the Moslems of culture and progress under the avalanche of savagery which issued from the wilds of Tartary in the thirteenth century, overwhelming the whole of Asia with ruin and desolation." Having identified the Mongol invasions of the thirteenth century as responsible for Muslims' deviating from Quranic rules regarding women, he looked forward from the nineteenth century with great optimism: "If [Muslim women] do not in another hundred years attain to the social position of European women, there will be time enough to declaim against Islam as a system and dispensation."[105]

Ameer Ali identified four specific charges in Reichardt's article—"viz. the seclusion of women and the low status assigned to them; the plurality of wives and the facility of divorce"—all elements of the "old oft-repeated story which has formed the burden of ecclesiastical attacks on Islam for several centuries." In this article, as elsewhere, he responded to each charge by demonstrating precisely how it pertained to a misapplication of the original intent, or of the true spirit, of Islam. To take the example of polygamy, "which is always cast into the teeth of Islam by unthinking antagonists," he pointed to the prevalence of unchecked polygamy in all communities, including Jewish and Christian, at the time of the Prophet Muhammad. The Quran actually limited to four the number of wives a man may have at the same time, he explained, and furthermore stipulated that if he cannot treat them all with equity and justice—which the Quran recognizes as the most likely scenario—then he *shall* have one. "It is a calumny, therefore," he continued, "to say that the Islamic system has lowered the status of women." He added,

> The Teacher who, in an age when no country, no system, no community gave any right to woman, madden [maiden] or married, mother or wife—who, in a country where the birth of a daughter was considered a calamity, secured to the sex rights which are only unwillingly and under pressure being conceded to them by civilised nations in the nineteenth century—deserves the gratitude of humanity.[106]

While in England, Ameer Ali met Henry Channing, nephew of the renowned US theologian William Ellery Channing. A social reformer who had been engaged in antislavery and women's issues, Henry Channing took interest in young Ameer Ali's discussions about Islam and encouraged him to write a book to correct prevalent European misconceptions about Islam. And it was thus that Ameer Ali wrote *The Critical Examination of the Life and Teachings of Muhammad,* published in 1873, just as he was preparing to return to India. Ameer Ali later expanded this slim book into *Life and Teachings of Mohammed, or The Spirit of Islam* (1891). He intended it primarily "to assist the Moslems of India to achieve their intellectual and moral regeneration under the auspices of the great European power that now holds their destinies in its hands." He concluded chapter 13, devoted to the status of women, by repeating his observation that "taken as a whole, her status is not more unfavourable than that of many European women, while in many respects she occupies a decidedly better position." The disadvantages in Muslim women's lives he attributed to a "want of culture among the community generally, rather than of any special feature in the laws of the fathers."[107]

Upon his retirement in 1904 as judge of the Bengal High Court, Ameer Ali moved back to England with his English wife, Isabelle Ida Konstam. The important contacts he had built up over the years allowed him to lobby fairly effectively in Britain on behalf of Indian Muslims, for instance, for special representation in the form of separate electorates. The Bengal that Ameer Ali left in 1904 would the following year be partitioned by the colonial government under Lord Curzon, further strengthening distinct Hindu and Muslim identities, though of course not everyone lined up neatly along communal lines. At a meeting in Dacca in East Bengal in December 1906, elite Muslim Bengali men would establish the Muslim League, which, by the middle of the century, would lead the movement for Pakistan.

The new century also saw the beginning of the active engagement of Muslim Bengali women, including women's rights advocates, with print media. These women had to fight not only against restrictions imposed by their own community in the name of religion and tradition but also the notion of Muslim backwardness that had emerged by the late nineteenth century among British colonial authorities, British missionaries and feminists, the Hindu elites, and of course many male Muslim reformers. For example, following the First Missionary Conference on Behalf of the Mohammedan World held in Cairo in April 1906, women missionaries released a united statement regarding their duty to alleviate the plight of Muslim women: "There is no hope of effectually remedying the spiritual, moral, and physical ills which they suffer, except to take them the message of the Saviour, and that there is no chance of their hearing, unless we give ourselves to the work. *No one else will do it.* This lays a heavy responsibility on all Christian women." The collection of reports on Muslim women "from all parts of the Moslem world," including India, if not Bengal specifically, was published the following year under the telling title *Our Moslem Sisters, a Cry of Need from Lands of Darkness Interpreted by Those Who Heard It.* The book's final chapter asks, "What we must do?" about "our broken-hearted sisters, that they might be comforted," and concludes, "When this [Christian] Life becomes theirs, Our Moslem Sisters will be our own sisters in a new sense of the word, and we shall see the evangelization of the Mohammedan home and of all Moslem lands."[108] Subtler forms of such racialized condescension toward women of the East would be on display also in more secular contexts in the early twentieth century. Unlike the missionary meetings, however, women from Eastern countries would be present at the international women's conferences and deliver a fierce response.

FIVE

Writing Feminism, Writing Freedom

MUSLIM BENGALI WOMEN TOOK UP THEIR PENS with zeal at the turn of the twentieth century. They also engaged in activism, in the streets and from their homes, alongside women of other backgrounds. They did so in the context of major political upheavals in Bengal, India, and the world. Among these were the Partition of Bengal in 1905 (and its revocation in 1911) and the resulting boycott of foreign goods such as British cotton textiles in favor of swadeshi products (made in one's own country); the Khilafat movement to preserve the Ottoman sultan's authority as the caliph of Sunni Muslims around the world in the face of the European powers' dismemberment of the Ottoman Empire; and the anti-British nationalist movement that culminated in the formal division of British-colonized India into two new ostensibly Hindu- and Muslim-majority countries, India and Pakistan, in 1947.

EDUCATION, "THAT PRICELESS JEWEL"

This effervescence in published work by Bengali Muslim women grew out of the dramatic changes that had unfolded in the latter half of the nineteenth century in female education in Bengal and in the increased opportunities to publish their writing.[1] The earliest published prose by a Bengali Muslim woman was a short essay in a magazine launched by the Brahmo association Bamabodhini Sabha (Society for the Enlightenment of Women), established in 1863 to promote female education. The Sabha's strategies included a monthly magazine for women as well as the publication of instructive materials on topics deemed suitable for female readers in the zenana, or *antahpur*—on history, geography, science, and astronomy, as well as child care, housekeeping, and religion. The goal was to coax women out of their lives of seclusion and isolation through what amounted to a correspondence course. The magazine, *Bamabodhini Patrika* (Journal for the enlightenment of women), was launched in August 1863 and would continue until 1922. Its founding editor was the twenty-three-year-old Umesh Chandra Datta, a devoted follower of Brahmo reformer Keshab Chandra Sen.[2]

One of the first journals for women in Bengal, *Bamabodhini Patrika* sold out all one hundred copies of every monthly issue for several decades. Its second editorial announced that it intended, in time, to be a journal by women for women rather than have men speaking for women, as had long been the case in Bengal.[3] One of the first essays by a woman to appear in the magazine, a lengthy letter to the editor, published in early 1865, was written by a Muslim woman who identified herself as Bibi Taheran Lessa (more commonly written today as Taherannesa), a student in a girls' school in what is now Bangladesh. We know that she originally submitted the letter in late 1864 because there was an announcement in the October–November issue from the editor requesting six named women writers to provide proof that they had actually written the articles they had submitted for publication. The editor warned that the articles would not be published without such verification. Taherannesa must have provided adequate evidence, for her letter appeared shortly thereafter.[4]

Taherannesa's letter focused on women's need for education, "that priceless jewel." Education would teach women to shun "wrong practices," how to behave appropriately "towards their parents, husbands and elders," and how to take care of their own health as well as that of their children. To support her case Bibi Taherannesa cited classical Hindu texts and invoked celebrated women from the Hindu tradition, "ancient women of this land"—the mathematician Lilavati, the astronomer Khana, and the ascetic Shabari—as an indication of the shared culture of educated Muslims and Hindus in Bengal. She concluded by pleading with the "civilized men of this land…not [to] remain neglectful of educating women" and "to adorn your women with the ornament of education." Despite the power and eloquence of this letter, there is no evidence that Taherannesa ever published anything else.[5] Over the years women of all religious backgrounds and from all over undivided Bengal, from Dacca and Calcutta as well as smaller towns and villages, would submit essays to *Bamabodhini Patrika* and weigh in on the content and the challenges of *antahpur* education.[6]

In the late nineteenth century, despite the efforts of colonial authorities and elite Muslim men to establish educational institutions for Muslim girls, wealthy Muslims continued to rely on private tutors to teach their daughters at home. This not only allowed the girls to maintain purdah but also granted the family some control over the curriculum. Faizunnesa Chaudhurani's father, however, surprised his contemporaries by hiring male Indian tutors for his daughters rather than English governesses, as had become increasingly fashionable among the elites.[7]

Initially with the tutors, and later on her own, Faizunnesa studied Arabic, Sanskrit, Urdu, Bengali, Islamic history and law, and Hindu religious texts and epics. Her teachers included one Ustad Tazuddin, whom she would recall with much affection and admiration in the preface to her epic ballad *Rupjalal,* which is recognized today as the earliest surviving published literary work by a Bengali Muslim woman. After her father's early death from tuberculosis, her mother assumed the reins as *jomidar* (Bengali form of zamindar), clearly serving as a powerful role model to her daughters.[8]

In 1873 Faizunnesa worked with Brahmo social worker Kalicharan Dey to use her family wealth to set up a school specifically for Muslim girls. It was predated only by the Victoria School in Bhopal, established several years earlier by that princely state's female nawab, Sikandar Begam, and named after the British sovereign, to provide technical training—such as gold and silver lace making, silk embroidering, shawl weaving, and shoe making—and basic academic and Quranic instruction to girls from low-income communities. At Faizunnesa's school classes were taught in Bengali, the language of the general population, as opposed to Urdu or Persian, the languages preferred by the educated Muslim elite of Bengal and north India. The school also offered English, which Faizunnesa justified given the larger context of colonial rule, a revolutionary move at a time when many members of the Muslim elite still held reservations about the study of English. In 1893 Faizunnesa established a women's zenana hospital, staffed by British missionary doctors and nurses.[9]

While legend holds that Faizunnesa's great-grandfather Mozaffar Gazi had chosen to take his own life rather than work with or under the British, she recalled in the preface to *Rupjalal* that her father was "on friendly terms with many British governmental officials who used to spend time as royal guests in our estates."[10] Faizunnesa herself accepted the title of "Nawab" from Queen Victoria in 1889 in recognition of her important social projects in the area, after having rejected the British government's initial offer to make her a "Begum." She had responded that she was already recognized as "Begum" by her subjects and so should be given the same title the government would have bestowed on a male ruler for comparable accomplishments as a zamin-dar. After all, in the princely Kingdom of Bhopal in central India, a dynasty of powerful women had been ruling as nawabs or nawab begums since 1819.[11]

THE STORY OF *RUPJALAL*

Faizunnesa's great legacy to future generations, in addition to the school and hospital she established, was *Rupjalal.* The book was published in 1876, the same year that British prime minister Benjamin Disraeli proposed declar-ing Queen Victoria empress of India. The title became effective on the first day of 1877, which marked Victoria's golden jubilee on the throne.[12] Believed to be the first published book by a Bengali Muslim woman, *Rupjalal* was an enormously courageous and innovative text for that time. Faizunnesa wrote it in Bengali—when even her own brother, for example, wrote in Persian—and the more common *mishrabhasha* (mixed languages of Bengali and Persian or Arabic) used in traditional *punthis* (oral ballads of Bengal) and by many male Muslim poets and writers of the time. In addition, she experimented with form and language, combining fiction with autobiogra-phy and folklore, myth, and fantasy in the style of verses from the *punthis,* with prose text and social commentary. In creating the world of *Rupjalal,* she drew on the rich and varied cultural currents that coexisted in late nine-teenth-century Bengal: Hindu epics, the Quran, the Bible, local legends, and the *Arabian Nights,* which had been translated into Bengali around 1830. Although the main characters have recognizably Muslim names, her book is populated with saints, ogres, jinns, fairies, gods and goddesses, and Satan from the shared worldviews of local and rural Hindus and Muslims. Fatima, the Prophet Muhammad's daughter, appears alongside Radha-Krishna and Ram-Sita of the Hindu traditions.[13]

That *Rupjalal* was inspired by her own unhappy experiences with love and marriage, as she revealed in the book's preface, renders her candid account of sexuality and desire, including those of women, all the more transgressive. She recounted how Ghazi Chowdhury "fell in love [with her] instantly" and, when his first marriage proposal was declined, "left our estate with a broken heart." Discussing her "reasons for writing this book," she recalled spending the first few years of marriage "in utter happiness," during which her hus-band "loved me more than anything else in this world." Following the cow-ife's use of "black magic," however, her husband "who could not live away from me for a single moment, started hating me." It was this pain and sorrow that she wished to share with her readers through the story of Prince Jalal's deep love for Princess Rupbanu.[14] In the main text Faizunnesa describes, for example, how the "beautiful bride" Hurbanu, whom Jalal has been forced to marry despite his love for Rupbanu, "awaited all night to be passionately caressed / By her husband.... She burnt with desire, like the morning dew / That burns silently with the touch of the morning sun." Hurbanu's attendants approach Jalal to ask him, rather directly, "O Prince, why don't you have sex?"[15] By contrast, the popular conduct books and novels of the era, both heavily dominated by men, projected an ideal Indian Muslim woman whose sexual restraint would have been applauded by the British authors of conduct manuals for Victorian women.[16]

TOWARD LADYLAND

In 1905, the year of the Partition of Bengal, Rokeya Sakhawat Hossain published "Sultana's Dream," a parable about a utopian society called Ladyland, a land without religious conflict, war, bloodshed, crime, poverty, or even mosquito bites, where all the men live in seclusion in *mardanas* and women run society, using science and technology responsibly and ethically. Hossain's short story appeared in *Indian Ladies' Magazine,* published in Madras (today Chennai), the first English-language magazine for Indian women and one of the first to be edited by a woman.[17]

Roquiah Khatun, or Mrs. R. S. Hossein, as she signed her name in English (popularly known today as Rokeya Sakhawat Hossain, or Begum Rokeya), was born in 1880 into an educated and powerful jomidar family in the village of Pairaband in Rangpur, East Bengal, in what is now Bangladesh. Her father, like other learned men of the landed elite of his time, had studied Arabic, Persian, and Urdu. He had four wives—one of whom bore no children and one of whom was European—and a total of nine sons and six daughters. Begum Rokeya's mother, Rahatunnesa Sabera Chaudhurani, was his first wife.[18]

Rokeya's brothers were educated locally and then sent to college in Calcutta, three hundred miles away but connected to Rangpur by railway.[19] Abul Asad Ibrahim Saber, her older brother, attended Saint Xavier's College in Calcutta, where he encountered the ideas and activism of Syed Ahmed Khan and Syed Ameer Ali. In Rangpur he met and was influenced by the

FIGURE 10. Karimunnesa Khanam.
Courtesy of the Ghuznavi family.

Brahmo Krishna Dhan Ghose, who was part of the small group that had traveled to Britain in 1870 with Keshab Chandra Sen but had stayed and received a medical degree from the University of Aberdeen. Among Ghose's children was the philosopher and nationalist Sri Aurobindo. These important encounters and influences, it would seem, persuaded Ibrahim Saber to defy his father's wishes and teach English and Bengali to his two sisters in secret, by candlelight in the night.[20]

As a child, Begum Rokeya's much older sister, Karimunnesa Khanam, was taught only Arabic so that she would be able at least to fulfill her responsibilities as a Muslim and recite the Quran. But Karimunnesa resolved to teach herself Persian and Bengali by watching and listening to her younger brothers and practiced writing by drawing the lines of the Bengali alphabet in the dirt. Although her father was somewhat supportive when he first learned of her efforts, local religious leaders and neighbors soon pressured him to marry her off. When Karimunnesa was only fourteen, he arranged her marriage to the son of the jomidar Ghaznavi family. The year was 1869, the year that Syed Ameer Ali began his first sojourn in England and John Stuart Mill published *The Subjection of Women*. Karimunnesa was fortunate in that her husband, Abdul Hakim Khan Ghaznavi, and his family encouraged her to learn Bengali properly. Her later poetry suggests that it was a happy marriage, but tragically her husband died after nine years of married life, leaving Karimunnesa with two young sons. Determined to give the boys the best education possible, she moved to Calcutta so that they could attend school. When her older son was about fourteen, she sent him to England for further studies (and subsequently France and Italy), over the objections of many around her.[21] The novelist Mir Mosharraf Hossain, who served as her manager on the estate until 1894, set his novel *Gazi Miar Bostani* (1899) around a jomidar family in northeastern Bengal and included in it an educated aristocratic Muslim female character that was undoubtedly based on Karimunnesa.[22]

Karimunnesa continued her intellectual pursuits, studying Bengali, Arabic, Persian, and even some English after her husband's death while also shouldering her considerable jomidari and family responsibilities. As she later explained to Begum Rokeya in a letter, she decided at the age of sixty-seven to learn Arabic properly so that she could actually understand what she read in the Quran rather than merely recite it "like a parrot." She helped to finance the journal *Ahmadi,* first published in 1886, with the objective of fostering Hindu-Muslim amity.[23] Karimunnesa also wrote poetry and essays that she never undertook to publish herself. In 1923–24 Begum Rokeya published a few of Karimunnesa's poems anonymously in a journal.[24] Karimunnesa's son Abdul Halim Ghaznavi would be one of the leading Muslim supporters of the swadeshi nationalist movement in Bengal.[25]

According to her recollections in *Aborodhbashini* (Women in seclusion), a book she dedicated to her mother, Begum Rokeya was made to start observing purdah when she was only five years old. While it could not have been easy, we should keep in mind that at least for the women of elite families, seclusion did not mean being confined in a small dark space but rather a demarcation of distinct male and female spaces in a vast home and estate. Begum Rokeya would remember, "We rise to the cry of the morning birds; the call of the foxes signals that Maghreb (evening) prayer is near....Our childhood passed in bliss in the midst of shady forests in rural Bengal."[26]

Rokeya later described her education at home as learning the Arabic alphabet, followed by reading the Quran. Comprehension was not an objective, let alone a priority. The furthest a woman might get with Arabic, with her father's encouragement, was to become a *hafeza,* one who had memorized the entire Quran. As for Persian and Urdu, she remarked, it was difficult to make progress because there were no easy books for new learners. Finally, she complained bitterly, "even in Bengal, young girls are not taught Bengali in a systematic manner."[27]

Begum Rokeya's protégée and first biographer, Shamsunnahar Mahmud, later reported Rokeya's deep gratitude for her siblings' "love and care" in the matter of her education.[28] Although the educated Muslim Bengali elite of her time frowned on Bengali and preferred Urdu and Persian—because they felt Bengali was not sufficiently Islamic—the young Rokeya had the opportunity to master both Bengali and English with the help of a support- ive older brother, older sister, and husband. She dedicated the second vol- ume of *Motichur,* her collection of previously published essays, to her *apajaan* (beloved older sister) Karimunnesa, in appreciation for the "grace of your affection" and "blessings" that allowed her to learn Bengali despite the hos- tility around them and to learn it well enough that she didn't forget it during her "14 years in Bhagalpur, where I didn't find a single person with whom to speak in Bengali."[29] Similarly, for his role in her education, she dedicated her 1924 novella *Padmarag* (The ruby) to her older brother, Ibrahim Saber, who "moulded me single-handedly" and was "my only instructor."[30]

In 1896, when Rokeya was sixteen, Ibrahim arranged her marriage to Syed Sakhawat Hossain, a member of the Bengal Civil Service. Although raised speaking Urdu in Bhagalpur in Bihar, Sakhawat Hossain had learned a little Bengali while studying at Hooghly College in Bengal. He had also traveled to England on a government scholarship to study agriculture. A widower with a daughter, he was some twenty years older than Rokeya. Ibrahim had met him when he was stationed in Rangpur and must have concluded that he would be supportive of his sister's intellectual interests. Indeed, Sakhawat Hossain actively encouraged Rokeya's continued education, and she was able to over- come her homesickness by channeling her energies into writing. Rokeya gave birth to two daughters, but neither survived beyond a few months. These losses, combined with her husband's diabetes, failing eyesight, and finally his death thirteen years into the marriage, made for a relatively brief and unhappy married life. However, she remained grateful for Sakhawat's active support. He encouraged Rokeya to socialize with educated women of the Hindu and Christian communities in Bhagalpur, and this no doubt helped Rokeya gain a broader perspective on women, education, and religion.[31]

Sakhawat passed away in 1909, leaving Rokeya a large sum of money to be used specifically in support of women's education. She founded a girls' school in Bhagalpur that same year, but a family dispute soon forced her to move to Calcutta. There, in 1911, she started the Sakhawat Memorial Girls' School. Other Bengali Muslim women—invariably of well-connected wealthy fami- lies—had started schools in recent decades, but the only two to have survived

FIGURE II. Begum Rokeya Hossain.
Courtesy of Roushan Jahan.

to that point were the Nawab Faizunnesa Girls' School and the Suhrawardy Girls' School. The latter was founded in 1909 by Khujista Akhtar Begum, who had studied closely with her father, Obaidullah al-Obaidi Suhrawardy, the first superintendent of the Dacca Madrasa and a teacher of Syed Ameer Ali and others. Her son Hussain Shaheed Suhrawardy would serve as prime minister of Pakistan.[32]

Alongside her work with the school, Rokeya became involved in several women's organizations. In 1916 she founded the Bengal branch of Anjuman-e-Khawatin-e-Islam (All India Muslim Ladies' Conference), whose primary purpose was social work, including literacy training, among poor women. It was the first organization in Bengal founded specifically to bring together Muslim women, much to the consternation of the *samajpatis*—literally, lords of society, as she called the powerful conservative men who opposed her efforts. Over the years the Bengal branch would operate increasingly autonomously of the original Anjuman based in Aligarh. She was also involved in several organizations that brought together women of different religious communities, such as the Bangiya Nari Samaj (Bengali Women's Society) that campaigned for female franchise in Bengal, the Bengal Women's Education League, and the All India Women's Conference.[33]

Begum Rokeya wrote primarily in Bengali and started publishing in 1902, mainly essays on social issues. Her 1903 piece "Alonkar na badge of slavery" (Jewelry or badge of slavery), marked the start of Rokeya's explicitly feminist writing. It was published in the Calcutta journal *Mahila* (Woman), edited by Girish Chandra Sen, a Brahmo who, interestingly enough, had been the first to translate the Quran into Bengali. In "Alonkar" Rokeya warned women against allowing themselves to be belittled and bribed with trinkets and jewels, which were nothing but marks of "slavery on our bodies," much like the "iron shackles" of prisoners.[34]

A modified version of the essay appeared as "Amader Abonoti" (Our degradation) in September 1904 in *Nabanoor* (New heavenly light), edited by Syed Emdad Ali. One of the earliest periodicals to be published by Muslim intellectuals in Bengal, *Nabanoor* ran between 1903 and 1906 and actively invited women to participate and "assist us in our literary efforts and lead the nation to greater development."[35] Begum Rokeya heeded the call, along with many other women, Hindu and Muslim. Another version of this article, with the title "Strijatir Abonoti" (The degradation of women), was included in her first collection of essays, *Motichur* (A string of pearls), also published in 1904. In the course of the revisions and modifications, five powerful paragraphs were expunged because of the furor they had already provoked, no doubt because they were critical of religion: "Whenever a sister has tried to lift her head, her head has been pulverized with the excuse of religion or the force of utterances from holy texts.... It must be said that, ultimately 'religion' has strengthened the bonds of our enslavement; men are lording over women using the pretext of religion."[36]

These passages were removed because they outraged many readers. With her criticism of "religion" generally, she had offended not only her fellow Muslims but also members of the other communities among whom she lived in early twentieth-century India. Even though she was writing in a period of growing Muslim nationalist sentiment among some elite Muslim males that would culminate in the 1905 Partition of Bengal, Rokeya had no interest in claiming the superiority of women's rights under Islam in such matters as inheritance or the right to contract. For her all religions, including Islam, were inherently problematic for women. Even though she was writing in the early years of the Indian anticolonial nationalist movement, Rokeya did not subscribe to the Indian nationalist position that the Indian private sphere, and hence its denizens, women, were morally and spiritually superior to their Western counterparts.[37] Finally, writing at a time of imperial Britain's preoccupation with downtrodden Indian and Muslim women, she was not particularly impressed with the Western model of women's emancipation or the efforts of some Indian male reformers to usher in modernity simply by unveiling women. In "Strijatir Abonoti" she wondered whether the Parsi (Zoroastrian) women of India, who had been among the first to unveil and wear Western dress, were "truly free from mental slavery." Her response: "Certainly not! Their unveiling is not a result of their own decision. The Parsi men have dragged their women out of purdah in a blind imitation of the Europeans. It does not show any initiative of their women. They are as lifeless as they were before. When their men kept them in seclusion they stayed there. When the men dragged them out by their 'nose-rings' they came out. That cannot be called an achievement by women."[38]

In contrast to many of her male contemporaries across religious communities, Rokeya wanted to educate girls and women to develop their intellectual faculties and help them attain economic independence.[39] For example, the daughter of Brahmo reformer Keshab Chandra Sen would later describe the curriculum at the college her father had founded in Calcutta—and named after Queen Victoria—as focused on teaching girls only what would be useful in their roles as wives and mothers.[40] While Begum Rokeya acknowledged the reality that most women of her time would marry and become mothers, she, like feminists before her, deplored the vast gap between the education of men and that of women: "When the man measures the distance of the sun and the stars from the earth, the wife measures the size of a pillowcase (for sewing). When the husband, through his flights of imagination travels the solar sphere surrounded by the planetary system, measures the dimension of the sun...and detects the movements of the comets, the wife loiters in the kitchen, weighs the food items for cooking and observes the movements of her kitchen help."[41]

And, indeed, the curriculum at Begum Rokeya's school was quite broad. As someone familiar with the school explained in a letter, "Everything is taught at the school, from Quran recitation and its *tafsir* [exegesis] to English, Bengali, Urdu, Persian, Home Nursing, First Aid, Cooking, Sewing and whatever else are essential for Muslim girls to learn." Rokeya had decided that geography, history, and health science were also necessary. However, in her presidential address at the first Bangiya Nari Shikkha Samiti (Bengal

Women's Educational Conference) in February 1927, Rokeya lamented that the girls often performed badly in these subjects. She explained that this happened "because they do not get to see any other place in this world except for their school campus and the private quarters of their own homes, and remain unaware of the rest of the people of the world except for their own father and brothers." What they needed was a "good education."[42] For Rokeya and her contemporaries, education was far more than literacy: it was the very means to women's greater presence and participation in the larger society.[43]

Thinking pragmatically, however, she provided curtained transportation for her students because she knew that without it many girls would not be allowed to attend at all. Although she never came out of purdah herself—that is, she always covered her hair—she was fiercely critical of the practice of seclusion, whereby women had separate quarters in elite homes that they were not allowed to leave. As she noted in her presidential address, seclusion curtailed women's knowledge of the world. At the same time, as her comment about the Parsis shows, she recognized the superficiality of the liberation bestowed on women by male reformers who were eager to impress Western powers.

In Rokeya's eyes the ill-treatment of women was a worldwide problem that afflicted not only the women of India—Hindus, Muslims, Christians, Buddhists, and Parsis—but also the women of imperial Britain. In "Ardhangi" (The female half), first published in the monthly magazine *Mahila* (Woman) in 1903, she wrote of Christian women who, despite all the opportunities for education available to them, "cannot rid themselves of mental slavery" and remain "preoccupied with the thoughts of buying a new bonnet," oblivious to the "prosaic reality of the load of debt."[44] Her novella *Padmarag* (1924) is similarly populated with female characters of various religious backgrounds. This "gallery of oppressed wives" includes Helen Horace, a White British woman whose story was inspired by the newspaper reports of the real-life ordeals of Cecil Rutherford. Upon hearing about Helen's unhappy experiences, a Muslim character called Sakina laments, "This England—this noxious, putrid England—claims to be civilized!"[45]

Rokeya's partial translation to Bengali of the 1896 novel *Murder of Delicia*, by the best-selling and prolific Victorian author Marie Corelli, also represented an effort to prompt her readers to look anew at women's lives in both Britain and India. Rokeya chided Indians who subscribed to the notion of European civilizational superiority and assumed that women there are "free, exceptionally talented, equal to men, honoured in society and what not." She pointed out that Delicia's story revealed a very different situation, not unlike that in which Indian women found themselves: "Everything is hollow!...In London, the site of civilization and liberty, hundreds of Delicia murder stories are being staged. Alas! Women are defenseless everywhere in the world!" In both India and England, despite the veneer of egalitarianism in the latter, laws and institutions discriminated against women and left them vulnerable to the machinations of unscrupulous male relatives.[46] In both contexts, Rokeya demonstrated, the ideal woman was docile and subservient, and women tended to remain as such since the laws, to quote Corelli, were "made by men for themselves and their own convenience."[47] Ultimately, having identified common problems, she seemed to see Delicia as worse off in many ways than the Indian Muslim character Mazluma. For example, as a Muslim woman, Mazluma, unlike Delicia, had no obligation to contribute to her husband's or even her household's expenses. "Is this civilization? Is this chivalry?"[48]

Closer to home, Rokeya recognized the problematic treatment of women in the Hindu religious texts and often in practice but also noted the advances that the Hindu community had made recently in female education. In an English article published in the *Mussalman* on 6 December 1927, aptly titled "God Gives, Man Robs"—the title a bitter reversal of the old saying "Man proposes, God disposes"—she challenged Muslim men to do better for Muslim women. "It is an irony of fate," she wrote, "that the Hindus who are bound by their cartload of Shastras to treat the women like slaves and cattle and to get their daughters married before they were hardly above their girlhood, i.e., within ten years of age, are, as a matter of fact, allowing the greatest liberty to their womenfolk and giving them high education." She reminded her readers that Islamic scriptures already called for more rights for women than they currently enjoyed, that God "has made no distinction in the general life of male and female," and that the Prophet had stipulated that it was the duty of both men and women to acquire knowledge. Yet, she lamented in this and other articles, Muslim men continued to violate Muslim women's rights under Islam, such as the right to consent to a marriage and the right to inheritance. For her, however, the "worst crime which our brothers commit against us is to deprive us of education."[49]

In an effort to persuade the Indian Muslim opponents of female education that Muslim women enjoyed a God-given right to education, that its very idea was grounded in Islam, not copied from the West, Rokeya eagerly pointed out how other Muslim countries had advanced the cause of female education. Her 1927 presidential address to the Bengal Women's Educational Conference, mentioned earlier, identified Egypt and Turkey as countries that were once "opposed to women's education, but having lost and learnt from their mistakes, they have now returned to the right path," a reference no doubt to the right path of Islam. Moreover, "Turkey did not follow directly in America's footsteps; rather, it fulfilled one of the inviolable teachings of our religion, because the first person to ever mandate giving equal education to both men and women as a duty was our revered Prophet." Rokeya went on to criticize the hypocrisy of Muslims: "the same Muslims who are willing to lay down their lives in the Prophet's name (or even at an insult of a piece of brick [thrown] at a dilapidated mosque), why are they reluctant to follow an authentic guidance from the Prophet?" To appeal to Muslim men's sense of competition with the other communities—in education, employment, and political power—she quoted Shaikh Abdullah, who with his wife, Wahid Jahan Begum, had founded a girls' school in Aligarh in 1906 and was a close associate of Syed Ahmed Khan's: "How can a community that keeps half its population ignorant as well as imprisoned in the form of purdah compete in the affairs of life with those who have introduced equal opportunities for their women?" She called out Muslim men's willingness to donate generously to prestigious institutions of higher learning designated for men and yet claim poverty when she asked for money for female education: "The Muslim men think that they can enter heaven by relying on a few graduates from Aligarh University, Dacca University and the Islamia College in Calcutta, and will be able to carry their wives and sisters stuffed in a handbag while traversing the causeway." But since each Muslim was responsible to God for himself or herself, "instead of hoping to enter heaven riding on another's shoulder, women should focus on the education of their daughters."[50]

Begum Rokeya's vision for the future extended far beyond her immediate community of Bengali Muslims to encompass Indian women generally and toward an India in which the various communities could progress together while retaining their differences. As she put it in her essay "Sugrihini" (The good housewife), "We are not only Hindu or Muslim or Parsi or Christian nor are we only Bengali, Madrasi, Marawari or Punjabi—we are Indians. We are first and foremost Indian, and then Muslim, Sikh, or something else."[51] Even "Sultana's Dream" opens with the narrator "thinking lazily of the condition of Indian womanhood," while her essay "Ardhangi" concludes with a rousing call to education for all women in India, since "unless the Indian women awake, India cannot arise." She clarified, "I want the best for my sisters, and do not intend to encroach upon the social and religious ties.... To progress mentally, a Hindu doesn't have to renounce her Hindu identity or a Christian her Christian identity. We can liberate the mind while retaining our respective ethnic differences." The problem, she believed, was "our lack of education," which, as she wrote in the original "Strijatir Abonoti," denies women the "qualifications to be sages and saints" themselves and to blindly accept "these religious texts [that] are nothing but rules and regulations created by men."[52]

Despite her dependence on the colonial government for its formal recognition of her school and for funding, Rokeya did not hesitate to speak out against British colonial rule, though often in subtle ways and typically in conjunction with her main passion, women's rights and especially women's education. Her story "Gyanphal" (The fruit of knowledge), for example, is the allegorical story of an island, Kanak, which receives visitors who are "beautiful looking, but except for their physical beauty...didn't have much to boast about." The trade arrangements established by these visitors led to famine. The story concludes not only with the liberation of the Kanak people from the exploitative outsiders but with an admonition that the society will not prosper unless women are granted full access to the fruit of the knowledge tree.[53]

Similarly, "Nurse Nelly," based on a true story, is the story of a cleaner in a women's hospital in the North Indian city of Lucknow. Once a homemaker in a middle-class Bengali Muslim home, Nayeema had been converted to Christianity by nuns, renamed Nelly, and brought to Lucknow. In recounting Nayeema's suspenseful if melodramatic metamorphosis, the narrator bemoans the dangers posed both by missionaries and by the low levels of education among women. While sightseeing in Agra, the narrator supports her point about the need for education for men and women alike by comparing Mumtaz Mahal, "the woman who lies buried in that far-famed mausoleum [the Taj Mahal]" built for her by her husband, Mughal emperor Shah Jahan, with the earlier Empress Nur Jahan, whose "humble, ordinary tomb lies neglected...in a little-known place in Lahore." It was education, not a grand tomb, that "has made [Nur Jahan]...immortal.... It is the grace of education that has made her a radiant and renowned figure. God forbid, the Taj Mahal can be destroyed by an earthquake or by war, but Nur Jahan's glory will last forever."[54]

Toward the end of her life, with the Indian nationalist movement in full sway, Rokeya alienated many Indians with her refusal to condemn the US writer Katherine Mayo's book *Mother India*. Mayo, whose trip to India had been set up in collusion with British colonial authorities, argued in her 1927 book that Indian practices such as child marriage essentially rendered the country unfit for self-rule or independence. Bengal, as the "seat of bitterest political unrest," received special attention as "among the most sexually exaggerated regions of India." The book provoked a flurry of furious and critical reviews, including one from Gandhi himself, titled "Drain Inspector's Report." British colonial officials, for their part, encouraged its circulation among Muslim readers in the hope that a book focused on ostensibly Hindu social evils would help to create a rift between Hindus and Muslims in the nationalist movement.[55] In her essay "Rani Bhikarini" (The beggar queen), Rokeya upbraided the Muslim men who seemed to think that the problems Mayo described pertained only to the Hindu community: "Take a look at yourselves in the mirror. Look how you too have dressed the queens of your society in the garb of beggars. Let alone granting women their rights, there is no country, no race, no religion in this wide world which has acknowledged women's sense of self." Not only did Rokeya refuse to allow nationalist concerns to force the question of women's rights to the background, but she also dismissed the idea that the status of women was an indicator of a country's ability to govern itself, given women's lowly status everywhere.[56] For Rokeya, then, women's emancipation and anticolonial and anticommunal struggles were deeply intertwined and indeed analogous. As she put it with some bitterness in her 1927 Bengal Women's Educational Conference address: "As the altruistic British government cannot suffer the aspirations of the Indians… and our non-Muslim neighbours often cannot put up with the rights and claims of the Muslims, so the Muslim men cannot grant any wish to their women to prosper." Given "how intimately connected to with one another" we are, she continued, "as long as the Muslim men pay no heed to the aspirations of their women, the two hundred and twenty million other Indians will…ignore the eighty million Muslims in the country [and] the British government also will not yield to their demands."[57]

THE SUNDERING OF BENGAL
AND NATIONALIST POLITICS

While Begum Rokeya's contemporaries similarly underlined the need to improve Muslim Bengali women's access to education, many also wrote forcefully about British colonial domination and growing nationalism among Indians. In July 1905 Lord Curzon, then viceroy of India, partitioned Bengal, the largest province in India, into predominantly Muslim and Hindu halves. Although he presented it as both a concession to Muslims still pining for the power and glory of the Mughal era and a decision motivated by British concern for administrative efficiency, there was little doubt that his administration had come to fear the anticolonial nationalism brewing in Bengal and that this partition was ultimately a political decision. As his home secretary Herbert H. Risley had put it in December 1904, "Bengal united is a power; Bengal divided would pull in different ways... one of our main objects is to split up and thereby weaken a solid body of opponents to our rule."[58] The move was supported by men of the Muslim elite in Bengal, such as Nawab Salimullah of Dacca. But large numbers of educated Hindu and Muslim Bengalis rose in opposition to it. Emboldened by recent international political events such as the Anglo-Boer Wars, the Japanese defeat of the Russians, and the Chinese boycott of US products, women and men in eastern and western Bengal cited a shared language and culture as they lent their support and energy to the swadeshi movement. Dramatic bonfires were held to burn imported cloth, resulting in a 25 percent decrease in cotton goods imported.[59] Although this partition was revoked in 1911, Bengal would once again be divided in 1947, when the entire subcontinent would be partitioned into India and East and West Pakistan.

Bengali Muslim women's grievances mounted during and after the 1905–11 partition, especially as Muslim elite men in Muslim-majority eastern Bengal began to benefit from new opportunities. These included Dacca University, established in 1921, and new jobs for educated Muslim men in the colonial government. In the many magazines that flourished in Bengal in the early twentieth century, Muslim women published articles articulating their demands for greater access to education for women of different classes and their frustration at Muslim men's disregard for women's urgent need for education. Many advocated for more education and opportunities for women using an argument similar to that used by what has been called the "first wave" of feminists active in other parts of the world. As we saw in Begum Rokeya's "Sultana's Dream," they argued, for instance, that women are less likely than men to engage in war and aggression and are more attuned to nature and the environment and thus could help shape a very different future.

The concerns and priorities of colonized women differed, however, from those of feminists of colonizer nations such as Britain. In 1938 even the generally anti-imperialist and feminist (though she abjured the latter term) English writer Virginia Woolf could write, "As a woman I have no country. As a woman I want no country. As a woman my country is the whole world."[60] This declaration might easily be read as ignoring the multiple constraints within which women in colonized countries such as India had to advance their cause and that the fight to rein in, and later overthrow, colonial rule was of great significance and integrally tied to the fight for women's rights. Muslim Indian women faced the additional quandary of how to best engage with an anticolonial movement that often relied on heavily Hindu, and even overtly anti-Muslim, symbols, such as the hymn and chant "Bande Mataram" (I bow to thee, Motherland), to mobilize Hindus across castes and classes.[61] There was, of course, no united voice even among Bengali Muslim women writers, and many positions evolved over the first half of the twentieth century. We can see, however, that there was some agreement in those first decades that true emancipation would come not from education or women's rights alone but when combined with freedom for their nation.

Among those active in the first decades of the twentieth century was Khairunnesa Khatun, the principal of Sirajganj Hosainpur Girls' High School. A fierce advocate of female education, she also wrote in favor of the nationalist swadeshi movement and enjoyed her husband's support in both her writing and her work at the school. As the Partition of Bengal unfolded in 1905, Khairunnesa Khatun walked from village to village and even participated in the antipartition rallies organized by the Indian National Congress, undeterred by rules of seclusion. That same year she published an article, "For the Love of the Motherland," in the Bengali magazine *Nabanoor*, in which she urged Bengali women of all religious backgrounds to support the swadeshi movement even from the privacy of their own homes. She blamed the sorry state of the country on the partition and reminded women of their "equal right to participate in these matters" and their "responsibility to try to do as much as we can": "Sisters! Come, let us pledge to give up saris made from foreign cloth; scorn British bodices, chemises, and socks; start using rose water and attar [a fragrant oil traditionally made of natural essences] instead of lavender, and free ourselves from wearing shoes meant for foreign ladies that make us stumble. Only then will we be able to benefit our country."[62]

To turn away at this time of need, she continued, would be offensive to God Almighty. By buying only Indian products, she noted, Indian women would also be supporting "India's dormant industries." She went on to describe how many British goods were actually bad for one's health, specifically mentioning enameled utensils, imported tinned milk and sugar, and, quite presciently, cigars and cigarettes. "Seeing that we are such simpletons, the merchants of America, England, Scotland, Germany, Australia, Switzerland and Japan are constantly trading paltry articles for the crops we produce with hard labour, taking them home, even as we go begging from door to door for a fistful of rice! Unless we liberate ourselves from the dishonest clutches of these merchants, we will continue to remain in this abyss of despair!"[63]

Masuda Rahman, who was active in the short period between the end of World War I and her death at only forty-one in 1926, also wrote passionately about the freedom of both the country and women. She was married off at a very young age (sources suggest between eight and eleven) to a jomidar but was inspired by reading the works of Begum Rokeya and by her own friendship with the emerging poet Kazi Nazrul Islam, who had recently returned from Karachi, where he was stationed as a member of the British army's Forty-Ninth Bengalees Battalion. Nazrul Islam, who would go on to become the renowned "rebel poet of Bengal," published many of her articles in his short-lived biweekly magazine, *Dhumketu* (Comet). She facilitated his marriage in 1924 to Pramila Sengupta, a young Hindu woman and Indian nationalist he had met in Comilla, and paid for the wedding expenses herself. After Rahman's untimely death from smallpox in December 1926, Nazrul Islam wrote in the periodical *Saogat* about not only their personal relationship but also her great literary talent. In keeping with the principles of the swadeshi movement, Rahman wore *khadi* (homespun cloth) and even requested that her shroud be made of it.[64]

Rahman regretted that she wasn't taught the Quran properly and mocked men who bragged that their daughters had read the entire Quran, when these girls "might not be able to make sense of a single word in the book." In articles such as "The Great Fire" ("Bijoli," 1922), Rahman openly criticized the corruption of religious men, declaring that "they live with untruths" and were "blinded by self-interest." She recommended that society "pack the conservative old men off to the forests with their rosaries, snatch the religious texts from the hands of the hypocrites and lawyers, drive the offenders away from the sacred podium of this temple we call society." Her criticisms were not directed at religion as such but against those who had assumed sole responsibility for guiding their respective communities, those who "have the so-called sacred thread around [their] neck" (a reference to Hindu Brahmins) as well as those who "have a few strands of hair like a goat on [their] chin" (a reference to bearded Muslim leaders). Like other Muslim Bengali women writers of that era, Rahman invoked female figures worthy of emulation from both Hindu and Muslim religious texts to strengthen her arguments—both Draupadi and Zainab; Shiva's wife, Uma; and the Prophet's daughter Fatima. Rahman also called on women to delay marriage and strive for financial independence. In "Our True Nature" she demanded of her women readers: "What did your husbands give you? Are you their life partners and house-keepers, their friends and the mothers of their children, or are you like house-hold pets, ready to endure insults and abuse, the kicks and the stick, for the sake of a piece of leftover fish and milk?"[65]

Rahman's feminism was intertwined with her anticolonial nationalism. In a 1922 article titled "Amader Dabi" (Our demands), she reminded women that colonized Indian men, from whom women demand rights, "do not have any rights themselves.... [They] have entrammelled themselves in the serpentine coils of slavery" and were in no "position to give us our rights" or "help us achieve emancipation." She wrote elsewhere of her dream of the "flag of liberation, high above, kissing the skies."[66] True freedom for women, to her mind, required India's freedom.

Another prolific writer of this era was Razia Khatun Chaudhurani. Only twenty-seven when she died in 1934, she left behind an impressive corpus of literary work, prose and poetry, and essays on topics such as women's education, motherhood, purdah, and sexuality. Like Begum Rokeya, she didn't attend school but benefited from the care and attention of many around her. From her teachers, among them the imam of the local mosque and her maternal grandfather and uncle, she learned Arabic, Bengali, English, and Persian. Like many elite Muslim women of her time, she wore a burqa, but hers, interestingly—though probably not uniquely—was designed to mimic the attire of the deceased British sovereign. Her sister Safura Hussain would later describe her burqa as "styled after Queen Victoria's official dress. It had a black petticoat trimmed with lace, a coat with sleeves also black, and a white lace veil."[67]

Given both her father's and her husband's active participation in local, regional, and national politics, Chaudhurani observed major political developments from a prime vantage point. Her father, Abdur Rashid Khan, was a close associate of the Bengali nationalist leader Chittaranjan Das and was among the Noakhali-based leaders of the Swaraj (Self-Rule) Party

FIGURE 11. Razia Khatun Chaudhurani, a 1933 painting commissioned in Calcutta. Courtesy of the Chaudhury family.

and Noncooperation movement. In 1925 she married Ashrafuddin Ahmed Chaudhury, the scion of a jomidar family in Comilla, then part of Tipperah District in eastern Bengal. Chaudhury had studied law at Calcutta University but, following his return to Comilla in 1919, became active in the anticolonial nationalist movement. He organized local peasants in the Tipperah Krishak Samiti and participated in the Khilafat and Noncooperation movements that helped to create pan-Indian elite Muslim support for the nationalist movement. He was also in a faction of the Bengal chapter of the Indian National Congress headed by legendary anticolonial nationalist leader "Netaji" Subhas Chandra Bose. Chaudhury's commitment to anticolonialism meant that he spent their brief married life of nine years in and out of British colonial jails, while Chaudhurani lived in Comilla with her in-laws and wrote to him regularly. She bore five children but lost her older son when he was very young. She died just months after the birth of her youngest, a daughter she affectionately called Julie because she was born in July.[68]

Chaudhurani's writings reveal a grounded sense of both her cultural and religious identities. Like Begum Rokeya, Chaudhurani refuted the notion that British women offered the best model of freedom for Indian women, but she also defended Islam more forcefully than many of her contemporaries from charges that its teachings were to blame for Muslim women's current plight, as in this 1929 essay in *Saogat*:

> The first thing we note in their religious text, The Bible, is that women are described as "the root of all evil."...According to the Bible's Old Testament, a woman's not bearing any children is a grievous sin. If a woman finds no place in her husband's home or has not the capacity to earn an independent income, then a woman in England becomes totally helpless; the law does not grant her the right to expect even one basic meal in her father's home. Right to his property is a far cry. This is how an educated and civilized society treats its women....Justice and honour for women [are] ordained by Islam alone.[69]

Chaudhurani's refusal to see Britain as the epitome of progress and a model to emulate is clear in her discussion of the double standard inherent in the concept of *satitva* (chastity). "It is applied at random to women," she wrote, "but there is no equivalent word for men in Bengali, nor even in the 'civilized language' English."[70]

The Khilafat movement that sought to provide financial and moral support to the waning caliphate after the end of World War I and that took up so much of Chaudhurani's father's and husband's time and energy also mobilized women around the country, although only a few women had public roles, most notably Bi Amman, the mother of the North Indian leaders Mohammad Ali Jouhar and Shaukat Ali.[71] Among the women swept up in the politics of the movement and in Mustafa Kemal Ataturk's subsequent efforts to modernize Turkey through its women were the grandmother and mother of Hameeda Hossain, who would emerge as a leading feminist and human rights activist in Bangladesh in the final decades of the twentieth century. Born in Sindh, on the far western corner of the Indian subcontinent, Hossain's grandmother Ghulam Fatima Shaikh traveled with her physician husband and two young children to Ottoman lands in support of the caliphate and lived in Madina in the Hijaz (in what is today Saudi Arabia) and Adana (in what is now Turkey).

Hossain grew up hearing her mother, Mariam Shaikh, tell the story of how, while she was a schoolgirl in the new Turkey, the authorities took it on themselves to cut off her hair so that she would appear modern when Ataturk came to visit the school—much to Ghulam Fatima's chagrin.[72]

A NEW GENERATION

The life and accomplishments of Shamsunnahar Mahmud, Begum Rokeya's protégée and first biographer, extended past the British colonial period. She emerged as a great force for Bengali women's education in East Pakistan following the 1947 partition, though her path was not an easy one. Efforts on behalf of zenana education by both her grandfathers, as part of the Dacca Mussulman Suhrid Sammelani (Dacca Muslim Friends Society), had made it possible for her grandmother, mother, and aunts to study at home for several years and take exams to confirm promotion to higher grades. Shamsunnahar was the first girl in the family to attend a school. She and her older brother, Habibullah Bahar, were very young when their father died and their mother moved in with her parents in the southeastern port city of Chittagong. Shamsunnahar was enrolled in Khastagir School but had to withdraw when she turned nine because her grandfather, despite his activism on behalf of girls' education and his position as divisional school inspector of Chittagong, was unwilling to have his female relatives violate purdah for the sake of school education. She later remembered with anguish how, while she "sat at home," she watched her "classmates—Hindu, Brahmo and Christian girls— move around freely, get promoted from one class to the next" and go on to attend colleges in Calcutta. "I felt that we are creatures of the dark while they were citizens of a lighted world. The rebel in me groaned inside, for days together." Her grandfather finally relented and hired an elderly tutor for her. While teacher and pupil sat at the same table, a heavy curtain separated them in keeping with the practice of purdah, which literally means curtain. Shamsunnahar persevered and eventually passed the national matriculation examination with flying colors.[73]

In late July 1926 the eighteen-year-old Shamsunnahar found herself in the presence of the poet Kazi Nazrul Islam when he stayed in her grandfather's home in Chittagong for a few days shortly after her grandfather's death. Although she wasn't permitted to meet him directly, she was able to hear him recite and sing from the inner quarters to which she was confined. Keenly aware of the unjust rules that had prevented them from meeting properly, the poet sent Shamsunnahar an inspiring and memorable letter after he returned to Calcutta. Bemoaning the strict seclusion of women, he urged "women to rebel." He composed the poems that constitute the collection *Sindhu Hillol* during this visit, and he dedicated it to the brother and sister, Bahar and Nahar.[74]

In 1927 Shamsunnahar's mother arranged her marriage to a physician, Wahiduddin Mahmud. With his support she continued her formal studies at the Diocesan College in Calcutta, attending classes in her burqa, much to the amusement of her more urbane schoolmates. She earned a bachelor's degree in 1932 and a master's in 1942. Begum Rokeya organized a reception at the Shakhawat Memorial Girls' High School to celebrate Shamsunnahar's new bachelor's degree. In 1939 Shamsunnahar joined the new Lady Brabourne College as head of the Bengali Department. The government of Bengal, under the leadership of Bengal chief minister Abul Kasem Fazlul Huq, had established the college that July, specifically to meet the needs of female Muslim students who had long complained of being unwelcome, as Muslims, at the much older Bethune College as well as at other women's colleges in Calcutta. While women of all communities could attend the new college, Arabic, Persian, and Urdu were part of the curriculum from the beginning, and the hostel was set aside for Muslim students.[75]

Shamsunnahar became active in a variety of social and political causes and literary pursuits even as a student. She joined Begum Rokeya's Anjuman-e-Khawatin-e-Islam soon after her arrival in Calcutta and, over time, became progressively more involved with the All India Women's Conference. In addition, she joined her elder brother as coeditor of a magazine called *Bulbul* (Nightingale) that was published from 1933 to 1938.[76] Following his marriage in 1938, she developed a close friendship with her sister-in-law, Anwara Bahar Choudhury, a noted educationist and social activist. Anwara Bahar's aunt, who raised her, had taught at Begum Rokeya's Sakhawat Memorial Girls' School in Calcutta and enrolled her there as the first student in the Bengali section. After studying at Bethune and Scottish Church Colleges, Anwara Bahar taught Bengali briefly at Lady Brabourne College and served as a teacher and eventually principal of Sakhawat Memorial Girls' School. She was also secretary of Anjuman-e-Khawatin-e-Islam. After partition the family moved to East Pakistan, and Anwara Bahar remained involved in education, serving as principal of several highly ranked Bengali-language girls' schools in Dacca and Mymensingh, even while her husband, Habibullah

Bahar, served in the cabinet as health minister. Deeply committed to advancing Bengali music and dance, she established a music and dance section in one of her schools and cofounded the Bulbul Academy of Fine Arts, named after famous dancer Bulbul Chowdhury.[77]

The best-known woman activist of this generation was undoubtedly Begum Sufia Kamal, whose life would span the late colonial era, partition, the East Pakistan period, and almost three decades of independent Bangladesh. Her father left home when she was only seven months old, compelling her mother, Sabera Khatun, to return with her two children to her parents' estate in the Barisal region of eastern Bengal. Like other jomidar families of that time, her relatives spoke Urdu, and zenana education included Arabic and Persian, but Sabera Khatun took it on herself to teach her children Bengali. Young Sufia's uncle had a vast library with books from around the world, but, given his strong opposition to female education, young Sufia had to sneak into the library to read. For a short while the adults let her dress as a boy, with a hat, a long coat, and pants so that she could accompany her male cousins to the local village school; that ended once the boys moved to town for further study. On a visit to Calcutta when she was seven, she met Begum Rokeya at her aunt's house. The older woman recognized the young girl's potential and tried to recruit her into her new school, but it was in vain since Begum Sufia and her mother had to return to Barisal.

Sufia was only twelve when she married her cousin Syed Nehal Hossain in 1923. The young couple moved from the family estate to the town of Barisal, where she was pulled into the Noncooperation movement. In 1925 she met Gandhi himself and, dressed like the Hindu women around her, down to the vermilion on her forehead, offered him some of her homespun cotton; because she always wore a burqa outside the home, nobody recognized her. Her husband submitted some of her writing to a magazine, and a short story and poem by "Mrs. S. N. Hossain" appeared in print shortly. The couple then moved to Calcutta for Nehal Hossain's studies, and there Sufia Hossain encountered the writers Kazi Nazrul Islam and Rabindranath Tagore, *Saogat* editor Mohammad Nasiruddin, the nationalist leader Subhas Chandra Bose, Shamsunnahar Mahmud, and, of course, Begum Rokeya. Like Shamsunnahar Mahmud, Begum Sufia became involved in Begum Rokeya's Anjuman-e-Khawatin-e-Islam and its various welfare and reform activities. After her husband's premature death from tuberculosis in 1932, she found a job as a teacher to provide for herself and her young daughter. Following her second marriage in 1939, to Kamaluddin Khan of Chittagong, she changed her name to Sufia Kamal, the name by which this leading writer and feminist activist came to be known to later generations.[78]

THE QUEST FOR POLITICAL EQUALITY

The interwar period saw women organize most coherently around the causes of anticolonial nationalism and women's suffrage. The best-known, and perhaps most-revered, women activists of this era were undoubtedly the young women student revolutionaries such as Kalpana Dutt, Dipti Medha, Shanti Ghosh, Suniti Chaudhury, and Pritilata Waddedar, who carried out attacks on British officials in eastern Bengal.[79] Others threw their energies into the campaign for women's suffrage.

The resolution for (limited) female suffrage passed in the Bengal Legislative Council in 1925, after having been defeated in 1921. Both times Muslim men on the Bengal Council constituted the main opposition. Some put forth the argument that conservative men (and women) have made all around the world—that women's greater engagement with the public world of politics would detract from their domestic responsibilities. For others, however, the bigger concern was the system of communal electorates established by the recent British colonial reforms that set aside seats for Muslims and other groups: they feared that with purdah more prevalent among elite Muslims, eligible Muslim women would not exercise the right to vote to the same degree as Brahmo and Hindu women and thereby lead to a lowering of the Muslim quota.[80] Their fears about women's low voter participation proved true in the first elections, leading Begum Rokeya to fume during her 1927 Bengal Women's Educational Conference address that "women have now been given the right to vote, but Muslim women relinquish that right voluntarily. In the last election, only four women had cast their votes in Calcutta. Is that a matter of pride for the Muslims?"[81]

The issue of separate electorates also posed a problem for national women's organizations. Muslim women's participation in organizations such as the All India Women's Conference (AIWC) served to erase differences of religious community (and class and caste) between Indian women, but the reality of Hindu dominance meant that Muslim concerns were regularly sidelined. Nonetheless, activists such as Shareefah Hamid Ali joined other leading members of the AIWC in rejecting the colonial authorities' proposal for women's suffrage along sectarian or communal lines, arguing that it would be "degrading" to be elected "as a 'Muslim' only" rather than as an "Indian." Jahan Ara Shah Nawaz, however, decided to participate in discussions with the colonial government and ultimately to work in favor of Muslim representation specifically, helping to establish the women's wing of the Muslim League in 1935.[82]

The comparatively rapid progress of the Indian campaign prompted frustration in Britain between 1918, when British women received partial suffrage, and 1928, when the earlier qualifications were removed. British suffragettes, after all, had been using the image of the meek and oppressed Indian woman to make the case for political empowerment, arguing that their greater participation in their imperial politics would put them in a better position to save their hapless Indian sisters.[83] An editorial in the *Times* of London in August 1926 remarked on the irony of the situation whereby a "country whose women still keep *purdah* or are confined to the harem should give them a greater share of political freedom than is employed by their European sisters."[84]

A few months after the Government of India Act of August 1935 expanded women's suffrage (albeit with qualifications), Shamsunnahar Mahmud published an article in *Saogat* in which she compared the different experiences of Indian and English women activists in attaining suffrage: "I thank our providence when I think about the women of England. Their free way of life is perhaps something that many women desire. But we are astonished when we hear that they had to strive so hard even to gain those rights that we have got so easily." She described how British women had had to struggle tirelessly for a half century and overcome a variety of obstacles before obtaining clear and unconditional rights as recently as 1928. One important lesson was that "nobody simply handed [British] women their rights." Rather, she continued, the activists persevered despite many setbacks and never gave up: although Indian women had received the right to vote and stand for election relatively quickly and easily, there still remained too many qualifications, of educational attainment and property ownership, that excluded the vast majority of women and therefore needed to be challenged.[85]

A CHERISHED GIFT TO WRITERS AND READERS

The newspaper *Saogat* (The cherished gift), as we saw previously, emerged as a valuable forum for Muslim Bengali women writers and as a chronicle of their interests in the early twentieth century. The Bengali journalist Mohammad Nasiruddin launched *Saogat* in 1918, as World War I was coming to an end in Europe, because he wanted to privilege Bengali over Urdu and also, as he put it, to fight superstition and outdated thinking. To encourage women to become actively involved in writing and journalism, he established a page dedicated to women, "Zenana Mahfil" (Women's forum). This Urdu title was later replaced with the Bengali title "Mohila Jagot" (Women's world).[86] The women's page regularly featured illustrated local and international news that would be of interest—and no doubt instructive—to women. A 1927 issue included a photo of the wedding of the Brahmo Aruna Ganguly and Muslim Asaf Ali, with a comment that interreligious marriages such as this would do much to bridge the communal divide in the country. One 1929 issue shared news of a new Muslim girls' school in Dinajpur in northern Bengal and an announcement about the successful campaign for female suffrage in Japan. Debates regarding the content of women's curriculum regularly animated its pages. In a 1927 article a writer named A. F. M. Abdul Hakim expressed his concern that Western education and higher education would distract Muslim women from their domestic responsibilities. Nasiruddin responded directly, writing, "The aim of higher education is to expand one's mind," and it would "be unethical to restrict women on grounds of their child-rearing and home-making duties."[87] Special monthly issues in which all the writers were women (Muslim and non-Muslim) were published in the 1930s. A special issue from 1935, for example, included both poetry and prose by Sufia N. Hossain; translated excerpts from *The Cause,* the British feminist Ray Strachey's 1928 history of the women's movement in Britain; extended profiles of the Turkish writer and women's rights activist Halidé Edib (who had visited India that year) and French-Polish two-time Nobel Laureate scientist Marie Curie; articles on women in Egypt, Japan, Russia, and Turkey; photos of international female athletes and notable Indian women of different regions and religious backgrounds who had risen to new professional or educational heights or traveled overseas; sections on style and fashion as well as health and well-being; and a photo gallery of the women writers who had contributed to that particular issue.[88]

In 1945 *Saogat* started another special section, "Muslim Jahan" (Muslim world), which provided news of other Muslim countries, especially visual evidence of changes in the lives of women in Turkey, Egypt, Iran, Morocco, and Albania.[89] This contributed to a broader understanding of Muslim lives, of the different ways Muslims understood their relationship to their faith, and, indeed, of the different ways of being Muslim.

A "PANORAMIC VIEW" OF MUSLIM WOMEN

Through this period Indian Muslim women activists continued to learn about and interact with the world through the many foreign women who visited India, from the notorious Katherine Mayo to the much-admired Halidé Edib. When Ruth Woodsmall arrived, the country was still reeling from the visit of her fellow American. In letters Woodsmall wrote of her resentment that "Miss Mayo has set the clock back in friendly relations and has created a defense attitude of Indians against Americans," complicating her own efforts "to gain a fair idea of what women were doing and thinking." Woodsmall's approach was certainly more academic and lacked Mayo's overt hostility to Indian nationalism. Indeed, she recognized that the "growth in political activity of Indian women has come as the inevitable result of their awakened social consciousness and passion for national progress." Not surprisingly, she failed to please a US editor eager for a piece on Muslim women's "concentrated life of religion and sex," a comment that is not unfamiliar to writers even today.[90]

Woodsmall had first visited India in 1916 as part of a tour of India and East Asia following several years of teaching. Almost two decades later she returned with a Rockefeller fellowship that took her to several Arab countries, Turkey, and Iran. Her objective this time was to study and offer a "panoramic view" of the rapidly unfolding changes in Muslim women's lives. An educated, professional single woman from Atlanta, Georgia, who traveled widely and had worked with women around the world, Woodsmall in many ways evoked the missionary women of the previous century. Her nine years of working with the YWCA in Syria and Turkey had instilled in her an acute awareness of the diversity of Muslim lives across classes and regions and the impact on these lives of larger social, political, and economic changes. Put differently, she seemed to understand that Muslims' understanding of Islam varied and changed over time, and, in any case, Islam alone did not determine Muslims' decisions, opportunities, and lives. She was aware too that "no outsider, however sympathetic, can penetrate the inner secrets of another life and culture foreign to his own" and that "this book can only give the observation of one who has seen the East frankly and sympathetically though the eyes of the West. A Moslem woman would write very differently of her changing world."[91]

Yet, as Woodsmall made clear in her book about her fourteen-month study tour of the Middle East and India, *Moslem Women Enter a New World* (1936), she could not overcome her conviction that the "social systems of the East and West are established on diametrically different principles. The pivotal difference is the difference in the position of woman." While she conceded that dramatic changes were at long last afoot in Muslim societies, it was still the "veil" that was the "barometer of social change in the Moslem world." She found hope in the fact that, even in India, which to her represented the "extreme of conservatism" in terms of the practice of purdah and seclusion, there were "rumours everywhere of change."[92]

A year later the Turkish writer Halidé Edib published an account, in English, of her own tour of India. Muslim intellectuals at the Jamia Millia Islamia (National Muslim University) in New Delhi—which she described as the "offspring, though a rebellious one" of Aligarh College—had invited her to deliver a series of lectures in January 1935. She arrived in India filled with the knowledge she had accumulated from her English governess, whose husband had been a "tea-planter" in India; from the fictional works of British and Turkish writers; and from Indians she had met in Turkey and in her travels overseas. Indian men had traveled to Turkey as members of the Indian Red Crescent deployed in 1912 after the Balkan Wars and again in 1918 as members of the occupying forces after the defeat of the Ottomans. Edib had also followed the rise and fall of the Khilafat movement in India from a distance. In New York she had briefly met the Indian poet and nationalist leader Sarojini Naidu who, along with "Mrs. Sun Yat-Sen...is the best known Eastern woman in politics."[93]

Among the questions Edib faced from journalists shortly after she disembarked in Bombay was one about her views on birth control, and she was grateful that the "interview came to an end without another ultra-modern sex problem in education being raised." The question was no doubt inspired by the concurrent visit of British suffragist Edith How-Martyn, who had arrived two months earlier and was traveling the country advocating for birth control. How-Martyn would return to India later that year with Margaret Sanger, who, like Woodsmall, would feel compelled to explain that she too hoped to "undo" the damage done by the visit and book of her compatriot Katherine Mayo.[94]

Edib encountered several prominent male leaders—Mohandas Karam-chand Gandhi, Mahadev Desai, and Muhammad Iqbal, for example, chaired her different lectures in Delhi—and an impressive range of female activists. In Bombay she was welcomed by the nationalist, women's rights, and arts activist Kamaladevi Chattopadhyay. While she stayed in Delhi, her fellow guests at the home of her old friend Dr. Mukhtar Ahmad Ansari, a veteran of the Indian Crescent Mission in Turkey, were Sarojini Naidu, the English suffragist and preacher Maude Royden, and English suffragist and International Alliance of Women president, Margery Corbett Ashby. Over tea one afternoon she also met some of Naidu's guests, such as Begum Shah Nawaz, who had been the Muslim woman delegate at the recent London Roundtable Conferences, and the young political activist Aruna Asaf Ali, a "lovely Hindu woman married to a Muslim." Her travels around India took her to Calcutta in late February, where she met Shamsunnahar Mahmud and the renowned young singer Noor Jehan, among others.[95]

Whether Edib's admirers across India knew of the controversy surrounding her work with Armenian orphans in Lebanon following the Armenian Genocide is unclear.[96] If they did, the knowledge did not appear to detract from her stature as an exemplary modern Muslim figure in interwar India. Shamsunnahar Mahmud, then a young mother freshly equipped with a bachelor's degree, was thrilled by the opportunity to meet this iconic figure and would cherish the memories all her life. She recalled the immense crowds of men, and some women, who came to Ashutosh Hall at Calcutta University to hear Edib speak, this "wonder of the world, radiant and dignified in her head-to-toe grey attire that revealed only her face." Mahmud helped to organize a reception for Edib at the YWCA on behalf of the two organizations with which she was actively involved, AIWC and the Bengal Anjuman-e-Khawatin-e-Islam. (A decade after Edib's visit, my own grandparents chose to name their eldest daughter, my mother, Khaleda in her honor.) Nearly two decades after Edib's visit, Mahmud would seek out Edib once again while on an official visit to Turkey.[97]

A year after Woodsmall's and Edib's books appeared, Syed M.H. Zaidi of Calcutta published *The Muslim Womanhood in Revolution,* which he described as an "exhaustive survey of modern movements among the Muslim women all over the world with special reference to their social, educational and political awakening." The book, which covered Muslim women from Albania to China and Java, began with a reminder that the "legal position of Muslim women…—though instituted over thirteen centuries ago—is far ahead of times even to-day, and this is still denied to women under other religious governments." To support his case he chose to cite the "famous Judge Crabites of the USA." Indeed, just a few years earlier, while serving as a judge of the Mixed Tribunal in Cairo, the New Orleans-born Pierre Crabitès had felt compelled to respond in the *American Bar Association Journal* to the "idea [that] is prevalent in the Occident that the Oriental woman is a toy made to pander to the pleasures of man." Despite clear inequities, he wrote, "the reciprocal rights and duties of the Eastern husband and wife place upon the woman no charge, submit her to no disability and make no demand upon her which, if carefully analyzed, tend to place her in a position inferior either in dignity or power to that enjoyed by her Western sister in respect to her Western husband." Invoking Blackstone on the legal infirmities of Anglo-American women, Crabitès pronounced the "Muslim wife," in matters of property ownership and control, to be "as free as a bird."[98]

According to Zaidi, the "present world-wide awakening" of Muslim women was nothing short of a "glorious manifestation of the spirit of Muhammad's scheme of life for women." However, because he understood Muhammad's message to be accompanied by a "caution to occasion no scandal by exceeding the limits of prudence and moderation," Zaidi could not support dramatic changes such as the discarding of purdah. For example, after several pages on the accomplishments of Muslim women in Bengal, he concluded that these successes "are a standing challenge to those who, through wisdom or unwisdom, aver" that attainments such as these "can be achieved by women only when the barriers of purdah and seclusion are removed from their way."[99] In short, he saw no need to challenge the practice of purdah for women to advance.

INTERNATIONAL ALLIANCES AND TENSIONS

In the early twentieth century, South Asian Muslim women, primarily through organizations such as the AIWC, began their engagement with the recently established international women's and feminist organizations and networks that had become interested in expanding beyond their elite, Christian, Euro-American constituents to encompass feminists of other backgrounds. For instance, the self-avowedly feminist International Woman Suffrage Alliance (IWSA), founded in Washington, DC, in 1902, in the presence of delegates from several European countries as well as Turkey, Chile, and Russia, formally welcomed women "of whatever race, nativity, or creed" a decade later.[100] After a 1904 meeting in Berlin, IWSA was renamed the International Alliance of Women for Equal Citizenship (IAWSEC or, more commonly, IAW). With a clear goal of female suffrage, IAW organized meetings or international congresses every two or three years. In 1906 it also established the journal *Jus Suffragii* to keep its members around the world informed about developments elsewhere.[101] The existing leadership none-theless remained torn between the ideas of universal sisterhood and a sense of responsibility among both US and British feminists to "save" the poor oppressed women of the world, in particular, in areas within their coun-tries' domains of imperial control, such as in the Philippines and India, respectively.[102]

In an effort to encourage women from other countries to join the IAW, Carrie Chapman Catt, the organization's US founder and president, and Aletta Jacobs, a Dutch feminist and the first woman physician in the Netherlands, set out from Madeira in 1911 on a fifteen-month trip to Asia and Africa.[103] The trip proved transformative for the two women. As Catt would later recall in a speech at a suffrage convention in Newark, New Jersey, "Once I was a regular jingo but that was before I had visited other countries. I had thought America had a monopoly on all that stands for progress, but I had a sad awakening."[104]

Preconceptions about Muslim women inevitably influenced Catt and Jacobs during their world tour. Catt wrote in *Jus Suffragii* about the "fos-silized humanity" in Palestine and how the two women "wondered what the veiled women we met in the street were thinking." She reported with some relief that, after having had some private meetings with such women, she could say with confidence that the "seeds of rebellion have already been planted in the hearts of those mysterious women behind the veil." The cele-brated Millicent Garrett Fawcett, who, as we saw earlier, had worked closely with Syed Ameer Ali in London, visited Palestine in 1921 and drew a sharp contrast between the "unorganised, inarticulate, little-educated Moslem women" and the "progressive women" of the Jewish Women's Equal Rights Association.[105] Seemingly oblivious to the political tensions on the ground, some British feminists saw the settlement of Zionist women in Palestine as a positive development. In a *Jus Suffragii* article titled "The Holy Land" in January 1912, Catt described the Zionist colonies "like bits of the new world transplanted into the old" and, despite her usual disdain for religious estab-lishment, shared with her readers her conviction that Christian missionar-ies and Zionist women would help move the Palestinian women forward.[106]

Jacobs, a staunch Dutch nationalist, described how friends had persuaded her to visit British India so that she might see for herself how much better Dutch colonial administrators were than the British.[107] Following her visit to India, she conceded that the Dutch presence in Java had indeed rendered that area more hospitable to Europeans, but, as a feminist, she worried that the Dutch had done less for local women than had the British in India.[108] Nonetheless, in her letters to a Dutch newspaper, Jacobs recalled with much admiration the Muslim women she had encountered in the Padang highlands of Sumatra in the Dutch Indies: "For us the sight of these hard-working women was particularly interesting, because these happy people formed such a wonderful contrast with the gloomy women of Egypt and British India, who looked so miserable."[109] While this observation suggests that Jacobs did not see Muslim women as an undifferentiated group across India and Indonesia, her subsequent sentences are a stark reminder that perhaps what she really appreciated about the Padang women was their presence in the public sphere, a central tenet of Western feminism at that time. The passage is worth quoting at length:

> If you want to be convinced that women are only happy when they have responsible work to do, that it is in woman's nature that they are only satisfied in circumstances where they have useful work, you just need to visit the Padang highlands and compare these women to those in countries where they are excluded from useful work by the development of industry, or by traditional customs and habits. The whole women's movement, despite appearing to function differently throughout the civilized world, in fact has the sole cause and goal of regaining the meaning that women originally had for the human race. Our aim is again to participate in working for the general interest and to be responsible for half of the labor that has to be done for the preservation of the species and the progress of humanity.[110]

In January 1913 *Jus Suffragii* announced "invited delegates...from Egypt, India, Burmah, China, Japan and the Philippines" were expected at the conference that year in Budapest. "For the first time in the woman movement, it is expected that Hindu, Buddhist, Confucian, Mohammedan, Jewish and Christian women will sit together...uniting their voices in a common plea for the liberation of their sex from those artificial discriminations which every political and religious system has directed against them." But no "Asiatic" delegates attended the 1913 congress. Perhaps they were alienated by the constant litany of the supposed horrors of the non-Western world— cannibalism, sexual slavery, the veil—that were repeatedly invoked to highlight how far advanced Western women were in their own emancipation and to justify Western dominance of the leadership of the global feminist movement.[111]

Organizations from other countries were invited to join the IAW, and eventually they did, but leadership long remained limited to Europeans and Americans. India, Egypt, and Palestine joined in 1923, Turkey in 1926, and Ceylon, Dutch East India, and Syria in 1929. Huda Shaarawi of Egypt and Dhanvanthi Rama Rau of India eventually joined the board, and Shaarawi would be the only Muslim woman to play a prominent role in IAW for some time.[112]

By the mid-1930s the IAW appeared willing to concede that the women of the East were capable of identifying—and organizing to resolve—their own problems, but even their laudatory statements retained hints of maternalism. The April 1935 issue of *Jus Suffragii,* for example, celebrated the Indian Muslim writer and IAW delegate Iqbalunnisa Hussain as "one of the leading educationalists in Mysore"—despite, the article explained, the strict purdah of her childhood, early marriage, and a large family. A few months later the journal noted with seeming greater confidence: "India has great problems, problems made more difficult by her vast territory, by the magnitude and variety of her population and traditions. But one never reads about Indian women without feeling that they hold the solution to those problems."[113]

The 1935 IAW congress met in Istanbul, the first to be held outside western Europe. The new state of Turkey, under Mustafa Kemal Ataturk, had recently granted women suffrage, and the elections held a month earlier had brought eighteen women to its assembly, the highest proportion of women legislators in Europe at the time. Yet one US news agency felt compelled to invoke for its readers an older image of Eastern women with this headline: "Women of thirty-five nations met today in the old Yildiz Palace, once the world's greatest harem, to work for emancipation of women." The Istanbul congress welcomed four new societies: the Union of Patriotic Women of Persia, Union of Féministe Arabe of Syria, Union of Féministe Arabe Palestinienne, and the All India Women's Conference. The resolutions adopted by the congress included a statement of the IAW's commitment to support the "Women of India in their demand for the abolition of all sex qualifications in regard to their civic and political rights" as well as formal protests against polygamy and child marriage.[114]

While some European and US feminists undoubtedly saw these international conferences as a forum for undertaking tutelage of their Eastern sisters, others saw the increased presence of Asian delegates at these international gatherings as an opportunity to learn more about them directly from them. As Ruth Woodsmall later put it, where at earlier conferences, "Western women...often represented the East," today they "would not have the temerity to try to interpret the changing East, since Eastern women themselves now represent the East." She went on to describe the exciting presence of "three women from India (as it happened all three were Moslems), a young woman from Teheran, a number from Egypt, both Moslems and Copts, a large delegation of Syrian women, representing Christians and Moslems, and also a group of students from the American Junior College in Beirut—all these Eastern delegates together with a group of very active Turkish delegates, the total number of Eastern women constituting perhaps half of the Congress, gave one the very definite impression of the active participation of women of the East in international life."[115]

Many of these women arrived in Istanbul with a fair degree of experience in international organizing. Shareefah Hamid Ali had been one of fourteen women (all Indian, with the exception of the Irish Theosophist and feminist Margaret Cousins) to issue an invitation to thirty-three Asian countries (including Palestine, Syria, and Iraq) to send delegates to the first pan-Asian women's conference in Lahore in January 1931. Perhaps they had been inspired by the Oriental Women's Congress in Damascus in July 1930, which had hoped for delegates from as far as India, Japan, and Java, though only women from Arab countries, Iran, and Turkey participated. The Indian invitation had declared that "it is fully time" to work together to "develop among ourselves a spirit of Asian sisterhood, with the object of preserving all that is valuable in our age-long national and social cultures and of discriminating what is best for us to assimilate from outside Asia." While attendance was disappointingly low, these small conferences provided an important opportunity for feminists in these regions to set their own agendas and discuss issues that mattered to them, including polygamy, child marriage, suffrage and citizenship, and access to work and education.[116] The Asian feminists carried lessons from their own national and regional meetings into the larger conferences with European and US women.

In an article about the Istanbul congress in the Egyptian Feminist Union's journal, *L'Egyptienne,* its editor, the Egyptian feminist Saiza Nabarawi, credited Begum Kamaluddin and Shareefah Hamid Ali of the All India Women's Conference for the resolution against polygamy. In her role as cochair with Huda Shaarawi of a session on "The East and West in

Cooperation," Iqbalunnisa Hussain spoke of the long history of contact and fusion that had produced modern civilization. In their speeches Hamid Ali, Hussain, Shaarawi, and Julia Dimashqiya of Syria, among others, conceded that, to quote Shaarawi, "the movement of Western women for peace, and the equality of rights" had progressed further than had the movements in their own countries, and they reaffirmed their support for the feminists of the West. At the same time they reminded their European colleagues that the latter's efforts for women's equality had progressed in conjunction with their nations' prejudices and imperialism and—again quoting Shaarawi— with "the faults committed by your governments." Katherine Mayo's recent aspersions about Indian women might well have been on her mind when Hamid Ali stated even more bluntly, "May we hope to have you with us as friendly and not enforced guides—that we shall have from you cordiality and human fellowship, and not 'tutelage' and 'patronage'?"[117] Many of these tensions over the delineation of women's rights and feminism would resurface in the United Nations conferences of the late twentieth century, as we'll see in chapter 8.

When looking back in 1955 on fifty years of the IAW, the organization's honorary vice president Adele Schreiber began by listing the many problems that the IAW had helped to eradicate over the years. Its "courage, devotion, sacrifice, and enthusiasm" had "brought final victory and released women from so many forms of slavery—crippled feet, seclusion and veiling, child marriage and the sale of girls, the burning alive of widows, to mention but a few." While she went on to concede that "sex equality is far from achieved" and there remained problems everywhere, from the "White Slave Traffic" and the "overburdening of mothers and housewives" to the "greatest of all evils—war," the image of Western feminists mentoring the rest of the world, where these peculiar, unfamiliar, and exotic practices had long held sway, remained vivid.[118]

Among the specific accomplishments of IAW that Schreiber listed was Huda Shaarawi's decision to remove her veil: "Though unenfranchised, Egypt had made spectacular progress. Hoda Charaoui Pasha, a beautiful and talented member of the nobility, attended her first congress at Rome. She was so much impressed by what she saw and heard there, that she took off her veil on the way home and never wore it again."[119] In the mid-twentieth century the veiling of Muslim women remained in the eyes of many Western feminists an obstacle to be overcome on the *Journey towards Freedom,* as the jubilee book was titled. For Western feminists unveiling was a cause for celebration, regardless of the view held by feminists and women's rights advocates, individuals and organizations, in Muslim societies around the world.

To be sure, in the early twentieth century Muslim women in Bengal, and India more generally, also wrote with real concern about the issues of purdah and seclusion. But for them purdah was a problem only when it hampered women's mobility and limited their opportunities for education and employment. Their concerns and resolutions were both far subtler and more complex than the automatic association of unveiling with emancipation under which many Western observers, even the more astute and thoughtful observers like Woodsmall, labored.

The Bengali mathematician and educationist Fazilatunnesa Begum explicated well—without touching once on the issue of veiling—the nuanced relationship between *mukti* (freedom), education, and women's empowerment in a 1929 piece in *Saogat* titled "Muslim Narir Mukti" (Freedom for Muslim women). Having reminded her readers of the "extraordinary challenges that the Muslim community has had to face in this country," she wrote, "'freedom' stands for the freedom of the soul, and freedom of the soul means the independence of thought and expression that can be useful for society and the world at large, which can stimulate one's own reasoning and intellectual growth." She described the changes that had overcome the "age-old dormant spirit of the Muslim woman," such that she "shall no longer remain an object of another's sensuous gratification, [and] she will not forget her womanhood and selfhood." What mattered was not how women dressed but the "veil of illusion" and the "noose of fragility and luxury" that have kept women from enjoying the larger "beauteous world." To "establish contact with the world outside," Muslim women required the "very weapons of this battle, that is, education and knowledge." For Fazilatunnesa education did not mean "being stamped with a certain number of degrees; education is that which trains and nurtures the mind, directs and polishes the ability for reason: that is education; it is that which gives strength to the personality and dignity to a being."[120] Fazilatunnesa herself had been the first Muslim student at Bethune College, where she earned her bachelor's in 1923, and the first Bengali Muslim woman to earn a master's, which she did at Dacca University, receiving the highest marks of all the men and women in her class

ফজিলতুন্নেছা জোহা এম-এ
বাঙ্গালী মুসলিম মহিলাদের মধ্যে ইনিই সর্বপ্রথম
এম-এ পাশ করিয়া শিক্ষা বিষয়ে অভিজ্ঞতা লাভের
জন্য বিলাত গিয়াছিলেন ।

FIGURE 13. "Fazilatunnesa Zoha, M.A. among Bengali Muslim women, she was the first to complete her M.A. and go abroad for further training in education." *Saogat* 11, no. 9 (1935): 480. Heidelberg University Library.

in applied mathematics before going to study in London. Khan Bahadur Ahsanullah, who had helped found Dacca University just a few years earlier and was then the director of public instruction for the undivided province of Bengal and Assam, arranged her scholarship for England; she married his son Shams uz-Zoha shortly after her return. She taught mathematics at Bethune College in Calcutta until partition, when she moved to Dacca with her family and became the principal of Eden College.[121]

For some Muslim Bengali women of this era, women's right to mobility or even education meant little without the political freedom that eluded them under colonial rule. In the 1940s Muslim women in Bengal, as in other parts of the country heeded Muhammad Ali Jinnah's call to women to join the movement for Pakistan. Among them were Shaista Suhrawardy Ikramullah, the great-granddaughter of Nawab Latif, who, as we saw in the last chapter, had been grudging in his support for female formal education. That Ikramullah would earn a doctorate from the University of London in 1940 and serve as a member of parliament and ambassador in independent Pakistan was testament to the rapidly unfolding changes within the educated Muslim elite of Bengal in less than a century.[122] Landless Bengali Muslim women also became politically mobilized in the 1940s and were among the six million or so sharecroppers of various communities who came together to fight for economic justice in the aftermath of the devastating Bengal Famine of 1943, most notably in the Tebhaga movement of 1946–47.[123] Following the end of British colonial rule, the division of Bengal and Punjab and, indeed, greater India into ostensibly Muslim and Hindu parts in August 1947, East Bengali Muslim women across classes would find themselves confronted with new privileges as well as unexpected challenges as citizens of a Muslim-majority state.

SIX

In the Shadow of the Cold War

SHAMSUNNAHAR MAHMUD FOUND much to admire and ponder during her tour of the United States in late 1956, although, as she frequently asserted, she believed her countrywomen should forge their own way forward rather than blindly copy Euro-American women. For instance, in a formal welcome address to Fatima Jinnah, who had accompanied her brother Muhammad Ali Jinnah to Dacca a few years earlier, Shamsunnahar Mahmud had reminded her listeners that "Islam gave women equal rights several centuries ago," and there was no need, in the continuing struggle to help improve Bengali women's lives, to turn to "England, America, Russia, or any modern European country" for ideas or assistance. An early protégée of Begum Rokeya Hossain's, by the time of her trip to the United States Mahmud was an established author, educationist, social reformer, and political figure in her native East Pakistan (as East Bengal had been renamed formally just a year earlier). Following the Partition of India in 1947 she had moved from Calcutta in West Bengal, India, to Dacca in East Bengal with her husband and two sons and thrown herself into helping to build the new nation of Pakistan.[1]

A NEW STATE—AND NEW CHALLENGES

Pakistan had been independent for just nine years at the time of Mahmud's visit to the United States. Carved out of predominantly Muslim areas in the northeast and northwest of undivided India, the new nation was the "truncated and mutilated moth-eaten Pakistan" that Jinnah had foreseen in a May 1947 speech denouncing the planned partition of Bengal and Punjab.[2]

Pakistan was supposed to be a homeland for the Muslims of the subcontinent, yet some thirty million Muslims remained in India and as many non-Muslims in Pakistan; the eastern and western wings of Pakistan were separated by some 1,300 miles of Indian territory; and, like Punjabis to the far west, Bengalis sharing a language, culture, and history found themselves divided by new national borders. The population transfer of non-Muslims to India and of Muslims to Pakistan was on a smaller scale, generally less violent, and far more gradual in Bengal than it was in Punjab. In both regions, however, Hindu and Muslim (and, in Punjab, also Sikh) women bore the brunt of sexual violence and abductions. Nazara Huq, a young mother in Shibpur, Howrah (in West Bengal, India), later recalled that during the riots of 1946, some of the women who took shelter in the Shibpur relief camp were "almost naked," others "grievously wounded." Many Muslims fled from West to East Bengal not necessarily because they had witnessed violence themselves but out of fear of the possibility of such incidents. Others, such as the physician father of Taiyeba Ahmed, moved to East Bengal because, as she later put it, "He wanted to contribute to the building of the new nation, Pakistan."[3]

Many Muslim migrants to Pakistan hoped the new country would be a "land of eternal Eid [celebration]," in the words of a Muslim poet of that time. There they would be able to live proudly as Bengali and Muslim, without British or Hindu dominance, and with the promise of an agrarian utopia, liberated of the old socioeconomic hierarchies and exploitation.[4] The euphoria inspired by the new nation and the new possibilities it represented was palpable in a November 1949 article by the young Moshfeka Mahmud in the Bengali women's magazine *Begum* about the significance of 14 August 1947. In her article Mahmud recalled the moment of Pakistan's birth at the stroke of midnight some two years earlier and the sheer joy and pride that had enveloped her and everyone around her as they "cast off the shackles of servitude" and emerged "as *azaad* [free] inhabitants of an *azaad* Pakistan." No longer would she have to "lower her head in shame" when meeting citizens of independent nations. Instead, "now we will be able to hold our head up high and walk alongside the rest of the world as we move forward." As she prepared to attend a ceremony of the hoisting of the new flag at dawn, she came across a poor, emaciated woman with her child. It "made her happy" to be able to help her because "there ought to be a smile on everyone's face today"; as Mahmud continued to her destination, she felt confident that poverty and exploitation would not be part of this new nation.[5]

Yet fissures in the new nation appeared quickly. West Pakistani politicians and media alike proved generally apathetic to a serious food crisis in East Bengal in 1947, reminiscent of the 1943 Bengal famine, when British war priorities led to a famine that killed some three million people. In addition, the political elite of West Pakistan decided that its preferred language, Urdu, which was a minority language even in the western wing, should be the state language of Pakistan. In March 1948, on what would be his sole visit to East Bengal, Jinnah reiterated West Pakistani opposition to the Bengali language in a number of public speeches. He also suggested that any attempt to advocate for state language status for Bengali—which many in the western wing saw as a "Hindu language," given its script related to Sanskrit rather than Arabic—represented a conspiracy by leftists and others to rupture the new nation. Such developments led many Bengalis, a numerical majority in Pakistan, to wonder about their place in the new nation.[6]

Amy Geraldine "Dinah" Stock, who chaired the English Department at Dacca University for the first four years following the partition, witnessed the early stages of the *bhasha andolon* (language movement) from her prime vantage point in university quarters and with an open and curious outlook that she had developed as a student. While at Somerville College, Stock had been the only European at the Oxford Majlis, a debating society founded and dominated by South Asians, and an active member of the Oxford University Labour Party as well as various labor, antiwar, and anti-imperialist movements. In London she had worked closely with the future Kenyan nationalist leader Jomo Kenyatta. Eager to experience life in a newly independent country, she had quickly accepted the job offer from Dacca University. "Pakistan," she noted astutely upon her arrival in August 1947, "was due to be born in two weeks' time, and unlike India which had been preparing for independence for years, it had only just begun to believe in its own existence."[7]

While the vast majority of her colleagues and students were men, Stock encountered a few women at the university, as well as when she ventured off-campus with friends. On a visit to the southeastern district of Noakhali with Khorshed, a student in economics and English, she found herself the object of great curiosity among local women. Two widows, who had walked eight miles to see her, voiced their concerns about her future—because she had no husband or children. From an intelligence officer she met when her colleague Munier Choudhury was arrested, she learned of the significance of women's educational degrees to the new nation's male civil servants: the officer's younger sister was in danger of being divorced by her husband, a rising civil servant in need of an "educated wife for his career," if she failed to pass matriculation within two years. (Munier Choudhury, we should note, would be among the Bengali academics killed by West Pakistani soldiers and their Bengali collaborators in Bangladesh's war of independence in 1971.) Stock also noted that although female students participated actively in the language protests in February and March 1948 that preceded and followed Jinnah's visit to Dacca, even the staunchest activists "were accustomed to purdah, did not go to the cinema without a chaperone, [and] did not normally speak to the men who sat in the same classroom."[8]

The East Pakistan Youth League, established in March 1951, emerged out of East Bengali restlessness and frustration over a variety of West Pakistani policies. They demanded, for example, government provision of basic needs, a plebiscite to resolve the Kashmir situation, Bengali as an official language in education and public sector work, and the rehabilitation of refugee youth. The women members of the league added, "We, the young women, hoped that through legislation the Pakistan government will liberate us from social oppression, provide for our education and give us equal status with men in every sphere of life." They lamented the low literacy rate among women and pointed to the example of a "small Muslim state like Albania," which already enjoyed "free and compulsory primary education."[9] The demand for Bengali to be *a* national language (alongside the many languages of West Pakistan) was tied to pride in cultural heritage as well as concerns about future mobility, progress, and access to education and jobs that would allow them to better contribute to the new nation. Despite the league's efforts in the following months, politicians continued to insist on an Urdu-only policy—and students continued to protest.

On 21 February 1952 female and male students from local high schools, colleges, and Dacca University marched together in violation of the Pakistani authorities' ban on "unlawful assembly." Sufia Ibrahim, then a second-year student in the newly established department of Islamic history and culture, was there with a few friends, including Shamsunnahar Ahsan, "who always wore a black burqa," which was fairly unusual among women students in those days and thus worthy of comment. While they had orders not to arrest any women that day, the police, all male and most West Pakistani, used their batons on the women protesters. Ibrahim recalled being hit on her leg. She and her friends were also injured when climbing over barbed wire. They were trying to make their way to the Medical College to get first aid when they heard the first gunshots.[10] The men killed that day, most of them students, would be celebrated in East Pakistan, and later in Bangladesh, as language martyrs, while the date *ekushey* February (21 February) would be commemorated as Shaheed Dibosh (Martyrs' Day). In 1999 UNESCO declared the date International Mother Language Day.

A CHANGING OF THE GUARD

For Britain the independence of India and Pakistan meant the loss of its "jewel in the crown" and set in motion the dismantling of British global dominance. The conclusion of World War II paved the way for the ascendance of the United States and the Soviet Union, both of which, eager to distance themselves from the old European colonial powers, celebrated the sovereignty of the new states. Before long they would begin to vie for the loyalty of the majority of the world's population that inhabited what came to be known as the "Third World," or developing world, with implications for how the Soviets and Americans would write about and interact with women in other countries.

Pakistan's first leaders—Jinnah until his death a year after independence, followed by Liaquat Ali Khan until he was assassinated in 1951—declared repeatedly that Pakistan would steer clear of both the Americans and the Soviets. The US and British decision to support the creation of Israel in 1948 with little regard for the local Arab Palestinian population had enraged many Pakistanis in both wings. The joint Anglo-American overthrow of the democratically elected Iranian prime minister Mohammad Mossadegh in 1953 would only confirm their suspicions about Anglo-American apathy for Muslim aspirations. Communism, similarly, held no appeal, although Liaquat Ali Khan admitted Soviet-style land reform could help curb the feudal power of the remaining zamindars. In the end, however, economic need and fears about India's military dominance soon pushed the Pakistani state, if not its people, decidedly into the US camp—and into decades of military rule.[11]

The United States' relations with Pakistan were shaped by a combination of US fears of Soviet inroads in the Middle East and US concerns about the very nature of communism. Post–World War II religious zeal also helped to tilt the US government in Pakistan's direction. US Protestant leaders, already troubled by growing secular trends, saw Soviet communism as inherently dangerous. Evangelical Protestant preacher Billy Graham, for example, described communism as being "against God, against Christ, against the Bible, and against all religion."[12] For the majority of Americans, Dwight Eisenhower's 1950 Labor Day speech set the terms for the good-versus-evil rhetoric of the incipient Cold War. In his nationally broadcast address to an audience of some four thousand people in Denver, Eisenhower urged Americans to support the "crusade for freedom," "a battle for truth" against an enemy who "weaves a fantastic pattern of lies and twisted facts," "devilish libel," and "slander" about the United States. He described the enemy as "vicious" and a threat to his country's commitment to "freedom, opportunity, and human happiness," to the "blessings and opportunities of liberty," and to "free government" and the "dignity of the individual." He spoke of US soldiers who were "dying for ideals" in places like Korea to protect the US way of life and the "right of freedom" given by God. The Crusade for Freedom would raise funds for Radio Free Europe, which would fight the communist propaganda allegedly emanating from this evil enemy, the Soviet Union.[13]

While similar language would be deployed against Muslims decades later, in the postwar years the familiar monotheism of Muslims made them natural allies in the global fight against godless communism. A 1951 article in *Time* pondered the crucial role that Muslim-majority countries might play "in the struggle between the West and Communism." There was much to attract Islam, "the only great religion founded by a successful businessman," on both sides of the Cold War. "To the West, opportunity beckons from one side of Islam—its God, its acceptance of the moral code, its protection of private property. To the Kremlin, opportunity beckons from another side of Islam—its poverty and corruption, its long acceptance of tyranny, its ingrained hatred of Christendom." *Time* singled out Pakistan prime minister Liaquat Ali Khan as "probably the ablest Moslem political leader in office today."[14] Liaquat Ali Khan had impressed Washington and challenged stereotypes about Muslims and South Asians when he and his wife, Ra'ana Liaquat Ali Khan, had visited a year earlier, in spring 1950.[15] His assassination in October 1951 would throw the new nation into political turmoil and allow others to set the terms of the burgeoning US-Pakistan relationship.

Eleanor Roosevelt visited Pakistan a few months after the prime minister's assassination. US President Harry S. Truman had appointed her a "roving ambassador" to the Middle East, South Asia, and the Philippines. Her goal, as she recorded in her account of the trip, was to prevent the "awakening of the east" from leading to support for communism rather than democracy.[16] On 20 February 1952, the day before the repression of *ekushey* February, Eleanor Roosevelt arrived in Karachi, Pakistan, for a seven-day visit. Her hosts, members of the All Pakistan Women's Association (APWA), including founder-president Ra'ana Liaquat Ali Khan, were quick to impress on her the many rights women already enjoyed under Muslim law.[17] Although Roosevelt later noted in her memoir that the Quran governs all aspects of Muslims' lives and its teachings hold women as "lesser beings," she conceded Muslim women's long-standing rights of inheritance and within marriage. She also found it "curious" that, "considering how closely the custom of purdah is associated with the Moslem world...the Koran itself nowhere contains any mention of purdah." She lauded "enlightened Moslem leaders" such as Jinnah for having condemned the practice "unequivocally" as a "barbarous anachronism" and the efforts of women leaders to encourage women to participate in the "life of the world" through growing opportunities in education and employment, as well as the exercise of the franchise. At a "purdah party" she met two women who had "pioneered in the cause of women's rights, displaying the same sort of courage our own early suffragettes showed." She attributed the "emergence of the women of Pakistan—a major reason why their emancipation has progressed so much more rapidly and so much further than in the Arab-Moslem countries" to the dramatic social changes wrought by the partition and the refugee crisis. "The need was urgent and immediate—and the women rose to it."[18]

During her weeklong stay, Roosevelt visited East Bengal for only seven hours, an affront on the part of the West Pakistani organizers that did not go unnoticed by Bengali women. Her host for the day was the Austrian-born Viqarunnessa Noon, the wife of the then governor, the West Pakistani (specifically, Punjabi) Firoz Khan Noon. In her memoirs Roosevelt would describe Begum Noon as "charming in a soft pink sari" and recall that Noon and the Bengali women activists were adamant that East Bengal should have a domestic science-training school just like the one the Ford Foundation had funded in Pakistan's western wing.[19] Shamsunnahar Mahmud was among those Roosevelt met in Dacca. Mahmud's niece and Anwara Bahar Choudhury's daughter Selina Bahar Zaman, then a young girl, was part of a group of dancers who performed for Roosevelt and others at a luncheon aboard the *Mary Anderson,* a luxury yacht built in the 1930s and named after the daughter of the then British governor of Bengal.[20]

THE POSTWAR MUSLIM WORLD

Alongside their efforts to ally with the United States, Pakistan's leaders tried to use their unique position as a country established to be a sovereign Muslim

FIGURE 14. Selina Bahar Zaman *(second from left)*, Eleanor Roosevelt, and Viqarunnessa Noon *(third from right)* on the *Mary Anderson*, Dacca, February 1952. Courtesy of Nasreen Shams and Iqbal Bahar Chowdhury.

homeland to seize the mantle of leadership in the postwar Muslim world. To that end Foreign Minister Zafrullah Khan toured several Arab countries and offered to host a conference of Muslim prime ministers in Pakistan to discuss issues of common interest. Pakistan also hosted several Muslim world congresses in its first decade. Although many Muslim-majority countries, most prominently Indonesia and Egypt, ultimately chose to focus their energies on what became the Non-Aligned Movement following the conferences of Asian and African countries in Bandung (1955), Cairo (1957), and Belgrade (1961), the relationships with other Muslim countries facilitated by Pakistan's early outreach proved eminently useful for Pakistan's women activists.[21]

These encounters with Muslim women from other countries, whether at international gatherings or through travel, revealed to Mahmud and other Bengali women of her class and time diverse ways of being Muslim and different possible paths to legal, political, and economic rights for Muslim women. In the spring of 1952, for example, women delegates from Egypt, Indonesia, Iraq, Lebanon, and Turkey traveled to Lahore for the annual conference of the recently established All Pakistan Women's Association. This "historic conference of women from all over the Muslim world," as one effusive report put it, was "the first of its kind to be held in the Pakistan-Bharat subcontinent." Foreign delegates appreciated this effort to establish the "corner stone of a better world." Several speakers recognized the problems shared by Muslim women across nations and hoped that "coming together gives them the opportunity to compare notes and to propagate and imbibe useful impulses."[22] Among the women Mahmud met there were the Iraqi pediatrician Laman Amin-Zaki Damluji and the Turkish lawyer Süreyya Ağaoğlu; the latter reassured Mahmud that she had no difficulty attracting both male and female clients.[23]

In late 1952 Mahmud visited Turkey on a goodwill mission as part of a cultural delegation of thirty Pakistanis, mostly students, from both wings. Among them was the young Sufia Ibrahim, who had marched in the *ekushey* February rally earlier that year. Mahmud was the only woman among the six senior members of the group, and the responsibility of representing her new nation weighed heavily on her. Just decades earlier, Mahmud recalled, Indians across the subcontinent had mobilized in support of the caliphate in Turkey, once the source of the "Muslim world's strength and inspiration." Today the new Turkey was an "unending fountain of courage and encouragement for all those who aspire to independence."[24]

One of the highlights of Mahmud's Turkish sojourn was the opportunity to see the writer Halidé Edib again at a tea party at Ankara Palas. Mahmud enthusiastically informed the older woman that much had changed since they last met in Calcutta in 1934. It was "with pride and joy" that she was now able to introduce to Edib an entire troupe of young Muslim women students from Pakistan who had "rushed to this distant land in search of knowledge." She also reminded Edib that, unlike when they had met last, she and her group had "traveled to your country as citizens of an independent nation." Edib reassured Mahmud that the souls of Pakistanis had always been free, for otherwise they would not have been able to overthrow those colonial shackles of subservience.[25]

THE LIVES OF US WOMEN

A few years later Mahmud was invited to participate in the Foreign Leader Program of the International Educational Exchange Service of the US State Department and learn about the lives and activities of US women. Invitations like this were common after World War II. Both sides of the

FIGURE 15. The Pakistan delegation to Turkey, with Turkish president Celâl Bayar *(center)*. Among the East Pakistanis present are Shamsunnahar Mahmud *(standing two spaces to the right of the president)*; next to her is Mustafa Kamal (so named by poet Kazi Nazrul Islam in honor of the Turkish nationalist leader), Leila Arjumand Banu, Khurshid Akhund, Kulsum Siddiqua Huda, Shafia Khatun, and Sufia Ibrahim *(seated, first from the right)*. Courtesy of Syed Refaat Ahmed.

Cold War deployed such instruments of public diplomacy, a term generally understood as propaganda efforts by governments (through official or private agencies) to win over the hearts and minds of the populations of other countries directly, without going through the governments of those countries.[26]

Mahmud's US itinerary reflected attention to her background and areas of interest. A biographical sheet compiled by the American Council on Education in conjunction with Mahmud's visit noted that she was one of the "first Muslim women graduates of undivided Bengal" and "one of the pioneers of women's education and emancipation movement among the Muslims of undivided Bengal."[27] Over three months Mahmud observed women volunteers at the YWCA in Boston, the League of Women Voters in Cincinnati, the Red Cross, and the Girl Scouts and visited the Yale School of Nursing, Connecticut College for Women, and University of California, Berkeley. She spoke with women workers in factories, hospitals, agriculture, and dairy farms and attended meetings of local chapters of the American Association for the United Nations. Mahmud's visit coincided with the invasion of Egypt by Britain, France, and Israel to overthrow the anticolonial Egyptian leader Gamal Abdel Nasser and to secure control of the Suez Canal, as well as US president Eisenhower's successful reelection bid. While she was impressed by

US women voters' level of awareness and engagement with the electoral campaigns, she was surprised by the low numbers of women in elected office. The US Congress had eighteen women at the time, while Pakistan's new constitution, promulgated just months before Mahmud's visit, had reserved ten seats for women in a much smaller unicameral parliament.[28]

In an interview with a local newspaper during her five-day visit to Oxford, Ohio, Mahmud spoke of how pleased she was with her US tour and how "despite the still wide differences in our way of living," she had identified "many things here which we can adapt." She bemoaned, for example, the dearth of opportunities for children in her country to receive citizenship training along the lines of US kids who served as class librarians and school safety patrollers and in school government. At the same time she expressed confidence that the close-knit and affectionate nature of families in her country protected children from the many dangers and temptations within the reach of US children. "In building our state and nation, we will accept from foreign countries only that which is good for us. If we are careful on this point, we will be able to steer clear of many dangers. Many of their problems will not even be able to raise their heads in our society."[29]

The US press's fascination with this visitor from a distant country is evident from a profile of Mahmud published in the *Christian Science Monitor* just days after the US presidential election and the Suez crisis. The article recounted in much detail the obstacles Mahmud had encountered in her relentless pursuit of education as a child and a young woman but also the support she had received from her grandfather and her mother. Mahmud was quoted at length on her analysis of the problems facing her new nation and her plans for helping her female compatriots. In announcing a forthcoming lecture by Mahmud, a September 1956 article in the *Hartford Courant* urged the "public" to come and hear from "this traveler from a land where women's freedom is new."[30]

What is striking in this era's press coverage of women visitors to the United States from Muslim-majority countries is the absence of reference to Islam as an obstacle to modernization. Indeed, neither the Americans— nor, indeed, the Soviets—seemed interested in the Muslim women of distant lands *as* Muslim women, even if they identified them as such. In other words, for the superpowers being Muslim posed no greater an obstacle than being of any other "traditional" culture. Muslims, like anyone else, could become modern. In the *Christian Science Monitor* article, neither Mahmud nor the profile writer, Jessie Arndt, invoked Islam or Muslimness, whether as a marker of Mahmud's or even Pakistan's identity or as a hindrance to Mahmud's dreams for herself or her country.[31] This was equally true of the US women's organizations that hosted many such international visitors and sent their own emissaries around the world. It is hard to imagine such an omission today. In the 1950s and 1960s, when both newly decolonizing nations and Western powers put faith in the promise of progress offered by technology and modernization and with the US government actively courting the leaders of Muslim-majority countries like Pakistan, Saudi Arabia, and Iran to join the fight against communism, the figure of the oppressed Muslim woman seemed to disappear. Western condescension and notions of superiority, however, persisted.

FOREIGN CORRESPONDENTS

US women less prominent than Eleanor Roosevelt also felt called in these early postwar years to travel to African and Asian countries and to bear witness to social transformation. While this eagerness for change generally presumed that the United States had already undergone this transformation and thus represented a model to emulate, some travelers and observers shared a degree of open-mindedness qualitatively different from the ethnocentrism and racism of the previous century. This willingness to try to understand unfamiliar cultures without judgment was perhaps more prevalent among those who recognized that the United States faced its own set of social problems. They accepted more readily that other countries might choose to forge their own paths rather than blindly copy a US or Western model that was far from perfect.

One such visitor was Ida Brooks Alseth. A former teacher and an award-winning journalist from Lake Preston, South Dakota, Alseth had been selected that fall by the State Department to travel to South Asia as part of an exchange program. Following her return to the United States, Alseth explained that her objective during her travels had been to counteract the "Hollywood versions of Americans....I wanted them to know that we worked and weren't all rich and lazy."[32]

"Hordes of people—going and coming along every road and street as if it were a special celebration or carnival. That is the way East Pakistan is every day." Thus began Alseth's first report to the *Daily Argus-Leader* of Sioux Falls, South Dakota, published on 12 December 1954. Her duties during her three-month trip included delivering lectures at Dacca University and several high schools and colleges, as well as meeting with members of local Rotary Clubs and women's organizations.[33] In Chittagong Alseth met the newspaper editor Maimuna Ali Khan, who had recently launched an English-language "one sheet bi-weekly." Although impressed with Khan, Alseth confessed to some uneasiness when, "as [her] toes played over the rich Persian rug" in the Khans' living room, both the editor and her husband, who owned a brick-manufacturing company, suggested that the United States should provide free assistance to projects in Pakistan.[34]

During her visit to the magazine *Begum*'s office in Dacca, Alseth marveled at the quality of the publication and lamented the absence of weekly magazines for women in the United States, though there were a few monthlies. The journalist Mohammad Nasiruddin, who had founded *Saogat* in 1918, had founded *Begum* in July 1947, just weeks before the partition, as a weekly magazine focused entirely on women's issues. The poet Sufia Kamal served briefly as its first editor and was succeeded by Nasiruddin's daughter Nurjahan Begum. *Begum* had moved from Calcutta to Dacca in 1950, following the emigration of most of its writers to East Pakistan.[35] Throughout the 1950s the magazine's articles and letters to the editor were an important chronicle of East Bengali women's growing politicization on domestic and international issues: they protested the rising costs of staples such as rice; voiced their objection to the growing inequalities between East and West Pakistan; declared as barbarous the French government's death sentence on young Algerian women freedom fighters; and demanded reforms in women's rights similar to efforts under way in Egypt, Tunisia, Turkey, and Iran. They also condemned the joint British, French, and Israeli attack on Egypt over the Suez Canal even though the Pakistan government, then led by Prime Minister Hussain Shaheed Suhrawardy, ultimately stood with the pro-Western alliance represented by the Baghdad Pact.[36]

At the *Begum* office Alseth spoke frankly about the many obstacles US women faced and encouraged Bengali women to persevere in their efforts. Inspired by the discussion, the *Begum* leadership and contributors decided that an organization centered on the magazine would be an ideal venue to gather and exchange ideas. The *Begum* Club was formally inaugurated on 15 December 1954, with just over sixty founding members and Shamsunnahar Mahmud as president and *Begum* editor Nurjahan Begum as secretary.[37] While in Dacca, Alseth also attended the first-ever cricket test match between India and Pakistan, held in the new Dacca Stadium on New Year's

Day 1955. She was moved by the warm welcome the Indian team received in Dacca, "with all the fans the Giants would get if they came to Sioux Falls or Huron to play."[38]

As part of a Ford Foundation–funded tour of six predominantly Muslim countries, the American Ruth Woodsmall returned to East Bengal three decades after her first visit. In Pakistan Woodsmall visited Karachi and Lahore in the western wing and Dacca and Chittagong in the eastern. Her new book, *Women and the New East* (1960), like the earlier one, identified purdah and polygamy as the most important concerns for women in Pakistan. Even Bayard Dodge, former president of the American University of Beirut, noted in his foreword, "It may not be an exaggeration to say the most fundamental movement of the twentieth century is the freeing of the women of Asia and Africa from *purdah* and the harem."[39]

Woodsmall was pleased to report that purdah was declining among educated elite Pakistanis, with the burqa almost unknown at Dacca University, and that seclusion was impractical for poor women who had no choice but to work outside the home. She also realized that Pakistani women's general unwillingness to be seen by male physicians had created a demand for female doctors that female students were eager to meet. "Ask any girl student in a school or college in Pakistan, 'What is your first choice of a profession?' and the answer is invariably 'Medicine.'"[40] With the exception of the obligatory focus on purdah, Woodsmall's chapter on Pakistan remains invaluable for its meticulous attention to the wide variety of social, economic, and political concerns occupying women in both wings of Pakistan. As a reviewer remarked at the time in a comparison with Woodsmall's earlier book, "The women considered here are still for the most part Moslem in faith and culture, but the word has been dropped from the title of this book, because it is no longer a determining factor in the status of women in these countries. In itself this is a revolution of which we in the West should be aware."[41]

East Pakistan also received visitors—and letters, newsletters, and invitations—from the New York–based Committee of Correspondence. Modeled on committees established in the decades before the American Revolution to build anti-British solidarity among the American colonies through the exchange of information, the mid-twentieth-century committee set out in May 1953 to counter communist ideas by direct personal correspondence with women around the world. With twenty active US members at its peak, many of whom had prior experience working or networking with such organizations as the Red Cross, the Woodrow Wilson Foundation, the YWCA,

FIGURE 16. "Students welcome a Gift from the US: Education for women gets high priority in Pakistan's plans. These Dacca University girls make good use of the reference library
assembled by the United State Information Service." Left to right are sisters Malka Perveen
Banu and Leila Arjumand Banu and their neighbor Sakina (surname not known, from
Bombay). Photo by Franc and Jean Shor, *National Geographic Magazine* 107, no. 3 (1955):
403, National Geographic Image Collection.

the Girl Scouts, and the League of Women Voters, the committee was exchanging letters with five thousand women in 140 countries by the mid-1960s.[42] Concerned more with the problems of women in other countries despite clear evidence of racial and socioeconomic injustice in their own, committee members assumed responsibility both for ensuring US presence at international women's conferences and for nurturing select women leaders in developing societies. By pulling these women leaders "from purdah to parliament," to use East Pakistani politician Shaista Ikramullah's expression, they hoped to divert them from the attractions of the Soviet model and to the side of the United States.[43]

Elizabeth Halsey, who visited Dacca on behalf of the committee in June 1955, met women leaders like Shamsunnahar Mahmud and visited the recently established Dacca Ladies' Club, which had received funding from the new San Francisco–based Asia Foundation to construct its first clubhouse. From her conversations Halsey quickly understood the emerging sense of bitterness among Bengalis regarding their relationship with West Pakistan. Just eight years after independence, they already felt that East Pakistan was like a "step-child," denied the "same consideration, [and] privileges" accorded the west. Halsey tried valiantly to initiate discussions about purdah, but found the Dacca women activists did not consider it an obstacle to the changes they sought in their new nation. Instead, Halsey discovered they were far more preoccupied with polygamy. Even the battle against polygamy—or, more accurately, polygyny—turned out to have international catalysts and connections.

ON THE WARPATH AGAINST POLYGAMY

The Pakistani envoy to Canada, Mohammad Ali Bogra, first met Aliya Saadi, his future second wife, in Ottawa in 1949. Bogra was from an aristocratic family in eastern Bengal, while Saadi's family had emigrated to western Canada in the early twentieth century from what is today Lebanon. He invited her to come work for him, and she joined him in Ottawa, then moved with him as his stenographer to Washington, DC, where he was appointed as Pakistan's ambassador to the United States, and then on to Karachi as his social secretary in 1953, when he was recalled to serve as Pakistan's prime minister. A Canadian news article described with excitement the opportunities this position had afforded the young woman from Edmonton, Alberta, to travel around the world and meet dignitaries. Saadi shared her observations of changes in Pakistan, describing how "women are taking an increased role in the affairs of thriving Pakistan. They have cast off the ancient veil to enter the professions."[44] Bogra quietly married Saadi in Beirut on 2 April 1955. A few days later the couple traveled back to Karachi, where, according to news reports, Saadi was given a room on the same floor as his first wife, Begum Hamida Ali, in the prime minister's residence. According to Begum Ali's private secretary, her employer was "considerably grieved" and ate dinner alone in her room.[45]

The wedding added fuel to the antipolygamy protests already under way. Activists in both wings of Pakistan had started mobilizing against Muslim men's legal right to polygamy the previous year upon learning of the second wives of two cabinet ministers and a popular cricketer. In late 1954 and early 1955, even US newspapers reported regularly on the formal agitation against the practice in Pakistan, with such headlines as "The Modern Mohammedan Wives of Pakistan Are on the Warpath against the Right of Men to Marry More Than One Wife."[46]

Pakistani women's groups like APWA—of which Begum Hamida Ali was a strong supporter—responded to Bogra's second marriage immediately and with fury, much as Indonesian organizations had just months earlier upon learning of President Sukarno's polygamous marriage. The renowned Egyptian feminist Doriya Shafiq, who had visited Karachi that January, sent a telegram pledging her support. In a second telegram she urged "feminist leaders" in East and West Pakistan not to vote for any man practicing polygamy.[47] APWA called for a comprehensive revision of marriage laws to restore to women the rights and status already bestowed on them by the Quran so that they might "play their part in the national life... shoulder to shoulder with their menfolk."[48] APWA announced a working committee to "deliberate on the growing evil of polygamy," followed by a conference in Karachi in February 1955.[49]

Significantly, despite growing East Pakistani resentment toward the policies of the West Pakistani–dominated central government, Bengali women activists worked with their West Pakistan counterparts to challenge Muslim men's license to take multiple wives. Calls to abolish men's right to polygamy appeared regularly in the pages of *Begum*. Some writers situated the practice in the early Islamic context of seventh-century Arabia, arguing that the Quranic verses did not provide an automatic license for today's men to take multiple wives. A 1954 essay listed the many negative consequences of polygamy "no longer unknown to any in at least the Muslim community," among them the destruction of happy marriages, a rising incidence of suicides, higher population growth, and greater economic costs. There was no support in the sharia, the article continued, for a man to leave his first wife *jibonmrito* (as dead although alive), for insulting and neglecting her, to take a second wife simply on a whim. There was, in the end, no scientific justification for keeping the practice alive in this day and age, and a thorough reform of marriage laws was needed. In a July 1955 article, contributor Ayesha Sardar demanded that the practice be "eradicated" and called on readers to pledge that they would rather die than marry a man who already had a wife.[50]

Among those who publicly defended the legal provision for polygyny was Princess Abida Sultan of the princely family of Bhopal. A good friend of the newly wed Bogra and Saadi, she had distinguished herself in her early years as an aviator and hunter and had recently served as Pakistan's ambassador to Brazil and as a member of Pakistan's delegation to the United Nations. In a statement to the Pakistani press, she argued that any bride who did not want her husband to have this right could simply stipulate it in the *nikah-nama* (marriage contract). To completely outlaw the provision, however, would create an entire class of "second rate sub-human beings," comprising unwed mothers and children with no legal standing because they were born out of wedlock. "Is this what our educated sisters would like to see established in Pakistan and call it Islam?" she asked and expressed her concerns regarding a "few educated women" choosing to "launch an agitation in the name of Islam, or to mislead their less fortunate sisters into believing that this modern rather Western interpretation is the correct interpretation of Islam."[51] Bogra defended his actions by similar reasoning, explaining that a "Moslem prefers polygamy to the Western custom of divorce, since it allows the first wife to maintain her status and dignity."[52]

The government responded by appointing a Commission on Marriage and Family Laws in August 1955 to examine whether "the existing laws governing marriage, divorce, maintenance and other ancillary matters among Muslims require modification in order to give women their proper place in society according to the fundamentals of Islam." The commission consisted of three women, among them Shamsunnahar Mahmud, and four men, one of whom represented the religious establishment. In its 1956 report the commission recommended that "changing realities and the influx of new and undreamed-of factors...require a modern approach, new rules of conduct and fresh legislation in almost all spheres of life and a radical remodelling of the legal and judicial system." Maulana Ihtisham-ul-Haq, the commission's religious scholar, issued a statement of dissent to the majority opinion, arguing that the report "undermine[d] the accepted tenets of Islam and the fundamentals of the Islamic Shariat." He strongly disagreed with the recommendations, which held out "false prospects of their rights in an attempt to push them again into the abyss of disgrace in which they had been rotting in the dark ages." Such disagreements led to the official report being shelved until March 1960, when the military government of Ayub Khan announced that it would finally act on the commission's recommendations, though with significant modifications and compromises. The Muslim Family Laws Ordinance, finally passed in 1961, remains a significant piece of legislation in both Pakistan and Bangladesh to this day.[53]

Following a change in government in late 1955, Bogra stepped down as prime minister and was reappointed ambassador to the United States. The commotion surrounding a 1954 visit by the king of Nepal had revealed that US authorities did not relish having to balance diplomatic relations against immigration laws that barred permanent entry to persons practicing polygamy. As a Canadian newspaper put it, "Uncle Sam's protocol experts in Washington are struggling with a new kind of problem for them—the eternal triangle.... Experts said diplomatic immunity would protect Ali [Bogra] from prosecution under US law but they were undecided whether to recognize wife no. 1, wife no. 2, or both."[54]

That Bogra was a good friend of the Americans made the situation all the more awkward. A 1962 *New York Times* profile described him as "one of Washington's best-liked diplomats." Dismissive of "old-fashioned diplomacy," he had advocated for "American-style frankness and outspokenness." His fondness for American style, according to associates, shone through in "his predilection for loud ties and his hobby of collecting electrical gadgets" and to his public championing of "American ways." He had even tried to switch traffic on Pakistani roads from the left side (as was the norm in former British colonies, plus a few other countries) to the right (as in the rest of the world, including the United States). More consequentially, as ambassador to Washington and as prime minister, he had worked hard to firmly align Pakistan with the United States in the Cold War.[55]

FIGHTING COMMUNISM THROUGH EDUCATION

The May 1954 Mutual Defense Assistance Agreement assured Pakistan of US military aid in exchange for acting as a buffer between the Soviet Union and the Middle East. This military assistance was accompanied by generous US funds to be used to win over ordinary Pakistani citizens. While most of this civilian aid was retained by the western wing, some found its way to East Pakistan, as did some Americans to help implement these US-funded projects. US women, for example, participated in efforts by the Ford Foundation and Oklahoma State University to establish professional institutions of modern home economics in East Pakistan against the backdrop of East Bengali women's activism for legal reform and in the Bengali nationalist movement.

Eleanor Roosevelt laid the cornerstone for the first home economics college in Karachi during her 1952 visit. She had been the main supporter of the first school of home economics in the United States, established as part of Cornell University in 1919.[56] While the discipline had emerged in the United States in the late nineteenth century as an organized effort to provide women with opportunities for further education and employment outside the home, US feminists of the 1960s and 1970s attacked home economics for reinforcing the idea that women's place was in the home.[57] During the 1950s, however, when Americans were helping to establish the Pakistani colleges, increasing economic prosperity as well as the escalating Cold War were establishing the ideal, if rarely the reality, of the male breadwinner and female homemaker, in a sense, updating the Victorian ideal. Professional home economists in the United States, for their part, continued to hold out hope that women armed with home economics degrees would also seek paid employment outside the home before marriage and "when her children are grown."[58]

Maude Pye Hood, head of the Department of Food and Nutrition at the University of Georgia, first visited Pakistan in 1954 as home economics adviser to the Ford Foundation. In Karachi Hood helped to establish the country's first college of home economics, quickly followed by one in Lahore, and a third in Dacca in 1961. Hood later described these colleges as "monuments to the progress of higher education for women." According to a contemporary US newspaper account of Hood's efforts, the US advisers on the project insisted that their objective was to help Pakistani leaders to develop "educational institutions suited to their own culture rather than transplanting the pattern of an American institution to their country."[59]

Mary Keegan and Frances Larkin both took leave from Long Beach State College in California to join Oklahoma State University's program in Dacca, arriving in late August 1961. As Keegan informed the local Long Beach newspaper, they had known little about East Pakistan, but just after they accepted the assignment, they came across a television program that "showed Dacca [as] a combination of modern and ancient buildings, unattended cows meandering down the main street, sari-clad women, the market place." The young women seemed unperturbed about the details supplied by the US consul in Dacca about his gardener recently having killed six snakes in the garden and said they looked forward to using their US knowledge to address local problems. "This is in keeping with our government's belief that we must fight communism through education; we must teach undeveloped countries how to use their resources." Both women had also absorbed the advice of a colleague already in Dacca, Doris Hanson, who wrote that they should not equate "illiteracy with inferiority. The Bengali mind is said to be one of the world's finest. No foreign visitor bearing an innate feeling of Western superiority goes undetected, no matter what kind of lip service is given to equality."[60]

By the late 1960s around seventy East and West Pakistanis had traveled in the opposite direction, for further training in home economics education in the United States. In August 1960 the *Arizona Daily Star* reported on the visit of five "Middle Easterners" to the School of Home Economics at the University of Arizona. The article, "Moslem Women Report: Harems Out of Fashion in Modern Pakistan," discussed the Pakistani visitors' views of marriage and women's roles in their home country and in the United States and the women's struggles to convince the "average American" that harems were quite uncommon. The "five women wearing rich green and yellow silken saris chuckled at American misconceptions of Middle East family relations." One of the married women in the group reported, "Americans tell me that if a woman here were to leave her husband for two years of study in another country, he would get a divorce." She discovered, however, that the Americans quickly explained away the greater openness of the Pakistani men by invoking polygamy: "Then they say," she continued, "But your husband has another wife or two to look after him while you're away." Zeenath Rahim of Karachi pointed out that "economy and psychology make it impossible" for men to meet the Islamic requirement that a man with more than one wife treat them equally, in terms of attention and finances, and therefore there were actually few polygamous households in Pakistan today.[61] Also in the group was Sultana Panni of Dacca, who was introduced to readers as the daughter-in-law of a Pakistani "maharajah." Speaking to a Lions Club meeting in Mexia, Texas, Panni praised the educational system in the United States as "very good, very practical." When asked about the rush to establish so many schools of higher education in the context of 80 percent illiteracy, she explained that the very purpose of these new institutions was to train teachers for the primary level. On the "social activities" of US college students, she stated quite firmly, "We don't approve of it because it hinders their studies."[62]

Young Pakistani women who had been selected for jobs as "stewardesses" on the newly launched Pakistan International Airlines also traveled to the United States for training. Pan Am's flight attendant college boasted a course on "image improvement" that was credited with helping a "girl who had ridden elephants, hobnobbed with maharajas and speaks fluent Hindu [sic]." One US trainer saw herself as "unveil[ing] the modern world of jet travel for a young and growing Eastern nation" by helping women who "only a generation ago ... were not permitted to appear in public without a veil or to work outside their homes."[63]

Pakistani women who traveled to the United States outside the bounds of carefully curated visits reported unpleasant surprises, usually in "those long blue aerogram letters" through which they maintained contact with families back home during their long absences. Shireen Huq, a prominent feminist activist in Bangladesh today, recalled how her aunt, the noted psychologist Mahmuda Khanum, went without food for two days when she first arrived in North Carolina in 1963. Khanum, who had left her six young children in the care of her mother and husband back in East Pakistan to take up a Fulbright fellowship at Duke University, arrived to find that the university cafeteria was closed for the weekend. A Duke retrospective on that period would simply say that she didn't eat because "she was too afraid to go out," but Khanum told her family that local restaurants refused to serve her—because she was a "colored" person. A few months later Khanum's concerns about where to spend winter break prompted the university to set up its first International Office (later renamed, more appropriately, International House) and arrange orientation and host families for future international students.[64]

STUDENT POLITICS AND PROTESTS

Younger Pakistanis studying in the United States in the 1950s and 1960s, while generally appreciative of US social life, spoke more openly about the relationship between the two countries than the older, often midcareer, Pakistani visitors. A 1957 survey found that many students saw the two countries engaged in a partnership to save "the world from atheistic communism," although a few expressed discomfort with what appeared to be an unbalanced relationship "between a charity-giver and a charity-taker." Others directly criticized US domination of Pakistani politics, especially foreign policy, and the Americans' "passive" role in the Kashmir situation. Pakistan, they felt, had "become a puppet" and was important to the United States simply as a "military base and a colony." While the Pakistani students surveyed appreciated the wealth, prosperity, and technological advancements of the United States, several recognized the racial and economic inequalities that marked the country, noting that "lynching is still practiced," "people believe in democracy, but draw the line at the colored people," and "the poor are oppressed by the rich business and industrial magnates." Over a quarter of the students reported they had experienced discrimination when seeking housing. Many also criticized Americans' materialism, openness with the opposite sex, lack of respect for their elders, and ignorance of other countries. Students were particularly dismayed at Americans' ideas about Pakistan: many Americans believed it to be "part of Arabia, India and even South America," where "people are dying of hunger...live in jungles and tents, have four wives...ride elephants...[and] wear grass skirts."[65]

Some 91 percent of students, male and female, had visited US homes and were impressed not only by the modern amenities and conveniences but also by the absence of servants and US men's contributions to household work. They were pleased to find that Americans were not entirely as Hollywood— or the recent widely circulated Kinsey studies on human sexual behavior—had led them to expect. All the women students interviewed in the 1957 survey expressed a great deal of admiration for gender equality in the United States and US women's hard work within their homes as well as in communities.[66]

In East Pakistan throughout this period, young, urban, middle-class women were being increasingly drawn into and preoccupied with the Bengali nationalist struggle against the cultural, political, and economic policies of the West Pakistani–dominated central government. Bengali had enjoyed state-language status alongside Urdu since 1952, but the West Pakistani hostility to the Bengali language and culture had persisted. Like students around the world in that turbulent era, young Bengali college and university students threw themselves into a fight to retain traditional aspects of Bengali identity even as they experimented with exciting new forms of art, sculpture, dance, and music.

In 1961 several local organizations came together to celebrate the birth

FIGURE 17. Chhayanaut's Tagore celebration. Among those on stage are Shakera Khan *(second from left)*, Sanjida Khatun *(on the harmonium)*, and Iqbal Ahmed *(third from right)*. Courtesy of Shakera Ahmed.

centenary of Bengali Nobel Laureate Rabindranath Tagore. In April that year Selina Bahar Zaman, who had performed in front of Eleanor Roosevelt in 1952, had just enrolled in a second master's program, this one in applied math, when she was cast in Tagore's dance-drama *Chandalika*. She was nervous because she had never received any formal training in dance but thrilled to be part of the celebrations. After all, she recalled, it was the first time Tagore's birthday was being celebrated in Dacca, and, even more exciting, Dacca had started its centenary events before Calcutta. Over several months Tagore's plays were performed, his songs sung, and his poetry recited in front of enthusiastic audiences. Not everyone, however, was supportive of these celebrations even in East Pakistan, and an acrimonious public debate ensued in the local newspapers, reflecting conflicting interpretations of Tagore's attitude toward Muslims and his ancestral relationship to East Bengal. In 1965 the central government used its war with India over Kashmir to ban the broadcast of Indian films and music and included Tagore in its definition of who and what counted as Indian. Finally, in 1967 the government issued a ban specifically targeting Tagore in East Pakistan. Young, urban women responded by wearing a *tip* (decorative dot on the forehead) and flowers in their hair and participating in public musical performances, often alongside young men—practices the West Pakistani authorities considered un-Islamic. Older women activists like poet Sufia Kamal and singer Sanjida Khatun were among those who created the space for these events through the cultural institutions they had recently founded, such as Chhayanaut Music School and, starting in April 1967, the Chhayanaut-sponsored open-air celebration of the Bengali new year in Ramna Park that endures today as a symbol of secular Bengali identity.[67]

RURAL ENCOUNTERS

While urban, educated Pakistani women interacted with Americans through their visits to each other's countries, schools, and voluntary organizations, women of the overwhelmingly rural majority in both wings of Pakistan encountered US power and friendship in their own villages in the form of development programs. In 1960 the Pakistan Academy for Rural Development in Comilla, East Pakistan, took what its director, Akhtar Hameed Khan, recognized at the time as a "truly revolutionary step" in launching a pilot program for and with women.[68] While the academy's work built on an earlier government project called Village Agricultural and Industrial Development (V-AID) that Khan had been involved with in the 1950s and that had also targeted women (though ineffectually), Khan's claim was not hyperbolic.[69] After all, the UN declaration announcing the First Development Decade (1961–70) had no specific reference to women. Indeed, there would be little formal academic or policy interest in women in development until the 1970 publication of *Women's Role in Economic Development* by the Danish economist Ester Boserup.[70]

Khan later recalled that he was pushed to start the program by the "seclusion and subordination" of the village women, who "for generations...have remained contented slaves." Moreover, "their exclusion from economic activity outside the home has overburdened the male breadwinners," while their "ignorance, weakness and helplessness" have directly affected the "character of their children." He denounced the "orthodox Islamists," who, by maintaining the "segregation of women," ensured the "backwardness of the Muslim community" even as "they proudly point out that our culture is superior to western culture because, unlike western women, our women are properly restrained and controlled." The academy, therefore, had deemed the "emancipation of village women" as "essential."[71]

US involvement in the Comilla Academy came in the form of generous funding and technical assistance and also Peace Corps volunteers. Sargent Shriver, President John F. Kennedy's brother-in-law and the founding director of the Peace Corps, visited the Comilla Academy in May 1961 on his world tour to launch the Peace Corps. He received a warm welcome and an enthusiastic request for volunteers from Khan.[72] Just a few months later, East Pakistan and the Comilla Academy received some of the first Peace Corps volunteers to venture out into the world.

In March 1963 US secretary of state Dean Rusk informed US missions in countries with volunteers that the Peace Corps was "not an instrument of foreign policy because," paradoxically, "to make it so would rob it of its contribution to foreign policy." Rather, the corps was an "opportunity for the nations of the world to learn what America is all about."[73] However, the notion that US women would also play a role in shaping the new image of the United States overseas was not without its US detractors, many of whom were concerned that female volunteers would present "romantic temptations," leading projects to fail. Nor, indeed, were all men deemed suitable for the enterprise. Vice President Lyndon B. Johnson had advised Shriver, when selecting new volunteers, to adopt the highly suspect and discriminatory methods Johnson himself had used with the Texas Youth Conservation Corps: "Keep out the three Cs... the communists, the consumptives, and the cocksuckers."[74]

The ideal volunteers would reflect the best of US "New Frontier" values—masculine, athletic, academic, and austere, with a pioneering and adventurous spirit—that distinguished them from both the stereotypical "ugly Americans" overseas, highlighted in Eugene Burdick and William Lederer's recent best-selling novel, and the British colonial administrators of old.[75] Americans, after all, were competing against dedicated men and women of their Cold War rivals. As the then senator John Kennedy had warned an audience of twenty thousand in San Francisco just days before the presidential election in November 1960, "Out of Moscow and Peiping [Beijing] and Czechoslovakia and Eastern Germany are hundreds of men and women, scientists, physicists, teachers, engineers, doctors, nurses, studying in those institutes, prepared to spend their lives abroad in the service of world communism."[76]

As it turned out, the new agency complemented all too well other endeavors under way in the early 1960s to project US power and progress. Modernization theory factored into its design and practices, most visibly in the corps' notion of community development to help reform what were seen as traditional societies. The youthful, energetic corps volunteers were quickly recognized as an effective weapon in the struggle against communist rivals for the hearts and minds of the poor. Modernization theorists advising the administration were confident that by meeting the dire need for technical expertise in so-called underdeveloped nations, the volunteers would in fact help accelerate the catching-up process. In addition, volunteers could help these poorer developing societies overcome their alleged cultures of fatalism and—as a team headed by Maurice Albertson, Colorado State University engineer and adviser to Shriver and Kennedy on the Peace Corps, put it—model instead the US tradition of being "self-starters" and such skills as "organizational ability" and "successful 'institution-building.'"[77]

While the new agency and President Kennedy were overwhelmed by thousands of letters of support and enthusiastic volunteers, the vast majority did not have the technical training the early US planners or the host countries had envisioned. Rather, most volunteers—70 percent of those accepted for Peace Corps training by 1965—were "B. A. generalists" or liberal arts graduates. The agency then shifted its programming to focus on teaching English, leadership skills, and community development, and Kennedy called on volunteers to assist the developing nations by lending them "a hand in building a society, and a glimpse of the best that is in our country." The very presence of these young, energetic Americans in these countries was expected to spur change.[78]

Thus it was that Florence "Kiki" McCarthy arrived in Comilla in October 1961 with a history degree from the University of California, Berkeley. She was part of a group of fifty-six volunteers sent to Pakistan, the first Peace Corps volunteers anywhere in Asia. Twenty-nine went to East Pakistan (twenty-four men and five women).[79] McCarthy was given the task of helping village women, in her own words, "to learn techniques and acquire knowledge which would enable them to become more effective in the areas of their responsibilities; i.e. their homes and families." This included "child care, home sanitation, kitchen gardening, poultry raising, sewing, literacy, the cooperative movement, handicrafts and so on."[80] She later recalled that, being twenty-one, unmarried, and fresh out of college, there were topics that she simply didn't know enough about to share with the women, even with her fairly proficient Bengali. Such limitations, however, didn't stop village

FIGURE 18. Peace Corps volunteer Florence McCarthy in a village woman's home, as women share what they have learned from their weekly training at the Comilla Academy. Photo by Charles Harbutt. Charles Harbutt Estate/Joan Liftin.

women from invoking her when arguing a point with other villagers—"Kiki Memsahib said so."[81] After completing her two years of service, McCarthy enrolled at Michigan State University for a master's in sociology that would bring her back to Comilla in 1966 for fieldwork; she would continue to write about Bangladesh well into the 1990s.

In the early years of the Pakistan Academy for Rural Development, US women were eagerly sought out for service. In a June 1964 interview for the *East Pakistan Peace Corps Newsletter* with volunteer Alberta Rosiak, then using her bachelor's in education to teach science and math at a Comilla school, Director Khan explained why he thought it was a "most splendid idea" that the Peace Corps send women to East Pakistan: "The people of East Pakistan like American girls. We need to emancipate our women. A certain amount of emancipation is taking place. Having brave American girls here is a great help.... Take a village girl the first time out and she sees Alberta Rosiak living in Faizunnessa [a village] with all the hardships so far away from her parents; and she will think you are brave. How would she think of this? Here is a girl not afraid of anything. I think they should send more women to East Pakistan."[82]

Whether intentionally or not, even the healthy bodies of the US women held lessons for the village women. In interviews with academy researchers, a woman named Rongomala described how "Miss McCarthy" had told them that people in her country "don't have boils and eczema" and "aren't so thin and sickly." Rongomala explained that, according to McCarthy, the reason for all the problems in East Pakistan was that "your country has so many people. You have so many children." When McCarthy came to their village, Rongomala continued, even "the men would say: 'Here comes the lady from Japan [sic]. The population of that country is small. The people are healthy. They don't eat much rice.'"[83]

Bengali women on the staff of the Comilla Academy, such as Ashrafunnessa Khatun and Tahrunnessa Ahmed (later, Abdullah), helped to orient and then worked with the US volunteers who rotated in and out. Ahmed, who had served as the associate instructor for the women's program, took charge of the Women's Section in July 1963 after McCarthy's term ended. Following a master's in social welfare from Dacca, Ahmed had attended the American University of Beirut with funding from the US International Cooperation Administration (which later became the US Agency for International Development) and obtained a diploma in public health. A Ford Foundation grant later sent her to Michigan State for a master's in agriculture and extension education. Ahmed would remain with the academy for nine years, until after the 1971 war of independence and the birth of Bangladesh.[84]

In November 1966, as part of her work at the academy, Ahmed published a pioneering study of village women in Bengali, *Palli Anganader Jemon Dekhechhi,* which was later translated into English by the future feminist leader Shireen Huq and published as *Village Women as I Saw Them.* Both Abdullah's book and Florence McCarthy's 1967 master's thesis at Michigan State University, "Bengali Village Women: Mediators between Tradition and Development," have proven to be precious resources for information and debates around women in rural development in East Pakistan in the 1960s.

Both based on fieldwork in Comilla, the studies differ most visibly in their discussions of purdah. Abdullah observed that rather than regard the burqa as an obstacle, rural women saw it as enabling them to move around more freely. Moreover, because purdah retained its power as a symbol of social rank and status, these same women expected their daughters to maintain purdah. Thus it made little sense for rural development programs to focus their energies on persuading poor women to discard the burqa. A more productive strategy would be to change attitudes toward purdah among the better-off in rural society and thus help diminish the value of purdah as a status symbol.[85]

McCarthy, by contrast, identified purdah as the primary obstacle to women's advancement, alongside a "rapidly exploding population." The strict practice of purdah, she wrote, affected all aspects of women's lives, "as they are less educated, less able to go out and experience the outside world or contribute to the family income, or have the positions and rights in regard to inheritance and property that women have in most other cultures." Interestingly, although she invoked the categories of modern and traditional throughout her thesis in discussing how the women in the program mediated between the two, she clearly recognized that the women did *not* hold up Western women such as herself as the ideal. Rather, she concluded from her conversations with the village women, the changes the women sought were to approximate the ideal Muslim woman—greater mobility, access to education, work opportunities, but all within the bounds of modest dress and behavior.[86] In this McCarthy's approach and conclusions, like Ruth Woodsmall's analysis in her 1960 book, departed quite significantly from those of the British colonial administrators and missionaries.

McCarthy's conclusions, while different from Abdullah's, echoed discussions that had been occurring in the weekly *Begum* by educated and mostly urban women. The frequent and heated discussions of purdah, specifically the strict form practiced by middle- and upper-class Muslim women, usually concluded with the assertion that the practice needs to be modified but not discarded.[87] The concerns expressed in *Begum* had less to do with actual dress than with mobility and access to educational and employment opportunities. There were also regular pleas to ameliorate the plight of oppressed village women; for instance, a November 1959 letter reminded the "educated sisters" of their responsibilities vis-à-vis the less fortunate rural women.[88] These different discussions, in short, made clear that even within

East Pakistan, Muslim women's views on the subject tended to reflect their class background.

US observers of the Comilla Academy were happy to congratulate themselves on the changes wrought by the women's programs. A 1970 report described purdah as "slowly yielding to the impact of the women's education and family planning programs" and noted that the "shy, burqa-shrouded, non-communicative village woman of yesterday" was giving way to the "serious and articulate woman of tomorrow."[89] From the perspective of Pakistani and US senior development officials who believed that the primary concerns of rural women in the region were greater mobility, self-confidence, and smaller families, the academy's programs had clearly proven successful.

FEMINISM AT THE HEART OF ONE SUPERPOWER

Even as US policymakers and volunteers were working to improve the United States' image abroad by promoting the education and modernization of women in decolonizing countries in line with US ideals of femininity, patriarchy at home was under attack. In 1963, the year that McCarthy finished her Peace Corps tour in Comilla and returned to the United States, Betty Friedan published *The Feminine Mystique* and the President's Commission on the Status of Women released its *American Women* report. In the 1950s US women had attended college in the context of societal expectations that, while they might work for a few years after graduating, the ultimate goal was to marry and then redirect their time and energies to taking care of their families. To give just one example, Wilbur Kitchener Jordan, president of all-female Radcliffe College from 1943 to 1960, had made a point of informing new students "that their education would prepare them to be splendid wives and mothers, and their reward might be to marry Harvard men."[90] (This attitude, you might recall, was akin to that of the Pakistani civil servant whose brother-in-law Amy Stock met in Dacca right around this time and who had given his wife two years to receive her degree and emerge as the educated wife he needed for a successful career.) In the postwar United States, powerful economic and political forces sought to restore the best-paid jobs to men returning from war by pushing women back into the home, from which they could demonstrate their superiority as US women by purchasing consumer luxuries denied to war-devastated Europe and the Soviet Union. After years of the Great Depression and war, US men and women were, of course, eager to enjoy this postwar peace and prosperity. Nonetheless, large numbers of US women of diverse racial backgrounds and classes remained active outside the home, in paid employment and in a variety of grassroots social movements.

The French philosopher Simone de Beauvoir's *The Second Sex,* published in the United States in 1953, struck a chord among many women. She put in words what they had been feeling: that they were defined, viewed, and assessed always in relation to men and never the other way around. The nation's growing preoccupation with the Cold War, however, meant that the book did not immediately galvanize renewed feminist activism. Even in 1960 Betty Friedan could publish an article in *Good Housekeeping* with the provocative title "Women Are People Too."[91] The situation would begin to change as younger women and activists from labor and civil rights movements entered the discussion. Friedan's 1963 best-selling book captured the "strange stirring" and "sense of dissatisfaction" with their limited opportunities that many mostly White, middle-class, college-educated US women had been experiencing for some time. Friedan articulated the question that she believed they were afraid to even ask themselves: "Is this all?" She reassured them that they were not alone and not wrong to feel as they did.[92]

The President's Commission on the Status of Women, established by President Kennedy in 1961 on the recommendation of Esther Peterson, assistant secretary of labor and director of the Women's Bureau, and chaired by Eleanor Roosevelt until her death in 1962, was tasked with making recommendations for "overcoming discriminations in...employment on the basis of sex" and for "services which will enable women to continue their role as wives and mothers while making a maximum contribution to the world around them." The report, released on 11 October 1963, on what would have been Roosevelt's seventy-ninth birthday, described itself as an "invitation to action" and made several recommendations that, with some tension, sought to address both women's role as homemakers and their growing presence in the paid labor force.[93]

Younger US women of that era were inspired and mobilized by the example of influential Black civil rights leaders such as Ella Baker, who helped to found the SNCC (Student Nonviolent Coordinating Committee); Jo Ann Gibson Robinson, a college professor who helped to organize the bus boycott following Rosa Parks's famous refusal; and SNCC activist Ruby Doris Smith Robinson. In November 1964 four White women activists in SNCC coauthored a memo criticizing gender discrimination within the organization. Two of them had had formative experiences while working abroad.

Elaine DeLott had been impressed by the greater gender equality and openness to sexuality she observed on an Israeli kibbutz she worked in between high school and college, though she had returned to the US disillusioned with the Zionist project. Emmie Schrader had learned Swahili and spent a year in Kenya as African independence struggles unfolded around her and traveled to Khartoum and the newly independent Algeria. Upon her return to the United States, she later recalled, she "saw nothing in America for me except joining the struggle against racism." The "Waveland Memo," written by DeLott, Schrader, Casey Hayden, and Mary King, drew a powerful analogy between sex discrimination and race discrimination. The authors hoped to provoke discussion such that, in the future, "the whole of the women in this movement will become so alert as to force the rest of the movement to stop the discrimination and start the slow process of changing values and ideas so that all of us gradually come to understand that this is no more a man's world than it is a white world."[94] This powerful feminist manifesto and subsequent restatements have been credited with catalyzing the feminist activism of the 1960s and 1970s.

Also in the fall of 1964, the journal *Daedalus* published a special issue devoted to "The Woman in America." In her contribution Esther Peterson of the President's Commission on the Status of Women redirected attention from "the suburban housewife, the college-trained woman and the professional" to the concerns of the United States' "25 million working women." These included limited job opportunities, lower pay than men for comparable work, and the lack of child care—problems that persist today, over a half century later.[95] Another article, by sociologist Alice S. Rossi, reveals how many US feminist writers of that era were not immune to the charms of modernization theory that informed the many projects targeting women overseas. In "Equality between the Sexes: An Immodest Proposal," Rossi lamented a lack of momentum in the US feminist movement since women won suffrage in 1920. She pointed to the failure to pass the Equal Rights Amendment, the declining enrollment of women in college, and the modest aspirations of those women who did attend college. She saw her article as a clarion call for a revival of feminist demands, the "claim to sex equality." She drew on recent social science research to argue that "traditional conceptions of masculine and feminine are inappropriate to the kind of world we can live in in the second half of the twentieth century." She felt justified in expecting equality between the sexes, given "the level our industrial society has now reached."[96] In short, the notion of change and progress in societies allowed Rossi and others to challenge the situation of women in the United States, much as the idea of the harem and seraglio had provided grist for Wollstonecraft nearly two centuries earlier. In 1966 Rossi, Friedan, legal scholar Pauli Murray, historian Carl Degler (who had also contributed to the *Daedalus* special issue), and others cofounded the National Organization for Women, which they hoped would represent the interests of women in the way the National Association for the Advancement of Colored People (NAACP) did for Black Americans.

WOMEN'S RIGHTS AND THE *OTHER* SUPERPOWER

Like the United States, the Soviet Union was also engaged in the battle for the hearts and minds of the world, including its women, and the space race between the two countries intersected with this battle. Valentina Tereshkova's seventy-one hours in space and forty-eight orbits around the earth in 1963 fired the imagination of women and men around the world, proving an additional source of consternation for a US government already working hard to woo the world away from the attractions of the Soviet model.

As an icon of women's empowerment, Tereshkova's feat would be hard to match, let alone surpass. Just a few years earlier, in July 1959, then US vice president Richard Nixon had extolled the virtues of the US kitchen to Soviet premier Nikita Khrushchev at the American National Exhibition in Moscow and argued for the superiority of the consumer choices available under the US system. A few months after Tereshkova's flight, Khrushchev declared with much satisfaction: "Remember the time when our country was economically backward, how many capitalist figures of the west scoffed at us.... And suddenly those who were considered clodhoppers, about whom it was said that they slurped up cabbage soup with their shoes, so developed the economy and science that they reached space before those who called themselves civilized!"[97]

The space flight had been strategically timed to precede, by a matter of days, the Fifth World Congress of Women meeting in Moscow in June 1963, organized by the Women's International Democratic Federation. Founded in Paris just after World War II but later based in East Berlin, the federation was a left-leaning international organization committed to fighting fascism and working for peace and women's rights. Organizers expected nearly two thousand representatives from 119 countries, including the United States. Fresh from the elaborate celebrations in Red Square of their safe return from their respective flights—a tradition established with Yuri Gagarin's first crewed space flight in 1961—Tereshkova and male cosmonaut Valery Bykovsky assumed positions in the congress leadership. In *Pravda* Soviet writer Anna Karavaeva spoke of the impact Tereshkova was expected to have on the foreign guests: "Upon seeing her, our lovely heroine, women of the already liberated countries—and of countries that are just preparing for liberation—will be enriched by the feeling of hope and moral uplift: these are the great wings that can grow in a woman's heart, this is what she can do when she is free and proud." Khrushchev's message to the congress reminded the delegates that "Soviet women have all the opportunities to fully participate in [the] political, cultural, and social life of the nation." Tereshkova was presented as a prime example of the Soviet commitment to gender equality. Delegates from around the world invoked the world's first woman cosmonaut in their own speeches.[98]

Tereshkova soon received invitations from more than thirty countries. In October 1963 she visited the United Nations in New York with Yuri Gagarin, en route from Cuba and Mexico to East Germany. The *New York Times,* which felt compelled to note "her high heels and upswept coiffure" and "her gray-green suit…decorated with two medals," stated that the cosmonauts received a "standing ovation" and "charmed" the press.[99] Although she never traveled to space again (nor did any other Soviet woman until 1982), Tereshkova continued to loom large in Soviet discussions of gender equality and to make public appearances at large international gatherings. One such event was the 1967 International Women's Day celebration in Moscow, at which the foreign delegates included Begum Sufia Kamal, the renowned poet and feminist from East Pakistan.

The year 1967 marked the fiftieth anniversary not only of the Russian Revolution but also of women's protests in Petrograd (formerly Saint Petersburg) over growing unemployment and the astronomically high cost of essentials that had precipitated the revolution and the fall of the tsar. The German communist leader Clara Zetkin had persuaded Lenin to declare 8 March a communist holiday in 1922, though it didn't become a nonworking holiday until 1965.[100] It was also in 1965 that relations between Pakistan and the Soviet Union, tense at best for most of Pakistan's existence, had taken a new turn. Upset by Pakistan's overtures toward China, US president Johnson had canceled his invitation to Pakistan's president, Ayub Khan. The Soviets quickly invited Ayub Khan to visit Moscow, and the new relationship was sealed with an agreement on new cultural and economic cooperation. The following January the Soviet Union brokered a meeting between President Ayub Khan and Indian prime minister Lal Bahadur Shastri in Tashkent, at which the two countries agreed to pursue normalization.[101] Upon receiving an invitation from the Soviets to send delegates to the 1967 International Women's Day celebrations in Moscow, the Pakistan government selected Begum Sufia Kamal from East Pakistan and Begum Zubeida Habib Rahimtoola, a founding member of APWA, from West Pakistan.

Begum Sufia Kamal recalled how, as the Pakistan International Airlines plane rose into the air, she was filled with excitement about visiting this "distant land of dreams, of fairytale kingdoms." At the same time she was anxious about the responsibility thrust on her to represent the women of East Pakistan, and she sent up a silent prayer to God that she might preserve the honor of Bengali women, "who are not timid, who are not afraid, who go into battle with courage and resolve, who go about at home and abroad with their heads held high." Just uttering the prayer had a calming effect, and she began to look forward to her time in a new land. She recalled the Russian fairy tales she had read as a child, stories about Saint Petersburg ("not Leningrad"), snow-covered Siberia, the land of Gorky, Tolstoy, Pushkin, Chekov, Gogol, so many writers, scientists, and, of course, the cosmonaut Tereshkova.[102]

Upon arriving in Moscow Begum Sufia was rushed directly to the Kremlin Palace of Congresses, where the International Women's Day celebrations had been under way since 3 March. Nina Popova, chair of the Soviet Women's Committee, welcomed her warmly and introduced her to other attendees as a beloved poet and important social activist from East Pakistan. Throughout her time in Moscow, Sufia Kamal was constantly struck by the Soviets' near-religious reverence for their cultural and nationalist leaders, famous and ordinary, and lamented how, by contrast, "we have neglected Rabindranath, Iqbal, Nazrul, and Begum Rokeya."[103]

For Begum Sufia this was a land where "everyone was equal." She admired the Soviets' dedication to hard work, which had raised them to such great heights in knowledge, science, and culture. Surely, she thought, God would reward them for this. The warm hospitality of the Soviets brought to mind the grand arrangements she had seen among the aristocracy of her childhood, but the difference here, she pointed out, was that the work was being done not by servants and laborers but by beautiful, well-dressed, educated women. She silently prayed that "we, our country, may become like this."[104]

At the main women's day event in the Friendship House on 8 March 1967,

Begum Sufia was excited to be in the presence of women from eighty-five countries. She developed goosebumps upon seeing the flag of the newly independent Algeria. She exclaimed "Djamila!" as she embraced the Algerian delegates and recalled Halidé Edib and Ataturk when she met the representatives of Turkey. Begum Sufia listened with rapt attention as women from different lands shared their experiences over the next few days. The Vietnamese delegates, for example, described their struggles and sacrifices in their fight for their homeland. Some foreign guests wore national dress; others did not. Some spoke in English, others in their own language. She wondered about the limited nature in which her own country had been able to implement the message of Islam, of unity, friendship, and equality. In the midst of these speeches, the unannounced appearance of Valentina Tereshkova was met with awed silence. When the cosmonaut stepped off the stage after speaking about her experience in space, Begum Sufia was compelled to follow her outside and embrace her warmly. She gave Tereshkova a small present she had in her bag, offered her greetings from the women and girls of her homeland, and invited her to visit East Pakistan.[105]

Begum Sufia gave her own speech in Bengali. Over the past fifty years, she noted, awakened and mobilized Soviet women had struggled and contributed to the current exalted status enjoyed by their great country. Although her countrywomen had been liberated for only twenty years at that point, she pointed out that they too were keeping up, studying, taking up a variety of occupations. The women of her country had struggled alongside men in times of shortage and famine, for independence, and for their language, and they would continue to improve themselves and their society. She later recalled how simply uttering the name of Begum Rokeya Hossain had given her inner strength as she spoke and how describing the accomplishments of contemporary women had filled her with pride.[106]

The Soviet consulate in Dacca held a reception in Begum Sufia Kamal's honor shortly after her return. In a speech there she described her joy at seeing with her own eyes the Soviet achievements she had previously only heard about. She spoke of her special delight in witnessing the "unprecedented power and influence Soviet women enjoyed, in seeing them responsible for the smooth functioning of mills, factories, workshops, trade unions, cooperative workplaces. As a mother, I felt proud of these accomplishments by women." She attributed the great successes of the Soviet Union—"its place on the highest rung of civilization"—largely to its women, who were today "completely independent" and who worked alongside men in all spheres of life, including politics and government. She proposed that by following in the paths of Soviet women and their ideals, the women of *anunnoto* (undeveloped, backward) countries such as her own could one day also attain a position of pride in the world.[107]

Begum Sufia spoke also of how impressed she was by the elevated status enjoyed by poets and writers in that land of near universal literacy. Indeed, unlike in many Western countries, she continued, where even successful writers often remain poor, Soviet writers seemed financially secure. She remarked too on the responsibility taken by the Soviet state, not only for producing machinery but also for producing human beings and reproducing society. While most women in her own country worried every morning about how to feed their children, citizen cooperatives in Soviet cities were in charge of feeding, educating, and providing exercise and recreation for thousands of children.[108] In these public speeches and even in her memoir, Begum Sufia did not comment on the absence of dissent from the official narrative of the Soviet authorities, though she must have been aware that her visit to the Soviet Union was as curated as those of her contemporaries who traveled to the United States on official visits.

TOWARD A GLOBAL CONVENTION IN SUPPORT OF WOMEN

At the United Nations delegates continued to discuss ways to pressure national governments to address women's issues. In November 1963 twenty-two countries of Eastern Europe and the developing world had sponsored a resolution at the UN General Assembly, calling for a declaration on eliminating discrimination against women. Remarkably, no major Western nation was among the countries that forwarded this resolution, which, by 1980, would evolve into the Convention on the Elimination of All Forms of Discrimination against Women—perhaps initially they saw no need for international oversight on women's issues in their own societies. Also significant is that six of the twenty-two countries were Muslim-majority, including Indonesia and Pakistan, the two largest Muslim countries in the world.[109]

A 1967 news article titled "Women Need Equal Rights in 'Advanced' Nations, Too" captured the dawning realization among US and European women that their complacency was premature. The author, journalist Aline Mosby, had started her career on the Hollywood beat and was widely credited with helping to push Marilyn Monroe's rise to superstardom. Now assigned to the United Nations in New York, she discussed the discriminatory laws still in place in many European countries and US states, covering issues on which many developing countries had demonstrated greater gender equality. According to Margaret Bruce, the British-born head of the Status of Women Section at the United Nations, whom Mosby interviewed for the article, "The more advanced countries are getting a bit smug and don't see the need for work in giving women equality. Perhaps it's because young Western girls these days don't take the status of women's problems as something to be concerned about." As Bruce pointed out, Libya and Gabon guaranteed equal pay for men and women, whereas only thirty states in the United States did the same.[110] A few decades later, however, the mobilization of a new generation of US feminists would coincide with growing anti-Muslim sentiment in both the US government and the general population, propelling a shift in US ideas about their own accomplishments in women's rights, especially vis-à-vis Muslim women.

SEVEN

Encounters in Global Feminism

THE FORUM OF NONGOVERNMENTAL ORGANIZATIONS and individuals that convened alongside the first UN Women's Conference in June
1975 reminded Rounaq Jahan of a _mela_. While this word (in Bengali and several other north Indian languages) is usually translated as a "fair" or "festival," Jahan clarified that, for her, _mela_ applied to the Mexico City gathering
because it "meets for a short time" and "various people come with divergent
objectives, but by the time it ends a strong sense of community has emerged."
A US-trained political scientist who had returned to the newly independent
Bangladesh to teach at Dacca University, Rounaq Jahan traveled to Mexico
City to join Indian economist Pushpa Nand Schwartz as official observers on
behalf of the Society for International Development.[1]

In the final decades of the twentieth century, the United Nations' form of
international feminism provided important financial and ideological support
for women's issues around the world. Its four world conferences for women
also proved to be important—and often productive—sites of encounters and
clashes between women from the wealthier countries, primarily in Europe
and North America, and women from the poorer majority of the world,
which included most Muslim-majority countries, over what constituted legitimate "women's issues."

Over the course of the 1970s and 1980s, Bangladesh, which had gained
independence after a brutal and bloody war in 1971, remained quintessen-
tially "Third World" rather than "Muslim" in Western eyes. It remained
largely untouched by the dramatic changes in Western ideas about Islam,
Arabs, and Muslims over the issues of oil, revolution, and female genital surgeries. Bangladesh's manufactured and natural devastations in its first years
ensured that the women of Bangladesh came to be seen as archetypal "Third
World women," assumed to be impoverished, illiterate, and overly fertile and

FIGURE 19. "Unholy Matrimony," by nationally syndicated Indian cartoonist Enver Ahmed, from his 1971 booklet, *The Anatomy of Betrayal*.

in dire need of population control, development initiatives, and Western aid.[2] Bangladeshi feminists, for their part, carved out their own agenda in the context of increased international funding and scrutiny, from Western as well as from Muslim donors, and helped to found international networks that challenged the mainstream narrative of women in development as well as newly enacted male-biased national laws. Bangladesh formally joined the Non-Aligned Movement at the Algiers meeting in 1973 (six years before Pakistan) and embraced its Third World identity to assert, not the poverty and backwardness that wealthier countries associated with the term, but membership in a shared project by the majority of the world's population to resist the influence of both superpowers and a shared commitment to peace, equality, and human rights in accordance with UN conventions.[3]

WESTERN FEMINISTS AND THE RAPES OF 1971

News of the mass rapes in the Bangladesh war reached Americans in the fall of 1971. In January 1972, a month after the war ended, the *New York*

Times reported that about two hundred thousand rape survivors were facing rejection by their families.[4] Women around the world wrote letters and organized rallies to raise awareness of the Bengali women's plight. In Great Britain, feminist journalist Jill Tweedie's *Guardian* article on the rapes prompted a flood of donations to the London office of the International Planned Parenthood Federation for forwarding to the Bangladesh Women's Emancipation Programme in Dacca. The contributions ranged "from £1,000 from one anonymous donor to 25 pence from a pensioner who wished she could have afforded more as she was so upset at hearing of the plight of the Bangladesh girls."[5]

While several international news reports noted that Bengali women needed help because "Moslem" men had committed the rapes and "Moslem" husbands and communities were rejecting them, Western feminists involved in antirape activism focused primarily on the universal and shared oppression of women rather than that they were Muslim. Describing the horrors discovered in Bangladesh, Australian feminist writer Germaine Greer noted in the London *Sunday Times* in April 1972 that "Bangladesh is paying as other nations have paid before, the price of having reared its women in a tradition of powerlessness and servility."[6] US radical feminist Charlotte Bunch invoked the Bangladesh mass rapes to warn against subordinating feminism in a fight against war and imperialism. In a 1972 article in the monthly the *Furies* that she had cofounded with her partner, Rita Mae Brown, Bunch argued that "male domination was and is the original imperialism." While she recognized the importance of a "critique of imperialism" and the urgency of opposing the Vietnam War, Bunch saw a "conflict between building our movement and spending time actively working against the war." In the end the "strong feminist movement here" would be able to "challenge all imperialisms." She gave the example of a pregnant rape survivor of the recent war in Bangladesh who was made an "outcast, because a woman violated by another man was not fit to be the wife of a liberated Bangla Desh man!" For Bunch this was further proof that even in "liberation struggles...male prerogatives were still paramount. All the leftist sympathies and relief money did little to alleviate her plight." In short, rather than dissipate women's energies by "dabbling in all the worthy causes and also carrying out an offensive against sexism...we must choose to win this time."[7]

The newly launched *Ms.* magazine turned its attention to Bangladesh in August 1972 with a photo essay by Jason Lauré and Joyce Goldman, simply titled "Women of Bangladesh." Goldman, a freelance writer based in New

Jersey, repeatedly drew comparisons with the US context more familiar to her readers as a way to highlight what she saw as the shared problems of women. Even before her trip the limited news coverage of the topic led her to realize that, "like rape victims in our own culture, women had been the subject of one sensational report, and then conveniently forgotten." She found that the Bengali attitude toward raped women was simply a "morbid exaggeration of our own attitudes." That the rape survivor herself may be held somehow responsible for the rape "is not unfamiliar to us," she wrote.[8]

A few months later poet and feminist Adrienne Rich alluded to Goldman's article in an essay in the *New York Review of Books* to remind her predominantly US readers that the distance between the women of the United States and Bangladesh was far shorter than one might think. "It goes without saying," she pointed out, "that for 'successful' women, male hostility usually takes forms less physical and literal than it does in the lives of their 'unliberated' sisters." She continued, "Every one of these [Bengali] women was raped twice: first physically by the enemy soldier, then psychically by the enemy in her own household. I wonder how many women there are, however free and fortunate they consider themselves, who would not respond to that double jeopardy with intense and painful recognition."[9]

The *Ms.* article on Bangladesh even made an appearance in the 1973 classic text of feminist theology, *Beyond God the Father,* in which Mary Daly analyzed the misogyny inherent in the Judeo-Christian tradition. For Daly the rapes of the Bangladesh war served as an example of masculine power driving the "most unholy trinity: rape, genocide, and war," and she agreed with Goldman, who regarded the suffering of Bengali women as only a collective, exaggerated form of "what individual women in this and other 'advanced' countries know from their own experience." To forestall her readers from "unseeing this...by protest[ing] that it happened in another culture, in a Moslem country," she provided a recent example from the *Times* of the horrific rapes of two young South Bronx sisters and the brutal death of the younger girl. She objected also to the large advertisement on the same page glorifying the masculine power of three well-dressed men, all too reminiscent of the three White teen boys responsible for the rapes of the young girls. Addressing "'informed' Christians and Jews [who] may protest that rape and brutality are alien to our own heritage," she pointed them to the many passages in the Bible "which tell a different story, namely that there is precedent for looking upon women as spoils of war."[10] In her 1978 book, *Gyn/Ecology,* Daly would turn her attention to *"suttee"* (sati) as an example of women's universal oppression and invoke the "excellent" and "exceptional" work of Katherine Mayo, whom we met in chapter 5.[11]

Through the early 1970s US feminist groups organized hundreds of speak-outs and conferences about rape, helping to establish rape crisis centers and demanding reforms in the US legal system. "Castrate rapists" buttons became popular. Journalist Susan Brownmiller's book *Against Our Will: Men, Women, and Rape* was published in 1975, having taken four years to complete rather than the one year she had expected. Her argument about rape, quite simply, was that "it is nothing more or less than a conscious process of intimidation by which *all* men keep *all* women in a state of fear."[12] While there was certainly much to criticize in the book—historians, anthropologists, sociologists, and prominent feminists such as Angela Davis and bell hooks would lambast its simplistic treatment of men, women, power, and race—it is undeniable that it helped to transform the manner in which rape was publicly discussed, in the United States and around the world, and energized activists who were already addressing the issue.

Even with just under eight pages devoted to the case of Bangladesh, *Against Our Will* brought the story of the "hit-and-run" rapes of 1971 to a much larger audience. Feminists and scholars in Bangladesh drew on her discussion for several years and, later, also challenged many aspects of it. For Brownmiller the significance of the Bangladesh case—to her mind, an "obscure war in an obscure corner of the globe"—lay as much in the mass rapes as in the new government's willingness to speak about them and its "acceptance of abortion as a solution to unwanted pregnancy."[13] At the same time the book helped to sear into US minds the image of Bangladeshi women as extraordinarily vulnerable—not only to masculine power but also to dire poverty, unbridled fertility, and, by the time Brownmiller's book appeared, also to devastating floods and famine. In 1975 Bangladesh entered a period of what would be fifteen years of military rule, and the window on the rapes and other war crimes of 1971 was temporarily shuttered.[14]

ABORTION, POPULATION CONTROL, AND WOMEN'S RIGHTS

In the early 1970s British and US feminists followed with great interest—and some wistfulness—one specific aspect of Bangladesh's response to the survivors of the mass rapes of the 1971 war: the government's relaxation of the law on abortion. Abdur Rab Chaudhury, the prime minister's coordinator for external assistance for relief and rehabilitation, had explained to *Ms.* that the government's new openness stemmed directly from its concern for rape survivors: "These women have been harassed and punished through their violations, and we can't punish them any more."[15] Although abortion was a criminal offense under the colonial-era Penal Code of 1860, the government's decision was no doubt made easier by the permissibility of abortion in Hanafi Islam, the dominant school of jurisprudence in South Asia, before the fetus is ensouled (believed to occur 120 days after conception) and in case of any danger to the mother's health, as determined by a physician.[16]

In addition to sending funds to Bangladesh just after the war ended, the International Planned Parenthood Federation also sent physicians, medications, and mobile clinics to help the survivors of wartime sexual violence. The organization already had an established and clearly influential presence in the country. As one family-planning expert had put it in 1970, "East Pakistan is a special crisis on a crisis subcontinent. It's got 72 million people jammed into a space just a little bit larger than Arkansas, which has only two million." A comparison with the western wing of Pakistan had brought such experts little comfort: the eastern part had twelve million more people although it was a fifth the size of the western wing. Some good news, however, according to a 1970 report in the *New York Times,* was to be found in "evidence that the less tradition-minded East Pakistanis have been more receptive to at least some of the new family planning techniques," making possible close to a million vasectomies in a "male-oriented Moslem culture." Authorities attributed the vasectomies to incentive payments, an awareness of the greater population pressure in their area, and "the fact that women have more influence in the family in East Pakistan than in the western section."[17]

Among those who traveled to Bangladesh on the 1972 "mercy" or "humanitarian mission" were the International Planned Parenthood Federation's first medical director, Malcolm Potts; the Los Angeles–based abortionist Harvey Karman, who had developed a new procedure for early abortions using his own invention, a flexible tube called the cannula; and the Australian Geoff Davis of the International Abortion and Training Centre in London, who had experience with late-term abortions. Davis later recalled a letter he received from Abdur Rab Chaudhury himself, "authorising my work there. It mentioned that anything I wanted to do was perfectly legal and they will give me all assistance.... I thought it was important since I was never going to see anything like that ever again as long as I lived. So, I better keep those."

At the time abortion had only recently been legalized in most of the United Kingdom and Australia and was still illegal in much of the pre–*Roe v. Wade* United States.[18]

In her *Ms.* article Goldman described Karman's role in providing abortions and in training thousands of local women paramedics to do the same, using techniques "that may be safer and easier than some other methods available to women in the United States."[19] That Karman, in addition to using the cannula on early pregnancies, had also tested his newer supercoil method on second-trimester pregnancies among Bengali women, remained uncontroversial until the "Philadelphia incident"—dubbed the "Mother's Day Massacre" by antichoice groups—in May 1972, when the use of the supercoil on fifteen poor Black women from Chicago led to severe medical complications.[20]

The Bangladesh government's decision to facilitate women's access to abortion stemmed also from its distress over the country's growing population. Bangladesh's First Five-Year Plan of 1973 firmly stated, "No civilized measure would be too drastic to keep the population of Bangladesh on the smaller side of 15 crores [150 million] for [the] sheer ecological viability of the nation." Thus, although abortion remained illegal, the first administrations permitted menstrual regulation (MR) alongside improved contraceptive access funded by foreign donors. MR relied on the very technology of uterine aspiration that Karman had used with rape survivors. Since it could also be used for other purposes, such as conducting a biopsy or completing an improperly executed abortion (permitted to prevent the woman's death), the fact that it could also be used to terminate a pregnancy in its early stages was simply less publicized. By defining MR as an "interim method to establish non-pregnancy" rather than a form of abortion, the Bangladesh Institute of Law and International Affairs also ensured that the procedure was not governed by the 1860 Penal Code.[21] Following the passage of the 1973 Helms Amendment to the Foreign Assistance Act, which prohibited the use of US federal dollars for abortions, Reimert Ravenholt, director of the Office of Population at USAID, turned to private and multilateral organizations. By 1978 USAID had distributed some 175,000 MR kits, which were used for around five million procedures worldwide. The distribution and use of MR kits was particularly successful in Bangladesh, where trained village women workers, many of them survivors of wartime rape themselves, were employed to go door to door.[22]

In the United States radical feminist self-help health groups were excited about their own access to this technology because it obviated the need for professional medical assistance or legal oversight. California activist Lorraine Rothman tweaked Karman's equipment to make it even easier for women to perform what US feminists called menstrual extraction (ME). As Rothman recalled in a 2002 interview, menstrual extraction gave them a way to "stop the humiliation of trying to persuade the powers that be to legalize abortion" and "to be in charge of our own reproduction."[23] In celebrating their newfound power, agency, and freedom from the medical profession and the legal system, US feminist health activists distinguished their own communities from those "areas and countries where people are most defenseless" and themselves from the undifferentiated mass of poor women in poor countries who were subject to experimentation by global population-control organizations. At the same time some US activists were furious since, even though the success of the MR program in Bangladesh had revealed the device's potential for use in any self-help movement, US women were still being taught that only proper doctors were qualified to perform abortions. US feminist Lolly Hirsch fumed in her magazine *Monthly Extract: An Irregular Periodical,* "We are intimidated into believing that laywomen in the United States are too dumb, too uneducated, too dry, too infection-prone, too inept, too unmechanical, too averse to technology to learn how to do an abortion."[24]

By the time of the 1974 World Population Conference in Bucharest, the Bangladesh government had already deployed thirteen thousand trained family-welfare workers to go door to door, distributing birth control as part of a package with smallpox and malaria medication. With Bangladesh in the midst of a deadly flood and famine when the conference got under way in Bucharest, the Bangladesh delegation enthusiastically endorsed the original draft of the conference's Population Plan of Action. The initial version had called for "substantial national and international efforts to reduce fertility," but opposition from countries in eastern Europe, Africa, and Latin America, led by Algeria and Argentina, led to the adoption of a milder plan of action that focused more on social and economic development. In the words of the Indian minister for health and family planning, Dr. Karan Singh, whose delegation also objected to the original draft, "Development is the best contraceptive." Australian feminist Germaine Greer complained that the original draft had depicted women as "baby-factories," the only difference being these particular factories were being called on to cease production, while Bangladeshi feminist Rounaq Jahan, also at the conference, called for a balanced approach to the population issue and the importance of paying attention to women rather than abstract notions like development: "We have learned from the West that even after you have a full level of development you don't necessarily have equality of the sexes. This is important so we can better decide which strategies for betterment we should use and which we should avoid." Almost all countries supported an amendment that called for an improvement in the status of women.[25]

The steady stream of funds targeting women and development in Bangladesh and elsewhere, starting in the 1970s, was the result of feminist intervention in US policy discussions. Danish economist Ester Boserup's 1970 book *Women's Role in Economic Development,* which had recently become available in the United States, was helping to challenge ideas about the presumed benefits of development and modernization for the world's poorest women, when development scholar Irene Tinker was invited to a briefing at the State Department on the upcoming UN International Women's Year. Thoughtful, empirically based presentations like Tinker's on the "detrimental impact of development on women" encouraged female civil servants to push for an amendment to the 1961 US Foreign Assistance Act that would pay greater attention to women. They chose Republican senator Charles Percy to introduce the amendment, which would require USAID to give priority to development projects that benefit women and better integrate them into their national economies. Intense lobbying by women's organizations such as the League of Women Voters helped to ensure passage of the Percy Amendment. Also at the State Department briefing was Arvonne Fraser, a dedicated feminist who had served as president of the Women's Equity Action League. She persuaded her husband, Donald Fraser, a Democratic representative on the House Foreign Affairs Committee, to organize hearings about women in developing countries, and this helped to build support for the Percy Amendment. US diplomats, for their part, were happy to try to use women's issues to court Third World nations away from any pro-Soviet proclivities.[26]

The Percy Amendment ushered in a new era of formal US attention to women in its development projects, with consequences for women throughout the developing world. In keeping with the modernization ideology that had dominated development efforts since World War II, the new amendment sought to help women around the world become more modern, more Western. Feminist critics would soon point out that because such efforts did little to challenge larger political and economic inequalities, they could not effect meaningful, lasting change in women's lives.[27]

IRAN, OIL, AND US IDEAS ABOUT MUSLIMS

While Americans viewed Bangladesh primarily through the lens of poverty and development in the 1970s, Iran served as a window on a Muslim society that, to US eyes, was both modern and exotic. Then, as now, the United States had its select allies among the leaders of Muslim-majority nations, and the most charismatic among them were undoubtedly the shah of Iran, Mohammed Reza Pahlevi, and his glamorous consort, Farah Diba. In October 1973 the Italian journalist Oriana Fallaci interviewed Pahlevi on his views on kingship, his regime's foreign policy, its brutal treatment of domestic dissidents, and women and the women's movement. Pahlevi spoke with pride of his White Revolution of 1963—coincidentally, the year that *The Feminine Mystique* was published—that had sought to modernize Iranian society, including women's rights. Later assessments would reveal, unsurprisingly, that urban, elite women had benefited at the expense of the rural poor. It was, however, his contemptuous statements about women's abilities that irked Fallaci and, later, readers of the published interview, among them Betty Friedan. He saw no point in "this Women's Lib business" and the demand for equality, since "I don't want to seem rude, but... you may be equal in the eyes of the law, but not, I beg your pardon for saying so, in ability." While he dismissed as a "stupid, vile, disgusting libel" the rumor that he had taken a second wife, he defended Muslim men's right to polygyny if the second marriage was contracted legally—that is, "so long as the first wife agrees and the court approves." After all, he reminded Fallaci, men in Western society often take a mistress "or even more than one" when dissatisfied with their first wife.[28]

By the time Fallaci's interview with the shah appeared in the December 1973 issue of the *New Republic,* the oil-producing Arab states had slashed production and announced a 70 percent hike in the price of their oil and an embargo on oil exports to the United States. This was in retaliation for the US decision to support Israel in the 1973 October War, also known as the Ramadan or Yom Kippur War, when Egypt and Syria crossed the Suez Canal in a surprise bid to reclaim territories occupied by Israel in 1967. The price hike was also a defiant act of economic independence by several members of the developing world.[29]

Having enjoyed cheap and plentiful gas in the recent past, Americans were outraged. In a mid-November cover story, *Time* described the shock experienced by Americans:

> Rushing to work last week, John Doe, American, swung his car onto the freeway—only to discover that the posted speed limit had been reduced from 60 m.p.h. to 50 m.p.h. When he stopped at a gas station for a refill, he learned that overnight the price had gone up 2¢ per gal. At his office he felt unusually cool because the thermostats had been pushed down a couple of degrees, to a brisk 68°. Later, when he finished work and was driving home, he noticed that the lights on outdoor advertising signs had been doused. In his living room he was greeted by his children, who gleefully reported that their school would be closed for a month this winter—in order to save oil.

These new inconveniences were attributed to the "backward but wakening desert kingdom of Saudi Arabia." The magazine cover that week was a grim image of Saudi King Faysal, described as "The Hand on the Valve."[30] Faysal, who would be assassinated by his nephew just fifteen months later, was portrayed as the man controlling Americans' access to the life to which they had become accustomed, premised on a car culture that promised unfettered mobility. Along with Indonesia, Nigeria, and Venezuela, the Middle Eastern states of Iran and Iraq continued to sell to the United States—and benefit from the higher oil prices, which had increased fourfold by the time the embargo was lifted in March 1974.

In May 1974 Betty Friedan, Germaine Greer, and the Finnish UN diplomat Helvi Sipilä visited Tehran at the invitation of the Women's Organization of Iran (WOI), then led by Mahnaz Afkhami and the shah's twin sister, Princess Ashraf, who was Iran's ambassador to the United Nations and the primary financial sponsor of the International Women's Year conference, scheduled for June 1975. This earlier gathering was a preliminary meeting to prepare for the 1975 conference. Some forty years later Afkhami recalled selecting these representatives of "Western feminism" to share their ideas and experiences with activists in Iran. Kate Millett had been on the list too, even though Afkhami was concerned that the "language and concepts that some Western feminists such as Kate Millett used in books such as *Sexual Politics* were less appealing to women in our region—perhaps even counterproductive." Friedan, by contrast, "had an important message based on the reality of middle-class women in suburban America that reflected the problems of patriarchy. She did not focus on the individual as the center of the family, community, nation, or universe, or on sexuality as the focal point in studying the challenges women face. In this sense she was closer to feminists from the rest of the world than feminists from the West." While recognizing that local culture, issues, and needs were different, Afkhami was convinced that the "universality of women's condition around the world" meant that there was much for Iranian women to gain from hearing from these Western visitors. Some WOI members worried that such an event might bring charges of *gharbzadegi* (Westoxification) against WOI, but the invitations went out in the end. When Millett was unable to attend, Afkhami extended an invitation to Greer as an equally suitable "representative of the more radical wing of the feminist movement."[31] Friedan, Greer, and Sipilä arrived in Iran very much aware of recent news reports about political suppression, torture, and even disappearances by the shah's secret police as well as Fallaci's recent interview with the shah.

Friedan wrote about the visit in an article for *Ladies' Home Journal,* predictably titled "Coming Out of the Veil." There she reported her delight in the "real Iranian caviar on the menu" at the Tehran Hilton and how she felt "strangely at home" in her interactions with the elite women of the city. When some local women persuaded her to try on a chador, she found herself reflecting on "those invisible veils trapping our spirits in the West." She was thrilled to learn that the empress Farah Diba had already read *The Feminine Mystique*—"originally in French in paperback"—and "agreed with it all." Friedan left the meeting, which lasted an hour and a half rather than the scheduled ten minutes, declaring her immense joy at having met an "Empress who is also a feminist." Friedan also met professional women and was surprised to learn that they typically kept their own names upon marriage, "without the fuss we've had to make to be 'Ms.' in America. It's an Iranian *tradition.* And it remains her legal name through life." While in Tehran, Friedan received an unexpected invitation to meet with the shah himself, during which he attempted to clarify his statements to Fallaci.[32]

Despite her qualms about the ulterior motives behind the shah's interest in women and her awareness of his suppression of political enemies, Friedan ended her article sounding almost wistful about the impressive levels of state support—"funds beyond our wildest dreams"—for women's causes in Iran.[33] Most members of WOI were wealthy, some even royal or aristocratic. While the WOI did work with women from more impoverished backgrounds, because the state wanted to appear modern on the international stage, it tended to downplay the deleterious effects of government policies on poor, rural women.[34]

EMERGING FAULT LINES

Disagreements between feminists in the West and those in the Eastern Bloc and the increasingly united members of the Third World over their understandings of gender equality became increasingly apparent even before the 1975 UN International Women's Year conference in Mexico City, when the schism dominated discussions and media coverage of the conference. Where Western feminists, generally speaking, focused on equal legal and economic rights, activists from the rest of the world insisted that women's equality could not be separated from other forms of oppression and injustice, such as racism, colonialism and imperialism, Zionism, economic development, war, and occupation. Many of these issues, moreover, directly implicated many European countries, the United States, and Israel. Given that the Women's International Democratic Federation (WIDF) and the Eastern Bloc countries had long argued for a broader understanding of gender equality and women's issues, it was understandable that women's organizations from the vast majority of the world's countries sided with them even when their own governments did not. Significantly, the very idea for an international women's year was first proposed by WIDF, which enjoyed consultative status with the United Nations. The proposal was formally presented by WIDF representative Shahnaz Alami, an Iranian poet who had been living in political exile in East Berlin since 1953, the year a CIA-sponsored coup overthrew the democratically elected government of Mohammad Mosaddegh and cemented Reza Pahlevi's monarchical rule.[35]

Even before Bangladesh's founding constitution was promulgated in November 1972 with its four pillars of democracy, nationalism, secularism, and socialism, it was clear that the new state was tilting more heavily toward the Soviet Bloc than Pakistan had during Bangladesh's Pakistan *amol* (Pakistan era). In the final days of the war, the Soviet Union supported India in its intervention on the side of Bangladesh, and Soviet Bloc countries were among the first to recognize Bangladesh, after its neighbors Bhutan and India. The Soviet Union extended its formal recognition on 25 January 1972.

US president Richard Nixon and secretary of state Henry Kissinger, for their part, had put the US government firmly on Pakistan's side during the war, even ignoring reports of genocide from US officials in Dacca.[36] To add insult to injury, in early January 1972 *New York Times* investigative journalist Jack Anderson revealed stinging references to Bangladesh as an "international basket case" by Kissinger and career diplomat U. Alexis Johnson in the transcript of a December 1971 meeting of the National Security Council.[37] Not surprisingly, when the renowned Indian writer Khushwant Singh visited Dacca shortly after the end of the war, in January 1972, and again that December, he saw anti-American slogans around the city and a hammer and sickle on the walls of the United States Information Agency.[38] Some sixty other countries had recognized Bangladesh by the time the United States finally did so on 4 April 1972.[39]

It was also in early April that the Bangladesh Mahila Parishad (BMP; Bangladesh Women's Council) convened its first international conference with guests from the Soviet Union, East Germany, Hungary, and India. The East Pakistan Mahila Parishad had been founded two years earlier in the midst of increasing mass agitation for greater autonomy in East Pakistan, its membership drawn primarily from young women activists from various leftist parties. Prominent international participants at the 1972 conference included Hertta Kuusinen, the Finnish-born head of the WIDF, and Ila Mitra, the celebrated Indian Bengali communist and peasant movement activist. A few weeks later the BMP sent its own representatives, Begum Sufia Kamal and Maleka Begum, founding president and general secretary, respectively, to attend the WIDF Council Meeting in Bulgaria. They would also make stops in East Germany and Soviet Russia to muster support for an ultimately successful bid for the BMP's induction into the WIDF. In Moscow Kamal was delighted to see Nina Popova again, whom she had met in 1967, as we saw in chapter 6.[40] In a visit in 1973, she would reconnect with Tereshkova.

The WIDF meeting that Sufia Kamal and Maleka Begum attended in Varna on the Black Sea coast was hosted by the Committee of the Bulgarian Women's Movement, which had been making a deliberate effort to reach out to women's organizations in Africa, Asia, and Latin America and selected individuals in Europe and North America. For instance, later that year the committee would host US civil rights activist, scholar, and communist Angela Davis, then on a tour of socialist countries following her acquittal on charges of kidnapping and murder.[41] Relationships forged in Varna would lead the delegates from Bangladesh, Bulgaria, and other nonaligned and Soviet Bloc nations to join forces three years later during the International

FIGURE 20. Chair of the Soviet Women's Committee, Valentina Nikolayeva-Tereshkova *(second on left)*, holding a reception for her guests, a delegation of the Bangladesh-USSR Friendship Society, headed by Sufia Kamal *(second on right)*. Moscow, November 1973. Sputnik Images.

Women's Year conference to object to US delegate Rita Johnston's proposal to add the word "sexism" to a list of obstacles to women's equality alongside terms such as colonialism and apartheid.[42]

In August 1972 the BMP sent two representatives—Sayeda Zohra Khatun, vice president of the BMP and the spouse of the country's first prime minister, Tajuddin Ahmad; and Fauzia Moslem, a member of the BMP's Central Executive Committee—to the Second Afro-Asian Women's Conference in Ulan Bator, Mongolia. At the first conference in Cairo in 1961, attended by women from thirty-seven countries, Egyptian activist Bahiyya Karam had expressed her delight at meeting "delegates from countries in Africa which imperialists had never allowed before to leave the boundaries of their land."[43] At the Ulan Bator meeting, delegates from some sixty countries and several international organizations discussed many of the issues that arose again in Mexico City just three years later, issues that would delineate a growing rift between Western and Third World feminists.

Recognizing that eleven additional countries had gained independence in the eleven years that separated the two Afro-Asian women's conferences, the delegates in Ulan Bator celebrated the "collapse of the colonial system" and the contributions of socialist countries and of women to national liberation movements. They acknowledged, however, that "dangerous hotbeds of

FIGURE 21. International Women's Year Tribune, 1975. Hameeda Hossain and Rounaq
Jahan *(seated, fourth and fifth, respectively, in the second row from the front)*. Courtesy of
Rounaq Jahan.

imperialist aggression continue to exist," the most prominent examples being
Indochina, where, "despite heavy defeats, US imperialism strives to realize
its criminal designs"; Zionist "aggressions against the Arab homeland"; and
apartheid and racism in South Africa. In outlining the "main tasks" of the
conference, the participants produced a list that would reappear almost ver-
batim in the 1975 conference: "A task of vital importance facing the developing Afro-Asian states today is to consolidate the victories of the national
liberation movements and to protect them against the unceasing encroachments of imperialism, colonialism, neocolonialism, racism, Zionism, fascism
and reaction." Delegates spoke of the need for economic and social progress beyond political liberation and the problems posed to the goal of "genuine national independence" by the continued presence of foreign capital.
Women, as workers in foreign-controlled factories, plantations, and world
markets, were "vitally interested in the solution of all these problems." The
BMP and the women of Bangladesh were among the countries and organizations that the conference formally recognized as having participated in
recent struggles for liberation and "national construction."[44]

In September two representatives of the Cuban Women's Federation visited Bangladesh at the BMP's invitation and, at a news conference in Dacca, spoke of their interest in forging a strong bond of friendship with Bangladesh.[45] A year later, at a meeting of the Non-Aligned Movement in Algiers, Fidel Castro greeted Sheikh Mujibur Rahman with warm admiration for his role in leading Bangladesh's independence movement. In 1974 this amity between the two countries—specifically, Bangladesh's decision to export jute bags to Cuba—led the United States to suspend a shipment of food aid to the already-struggling new nation and contributed to the escalation of an already catastrophic famine. By the end of 1974, with the worst of the famine over, women's organizations turned their attention to long-term rebuilding efforts and preparations for the International Women's Year.

THE QUESTION OF "WOMEN'S ISSUES"

In Mexico City in June 1975, US feminists were taken aback by the anti-American tenor of the conference. Smarting from the Watergate scandal and the US defeat in Vietnam, they arrived in Mexico clearly unaware of the many recent discussions among Third World women in other venues. Two days into the conference, Carole de Saram, the president of the New York chapter of the National Organization for Women, complained that "the true issues, the problems of women, are being forgotten here.... Instead, this conference is concentrating on political issues that represent the male mentality. The direction here is not coming from women, it's coming from men." New York lawyer Ronnie Feit reported that too many of the women at the tribune were focused on economic issues and world peace rather than women's issues such as equality, education, and employment opportunities.[46] Betty Friedan had felt confident that there would be no conflict between Western and Third World women because, as she put it, "We are our sister's keeper," and her goal was "to advance the world-wide moment of women to equality." Instead, she was shocked not only by the anti-Americanism but also by the passionate anti-Zionism of so many attendees; she later referred to the developments in Mexico City as "scary doings."[47]

A different perspective was offered by Hanna Kaiser Papanek, a German-born, US-trained anthropologist and feminist who had spent many years in both South and Southeast Asia. She had accompanied her husband, economist Gustav Papanek, to Pakistan in the mid-1950s, when he served as an adviser to the Pakistan Planning Commission, and also conducted her own doctoral research on the Khoja Ismaili community. In a short report on the conference in the inaugural issue of the feminist journal *Signs,* Papanek described the exciting and productive discussions that occurred outside the official sessions, in the parallel tribune as well as in informal settings all around. She recalled the "profound differences of opinion" one heard in "hotel dining rooms, over breakfast...between younger and older women from Muslim countries about the need to reform the status of women in Islam." Most of all, she wanted to share the "enthusiasm and excitement" and that "possibilities were opened up" simply from being in the midst of some five thousand women from around the world.[48]

Jennifer Whitaker, associate editor at *Foreign Affairs* magazine and a former Peace Corps volunteer, appreciated that the "divergent positions" on women's issues "signified that the event was taking place in the real world, not as an academic exercise or an oversized coffee-klatch." If Western women worried that women from the Soviet Bloc and the developing countries were distracting from or diluting women's issues by bringing in "political" matters such as colonialism and imperialism, the latter group of women were wary of Western women's narrow definition of "women's issues" and their apparent hostility to men. Whitaker reported that most representatives from the developing world, although typically members of their country's elite, refused to accept a feminism that was detached from larger political and socioeconomic issues such as poverty, foreign domination, apartheid, and Zionism. They saw the men in their communities not as enemies but as partners to fight these evils. That nationalism could be a more meaningful issue than a particular form of feminism came as a shock to US feminists, as did the realization that they themselves were perceived as being part of the privileged and problematic power structure oppressing much of the world.[49]

Whitaker equivocated on the subject of Islam and Muslims in her discussion of how different cultures and traditions had constrained women. She began by pointing out that the "religion which has notoriously curbed women, especially in the Middle East, is of course Islam. The religion of Mohammed, with its male domination and restrictive protection for women, is especially resistant to change in general and changing the position of women in particular." She conceded, however, that the "Muslim woman is freer than women in Christian cultures" since Islam lacks a "societally induced mystique of sentimental love binding the wife in service to the husband." This reference to Islamic marriage as contractual rather than a sacrament, which as we recall dates back to missionary writings of the early nineteenth century, appeared in a new light to Western feminists who were questioning once again the institution of Western Christian marriage.[50]

Many Black American feminists shared the Third World women's fury against US imperialism and economic power. Florynce Kennedy, described by *People* magazine in 1974 as the "biggest, loudest and, indisputably, the rudest mouth on the battleground where feminist activists and radical politics join in mostly common cause," was part of the US delegation to the NGO tribune. Outside the tribune site this lawyer and civil rights and women's rights activist led groups in song, including her versions of the US national anthem "The Star-Spangled Banner" and the unofficial national anthem "America." The former began with "Oh say can you see any heel marks on me?" while the latter emerged as "My country 'tis of thee / Sour land of bigotry / Of thee I sing. / Land of Indian massacre / Land of black slavery / Land of hypocrisy / Of thee I sing." In her hotel room Kennedy organized discussions about issues such as the government persecution of Black Panther Assata Shakur and the criminalization of sex work.[51]

The tensions of Mexico City resurfaced a year later at the Conference on Women and Development at Wellesley College in Massachusetts in June 1976. A largely academic event that drew little mainstream media attention, it is significant in the longer history of encounters between Western and Third World feminists for provoking the latter, among them Muslim-identified feminists, to articulate their perspective on the imbalance in these very interactions. A few months later conference participants Fatima Mernissi of Morocco, Nawal El Saadawi of Egypt, and Mallica Vajrathon of Thailand excoriated the conference in an open letter published in numerous venues. Mernissi and El Saadawi would soon become two of the best-known Muslim Arab feminists in the West, following the publication of their books in English, *Beyond the Veil: Male-Female Dynamics in a Modern Muslim Society* (1975) and *The Hidden Face of Eve: Women in the Arab World* (1980), respectively.

Their open letter began by describing the event as "'successful' precisely because it was a painful clash between well-meaning American women academicians who believed themselves to be ahead of American men, freed from colonial and imperialist limitations on one hand, and on the other hand, overly optimistic Third World women who had believed that the impossible dialogue between people of developed/developing nations could be restored by women, between women, and for women." It was naive and "unrealistic," they continued, to think that the "mere fact of being women is a binding enough characteristic to create instantaneous international sisterhood above and beyond political differences and unequal power distribution." In the end the Wellesley conference "was an American-planned and organized conference," at which "Third World researchers...were reduced to being passive, accommodating audiences rather than participants." The focus had been insistently on the "oppressive conditions of women in developing countries" but not on the "causes of oppression." When Third World women tried to bring up the problems caused by "so-called 'development' and 'modernization'" or the "role of the multi-national corporation," they were met with accusations "of being nonfeminist; of imitating the male in his political games; and 'splitting the spirit of sisterhood in the Women's Movement.'" The authors objected to the "absence of papers on American women, be they black, white or brown." Third World participants had expected to learn about the impact of the "development process" on US women, but what they got instead was "American 'scholars'...interpreting for us our condition, our cultures, our religions and our experiences." It was a repetition of the "hardly-healed colonial experience wherein the detached outsiders define your world to you."[52]

In a 1983 interview with Black American "scholarly activists" (as they described themselves) Tiffany Patterson and Angela Gillam, El Saadawi described her continued exasperation with the Western feminist obsession with the "oppression" of Third World women. At Wellesley she had had to listen to an "American woman" who, after just three months in Egypt, was "preaching and teaching about Egypt." In Vienna she had watched as "Germaine Greer, who had spent a few months in India," spoke "about Indian problems while Indian women sat there listening to her." She lambasted this "academic exploitation of Third World women" by Western women. "We feel as if we are guinea pigs or something to be researched by women from the First World, and we refuse to accept it." By contrast, the "very good feminists" of the "First World," according to El Saadawi, were those "who believe in an equal exchange and who really want to help. They understand the meaning of solidarity among women, international solidarity on equal grounds, etc. And they are political; they know how to combine the personal with the political, not to divorce these things as is happening in some countries."[53]

In 1984 El Saadawi, Mernissi, and Vajrathon came together again as contributors to US feminist Robin Morgan's *Sisterhood Is Global* anthology. Although published a few years after the Iranian Revolution, the anthology was more representative of an earlier era of mainstream White feminism in its approach to Muslims. In her introduction to the massive tome, Morgan proudly declared that the contributions from feminists in "seventy countries, plus the United Nations itself" provide "what may be the most fiery indictment of organized religion ever to sear its way across paper. No patriarchal religion is left unconfronted." Indeed, alongside the "profound misogyny inherent in fundamentalist interpretation of Islam," she listed the problems of the Catholic Church, the Russian Orthodox Church, Hindu and Buddhist theology and practice, Christian churches in Africa, and Protestant fundamentalists. She described the women of Iran, Ireland, and Israel as all surviving "under varying degrees of theocracy" and attributed the "miseries" experienced by women around the world to misinterpretations of the original messages of the founders of the religions—"Gautama Buddha, Moses, Jesus Christ, Mohammed"—who were "remarkably progressive for their own times." For instance, female genital excision, she explained, is not mentioned in the Quran, and yet many insist it is an "Islamic practice."[54]

FROM NEW ROCHELLE TO LAHORE

Critiques of Western feminists emerged not only from secular Third World feminists but also, on different grounds, from more religious Muslim perspectives. In April 1976, just months after the UN conference in Mexico City, Maryam Jameelah of Lahore, Pakistan, published a scathing critique of the Western women's liberation movement. This short book, *Islam and the Muslim Woman Today,* was widely read in Islamist circles worldwide, in its original English as well as in numerous translations. One of the earliest and most prominent Muslim women to write about Islam and society, politics, and the West, Jameelah was born Margaret (Peggy) Marcus and raised in a reformed Jewish family in New York.

Peggy Marcus's curiosity about Eastern cultures revealed itself early, in the pictures she drew as a young child, the music she listened to, and the books she read. Particularly fascinated by Muslims and Arabs, she increasingly found herself at odds with family and friends who supported the Zionist movement and the State of Israel. As a student at New York University, she tried to immerse herself in Orthodox Judaism and, when disillusioned with that, a Bahai group, but neither met her needs, spiritual or political. Following severe mental distress at nineteen, she revisited Islam, this time through the works of Muhammad Asad (born Leopold Weiss, an Austrian Jew who had converted to Islam) and New York University professor and rabbi Abraham Katsh.[55]

Marcus became increasingly involved with Islamic organizations in the New York area and also started writing to prominent male Islamic leaders around the world, among them Sayyid Qutb of the Muslim Brotherhood in Egypt and the Geneva-based Dr. Said Ramadan. In December 1960 she contacted Abul Ala Maududi, the founder and head of the Islamist party Jamaat-i Islami in Pakistan and informed him, "I am a young American woman, twenty-six years of age who has become so intensely interested in Islam as the only hope for the world that I want to become a convert." They began to correspond regularly about the role of Islam in addressing emergent social problems.[56]

In her letters to Maududi, Marcus wrote of her discomfort, even revulsion, at many aspects of contemporary US society, including expectations of men and women. For example, in a March 1961 letter she enclosed a recent article from *Look* magazine "about the latest fashions in women's dress, which to me are so repulsive that I refuse to conform and would rather be struck dead than seen wearing it." She accused "American and European fashion designers" of producing styles that make the "modern Western woman look like a street walker," though she added that "even professional prostitutes do not go to the extremes of these so-called 'respectable' women." At the same time she objected to the manner in which the communist system and, to a lesser degree, the Western world were pushing women into the workplace, including mothers of young children, and relying on nurseries to raise those children. While in full support of women being educated to the highest levels, she firmly saw women's primary role as revolving around motherhood and the home. Maududi, for his part, responded to her deep unhappiness with her present circumstances with messages of support. Referring to the "incompatibility between you and your society" in his February 1961 letter, he described her as an "equatorial sapling implanted into the Arctic Zone" and suggested that she either surround herself with like-minded people in the United States or migrate to a Muslim country, "preferably Pakistan," where he would assist her in finding a "virtuous young Muslim to be [her] life-companion." Marcus formally became a Muslim after Eid al-Adha prayers on 24 May 1961 and adopted the name Maryam Jameelah, which she described in a letter to Maududi as "my new name of which I am very proud."[57] Maududi was quick to recognize how powerful her example could be in bringing around his primary target audience, the "Muslim youth" of Pakistan who were "trying to westernize themselves despite their birth in a Muslim society."[58]

Like Maudud, Jameelah was harshly critical of Muslims like the nineteenth-century Egyptian Qassim Amin and the Indian Syed Ameer Ali, who had tried to reconcile Islamic tradition and doctrine with Western ideas about science, marriage, and gender. She also wrote disparagingly of the young students she met at the Muslim Student Association at Columbia University, where she regularly attended Friday congregational prayers, describing them as "blissfully unaware that the criticism with which they attack the traditional madrasas is a thousand times truer in the case of themselves... [for] they never do their own thinking but merely repeat in the most mechanical way what they are taught like parrots!" She was similarly critical of postwar US Jews who sought to assimilate and "to think, live, look and behave exactly like other Americans."[59]

In March 1962 Jameelah finally accepted Maudud's invitation to move to Pakistan, explaining, "I am a hopeless misfit. I just cannot live in this society." It was important to her, however, that Maudud first write to her parents to reassure them that she would live in his home in Lahore as a daughter and to disabuse them of the notions they hold, "like all other Westerners, ... that Muslims have nothing but contempt for women and keep them in abject subjection like chattel and that in Pakistan women are ill-treated and denied their rights as individuals." In his response to Maudud's letter, Herbert Marcus gave his and his wife's "full consent" to their daughter's decision to move to Pakistan, and shortly thereafter Jameelah boarded a Greek freighter departing from Brooklyn. In her first letter to her parents, Jameelah described the strong sensation of having come home that she experienced during her stop in Alexandria, Egypt, her first time in a Muslim-majority society. She would later write of her migration as an "escape" from a "bleak future in America," much as the Prophet Muhammad and his early followers had migrated to Medina to flee persecution in Mecca. In Pakistan she found "happiness" and appreciation of precisely "those qualities of character and temperament [that] Western society ridicules and scorns," though she conceded that, "like every other Muslim country," Pakistan was becoming "increasingly contaminated by the most noxious dirt from Europe and America."[60]

In 1976 Jameelah published *Islam and the Muslim Woman Today* to address misconceptions about the "social position of the Muslim woman as inferior" and to highlight the problems of the modern feminist and Islamic reform movements. She identified purdah and elements of Islamic marriage as the main issues inspiring "pity" among the "exponents of modern feminism" around the world and among "modernists" in Muslim countries like Pakistan. Alluding to legal reforms such as the 1961 Muslim Family Laws Ordinance in Pakistan, she denounced those who had pushed for restrictions on polygamy, arguing that such calls were "entirely the result of mental slavery to the values of Western civilization."[61]

Jameelah also attacked the conflation of women's emancipation with their unveiling, with "state-sponsored parades of unveiled girls in uniform marching through the streets of the capital waving banners and shouting nationalist slogans, ladies casting their ballots at election time, public 'beauty' contests where the seminude candidates are examined by the judges much as prize cattle at a fair or women dressed like men fighting in the army or working on a factory assembly-line." She vehemently opposed as contrary to Islam what she saw as efforts to confuse the roles of the sexes. "In Islam," she insisted, the "role of the woman is not the ballot-box but maintenance of home and family," allowing women to serve men as "helpers concealed from public gaze behind the scenes—a less exciting and more humble role perhaps, but no less essential from the preservation of our way of life." Turning her attention to the West, she quoted selectively from news stories to argue that feminism had already wreaked havoc in Western society and was poised to do the same in Muslim countries. "The movement for 'female emancipation,'" she warned, "should be recognized by all Muslims for what it is—a malignant conspiracy to destroy the home and family and eventually wreck our entire society."[62]

While Jameelah empathized with the women at Seneca Falls in 1848 who had demanded "their legitimate rights in marriage, control of property and earnings and equal pay with men for the same work," she found the feminists of the 1960s and 1970s "far more radical." She detailed with some horror the many demands and slogans of the US Women's Strike for Equality on 26 August 1970, the fiftieth anniversary of the Nineteenth Amendment, which had granted US women the right to vote. Unacceptable and contrary to Islam, in her eyes, was these new feminists' opposition "to any social roles being determined by sex," and she lamented the gradual encroachment of the feminist movement in Muslim countries, particularly visible in some women's decision to relax their observance of purdah, "revolting against their traditional roles, [and] patterning their lives more and more on the models of their Western sisters."[63]

Despite Jameelah's vociferous attacks on feminism as unnatural and abnormal for challenging what she saw as natural and God-ordained complementary differences between men and women, she appeared to concur with mid- and late twentieth-century US feminists on a few points, though there is no evidence that she recognized this convergence. When *The Feminine Mystique* took the United States by storm in the spring of 1963, Jameelah had already left for Pakistan. While she would certainly have dismissed White middle-class feminist concerns about being isolated in the home, she would have embraced the emerging feminist critiques of the beauty industry and beauty contests. Much like the members of the New York Radical Women who gathered at the 1968 Miss America pageant in Atlantic City and introduced the new feminist movement to the media—and the world—by unfurling a banner emblazoned with the words "Women's Liberation," Jameelah compared such pageants to a cattle auction. Indeed, the first of the ten points raised by the New York Radical Women was a rejection of the "Degrading Mindless-Boob-Girlie Symbol" and the similarities between the beauty pageant and the "county fair, where the nervous animals are judged for teeth, fleece, etc., and where the best 'Specimen' gets the blue ribbon. So are women in our society forced daily to compete for male approval, enslaved by ludicrous 'beauty' standards we ourselves are conditioned to take seriously."[64] Although, contrary to the enduring myth, no bras were burned that day, protesters did throw into a "freedom trash can" various "instruments of torture" to women, such as high heels, girdles, women's magazines, and beauty products.[65] No doubt Jameelah would have beamed with approval at that scene of women rejecting the beauty standards that she had found so uncomfortable in her younger days.

Jameelah also decried the Western feminist argument that liberation required women to participate fully in the workplace and public sphere. Her reasoning, interestingly, was similar to that used by the Cold War–era US government, and some US feminists, against the Soviet model of gender equality that had pressured women to enter the workforce but ultimately failed to provide a communal solution to their responsibilities in the home.[66] Jameelah pointed out that despite Western (and Soviet) efforts to get women out of the home, "this same propaganda insists that the emancipated woman's primary duty is still her home! In other words, this means that the modern woman must bear a *double burden!* In addition to earning her own living in full-time employment outside the home, she must at the same time somehow perform the near-impossible task of fulfilling all her obligations to her husband and children and keep a spotless house single-handed!"[67]

While Jameelah's books sold well and brought her valuable income, South Asian Muslim feminists generally ignored her because she spoke from within an Islamist framework. Through her writings in English and, later, translations into other languages, she came to be recognized as an important spokesperson for the Jamaat-i Islami. Her books' popularity derived not only from their content—their sharp criticisms of the West—but also from her very identity and background, the Jewish woman from New York who had converted to Islam and moved to Pakistan to become the protégée of one of the most influential Islamic ideologues of the twentieth century.

A NEW EPOCH DAWNS

As the 1970s drew to a close, US interest in Islam and Muslims focused on Iran's dramatic revolution. US feminist Kate Millett finally got her chance to visit Iran and arrived in March 1979 with an invitation to International Women's Day celebrations. In response to Ayatollah Khomeini's recent decrees regarding women, however, it became a day of mass protests. Images of the Iranian women's protests launched a new stage in US ideas about Muslim women's oppression by Islam as well as US views about the right kind of Muslim feminists. For Americans who saw Khomeini as both anti-American and cruelly misogynistic, Iranian women protesting in the streets against the new laws of the new Islamic republic made sense. What they overlooked was that many of these women had also protested against the shah. They wanted changes, yes, but they were not all looking to become the prototypical US feminist or US woman. As one Iranian woman, a chemist, told the *New York Times,* "We have our own tongues, our own demands. We can talk for us."[68]

Mim Kelber repeatedly reminded her *Ms.* magazine readers that "feminism in Iran was far from being a Western import," carefully suppressing any sense of US feminist superiority with her question: "Do we know…that Iranian feminists need our support—*and vice versa?*" She cited numerous Iranian feminists on the mixed effectiveness of the shah's much-heralded reforms and of the government-sponsored WOI. Yet, even in the midst of her otherwise-nuanced discussion, Islam emerged as the main villain, oppressive to Iranian women and feminists through its laws, along with the "Muslim men" who sought to implement them. She concluded, "For the women in Iran, for women all over the Islam [sic] world, threatened by a growing religious fundamentalism, and for international feminism, the five days in March can and must be the beginning of a new unity."[69] The hostage crisis that would unfold some eight months later at the US embassy in Tehran would only cement the US view of "Islam" as monstrously alien to the US way of life.

SEX AND THE MUSLIM WOMAN

Western fears about the Islamic threat emanating from revolutionary Iran were accompanied by Western fascination with female circumcision. When the World Health Organization first observed the practice in the early 1950s and alerted the United Nations, it used phrases such as "ritual operations," "ritual practices," and "operations based on custom."[70] Now, however, Western media quickly depicted the practice as a Muslim custom, even though it was known to have predated Islam, to be practiced also by non-Muslims in African and Arab countries (by animists, Copts, Catholics, Protestants, and Falashas, or Ethiopian Jews), and to be almost unknown in Muslim societies elsewhere.[71]

In March 1980 US feminist luminaries Robin Morgan and Gloria Steinem published "The International Crime of Genital Mutilation" in *Ms.* Following a later reprint of the article, Steinem would explain that they had delayed publication of the 1980 article out of concern that international attention might serve "to entrench the practice," and they had proceeded only after the World Health Organization had become more involved in the issue at the regional level. She also recalled that many activists working against the practice "in their own countries expressed relief that [their article had] placed FGM [female genital mutilation] on a continuum of patriarchal practices that included Europe and the United States."[72]

Although the 1980 *Ms.* article cautioned against assumptions that FGM was an Islamic practice or that such procedures were unknown in the West, the US examples simply reinforced the idea that this had been a problem in the United States only in the distant past. In a letter to the editor in the following issue, feminist biologists Ruth Hubbard and Patricia Farnes reminded readers that the practice was common "not only in the Third World...but right here in the United States, where it is [note the present tense] used as part of a procedure to 'repair' by 'plastic surgery' so-called genital ambiguities. Few people realize that this procedure has routinely involved removal of the entire clitoris and its nerve supply—in other words, total clitoridectomy." In the 1990s activists from the Intersex Society of North America would seek to ally themselves with US organizations campaigning against FGM but found feminists, journalists, and legislators consistently unwilling to draw attention to the links between the "scientific" and "medicalized" procedures routinely performed on intersex infants in the United States and the "barbaric" practices of distant cultures.[73]

Morgan and Steinem's article included an excerpt from a forthcoming English translation of Nawal El Saadawi's 1977 Arabic book *The Hidden Face of Eve*, published that same year in London.[74] In the book the Egyptian activist wrote about her observations during her many years as a doctor, as well as about the painful genital surgery she herself had undergone as a young child. El Saadawi later recalled how furious she had been at Steinem's selective editing of her article for *Ms.*, removing the "political, social, and historical analyses" to publish "only the personal statements, which put me in a very awkward position. People asked," she said, "How could Nawal write such a thing?" El Saadawi's US publisher had similarly cut the preface that had appeared in the UK version, making it appear "that I am separating the sexual from the political, which I never do. To me, women who think they are liberated but who are obsessed with sexuality are not liberated. They are living a new slavery. They are obsessed by not having men around just as they were obsessed with having them around. It is the other side of the same coin."[75] In the omitted passages El Saadawi made it clear that she "disagree[d] with those women in America and Europe who concentrate on issues such as female circumcision and depict them as proof of the unusual and barbaric oppression to which women are exposed only in African and Arab countries. I oppose all attempts to deal with such problems in isolation."[76]

FGM emerged as a topic of international discussion for the first time at the Mid-Decade UN Conference for Women in Copenhagen in July 1980. El Saadawi described the heated discussions: "In our workshops, we argued that clitoridectomy has nothing to do with Africa or with any religion, Islam or Christianity. It is known in history that it was performed in Europe and America, Asia and Africa. It has to do with patriarchy and monogamy." According to El Saadawi, Western feminists such as Fran Hoskens did not "want to hear any of this."[77] The Senegal-based Association of African Women for Research and Development also reacted sharply to the emerging Western approach to female circumcision, describing it as a "new crusade of the West... led out of the moral and cultural prejudices of Judaeo-Christian Western society." They called instead for an approach grounded in "solidarity," based on "self-affirmation and mutual respect."[78]

In a letter to the editor in the Copenhagen conference newspaper *Forum 80*, journalist Eugénie Rokhaya Aw pointed out that the Western world had its own share of problems, such as "battered women, abused children and rape," which its feminists rarely broached in such international gatherings, choosing instead to focus on the oppression of Third World and Muslim women in a manner that rendered the latter as inferior and in need of Western assistance. She wrote, "We, women, can avoid a split among ourselves, provided we are prepared to question our own visions of ourselves, to accept that we have differences but we are all worthy of respect and to be willing to learn from each other in order to better understand each other."[79] The overwhelming attention directed by US feminists in the early 1980s to the issue of female surgeries in Africa and the Middle East led to frustration and exhaustion among anti-FGM activists and feminists in those countries.[80] By the time of the Nairobi conference marking the end of the UN decade for women just five years later, much of the early goodwill that Steinem would later recall had dissipated, if it had indeed ever existed.

In 1985 Angela Davis traveled to Egypt on an assignment to write a chapter for a "world report" on the UN Decade. Davis's encounters during her college years had shaped her view of the world and struggles beyond the United States. In her 1974 autobiography, edited by Toni Morrison at Random House, Davis wrote of the many experiences that allowed her to view the United States from a fresh perspective and to come to understand that her relationship to the United States was different from that of her fellow US college students. She recalled, for example, these students' silence regarding the murder of four Black girls in a church bombing in Birmingham—girls from families she had known growing up—and her own muted reaction to Kennedy's assassination. One of only three Black students at Brandeis University, which she attended as an undergraduate student on a full scholarship in the early 1960s, Davis quickly made friends with Lalit, a young man from India; Melanie from the Philippines; and "Mac, a South Vietnamese woman about to be deported because she was opposed to Diem." Such friendships, she recollected, "helped me to understand concretely the interconnectedness of the freedom struggles of peoples throughout the world." Davis would experience more such connections the following summer when she stopped in Paris on her way to attend a youth festival in Helsinki.[81]

Davis had been looking forward to this opportunity "to leave the country in order to get a better perspective on things." When she moved around Paris, however, she read "with horror the racist slogans scratched on walls throughout the city threatening death to the Algerians" and recalled news of bombs in North African cafés and suspicious deaths. The parallels between European colonialism and White US racism were driven home when she attended a pro-Algerian rally near the Sorbonne. "When the *flics* [cops] broke it up with their high-power water hoses, they were as vicious as the redneck cops in Birmingham who met the Freedom Riders with their dogs and hoses. The new places, the new experiences I had expected to discover through travel turned out to be the same old places, the same old experiences with a common message of struggle."[82]

Davis began her second year of college with a sense of confidence and wisdom. "Meeting people from all over the world had taught me how important it was to be able to tear down the superficial barriers which separated us." She returned to Paris for her third year and, after college, attended graduate school in West Germany. Her early exposure to struggles around the world, combined with her academic study of philosophy and her intimate involvement in domestic activism, would shape her later interactions with women activists from the Third World, including Muslim women.

Davis's earliest encounter with Muslims had, not surprisingly, been with Black American Islam. She recalled a "gentle-looking, soft-spoken boy" in high school who, she was surprised to learn upon his arrest, was a "Black Muslim." She admitted that until then she had accepted the "prevailing propaganda" that Muslims were a "strange sect of people ranting and raving about Allah's future destruction of all white people" and who offered no real solution for racism. Then, during her first visit to Paris, she learned about the Algerian struggle for independence and, when she returned to campus, listened, with a mix of shock and fascination, to Malcolm X speak.[83] In 1973 she made only a brief stop in Cairo while in transit to Brazzaville but was able to return in 1985 for the report marking the end of the UN Decade for Women. In the course of the later visit she discovered firsthand the extent of Egyptian feminists' displeasure with the peculiar nature of Western feminist interest in their lives, sexual relations, and genital surgeries, compelling Davis to confront the implications of her privileged position as a US feminist, even if a radical and communist feminist of color.

Women: A World Report was organized by the UK-based New Internationalist Cooperative in cooperation with the United Nations. They sent ten feminist writers to different countries to reflect on women's experiences. In an effort to avoid replicating the more familiar practice "of the rich world ogling at the poor," they assigned as many Third World writers to study the

First World as they did First World writers to poorer countries. Among the more prominent writers who participated (and their assigned countries) were Anita Desai (Norway), Marilyn French (India), Buchi Emecheta (United States), Jill Tweedie (Indonesia), Nawal el Saadawi (United Kingdom), Germaine Greer (Cuba), and Angela Davis (Egypt).[84] Each writer was assigned a particular topic on which to focus—and that was where the project's lofty aspirations began to unravel.

It was Davis's first real visit to Cairo, and she was excited to learn about the lives of women there in the company of her hosts, members of the Arab Women's Solidarity Association, which had recently received formal recognition from the Ministry of Social Affairs. The association's president Nawal El Saadawi was away lecturing in the United States at the time. As she passed the vast City of the Dead, where a million Egyptians had taken up residence, Davis quickly understood that the housing crisis was one of the most urgent priorities for women.

Her assigned topic, however, as she soon revealed at a lecture organized by the association, was not a pressing economic issue such as housing but the "sexual dimension of women's pursuit of equality." Local feminists were furious. At a meeting Davis attended at the National Centre for Sociological and Criminological Studies, Egyptian feminist scholar Shahida Elbaz excoriated Western feminists for presenting circumcision as Muslim women's primary concern: "Women in the West should know that we have a stand in relation to them concerning our issues and our problems. We reject their patronising attitude. It is connected with built-in mechanisms of colonialism and with their sense of superiority.... They decide what problems we have, how we should face them, without even possessing the tools to know our problems."[85]

In her published report Davis insisted that she had not initially understood that "I would be expected to focus quite specifically" on sex and "clitoridectomy" and had even considered withdrawing after she found out. She was, after all, "very much aware of the passionate debate still raging within international women's circles around...[Western feminists'] crusade against female circumcision in African and Arab countries." She pointed out that, as an "Afro-American woman," she was "especially sensitive to the underlying racism characterizing the often myopic emphasis on such issues" and to the notion that women in these countries "would magically ascend to a state of equality once they managed to throw off the fetters of genital mutilation. Or rather once white Western feminists accomplished this for them." Davis highlighted the analogy with the birth control movement in the United States, long resented by Black American women weary of "being portrayed... as bestial and oversexed" and, through their fertility, as a threat to the numerical advantage of the White population. Davis bemoaned that most Americans, even those on university campuses, knew nothing about countries like Egypt and the Sudan beyond the practice of genital surgeries and yet seemed oblivious to the power of "male supremacist standards of beauty" that pushed US women to engage in practices and surgical procedure to alter their own bodies.[86]

Throughout her brief stay in the country, Davis struggled to understand Egyptian women's priorities in their own terms. She recalled a dinner in the home of Shahira Mehrez, at which "pandemonium erupted" once again when she mentioned her topic was "Women and Sex." Overcoming some initial defensiveness, she wrote, "I laboured to convince myself to refrain from attempting to defend my own position. Was I not in Egypt to learn about the way Egyptian women themselves interpreted the role of sexuality in their lives and their struggles? Was I not especially interested in their various responses to the unfortunate chauvinism characterising attitudes toward the sexual dimension of Arab women's lives in the capitalist countries?" Surrounded by many women who had followed her earlier travails with the US legal system with admiration and had come to meet her precisely because of who she was and what she had done, Davis began to respond in welcome solidarity, with open-mindedness and a willingness to learn rather than from the sense of superiority and condescension that more commonly characterized Western feminist writing on the subject. Yes, sexual liberation was important, she wrote, but more urgent for Egyptian women were fighting poverty, the housing crisis (what was the nature of sexual relations when a large family had to share a single room?), large-scale male migration to the Gulf countries, and economic policies that fostered ever-increasing dependence on more powerful Western economies. Prioritizing those issues over sexual liberation as defined by Western feminists did not make Egyptian women activists less credible feminists.[87]

EXPANDING WOMEN'S ISSUES BEYOND "CROTCH ISSUES"

The end of the UN Decade for Women was marked by the women's world conference in Nairobi in 1985. Never before in history had so many women gathered in one venue—well over fourteen thousand women from more than 160 countries. The very location of the conference no doubt helped to dampen some of the strong disagreements that had characterized the earlier conferences. As three feminist scholars who attended the conference remarked, "Observing firsthand the reality of Third World women's lives tempered the arrogance of many First World women. At the same time, Third World women were able to express their positions and concerns in a familiar environment." The changes in the global economy and international politics since the previous conferences—the rise of conservative religious movements in Latin America, the United States, the Middle East, and South Asia and economic crises in the United States and in the Third World—had had profound consequences for women in all these regions and also helped them recognize the interconnected nature of their problems. Dorothy Butler Gilliam, the first Black American woman reporter at the *Washington Post,* was among the nearly one thousand Black American women to attend the unofficial gatherings in Nairobi. In an article on this "historic gathering of women" for *Ebony* magazine, Gilliam wrote of the exhilaration of being "back in the Motherland" and of being present at the "birth of an international women's movement." Still, the conference was not without conflict and discord.[88]

Just weeks before the Nairobi conference, Black American feminist Flo Kennedy, who had attended both earlier conferences, warned of plans by the organizers to define "women's issues" narrowly and in a manner that did not reflect the real concerns of non-White, non–First World women: "It's a 'no no' to talk about women's issues other than crotch issues. Women are not going to be encouraged to talk about South Africa, apartheid, Ethiopia, certainly not the Arab/Israeli scene and so there again, women are being silenced." The official US delegation clearly espoused this narrow definition of women's issues. Maureen Reagan, the daughter of the US president and head of the official US delegation, announced early that political concerns would not be permitted to overshadow the "unique concerns of women." She also vowed to come "home with a document that did not have Zionism in it," and she succeeded. Although the United States once again found itself holding the minority position on issues on which much of the rest of the world agreed—Israel's oppression of the Palestinians, South African apartheid, and international trade restrictions—it ultimately endorsed the global plan of action that emerged from the official meeting. Participants from around the world also came together to oppose the US government's recent decision to restrict funding for organizations such as the UN Fund for Population

Activities that provided a variety of reproductive services, including abortion. Angela Davis protested that the official US delegation presented and represented only the current Reagan administration's conservative politics and included only five Black Americans in a delegation of thirty-six. Still smarting from the stalled ratification of the Equal Rights Amendment, US feminists were furious at Maureen Reagan's declaration that "all legal barriers to political equality have long since been eliminated" in the United States.[89]

Polygamy, population control, and female circumcision were important topics of discussion at the conference, but this time there was far stronger pushback from women who had previously been targeted for enlightenment, rescue, and empowerment by Western feminists. As Egyptian participant Nadia Atif put it, "What is needed from our Western sisters is not a denigrating, we-know-better approach, but the realization that mutilation of women is the actual order of the day. In the West it manifests itself as economic, psychological and spiritual mutilation, in Africa, it includes the physical. Let us then unite against all forms of female mutilation, beginning with ourselves and our children."[90] Polygamy proved a point of contention between African and Black American women. Gilliam reported in *Ebony*, "Black American women regarded [the practice] with disdain" and were "surprised" to hear African women defend it "as superior to the devastating extra-marital affairs among American couples." Dolly Adams, then president of the veteran Black American organization the Links, later described that interaction as a "revelation.... While I know the system needs to be improved to better protect the women, I can't be as critical as I once was."[91]

The greater presence in Nairobi of Third World feminist movements, including in leadership roles, led to less defensiveness and more open criticism on the part of Third World women of practices in their own communities and their own governments. Zimbabwean sociologist and participant Rudo Gaidzanwa came away with the sense that, compared to past interactions, there had been "little of the 'more feminist than thou' posture" among Western women but also less of the "more political than thou" position among Third World women. Nonetheless, she concluded that "as long as imperialism impoverishes the Third World, Third World feminism will be highly 'political,'" and it was high time that Western feminists directly addressed the "issues of racism and imperialism in the feminist movement and in western societies."[92]

This new organizational reality also enabled the creation of new coalitions between women's groups from around the world and especially in the Third

FIGURE 22. DAWN meeting in Bergen, Norway, in 1984, in preparation for the Nairobi UN conference. Participants included Neuma Aguiar (Brazil), Peggy Antrobus (Barbados), Rasil Basu (India/UN), Hameeda Hossain (Bangladesh, *standing third from left, front row*), Noeleen Heyzer (Singapore), Devaki Jain (India), and Claire Slatter (Fiji Islands). Courtesy of Hameeda Hossain.

World. Perhaps most prominent among these new international networks was DAWN (Development Alternatives with Women for a New Era), established in Bangalore, India, in August 1984. In Nairobi DAWN presented its framework, which connected the "past history of development policies and strategies to the current systemic crises—in the production and distribution of food, water and fuel availability, international debt, militarization, and growing conservatism opposed to women's changing roles" and suggested "alternative visions"; this was later published as the book *Development, Crises and Alternative Visions: Third World Women's Perspectives,* now a classic feminist text. Among the founding members of DAWN were the Moroccan feminist Fatima Mernissi, who had coauthored that devastating critique of the 1976 Wellesley conference, and Bangladeshi feminists Hameeda Hossain and Rounaq Jahan.[93]

Also founded in this period was the international network Women Living under Muslim Laws. Nine women—from Algeria, Bangladesh, Iran, Mauritius, Morocco, Pakistan, Sudan, and Tanzania—first met in July 1984

FIGURE 23. Regional South and South East Asian Women in Development Conference, Dacca, March 1977, organized by Rounaq Jahan (Bangladesh; *seated, third from left*). Also seated are Devaki Jain (India; *second from left*), Nasrah Shah and Satnam Mahmud (Pakistan; *fourth and fifth from left*). Among those standing are Ela Bhatt (India; *fourth from right*), Durga Ghimere (Nepal), and Elizabeth Uy Eviota (Philippines). Courtesy of Rounaq Jahan.

to discuss recent "violations of women's human rights" under Muslim law in India, Algeria, and Abu Dhabi. Under the leadership of Algerian leftist social scientist Marie-Aimée Hélie-Lucas, the network expanded into a source of support and a forum for women from different countries to share analyses of their respective struggles.[94] As early member Farida Shaheed of Pakistan recalled in a 2004 interview, among the most valuable purposes of regularly bringing together women from different Muslim societies was "to inform women about the differences that exist which all may be called 'Muslim.'"[95]

Bangladeshi feminists were also actively involved in several regional gatherings. For example, in March 1977 Rounaq Jahan organized one of the first events to bring together women from South and Southeast Asia. With Ford Foundation support she hosted the Regional South and South East Asian Women in Development Conference.[96] Conversations among activists in Nairobi spurred the founding of the Asia Pacific Forum on Women, Law and Development in Kuala Lumpur in 1986, with a mission to "use feminist analysis to dissect, engage with and transform laws, legal practices and the systems that shape and inform them." Hameeda Hossain of Bangladesh and Asma Jahangir of Pakistan were among the founding members.[97]

FEMINIST RESISTANCE TO DONORS, DEVELOPMENT, AND MILITARY RULE IN BANGLADESH

Over the course of the UN Decade for Women, the Bangladeshi state embraced the global agenda and, like the vast majority of the world's governments, created official departments focused on improving women's lives and incorporated women's issues into its national development plans.[98] In 1976 it established a Women's Affairs Division and switched from discussing women primarily as victims of the war and famine, in need of relief and rehabilitation, to productive citizens who could contribute to the nation's development.[99] Poor, rural, and urban women started to receive more attention from the government for their distinct potential roles in the country's economic development.

By the end of the UN Decade, Bangladesh was deep into its second military dictatorship. The country had experienced a series of coups and countercoups since the 1975 assassination of Sheikh Mujibur Rahman and most of his family before settling into an extended period of military rule marked by warm overtures to other Muslim-majority countries as well as the United States and western Europe. While both military rulers, Ziaur Rahman and Hussain M. Ershad, took advantage of the increased flow of funding from overseas to provide patronage and gain supporters, they also found themselves having to negotiate between the often-contradictory expectations of Gulf Arab and Western donors, especially on the subject of women.[100]

Under pressure from the World Bank and International Monetary Fund to switch from the previous regimes' import-substitution policy to an export-led model, Ershad introduced a new industrial policy in June 1982. A variety of factors, including the fall in supply from Sri Lanka (then embroiled in civil war), converged to encourage East Asian firms to invest heavily in apparel factories in Bangladesh. As had already happened in other Asian countries, large numbers of young women—attractive because they were low-paid workers, quick learners, and believed to be docile—were recruited to fill the factories.[101] Thus it was that, at the dawn of the neoliberal era ushered in by US president Ronald Reagan and British prime minister Margaret Thatcher—with unreined capitalism, increasing privatization, cuts in government-funded services, and brakes on labor organizing—the "Made in Bangladesh" label on readymade garments introduced a new image of Bangladesh to the world.

A dramatic consequence of these policies became visible on Bangladesh's urban streets. When US feminist and sociologist Shelley Feldman returned to Dhaka (the romanized spelling of the capital's name had been changed from Dacca in 1982) with a Senior Fulbright Award in 1984 after an absence of eighteen months, she did not recognize the city. In her earlier sojourns she had worked with the government and foreign donor agencies and also collaborated on research projects with Florence McCarthy, the former Peace Corps volunteer at the Comilla Academy. Feldman later recalled, "Perhaps most striking were the number of women who now walked along the road, often in groups of six or more, especially after a shift change at the recently opened garment factories that dotted the streets throughout the city. [This] ... was in stark contrast to my earlier experience when I was one of only a few, if any, women walking quickly along these same roads."[102]

Many Bangladeshi feminists appreciated the opportunities for research and policy interventions created by international donor attention to women's issues, though some were quick to realize the pitfalls of a donor-driven agenda. As early as 1984, Sultana Alam and Nilufar Matin denounced the hierarchical chain that linked Western feminists and development practitioners, urban Bangladeshi feminists, and poor, rural women. Just as the Western development community regarded Bangladesh's poor as an "idyllic, quiescent, suffering but harmonious mass of natives in need of 'help,'" Alam and Matin pointed out that the Bangladeshi elite, urban feminists, researchers, and activists "view[ed] themselves as working towards the salvation of rural women, rather than joining them in a mutual struggle." They also castigated the "narrow 'feminism' espoused by Western participants" that focused on purdah as the primary obstacle to change and neglected landlessness, rural unemployment, and increasing poverty in the countryside. Like the missionaries and colonial officials of yore who professed an interest in women's status in colonized countries but not their own, many of the Western women and development practitioners who were able to "swiftly move into positions of power" in Bangladesh "did not necessarily have backgrounds in organizing women back home or writing about feminist issues." This lack of experience with feminist concerns "back home" no doubt explained their refusal to even "hint at the true dimensions of marginalization [of women] in the economies of Europe and North America, leave alone hint at development patriarchy within the World Bank, the UN, USAID, [and so on]."[103]

Also, in 1984, a group of Bangladeshi activists interested in finding development alternatives that would take into account the needs of the most marginalized communities rather than donor and corporate priorities started UBINIG (Unnayan Bikalper Nitinirdharoni Gobeshona, or Policy Research for Development Alternative). Farida Akhter, one of the founders, recalled their distress over the negative environmental and economic impact of the World Bank's export-led policies. Commercial shrimp agriculture, for example, had salinized arable land, while weavers had lost their livelihood as a result of a burgeoning garment industry that relied on imported textiles. Working with local farmers, they launched the Naya Krishi Andolan (New Agriculture Movement), an ecologically and socially conscious form of agriculture akin to movements emerging in Europe and India. Women farmers were at the forefront of this movement because of their direct exposure to chemicals used in mainstream agriculture and their experience with a variety of health problems, including reproductive ones.[104] UBINIG also mobilized against the population-control establishment for flooding the market with contraceptives such as the high-estrogen Maya and the surgically implanted Norplant without full disclosure of the risks and without appropriate follow-up consultations and for offering financial incentives for procedures and contraceptive adoption to women and men whose poverty rendered their informed consent essentially meaningless.[105] Bangladesh had by then become the largest recipient of international population-control funds, and, with population assistance constituting over two-thirds of its national budget, the government had come to rely on it.[106]

AN INTERNATIONAL BILL OF RIGHTS FOR WOMEN

The Convention on the Elimination of All Forms of Discrimination against Women (CEDAW), adopted by the United Nations in December 1979, became an important issue for feminists in Bangladesh. CEDAW, often described as an international bill of rights for women, defines discrimination against women as "any distinction, exclusion or restriction made on the basis of sex which has the effect or purpose of impairing or nullifying the recognition, enjoyment or exercise by women, irrespective of their marital status, on a basis of equality of men and women, of human rights and fundamental freedoms in the political, economic, social, cultural, civil or any other field."[107] The following summer it was presented for government signatures at the mid-decade UN Women's Conference in Copenhagen. Sixty-four countries signed the convention that summer, including a few Muslim-majority countries, such as Afghanistan, Egypt, Indonesia, Jordan, and Tunisia.[108]

While the governments of some Muslim-majority countries invoked conflicts with Islam to justify not signing the convention, feminists from around the world, Muslim and non-Muslim, raised other concerns. One was CEDAW's privileging of the individual rights of women, which they saw as arising directly out of the Western feminist experience and not reflective of how women elsewhere envisioned their place in their communities. Critics also saw this focus on individual rights as too closely tied to modernization theory, which, since the early Cold War era, had sought to persuade countries to shed their own "backward" cultures and remake themselves in the mold of the West. Finally, as the fiery discussions at the first three UN women's conferences had revealed, there was no consensus on the very meaning of equality. CEDAW was clearly problematic for many women around the world for whom community and family connections, religion, and culture held great significance and for those who cared about larger social inequalities and injustices. Nonetheless, most feminist organizations chose to work with and around CEDAW rather than reject it outright.[109]

Bangladeshi lawyer Sigma Huda recalled the heavy campaigning by activists to pressure the government to sign CEDAW. Tactics included distributing eight thousand copies of a Bengali translation of CEDAW among women's organizations and activists. The Bangladesh government finally ratified the convention in November 1984, but with significant reservations. Like Egypt, which had ratified CEDAW in 1981 and many other Muslim-majority countries that would ratify in later years, Bangladesh justified its reservations by explicitly noting a perceived conflict with Islamic law.[110] In the years that followed, feminist historians and legal scholars of Islam around the world protested that the articles against which many Muslim countries had expressed reservations did not in fact contradict the Quran and that Islamic law was far from immutable and had to be interpreted and understood in context.[111] In reality, domestic and international political considerations played more important roles than religious interpretations, and, when the time was right, many countries withdrew their reservations.

In Bangladesh some twenty women's organizations that had come together in the late 1980s in preparation for the WIDF-sponsored World Congress of Women in Moscow in June 1987 consolidated as Oikyo Boddho Nari Shomaj (United Women's Forum) and issued a joint list of seventeen demands, including the ratification of CEDAW without any reservations. The list also called for a uniform civil code (in place of family laws based on the religion of the community into which one was born), the implementation of legal rights for workers such as maternity leave with pay as determined by the International Labour Organization, and a minimum wage for domestic workers.[112] A decade later, in July 1997, as part of an effort to fulfill pledges made at the Fourth UN Women's Conference in Beijing in 1995, the Bangladesh government finally withdrew its earlier reservations to the articles on family benefits and guardianship and custody of children. No doubt in an effort to appease both the women's groups and secularists demanding the withdrawal and the Islamist parties opposed to full ratification, the government chose to withdraw the reservations quietly, without any publicity.[113] In Bangladesh, as elsewhere, actual implementation, of course, has remained another matter.

Four decades after the UN adopted CEDAW, the United States is the only Western state on the very short list of countries that have not ratified the convention. The others are Iran, Somalia, Sudan, and South Sudan, and the smaller states of the Holy See, Tonga, and Palau. In several discussions on the Senate floor since President Jimmy Carter sent it there, participants have raised objections over the language around women's rights used by the rest of the world, which includes a critique of colonialism, racism, and Zionism, as we saw at the UN conferences. Others have voiced the assumption that US women already have all the rights and protections they need—even though there is evidence that CEDAW would enhance the provisions of existing legislation in such areas as domestic violence.[114]

FIGHTING ISLAMIZATION

As the 1980s drew to a close, many feminists in Bangladesh became engrossed with the government's ever-increasing efforts to Islamize law and politics. Indeed, women's groups were the first civic organizations to protest against the Ershad government's plans to introduce a constitutional amendment declaring Islam the state religion. As an April 1988 issue of the Dhaka-based English weekly *Holiday* announced, "This time the women have taken the lead."[115] The country's first military ruler, Ziaur Rahman, had removed secularism from the constitution in 1976, when the women's movement was preoccupied with the aftermath of the war, floods, and famine of the early 1970s. However, when his successor, Ershad, floated a proposal in 1988 to make Islam the state religion, women's organizations mobilized in vocal opposition. Several new organizations had emerged since the first International Women's Year conference, and they were some of the best-organized civic associations. Among those to join the venerable Mahila Parishad were the research and activist organization Women for Women, the professional group Bangladesh National Women Lawyers Association, and consciousness-raising and discussion-based Naripokkho, which translates as "On the Side of Women" or "Pro-women."[116]

The small group of well-educated, middle- and upper-class professional women who had founded Naripokkho had intended it to be an autonomous organization, distinct from the well-established and much larger Mahila Parishad, the women's wings of other political parties, and the NGOs that were already beginning to proliferate and take an interest in women's issues, albeit usually driven by donor agendas and UN priorities. The group's regular Tuesday discussions had allowed it "to tap into women's perceptions of their lives and situations to create an agenda that would speak on behalf of women," as cofounder Firdous Azim later recalled. In a 1989 interview (published in 1992) in the US radical feminist journal *off our backs,* cofounder Shireen Huq explained, "We decided deliberately to bring up the issues that people would rather avoid. Controversial issues, like sex outside marriage, abortion, you know, questions that are difficult in our social context." The discussions quickly made clear that "to launch a political fight based on only one issue," such as sexuality or economic issues, "is very restricting and piecemeal." A more "holistic" approach, by contrast, allowed Naripokkho to turn its attention to sex workers threatened with eviction, the coercive practices of the population-control establishment, and different forms of violence against women. Naripokkho gained new prominence in 1988 with its insistence on a secular polity that protected the rights of all citizens. As Azim later explained, "We used our standpoints on gender equality to talk about the equality of all citizens of the state, regardless of religion, and of the state's duty to treat all its citizens equally." The activists' fierce opposition to the proposed amendment was informed by their support for Bangladesh's original constitution but also, no doubt, from having observed the consequences for women of the recent Islamization drives in Iran and Pakistan.[117]

Bangladeshi feminists' activism against the expanding role of religion, specifically Islam, in law and politics went largely unremarked by international observers, who were preoccupied with Bangladesh's economic-development prospects. Bangladesh's "Muslimness," however, would soon become of great significance, given the prominent role of British Bengali Muslims in the outrage against Salman Rushdie's 1988 book, *Satanic Verses,* quickly followed by the furor over Bangladesh's own besieged writer, Taslima Nasreen.

EIGHT

In Search of Solidarity across Seven Seas and Thirteen Rivers

TASLIMA NASREEN (often spelled Nasrin) had understandably mixed feelings about being in Berlin. "To live alone in this unknown society is very difficult," she told the London *Independent* in late 1995. "The uncertain future disturbs me. I had never come to a Western country before. I think it is good for my writing. My experiences and my views have become broader....I miss my language. I write in Bengali, but I hardly ever speak it now."[1]

Two years earlier the writer and physician from Bangladesh had introduced herself to the readers of the *New York Times* in an op-ed titled "Sentenced to Death." Islamic groups in Bangladesh had announced a bounty on her life, forcing her into hiding, because they were outraged by her recently published novel *Lojja* (Shame) and an interview she had given in Calcutta. In the *Times* Nasreen announced that it was her "moral responsibility to protest" and said she would "not be silenced. Everywhere I look I see women being mistreated and their oppression justified in the name of religion." For Bangladesh to "became a modern country and find its place in the world," it had to fight the existing "reactionary attitudes" toward women.[2]

Although feminists in Bangladesh had been fighting against the growing Islamization of politics for several years by then, Nasreen's case brought international attention to the situation. More often than not, however, she and her foreign supporters presented her as fighting the good fight on her own, occluding the role of her Bangladeshi supporters as well as the far longer history of women organizing for their interests in that part of the world. Coming in the wake of Ayatollah Khomeini's 1989 fatwa against British novelist Salman Rushdie for his depictions of the Prophet Muhammad in the *Satanic Verses*, it was perhaps inevitable that Nasreen would be dubbed the "female Rushdie." And it also followed that Bangladesh, seen for so long as a land of poverty and disaster, and then of women factory workers and micro-credit users, came to be branded a land of militant Islam by the Western governments and media, just as Iran had following its revolution and the US embassy hostage crisis. The manner in which the Western media depicted Nasreen would be repeated time and again, hailing individual Muslim women for their bravery in speaking out against oppressive traditions, while minimizing or even ignoring organized activism on those same issues. A particularly egregious instance of this would occur in regard to Afghan women in the final years of the century, but the approach would become commonplace in the early twenty-first century following the attacks of 11 September 2001 and the launch of the so-called war on terror.

The world into which Taslima Nasreen cast her plea for help in 1993 had recently experienced other dramatic events. Relations between the West and the Muslim world, generally speaking, had entered a new phase, markedly different from the immediate post–World War II decades as well as the even earlier colonial period. These changes had implications for how Muslim women were depicted and discussed—and the different ways they, in turn, responded to these representations. In Bangladesh an extended mass prodemocracy movement had toppled the Ershad government in December 1990, ushering in a new era of democracy after some fifteen years of military rule. Bangladesh politics was now dominated by two Muslim women: Prime Minister Khaleda Zia, the widow of the first military ruler, Ziaur Rahman, who was assassinated in 1981, and Sheikh Hasina, head of the opposition and the daughter of Sheikh Mujibur Rahman, the leader of Bangladesh's independence movement who was assassinated in 1975. The Islamist party Jamaat-i Islami, banned from politics right after the 1971 liberation war for its wartime collaboration with West Pakistani forces in atrocities against civilians, had recently been rehabilitated by the new democratic government under Khaleda Zia's Bangladesh Nationalist Party. This promptly reenergized calls for a war-crimes tribunal, led by secular activists such as the poet Sufia Kamal and the writer Jahanara Imam.

In neighboring India, in December 1992, supporters of the increasingly powerful Hindu nationalist movement had razed to the ground the Babri Masjid, claiming that the sixteenth-century mosque had been built atop a temple dedicated to the deity Ram, setting off violent riots all over India and neighboring Bangladesh. This in turn inspired Nasreen's controversial novel, published in February 1993. Further afield the final Soviet withdrawal from Afghanistan and the fall of the Berlin Wall, both in 1989, had precipitated the end of the Cold War. Around the world millions watched as Germans celebrated on that cold November night, and they watched again as the United States led televised military operations in the Middle East in January 1991 to force Iraq out of Kuwait. In August 1992 details of the systematic mass rapes of predominantly Muslim Bosnian women started to appear in the US press.[3] In the fall the US presidential elections restored the Democrats to the White House after twelve years of Republican rule. In the summer of 1993, US political scientist Samuel Huntington published his article on the impending "clash of civilizations"—a term first used by the British historian Bernard Lewis—in *Foreign Affairs* magazine, arguing that, with the Cold War over, future global conflicts would occur along civilizational lines, most prominently between Islamic and Western civilizations.[4] Quickly embraced by media eager to replace the drama of the Cold War, such analyses were used to explain the ongoing conflict in the Balkans and the February 1993 World Trade Center bombing but also led to hasty assumptions that the Oklahoma City bombing of 1995 was the work of Arabs and Muslims. Taslima Nasreen was thus cast as a clear case of irrational, obscurantist Islam versus the democratic, progressive West in the latest, and most militarized, chapter in the story of global feminism.

THE PLIGHT OF MUSLIM WOMEN AS "A STICK WITH WHICH TO BEAT ISLAM"

Nasreen's *New York Times* op-ed had been arranged by Meredith Tax, a New York–based writer and veteran of the US women's movement. Born in Milwaukee, Wisconsin, in 1942, Tax had moved east to attend college at Brandeis and then on to London on fellowships. The distance from home helped sharpen her perspective on the United States, as she later recalled, "The thing about being in a foreign country is you see your country from afar and so you see everything that everybody else is saying about it." In London she participated in antiwar protests in front of the US embassy before she decided, "It was clear that if you wanted to build your life around being anti-imperialist and fighting the war in Vietnam, the U.S. was the place to do it, not England, at least if you were American."[5] Upon her return Tax became increasingly involved in the US women's movement and, in 1967, cofounded Bread and Roses, the first socialist women's organization in the country.

Outraged by the low number of women speakers at the 1986 Congress of International PEN, the international literary and human rights organization, Tax and a group of women including Grace Paley, Margaret Atwood, and Betty Friedan began a push for a women's committee. The PEN Women Writers' Committee was finally approved five years later.

The first case that Tax, as the new committee's chair, took up was that of five Croatian women writers, who had been harassed in the Zagreb press for writing about the wartime rapes and corruption in the former Yugoslavia. Disagreements with PEN led Tax and others to start an independent organization, Women's World Organization for Rights, Literature, and Development (Women's WORLD), that would focus on "gender-based censorship." In the midst of these activities, in late September 1993 the London PEN office forwarded to Tax a brief wire story about a Bangladeshi woman writer who had received death threats and asked her if she wanted "to do anything about it." Tax later acknowledged that the timing could not have been better. A case like Nasreen's would give her new organization precisely the kind of attention it needed to establish itself. She sought the help of feminists in Bangladesh to contact Nasreen, and within three days she reached Hameeda Hossain, veteran of the Mexico City and Nairobi conferences and a co-founder of DAWN and the legal-aid organization Ain-o-Salish Kendro, who responded with Nasreen's fax number.[6]

Although Nasreen's writing had been controversial—but also admired—within Bangladesh in the late 1980s, a major literary award in West Bengal in 1992 and then her 1993 novel *Lojja* (Shame) brought her a new regional level of notoriety. *Lojja* told the story of anti-Hindu violence by Muslims in Bangladesh following the Babri Masjid demolition in India. While the Bangladesh authorities banned the novel because they were concerned it would inflame Hindu-Muslim tensions, the Hindu nationalist Bharata Janata Party (BJP) in India distributed very cheap pirated copies to draw attention to the situation of the minority Hindu population in Bangladesh. Not surprisingly, the BJP's endorsement only further infuriated both the Bangladesh government and Bangladeshi Islamists. Then, in May 1994, just as the furor began to die down, Nasreen gave an interview—and an equally controversial rejoinder—in the BJP-owned Calcutta newspaper the *Statesman*. The paper quoted her as saying that the Quran was written by a human being and required a total revision. In her rejoinder just two days later, she clarified that *all* religious texts lacked contemporary relevance and said it was time to turn instead to humanism.[7] New death threats ensued, and the government charged her under the colonial-era Penal Code with having offended religious sentiments, forcing her into hiding.

Nasreen's global fame came as a surprise to critics and supporters alike, in Bangladesh as in the West. As Tax later put it, very little of her work had been translated into any of the "power languages." Nasreen had never traveled beyond India when the crisis erupted nor, as she told Mary Anne Weaver of the *New Yorker,* even met a non-Bengali until 1993.[8] Looking back on the intense drama of those years, Tax remembered how "the reporters I talked to seemed to want to use the story as a stick with which to beat Islam; I would talk about the rising tide of all kinds of religious extremism, Christian, Jewish and Muslim; but none of that ever got into a story. The Western press tended to portray [Nasreen] solely as a victim and symbol of the oppression of Muslim women, downplaying her courage and ignoring the work of the Bangladeshi women's movement."[9] Tax's later statements notwithstanding, the new popular concern with Muslim women's oppression made it easier for her to help Nasreen in those early years.

In the summer of 1994, Nasreen went into hiding in Bangladesh to avoid arrest for offending religious sensibilities. Hameeda Hossain's husband, Kamal Hossain, who had chaired the country's Constitution Drafting Committee in 1972, and their daughter, Sara Hossain, both highly respected lawyers, led the legal team defending Nasreen against the government's charges. Nasreen managed to send out faxes to her European and US supporters, pleading for help, and this launched a massive letter-writing campaign, similar to that undertaken for Rushdie following Khomeini's fatwa. Gabi Gleichmann, the head of Swedish PEN, who headed the campaign, later conceded he might have "overestimated the threat and in a way we destroyed her life." Susan Sontag, Milan Kundera, John Irving, Norman Mailer, Mario Vargas Llosa, and Günter Grass were among the several thousand writers who wrote to Bangladesh's prime minister, Khaleda Zia, asking her to help Nasreen in the spring of 1994. So eager were they to save this writer from the threat of fundamentalist Islam that they did not pause to think that Bangladeshi law might protect her if allowed to run its course. Instead, the overall effect of the letters was to portray Bangladesh as dominated by extremist Islamic ideology and Nasreen a solitary soldier in the fight against that ideology. This obscured the presence in Bangladesh of a vibrant secular movement, a legal system (even if sometimes imperfect), and a strong women's movement. In mid-July Salman Rushdie's open letter to

Nasreen appeared in several newspapers, including the *New York Times*. Tax and other women activists were furious that Rushdie had been brought in: "Well, this was the last thing in the world that Taslima needed. I mean she had enough trouble without being associated with Salman Rushdie."[10] The efforts of Nasreen's legal team and Bangladeshi activists, combined with international pressure, compelled the government to allow Nasreen to leave the country in early August 1994 to attend a conference in Sweden. She would not return for several years.

Before Taslima Nasreen several writers in Bangladesh had received fatwas and death threats from Islamists, among them Sufia Kamal and Jahanara Begum, but they had continued their usual writing, activities, and activism undeterred. They did not reach out to Western media or human rights organizations, nor did their stories capture the Western imagination. Nasreen's case, however, evolved very differently because of her particular decisions and actions in that historical moment and geopolitical context. Senior Bangladeshi journalist Shafik Rehman, whose weekly *Jai Jai Din* had published Nasreen's column and other writings, told the *New Yorker*'s Mary Anne Weaver in the summer of 1994: "The West wanted a female Salman Rushdie, an Islamic heroine, and you got it." Nasreen, he added, ended up serving as a symbol for both the fundamentalists and the West, a "demarcation line," and had been "catapulted into a political—not a literary—sky." He recognized, however, that it was the domestic political context of Bangladesh that "had allowed this to happen."[11]

Nasreen's criticisms of Islam appeared in her earliest interactions with Western journalists. In March 1994 she told columnist Pamela Bone of the Australian newspaper the *Age* that the "barbaric fascist forces of Islamic fundamentalism" were behind the attacks on women in Bangladesh.[12] While Nasreen often insisted that she was critical of all religions, she also conceded that she had the most experience with Islam. In a 1998 interview with the secular humanist journal *Free Inquiry,* she further explained why she saw no "difference between Islam and Islamic fundamentalists. I believe religion is the root, and from the root fundamentalism grows as a poisonous stem. If we remove fundamentalism and keep religion, then one day or another fundamentalism will grow again. I need to say that because some liberals always defend Islam and blame fundamentalists for creating problems. But Islam itself oppresses women. Islam itself doesn't permit democracy and it violates human rights."[13]

That Nasreen was a medical doctor was also a selling point to her Western supporters because she could be portrayed as representing European Enlightenment values of science and rationality, pitched against Islamic religion and superstition.[14] Nasreen took pride in having worked as a doctor, though she also made clear that the profession was chosen for her by her physician father. She cited examples of incidents she had witnessed in her work—from the cries of dismay she heard when a woman gave birth to a daughter rather than a son to the physical traces of rape she had observed on the youngest victims—as evidence of women's subordinate position in her society.[15]

Khushi Kabir, a staunch feminist who had been involved in grassroots work in rural Bangladesh since the early difficult days right after the war of independence, tried to make sense of the ambivalence toward Nasreen among members of the women's movement: "Taslima went for the jugular, and we're not ready for that. There's simply too much at stake. You have to learn how to deal with the situation—how to handle the bearded ones. And this is something that Taslima never understood."[16] Many worried that by inciting the rage of the Islamists, she was making things worse for the majority of women in the country, who were impoverished and lived in rural areas. Millions of women were struggling to overcome local objections from their families, neighbors, and often religious leaders to join NGOs whose funding came largely from Western governments and foundations. Feminists worried that Islamists enraged over Nasreen would turn their wrath to these NGOs, as many already had, and thereby threaten their work in the countryside. Kabir herself had started in 1972 with BRAC (originally short for Bangladesh Rural Advancement Committee, but now known simply as BRAC), today the largest NGO in the world, but, as she became concerned that BRAC was increasingly focused on delivering services to the poor rather than tackling the bigger questions of exploitation and corruption, she moved to the NGO Nijera Kori (We Do It Ourselves), which facilitates men and women's autonomous political organizing at the grassroots level.

Kabir's sister Sigma Huda, a prominent lawyer and human rights activist, was also concerned about the repercussions of Nasreen's actions for ordinary women: "She is a woman who used shock tactics and sensationalism, but these simply do not introduce lasting change in a patriarchal society like ours—they only alienate.... Smoking a cigarette on TV while you are reading the Quran only alienates people. You are not helping the cause. You are definitely not with the movement. Taslima's activities rendered everyone's work invisible. We lost a lot of ground."[17]

Despite the important work being done among the poor and among women in Bangladesh by organizations such as Nijera Kori as well as the government, Nasreen, in an interview with the Calcutta *Statesman* in May 1994, was initially unwilling to name a single Bangladeshi women's or human rights activist who had inspired her. She first responded, "I have no comments to make on this. You may write this." When journalist Sujata Sen pressed her on her views on respected activists such as Sufia Kamal and Jahanara Imam, Nasreen responded with scorn: "In Bangladesh most women activists are with a political party or an organization. Most are afraid of fundamentalists. They play limited roles. Following the Sharia is all they believe in. They are happy to live as housewives."[18] It was only on being pushed further that she mentioned Begum Rokeya Hossain, the Bengali Muslim feminist of the early twentieth century. Instead, the feminists she did admit to having read "a few chapters of" were Simone de Beauvoir and Virginia Woolf. Later that summer, she admitted to Mary Anne Weaver in the *New Yorker*, "When I started writing, I'd never read a book on feminism. I've had no experience with feminists at all."[19]

At the same time it is indisputable that Nasreen's early writings—in particular, her weekly columns in a Bengali-language newspaper—struck a chord among readers. Her frank and detailed discussions of sexual harassment in public spaces was a revelation for many women who had themselves suffered these assaults. Bangladeshi writer Shabnam Nadiya later recalled that she had read the great Western feminists like De Beauvoir, Friedan, and Millett, as well as Begum Rokeya, with great interest, but she had "consumed, judged and digested [them] at some intellectual level, connected to but not truly part of what it meant [to be a] woman…in Dhaka, on the bus, in rickshaws, in school, at home every day." Then she had encountered Nasreen's book *Nirbachito Kolum* (Selected columns) in the late 1980s and realized, "Taslima was the real thing…for me and countless others of my generation. We might not have agreed with everything she said, but that she said those things at all was, for then, enough." Young men and women alike idolized Nasreen for what she wrote and how she wrote it. "It was from that book that I—and so many others my age—first learnt in terms that we could relate to that our bodies and our urges were not things to be ashamed of, that the words we spoke, how we related to the world and the world to us were gendered down to the minutest detail." Some twenty years later Nadiya recalled, "I wept when I read Taslima describing a young man burning her arm with a cigarette in public.…I cannot begin to describe what that meant to a guilt-ridden teen, who lacked the knowledge that sexual harassment or molestation was not an isolated incident, that it happened everywhere every day, that it could happen to anyone. Twenty years ago—these were not things discussed in *bhodro* [polite, middle-class] society."[20]

Domestic politics, of course, also played a role in producing the Nasreen drama. It was, after all, the Bangladesh government that republished Nasreen's May 1994 Calcutta interview in one of its own newspapers, thereby circulating it among Bangladeshi readers who might well have not seen it otherwise. Since March that year Prime Minister Khaleda Zia had been confronted with calls from the opposition, led by Sheikh Hasina of the historically secularist Awami League but in alliance with the Islamist party Jamaat-i Islami, to agree to a new constitutional amendment requiring that the incumbent prime minister step down in favor of a caretaker government before the next election. Zia must have expected the Nasreen issue would break the alliance, but Sheikh Hasina did not speak up in Nasreen's favor, while all the Islamist parties came together in a powerful new coalition.[21]

On the international stage it was easy enough to see Nasreen as a female Rushdie and Bangladesh as another Iran. US poet and translator Carolyne Wright was in Bangladesh in 1989–91 on a Fulbright fellowship, collecting and translating the work of Bengali women poets and writers. She would later describe the Nasreen she met during that sojourn as "a human being, not a media phenomenon."[22] In the summer of 1994, she was startled to see "compelling photos in the *New York Times* [of] Bangladeshi women clad in burqah and veil, as if Bangladesh were an Iranian-style Islamic theocracy—when in reality very few women dress so severely."[23] For most other readers, however, that image of Bangladesh—and of Taslima Nasreen as the one brave person willing and able to take on the forces of "backwardness"—stuck. Bangladeshis abroad would confront this image as individuals and as members of delegations to international conferences such as the United Nations' 1994 World Population Conference and the 1995 World Conference on Women.

FORMULATING AN AGENDA UNDER WESTERN EYES

Taslima Nasreen's international story unfolded just as feminists in Bangladesh were celebrating the country's transition to democracy. The end of military rule also provided the women's movement with the time and opportunity for critical self-reflection, especially on issues of inclusiveness (the place in the movement for women of different classes, religious backgrounds, and ethnic communities such as that of the Chittagong Hill Tracts), and for a return to issues set aside during fifteen years of military rule. Paramount among these was undoubtedly the mass rapes of 1971. The new democratic context in Bangladesh, the movement for a war-crimes tribunal for 1971, the recognition of wartime rape as a crime against humanity in the Yugoslav and Rwanda tribunals of the mid-1990s, and discussions about sexual violence at the UN Women's Conference in Beijing all converged to enable Bangladeshi women's groups to revisit the errors of the war's aftermath. Leading feminist Shireen Huq later recalled her reaction to hearing a visiting speaker discuss "the mass rape of women in Bosnia, how it had been used as a means of ethnic cleansing… [and] how subsequently the government of Bosnia had announced that every child born to a Bosnian woman was Bosnian. It made us realise even more clearly how the pain that our *birangonas* [war heroine, the title Sheikh Mujib gave the rape survivors after the war] had been subjected to had been so utterly unnecessary." Specifically, Huq explained, the nation had forgotten these women in the decades since the war, except to repeat on national holidays that the country's independence was "gained in exchange of the honour of 200,000 mothers and sisters." Individual feminists and feminist groups like Naripokkho challenged the authorities to view the mass rapes as war crimes rather than the "loss of honour."[24]

Women's groups continued their work with ongoing forms of violence against women, mobilizing, for example, against domestic violence, fatwas (ostensibly religious decrees that invariably justified disproportionate physical punishments for women), acid attacks, sexual assault, and death in police custody. In addition, they came together in a broad alliance to support sex workers in their fight for rights and to build on the gains of the 1961 Muslim Family Law Ordinance, which, for example, had regulated but not outlawed polygamy, and push for further reforms in family law. There were even serious efforts in the late eighties and early nineties toward a uniform family code, led by Mahila Parishad and the legal-aid group Ain-o-Salish Kendro, to remove differences in the laws governing women of different religious communities.[25]

The acid attacks received the most attention from international media precisely because, as Shireen Huq of Naripokkho, which worked closely with several survivor-activists, recalled with bitterness, "The acid story… had shock value." US news outlets and magazines from CNN to *Ms.* carried reports on the acid attacks. ABC's *20/20* episode "Faces of Hope," which aired 1 November 1999, for example, framed the story of two survivors' trip to the United States for medical treatment as an escape from oppression to liberation, made possible by benevolent Western intervention, much like Nasreen's a few years earlier and even older missionary accounts of inspirational conversions. The filmmakers constructed this sensationalized narrative by depicting the Bangladeshi context as particularly abject, a British male physician in Dhaka as the main advocate for survivors, and the survivors' new life in the United States as the pinnacle of freedom. Reporter Connie Chung's comment that acid attacks were not sanctioned by Islam was rendered ineffectual by the images of mosques and burqa-clad women that flitted across the screen. The *20/20* version of the story failed to present the context of other forms of violence against women in Bangladesh and around the world, local feminists' work with the survivors, or, indeed, larger political and economic reasons for the attacks and for the use of specific acids in the attacks. Similarly, many in urban Bangladesh as well as in the West hastily attributed attacks on poor women and NGOs in rural areas to "Islam" when the real story was almost always far more complicated and connected to issues of local economic and political rivalries.[26]

Feminist concern with girls' and women's education, which had so preoccupied reformers a century earlier, underwent an important shift in this period. In the late twentieth century, the international development establishment, which set benchmarks such as the Millennium Development Goals, and the foreign-aid-dependent national government and NGOs all enthusiastically undertook efforts to provide girls with access to education. Advocates had found that not only did female education help with other development objectives such as lower fertility and healthier families, but it was also easier to support than, for instance, women's political activism in export-oriented factories. Some feminists, for their part, while continuing to monitor disparities in coverage across different communities and regions and in the various scholarships and incentives provided by the government, turned their attention to the very nature of the education that was being imparted to girls. Rokeya Rahman Kabeer, the founder of the NGO Saptagram, declared that she had been so disappointed in the locally available books that Saptagram had been compelled to create new books for their students. "Although we were on the threshold of the 21st century, there was still no acknowledgement of women's role. Instead, books were written about 'cowboys'...doing all the work. Or there would be Jack and Jill with Jill, as always, meekly following Jack."[27]

In the final years of the twentieth century, Bangladeshi feminists also took up issues pertaining to women's work, mobilizing for better pay and better working conditions in female-dominated sectors. On the topic of export-oriented garment-factory labor, activists in Bangladesh found themselves pitted against feminist, labor, and consumer activists in the countries of the wealthy Global North. Since the factories first appeared in the early 1980s, young women had coveted these jobs because they saw them as an opportunity to be self-reliant, to help their families but also be somewhat relieved of familial control, and "to work with dignity," as one worker put it—despite the many problems associated with factory work. Indeed, by the turn of the century, around a million and half women were working in the garment factories that plugged Bangladesh into the global market. Western efforts to enforce compulsory labor standards, however, directly threatened their livelihood. While some in the West pursued these efforts in the hope of improving working conditions, many others hoped to use the standards to remove the competition presented to their own manufacturing sectors by the cheap labor of places like Bangladesh, Honduras, Macao, and the Philippines.[28] Horrific accidents in Bangladeshi factories, such as the collapse of Rana Plaza, would return the issue to the international limelight two decades later.

INTERNATIONAL FEMINISM IN THE POST–COLD WAR ERA

Unlike the World Population Conference in Bucharest two decades earlier, the 1994 UN International Conference on Population and Development (ICPD) in Cairo was planned with input from women's groups. Rather than focus exclusively on population control and contraceptive access—as dictated by wealthy Western countries to poorer ones over the past half century and supported by many Third World national governments and elites—the emphasis had shifted to encompass women's general health, well-being, and reproductive rights. Women's groups argued that paying attention to girls' education, women's health needs and employment opportunities, and generally promoting gender equality would inevitably lead to fewer births.[29]

This very agenda, however, prompted unprecedented alliances and oppositions. The Vatican, Muslim leaders, and antichoice groups joined forces to oppose what they saw as an assault on their respective religious values. Pope John Paul II insisted that the conference proposals for curbing rapid population growth, which did not rule out abortion and supported reproductive services for unmarried women, were the "fruit of a hedonistic and permissive culture." In the months preceding the conference, he sent 140 papal envoys around the world to build opposition to what he described as the efforts of the wealthier countries to engage in "contraceptive imperialism." While Islamic scriptural injunctions regarding contraception and abortion are notoriously ambiguous, many Muslim countries assured the papal envoys of their support. Sudan, Lebanon, Iraq, and Saudi Arabia did not send delegates to Cairo, and President Suharto of Indonesia, the largest Muslim-majority country in the world, failed to attend because, a spokesperson announced, "He fell ill." Concerns unrelated to population growth appear to have been in play too: a papal envoy assured Muammar Gaddafi that the Vatican would intervene on Libya's behalf after Western nations accused Libya of masterminding the 1988 bombing of a Pan Am jet over Lockerbie, Scotland. The population-control establishment, for its part, criticized the "extreme" and "militant" feminists for not taking seriously the dangers of uncontrolled population growth. They argued that waiting for women's status to improve first would take far too long.[30]

For Islamists, as important as abortion was the ready availability of contraception in many Muslim countries, courtesy of the Western population-control establishment, and the fear that this would lead to the westernization of Muslim societies. In early September 1994 while the ICPD was under way in Cairo, advocate Abdul Razzaq of the Appellate Division of the Supreme Court of Bangladesh gave a keynote address at the Center for Human Rights in Dhaka that represented well the general Islamist opposition to the Cairo conference agenda. The program of action proposed by the ICPD, he warned, would result in a "society in which extra marital sex will be socially and legally permissible. Parents will have no control over their children." Such behavior, he continued, "has been prevalent in the West for the last half century and... had led to immoral behaviour, sexual anarchy, sexually transmitted diseases, more crimes, and more particularly sexually related crimes." The ICPD draft program would "export these western social maladies to the Eastern and Muslim countries in the name of population control and development." He concluded by declaring that "as far as Bangladesh is concerned these offending clauses of the document offend our religious feelings, our culture and above all our civilization . . . to agree to such a proposal would be . . . unconstitutional."[31]

In using "we" Razzaq suggested that he spoke for all Muslims, or at least all Muslims in Bangladesh. While many of his fellow Muslims and Bangladeshis remained uncomfortable with public acknowledgment of premarital relationships, his presentation in a Dhaka seminar, presumably to a predominantly Bangladeshi crowd, came across as an insistence that there was only one acceptable form of Islam, only one way of being Muslim, and it was not open to change or discussion. The reality, of course, was that there have always been premarital relationships in both rural and urban Bangladesh, in all classes and religious communities, and that young men and women in those relationships stood to benefit from reproductive services. Finally, Razzaq made the great leap from a broader definition of family and reproductive services for unmarried women to the destruction of the Islamic way of life and its lapse into Western sexual and social anarchy.[32]

This insistence on steering clear of "Western ways" was a response to women's growing visibility as garment-factory workers in Bangladesh's cities and as NGO affiliates in the villages.[33] Rather than acknowledge women's need—and, in many cases, desire—to work outside the home, conservative critics assailed their public presence as a mere imitation of Western ways. These same critics were also quick to label feminist mobilization as a Western import, thereby misrepresenting the long history of Muslim women working to improve their own lives, in Bengal and elsewhere.

Islamists were not alone in their opposition to feminist mobilization or greater reproductive rights. Halfway around the world, the conservative American Catholic politician and columnist Patrick J. Buchanan also spoke out vehemently against the ICPD's draft program, both in support of the Vatican's position and also out of what he described as a concern for the United States' future moral standing in the world. In a syndicated column published in US newspapers just a week before the start of the ICPD, Buchanan defended the Vatican's decision to seek an alliance with Muslim countries like Libya and Iran on the grounds that it was intended to "prevent a holocaust of Third World children." And he excoriated the Clinton administration for its misguided priorities at home and abroad: "Once America stood for freedom, liberty and a Judeo-Christian moral order. Next month in Cairo, the U.S. delegation will offer the world's poor IUDs, suction pumps, condoms and Norplant."[34] In criticizing the draconian nature of Indira

Gandhi's population policies in India and the consequences for baby girls of China's one-child policy, Buchanan was inadvertently aligned with Third World feminist activists concerned about the dangers of reproductive technologies. But he did not, unsurprisingly, embrace their larger analysis regarding the role of powerful countries like the United States in perpetuating their countries' political and economic problems.

As with the Islamist response to the Cairo agenda, the conservative Christian outcry in the United States had as much to do with social and political exigencies as with religious convictions. Buchanan, who had sought and lost the Republican presidential nomination in 1992—as he would again in 1996—was reacting to what he saw as undesirable changes wrought by the Western feminist movement, among them a fall in the birth rate. In a 2002 book dramatically titled *The Death of the West: How Dying Populations and Immigrant Invasions Imperil Our Country and Civilization,* he held feminism responsible for the demise of the West. Among the harmful consequences of feminist ideas that he listed were that "marriage is out fashion"; the "1,000 percent increase in the number of unmarried couples living together"; the fall in the number of nuclear families; and the rise in the number of single-parent households. And that was why, he warned, "the rise of feminism spells the death of the nation and the death of the West."[35]

On the other side of the dispute, women's organizations from different countries, continents, and religious backgrounds came together to push for a new vision of reproductive health. US feminist Ellen Chesler, for example, tried to clarify in the *New York Times Magazine* that "feminists do not object to family planning. It is specific practices we deplore—cavalier bureaucrats, misguided strategies and poor services that harm women."[36] For the Pakistani-born feminist and Muslim theologian Riffat Hassan, the ICPD in Cairo was "our most controversial conference in terms of the content— human sexuality and the underlying question of who controls women's bodies." Moreover, it was attended by "record numbers" of Muslim women because of its location, "one of the most important capitals of the Muslim world." Hassan saw the conference as a "victory for women," including Muslim women, over opponents like the Vatican and many Muslim leaders: "The fact that Muslim women forcefully challenged the traditional viewpoint in Cairo indicates they are no longer nameless, faceless, or voiceless.... We won our bodies in a major breakthrough. Women's voices were being heard, and a sense of momentum was building. I came back from Cairo very energized."[37]

Standing tall against the religious opposition and the advocates of traditional population-control policies was Nafis Sadik, the secretary-general of the Cairo conference and executive director of the United Nations Population Fund. Raised in a Muslim family in India until 1947 and then in Pakistan, Sadik cemented her desire for a career in medicine following an inspiring encounter with Muhammad Ali Jinnah in Calcutta. As a member of Pakistan's Family Planning Commission, she had organized a high-profile conference in Dacca in 1969, thinking that the city's dense population would be an effective argument for the need for population control. However, with East Pakistan in the midst of the pro-autonomy political turmoil that would culminate in the declaration of independence in 1971, curfews had kept the international guests sequestered in their hotel the entire time.[38] In Cairo a quarter century later, Sadik struck back at critics of the ICPD calmly but forcefully. She had hoped that having the three women Muslim heads of government address the conference would send a "powerful message" about their support for the agenda and about the diversity of positions regarding reproductive health among Muslims, but Prime Ministers Tansu Çiller of Turkey and Khaleda Zia of Bangladesh decided against leading their delegations. Benazir Bhutto of Pakistan almost canceled too, citing concerns about domestic opposition, but then changed her mind at the last minute and brought all her ministers with her.[39] Many of the conflicts around women's reproductive rights would resurface just a year later, at the Fourth World Conference for Women in Beijing.

With her signature white *dupatta* (scarf) partially covering her hair, Prime Minister Benazir Bhutto of Pakistan reminded her listeners at the opening session of the 1995 Beijing Conference that she was "the first woman ever elected to head an Islamic nation." In a rousing speech about the importance of this gathering of some forty thousand participants, she took a few minutes "to counter the propaganda...that Islam gives women a second-class status." To refute this she pointed to, among other things, the fact that there were now three women prime ministers of Muslim countries. "Our election has destroyed the myth built by social taboo that a woman's place is in the house, that it is shameful or dishonourable or socially unacceptable for a Muslim woman to work. Our election has given women all over the Muslim world moral strength to declare that it is socially correct for a woman to work and to follow in our footsteps as working women and working mothers." Bhutto spoke about the centrality of justice in Islam and the prohibition on injustice, the rights given to women by Islam some 1,400 years earlier, and the need to differentiate between Islamic teachings and patriarchal local cultures. In what was no doubt a veiled reference to the conference host's strict population policy in the context of a strong preference for boys, she cited the Quranic verses against female infanticide before lamenting, "How tragic it is that the pre-Islamic practice of female infanticide still haunts a world we regard as modern and civilized."[40] That a head of government would feel the need to put up such a defense of the status of women in Islam is evidence indeed of how besieged many Muslims felt by the mid-1990s by Western discussions of oppressed Muslim women.

The Beijing conference was the last of the large world conferences for women. It was also the first to be held after the end of the Cold War. In the earlier meetings in Mexico City, Copenhagen, and Nairobi, the political rivalry between the two superpowers had led to a certain degree of competition on women's issues and in efforts to define US and Soviet lists of feminist concerns and priorities. The Soviet insistence that true liberation for women entailed attention not only to patriarchy but to economic inequalities, colonialism, imperialism, and war had resonated with many in the Third World, in turn inspiring greater interest in women's issues from a US government loath to fall behind the socialist bloc. After the Cold War, however, the mainstream US liberal, and increasingly neoliberal, feminist worldview came to dominate, a feminism focused on equality of opportunity and antidiscrimination—rather than one that questioned larger systemic inequalities. The United States expended billions of dollars to foster civil society in former Soviet Bloc countries. Women's rights organizations featured prominently among the many NGOs set up in Eastern Europe, though, not surprisingly, as had already become clear in Bangladesh since the early 1980s, such NGOs turned out to be accountable primarily to their Western donors, not to the populations among which they worked.[41]

Crucially, the post–Cold War era allowed Americans to construct a new enemy, the "green peril" of Islam and Muslims to replace the "red menace" of communism, and to develop a new interest in the women of these communities. During the Cold War the United States had bragged about the greater femininity of US women, claiming that their greater adherence to traditional domestic roles rendered them superior to the ill-dressed peasant women and female factory workers of the Soviet Union.[42] In the 1990s Muslim women emerged not as rivals as Soviet women had been but rather as the collective object of pity of a West that saw itself as having won the Cold War, while Islam and Muslim men were vilified as existential threats to a Western way of life. The United States, after all, was not engaged in a close global rivalry with Muslim countries as it had been with the Soviets. To the contrary, as one century ended and another began, the United States came to exert economic and political—and, increasingly, military—power over more and more Muslim countries. It was within this larger context that Muslim women around the world became more organized and vocal about the problems they faced, as women and as Muslims.

This was also true of Muslim women in the United States. By the early 1990s there were an estimated five million Muslims in the United States, as growing numbers of immigrants and converts joined the much older African American Muslim communities. Outraged and frustrated over the attacks and discrimination against them, but also on the margins of both mainstream feminist groups and male-dominated Islamic organizations, Muslim women in the United States began to organize in a more systematic manner than ever before.

Sharifa Alkhateeb, born in Philadelphia to a Yemeni father and Czech mother, cofounded the North American Council of Muslim Women (NACMW), the first national organization for American Muslim women, in 1992. Its main objective was educating Muslim American women in the original sources of Islam, so they might "become confident and strong as individuals and as members of their families, and helping women to connect to the larger American society in a contributory way." For Alkhateeb the experience of being a minority in the United States meant dealing with non-Muslims who thought of the typical Muslim woman as having "huge sheets on and three children trailing behind her and her trailing behind her husband who just finished beating her." The all-female NACMW took on difficult issues such as different forms of domestic violence and, in 1993, conducted a survey on Muslim women's views of violence. Among the questions asked were "Do you recognize that there is such a thing as marital rape in a Muslim marriage?" and "What is the proper behavior of Muslims during war?" The latter emerged from the recently revived difficult discussions over the mass rapes perpetrated by Pakistani Muslim men and their Bengali Muslim collaborators during the 1971 war in Bangladesh, which in turn had received a boost from international rulings following the atrocities against predominantly Muslim women in Bosnia. Alkhateeb and NACMW participated in several panels at the Beijing conference.[43] Other US Muslim women's organizations present in Beijing included the California-based Muslim Women's League, also founded in 1992, and Karamah: Muslim Women

Lawyers for Human Rights, founded in 1993 by the philosopher and legal scholar Azizah al-Hibri.[44] Frustrated but ultimately energized by her struggles, Alkhateeb told the Australian-born writer Geraldine Brooks a few years later, "Muslim women are quite capable of speaking up for ourselves. We are not waiting for Western women to pour their loveliness into our heads."[45] Yet by then some of these "Western women" had already resolved to rescue the women of Afghanistan.

LETTING AFGHAN WOMEN "KNOW WE'RE COMING"

Barbara Bick of Martha's Vineyard and Washington, DC, was sixty-five when, in 1990, she embarked on the first of three trips to Afghanistan. A longtime political activist and feminist who had been a founding member of the antinuclear group Women Strike for Peace in the early 1960s, she was persuaded by an old friend to make the journey with an invitation from the All-Afghan Women's Council. The Soviets had withdrawn the previous year, and the Afghan communist government was embroiled in a civil war. Following the Taliban's seizure of power in Kabul in 1996, Bick became increasingly involved with the efforts of the Feminist Majority Foundation (FMF) to raise awareness in the United States about women in Afghanistan and would host a fund-raiser in her home in 1999.

Leading the Feminist Majority's efforts was Mavis Nicholson Leno. The situation of Afghan women under Taliban rule in the late 1990s reminded Mavis Leno of her father, who had been trapped in a mine some years earlier. He had emerged from the accident with broken ribs, but far worse than the physical pain, he told his daughter, was "that he had no way of knowing if anyone was looking for him." For Leno his experience and reaction were analogous to the suffering women in Afghanistan: "These women have been buried alive, and they don't know if anybody even knows they're there and is coming for them. We need to let them know we're coming."[46] Mavis Leno, who was married to the well-known American comedian and talk-show host Jay Leno, tended to avoid the celebrity limelight, quietly engaging in her own nonprofit work when not accompanying her famous husband. Then, at a 1996 lunch, she found herself seated next to Peg Yorkin, FMF cofounder, and shortly thereafter she joined the organization's board. The following year Leno took charge of the FMF's Campaign to Stop Gender Apartheid, and she and her husband donated $100,000—and a great deal of public attention—to the efforts.[47]

Founded in 1987, when Christian fundamentalist influence was growing in US politics, leading to increased state regulation of women's sexual and reproductive rights, the Feminist Majority focused almost entirely on domestic issues for much of its first decade. It led a public education campaign in support of the French "morning after pill" (RU-486), pushed for more women in elected office, and called on the Republican administration to address violence against women. By the early 1990s, however, national and international developments had pushed the Feminist Majority to turn its attention to women's issues overseas.

Organizations like the Feminist Majority did not take up the cause of women in Afghanistan because they believed they had already accomplished everything they had set out to do within the United States. Rather, US feminist leaders turned their attention overseas out of concern over divisions within the domestic women's movement, the general decrease in the number of new and younger recruits, and a conservative backlash. In genital surgeries, the rapes in Bosnia, and the severe restrictions on Afghan women's mobility, education, and employment, they saw a way to unite and energize the domestic movement and restore to it the vigor of the early 1970s. Attention to "bigger" women's problems in other countries gave US feminists a purpose at a time when domestic issues like sexual harassment and violence, the double day, poverty, and racism were proving intractable. International issues allowed them to raise funds even from those opposed to their domestic activism.[48]

In 1997 the FMF turned its attention to Afghan women and pulled together a "coalition of hope" of some 130 US organizations, including the National Organization for Women, Planned Parenthood, and the YWCA, in its fight against what it labeled gender apartheid in Afghanistan.[49] Leno's strategies to publicize the FMF's work on this "heartbreaking situation" included a letter to the nationally syndicated "Dear Abby" column in February 1999, because "everyone knows that if you want America to know something, you should tell Dear Abby." Leno told the story of how Afghan women had worn "contemporary clothes," attended co-ed schools, and worked in a range of professions until September 1996, when the Taliban took over and imposed "gender apartheid." Leno implored Dear Abby to "help bring these lost women back into the world." Five months later Leno wrote back with the news that forty-five thousand Dear Abby readers had joined the campaign, surprising reporters who had been unable to persuade US editors to publish stories on the topic, the Taliban itself, and "even the Afghan women, who thought Americans were their last hope." Leno shared with Dear Abby readers that the United Nations credited the FMF campaign with putting the issue "on the world stage," and the Taliban had responded by easing some restrictions on women's access to education and health care.[50] Other celebrities, such as Jane Fonda, Eve Ensler, and Oprah Winfrey, added their names and voices to the movement to delegitimize the Taliban by focusing on its imposition of the burqa, as did politicians from both sides of the aisle, such as Barbara Boxer, Sam Brownback, and Dana Rohrabacher.[51]

Afghan women had, of course, been trying to address their problems long before the Feminist Majority developed its interest in them and even before the Taliban came to power. The difficulties Afghan women faced could be traced to an earlier era, to the many decades of complicated British presence if not outright colonial control, followed by the direct intervention of both Cold War superpowers and the numerous national regimes, accompanied by the progressive weakening of the law-and-order situation and the worsening of the economy. In 1977, some twenty years before the Taliban seized Kabul, a twenty-year-old law student at Kabul University known as Meena had founded the Jamiat-e-Enqilabi-e-Zanan-e-Afghanistan (Revolutionary Association of the Women of Afghanistan, or RAWA). She had intended it to be an independent feminist organization, not affiliated with existing male-dominated student movements, and open to women of all classes and ethnic groups. Shaima, who had been one of Meena's high school teachers and was an early member of RAWA, recalled how many women had felt the need to come together "to [establish] a group movement to get rid of these inequalities." RAWA decided that education was the best way to change the situation, and long before the Taliban came to power and enacted their restrictive policies, RAWA members organized literacy classes for rural women who had recently arrived in urban areas such as Kabul and political education for all women.[52] Other Afghan women's groups also organized literacy classes, opportunities for women to earn a living, mosque study groups, and health clinics, all while following rules about wearing the burqa and having a *mahram* (the requirement to be accompanied by their husband or a close male relative). When a close relative was not available, women paid other men to play the role, often at great risk to both the man and the woman. For many Afghan men this was a valuable way to earn money and, as one put it, "of supporting our women, family and community."[53]

Also working to advance Afghan women's rights and against Taliban policies in the late 1990s was an organization called Support of Women of Afghanistan, or Negar (which in Dari translates to "Close Companion"). It was founded by Shoukria Haidar, who had left for France shortly after the Taliban came to power. A former athlete and member of the Olympic Committee, Haidar had found work as a physical-education teacher at a school outside Paris. At a 2000 conference in Dushanbe, Tajikistan, Negar brought together some three hundred Afghan women, most of whom were based in Afghanistan, with others from the growing diaspora. Together they drew on past Afghan constitutions as well as UN conventions to produce a Declaration of the Essential Rights of Afghan Women that affirmed that the "fundamental right of Afghan women, as for all human beings, is life with dignity."[54]

Because it saw the Taliban as the primary obstacle to a democratic future in Afghanistan, Negar was generally supportive of US efforts to oust the Taliban. RAWA, for its part, was deeply committed to both feminist and nationalist principles. Just as it had opposed the Soviet Union's occupation of Afghanistan that began in 1979, so it also opposed the US-funded Islamist resistance to the Soviets and, finally, the US invasion of 2001. As a RAWA member put it some years later, "We have learned from our Algerian and Iranian sisters, we cannot put the goals of the nation before women's rights."[55]

Meena's assassination in 1987 by the Afghan secret intelligence agency had driven the organization underground. Throughout the Afghan civil war of the 1990s, RAWA members covertly collected and publicized evidence, including photographs and videotapes, of human rights violations under the Islamists who came to power, including the Taliban in 1996. In need of funds to carry out their work, RAWA turned to the internet and established a website and email access, soon amassing a base of supporters from around the world. The US-based Feminist Majority Foundation was among the first and perhaps the most prominent organization to respond to RAWA's campaign.[56]

The FMF helped to coordinate the publication of articles on the plight of Afghan women in popular magazines like *Glamour* and *Teen,* while Mavis Leno met with President Bill Clinton and the Senate Foreign Relations Committee to persuade the US government to denounce the Taliban and put pressure on the California-based UNOCAL Corporation to withdraw from a consortium planning an $8 billion energy pipeline crossing Afghanistan. In a December 1998 press release, the FMF quickly claimed credit for what it described as a "stunning victory" in its campaign against gender apartheid, while UNOCAL representatives cited the drop in the price of crude oil as the "biggest reason" for the reversal. The FMF ended its press release by urging readers to visit "our Stop Gender Apartheid in Afghanistan Web page to find out what you can do to help free Afghan women!"[57] Absent in this celebration and in subsequent discussions were the long-standing contributions of Afghan women's organizations such as RAWA and their resistance to the Taliban's and others' efforts to suppress Afghan women. Also erased was the role of the United States (along with Iran, Pakistan, and Saudi Arabia) in funding the very *mujahideen,* or "freedom fighters," who fought the Soviets and gave rise to groups such as the Taliban.

The larger global interest in women's rights as human rights that took root around the World Conference on Human Rights in Vienna in 1993 and the Beijing World Conference on Women two years later, as well as in war crimes specifically targeting women as underlined by the magnitude of sexual violence in Bosnia, no doubt shaped the manner in which RAWA sought financial assistance from international feminists. RAWA communicated with women in Pakistan and Afghanistan primarily through its Dari and Pashtu quarterly magazine, *Payam-e Zan* (Women's message), with hard-hitting political articles generally critical of the successive pro-Soviet and then Islamist regimes, as well as accounts of resistance by Afghan women. By contrast, the information it shared with the outside world seemed well selected to showcase Afghan women's oppression and powerlessness and elicit outrage, sympathy, and much-needed funds.[58]

Shortly after the US invasion of Afghanistan in the fall of 2001, through which US president George W. Bush claimed to have liberated Afghan women, US activist and journalist Sonali Kolhatkar castigated the FMF's campaign for its focus on the "'barbaric' men of Afghanistan" and the "helpless women of Afghanistan." She was stunned when Helen Caldicott, an Australian physician, feminist, and antinuclear activist she had long admired, demanded to know about female genital mutilation among Afghan women. Genital surgeries were not practiced among Afghans, and yet this veteran feminist had learned from the FMF that it was a menace to be tackled in Afghanistan. Kolhatkar argued that continually portraying Afghan women as helpless and mute behind and because of the burqa allowed the FMF to speak and raise funds on their behalf, and yet the FMF kept as much as 50 percent of the proceeds as campaign costs. She noted, "Feminists like Helen Caldicott and the Feminist Majority approach the women of the Global South with short sighted preconceptions of feminism and their superiority. Helen Caldicott was more interested in exploring the fascinating desire of

Afghan men to treat women like dirt than in examining those forces (most often Western male-dominated governments) that have fostered misogynist religious extremism at the expense of women's rights."[59]

The spring 2002 issue of *Ms.* magazine included a lengthy article on Afghan women titled "A Coalition of Hope" that was intended to offer "readers an introduction to the organization that has become the magazine's new owner"—the Feminist Majority Foundation.[60] While it is indisputable that the FMF was responsible for bringing to general US attention the atrocities of the Taliban regime, it did so without placing the rise of the Taliban in its larger historical context, specifically, the role of US foreign policy in the region in facilitating its very rise. The FMF also chose to forge alliances with other Afghan Islamist groups such as the Northern Alliance, to which RAWA was as vehemently opposed as it was to the Taliban. An open letter addressed to *Ms.* editors by one Elizabeth Miller, available on the RAWA website, lambasted the magazine as a "mere mouthpiece of hegemonic, US-centric, ego driven, corporate feminism." It went on to criticize the FMF's "ego-centric and self-serving view of history" that suggested that "they, other Western women, and a handful of expatriate Afghan women have single-handedly freed the women of Afghanistan from an oppression that started and ended with the Taliban."[61]

The self-congratulatory celebrations of the FMF and the George W. Bush administration following the overthrow of the Taliban in late 2001 cleared the path for a new era of concern for "oppressed Muslim women" around the world and a renewed conviction that only the West could save Muslim women from their supposedly miserable lives.[62] Many US feminists embraced their new roles as saviors and ignored the continued efforts by Muslim women, secular and religious, around the world to improve their own lives— with the notable exception, as we'll shortly see, of a few women of Muslim background who were celebrated for their outspokenness and who, unlike RAWA, voiced their support for US foreign-policy decisions.[63]

THE DESIRABLE PRODUCTIVITY OF BANGLADESHI WOMEN

In the opening decades of the twenty-first century, women's groups in Bangladesh have continued to build new coalitions to work on the issues of LGBTQ+ communities, ethnic and religious minorities, and domestic, factory, and sex workers. The debates surrounding the garment-factory workers are an important example of the persistence of the figure of the Muslim woman in the new century, though this time deployed strategically by the Bangladesh government.

Increasingly dependent on trade earnings rather than foreign aid, the government became concerned that growing competition from other countries exporting to the United States was curbing Bangladesh's own access to the US market. These trade-related concerns, combined with the US focus on militant Muslims in the wake of 9/11, provided Bangladesh with an opening to request trade concessions by differentiating itself from countries like Afghanistan. The Bangladesh government turned to women as the marker of difference. In a December 2004 *New York Times* interview, a government minister proudly declared that a "silent revolution...has taken place in our country," which the reporter described as "one of the few Muslim democracies in the world." The minister went on to make clear the dangers of US trade restrictions and potential factory closures on these now-liberated Muslim women: "For the first time in a Muslim country, hundreds of thousands of women in their late teens and early 20's are wearing cosmetics, carrying handbags and walking to work every day.... There is no way in Bangladesh that this government or any other government can send them back to the kitchen."[64]

The rush to see women in Bangladesh as victims of Islamic doctrine rather than domestic and international corporate greed or a world trade order geared in favor of the wealthiest countries also obscured other forms of political engagement by women in Bangladesh. In February 2013, two months before the collapse of Rana Plaza, thousands of mostly young women and men started gathering at a busy intersection in Dhaka. They were there to protest what they saw as a suspiciously lenient verdict in a long-overdue war-crimes trial pertaining to the 1971 atrocities. The image of nonviolent and explicitly secularist protesters, among them hundreds of nonveiled women, didn't interest the US media, which focused instead on a later Islamist counterrally.[65]

The 2013 collapse of the Rana Plaza, which killed at least 1,100 garment workers and injured some 2,500, most of them women, ushered in a new era of Western interest in the poor women of Bangladesh. In contrast to the early years of Bangladesh's independence, when their Muslimness had retreated into the background, the post-9/11 interest in rescuing Muslim women added a new layer to these interactions. Responses to the accident from

Pope Francis as well as labor activists invoked slavery and the need to rescue Bangladesh workers from deplorable working conditions. Clothing companies in the United Kingdom and the United States jumped in to highlight that that their own merchandise was free of such "blood clothes." One particular image in the advertising campaign of American Apparel, undoubtedly designed to be both provocative and memorable, proved a stark reminder of the persistence of the figure of the oppressed Muslim woman. The Bengali American fashion writer Tanwi Nandini Islam described the image evocatively: "Maks, a topless model/merchandiser, stands in a classic dead-eyed AA pose. She's wearing the High Waist Jean, in case you hadn't noticed. The phrase 'Made in Bangladesh' covers her, punctuated by hints of nipple." The accompanying ad copy explained that Maks was born in Bangladesh but came to the United States as a young child. The High Waist Jean, in contrast to the clothing produced by the Bangladeshi workers Maks's very presence conjures, was crafted by "23 skilled American workers in Downtown Los Angeles, all of whom are paid a fair wage and have access to basic benefits such as healthcare." That Maks dared to bare was meant to convey that, in the move from Bangladesh to California, she had escaped to freedom and, specifically, sexual liberation—a narrative about Muslim women that has become increasingly popular in this century.[66]

THE NEW APOSTLES OF PROGRESS

A December 2004 *Newsweek* article titled "Rocking the Casbah," inspired by the 1982 hit song by the British punk band the Clash, conjured the image of an all-female Muslim rock band as the vanguard of the nascent movement to reform Islam and to usher the billion-plus-strong global Muslim community members into the modern age. Women, the authors argued, "may be the last, best hope for this generation":

> For more than 30 years, much of the Muslim world has been sliding backward, away from modernity. Maybe the West and Israel, defeat and humiliation, dictators, emirs or mullahs are to blame. Or maybe it's one of those cycles of fanatic religiosity that afflicts every society from time to time. Some voices of reason, however, have to stand up and say "Enough! There is a modern world and Muslims should be part of it." Some apostles of progress have to do more than bemoan their fate, bow to the diktats of intolerance, make excuses for willful ignorance or turn their backs on the faith altogether.

Well, at long last that chorus is growing among Muslims, and if you listen to the most strident voices, damned if they don't sound like an all-woman band. They're way out there on the edge of the faith; their message and their lifestyles are so far from the torpid Muslim mainstream they're almost in the desert.[67]

In the first decade of the new century, in the aftermath of the 9/11 attacks and the US invasions of Afghanistan and Iraq, the Ugandan-born Canadian Irshad Manji and the Somali-born Dutch Ayaan Hirsi Ali quickly emerged as the most celebrated of these "apostles of progress," with regular appearances on television and in widely circulated publications like the *New York Times, USA Today, Newsweek,* and *Time.* In a coauthored 2007 piece in the *Los Angeles Times,* Sam Harris, a self-proclaimed US atheist who had declared "Islam to be especially inimical to the norms of civil discourse," and the novelist Salman Rushdie, undoubtedly still traumatized by Khomeini's fatwa against him, described Ayaan Hirsi Ali as the "world's most visible and imperiled spokeswoman for the rights of Muslim women." The *Economist* called her the "world's most famous critic of Islam" and *Vogue* a "controversial freedom fighter." A 2008 *New York Times* article concluded that despite their contentious differences—Hirsi Ali sought to change Islam from outside, Manji from within—both women were fervent feminists. According to the *Times,* Hirsi Ali traced the problems facing Muslims today to the "sexual morality that we were force-fed from birth," while Manji saw the empowerment of women as the "way to awaken the Muslim world." The two women, the article continued, "might be considered crown jewels in the history of the modern women's movement.... As feminists, Ms. Hirsi Ali and Ms. Manji are demanding more than equality; they are very self-consciously challenging the foundations of an entire way of life."[68]

As though working from the same writers' manual, Manji, Hirsi Ali, and the other women of Muslim or Arab background who published best-selling memoirs in the years after the 9/11 attacks all recounted their personal stories of miserable lives filled with Islamic oppression and anti-Semitism, celebrated Israel and the West as feminist and progressive havens in direct contrast to Muslim societies, and generally ignored all recent scholarship on related subjects.

Manji recalled how, as a child, she "regularly imbibed two major messages—that women are inferior and that Jews are treacherous, not to be trusted." She described having fled an Islamic school in a Vancouver suburb that suppressed her ability to ask critical questions. Aglow from her 2002 visit to Israel, Manji discussed "Muslim complicity in the Holocaust" and praised Israel for being the only democracy in the Middle East and hosting the "only annual gay pride parade" in the region. Following a visit to the Temple Mount, she concluded that she "feels at home" and "more viscerally than ever, I know who my family is." Hirsi Ali, for her part, wrote about having escaped a forced marriage in Somalia to the freedom of the Netherlands. She remembered what "Sister Aziza told us about the Jews" and described images on par with the vilest European anti-Semitism. As a result, the first time she met a Jewish man, she was "astonished that he was an ordinary human of flesh and blood." For having "condemned the virtual enslavement of Muslim women in the name of Islam," Hirsi Ali was awarded the American Jewish Congress's 2006 Moral Courage Award, while Manji went on to head the Moral Courage Project at New York University and the University of Southern California.[69]

I am not suggesting that these women should not have shared their dramatic and often painful personal stories. Rather, the problem with such books is that these personal stories were presented as—and taken as—representative of all Muslim women and all Arab women. The stories of these individual women—Manji and Hirsi Ali as well as Nonie Darwish, Wafa Sultan, and Brigitte Gabriel, who presented themselves as exemplary victims of an Islam that was not only opposed to women and feminism but also anti-Semitic—became the single authentic story about the "Muslim woman." This opportunism, inability, and refusal on their part as well as on the part of their audience to grasp the internal complexity of the categories of Islam, Muslim women, and feminism has had profound political consequences for the public's approach to these topics and of government policies vis-à-vis Muslims within the West and in other parts of the world.[70]

The celebration of these writers as authorities on Islam, Muslim women, and feminism at all times and in all places came at the expense of a deeper understanding of the significant differences in domestic and global political, legal, and economic contexts within which millions of Muslim women across the entire globe operate. In presenting change in the Muslim world as possible only with intervention from the United States—either by force through the violent eradication of oppressive Muslim men or the less dramatic support of "moderate" Muslim groups and individuals—Hirsi Ali, Manji, and the larger cohort of media experts on the subject of Islam and Muslim women foreclosed the possibility of change from within Muslim societies. They studiously ignored or dismissed ongoing local efforts to confront injustices, such as those detailed in this book. Manji, for example, did not mention RAWA once in her long discussion of Taliban atrocities in her best-selling 2004 book, *The Trouble with Islam*. Instead, she referred to Muslims as an "army of automatons" and urged them to "wake up" out of the false consciousness from which they suffered. Hirsi Ali, for her part, made it clear early in her career as an expert that she had no time for Muslim women with views different from her own. On a January 2005 episode of the Dutch talk show *Meetingpoint*, Hirsi Ali pointedly told a young Muslim woman who disagreed with her methods and statements to "please go wake up."[71]

As this book has shown, Muslim women and men have long been struggling for change. Muslim activists have spoken out against both the self-aggrandizing revelations of these best-selling authors and those who have assumed the power to anoint them. For example, in November 2001, the Pakistani-born scholar, poet, and playwright Fawzia Afzal-Khan responded to Salman Rushdie's longing "for the voices of Muslim women to be heard!" by declaring,

> Well, I have news for Mr. Rushdie. Muslim women *have* been speaking out against the obscurantist Islam he decries in his essay, for years and years and years, although clearly Mr. Rushdie, and many others, have not paid them much heed. There are Muslim women who are feminists, theologians, writers, lawyers, activists, scholars both in the "Islamist" societies he paints with a broad brush, as well as in the "west," who have been engaged in a two-pronged struggle against *both* Islamic extremism as well as—and this is where their difference from Mr. Rushdie arises—the unjust foreign policies of the United States that have contributed, and continue to contribute, to the "hijacking" of Islam for terrorist ends.[72]

Similarly, in her scathing review of Hirsi Ali's *The Caged Virgin*, British Bangladeshi journalist Fareena Alam stated,

> It's obviously what I've been waiting for all my life: a secular crusader—armed with Enlightenment philosophy, the stamp of the liberal establishment and the promise of sexual freedom—swooping into my harem and liberating me from my "ignorant," "uncritical," "dishonest," and "oppressed" Muslim existence....
> Long before Hirsi Ali arrived in Europe, Muslim women were fighting against ignorance, religious prejudice and cultural misunderstanding. They are still pushing the boundaries, playing an increasingly important public role and advocating real long-term change—slowly but surely.... Many

Muslim women want to maintain a strong, spiritual connection with their faith, a choice Hirsi Ali seeks to deny them. These brave women sadly do not have the luxuries of monetary resources, bodyguards, spin-doctors and PR agencies that she takes for granted.[73]

What is crucial to understand is that not only do authors such as Manji and Hirsi Ali—and much of Western mainstream media—view Islam and Muslim women as monolithic and immutable categories, but also they assume that feminism comes in a singular, familiar package. Therefore, they write with a lack of understanding of the history and diversity not only of Islam but also of feminism within the West and around the world, including in Muslim communities, and of the connected nature of the different feminist efforts around the world.

By ignoring relevant histories of both the Muslim world and the West, these Muslim or formerly Muslim authors have, as "native informants," added new fuel to the old stories of Muslim women's subjugation. At the same time they have deftly displaced the charge of anti-Semitism from its historical European origins onto contemporary Arabs and Muslims. According to this worldview, where the West treats its women correctly and cherishes and protects Israel, this newly constructed Arab/Muslim East not only oppresses its women but now also is guilty of anti-Semitism. Israel is seen to be part of the West, a bastion of democracy and Western ideals, an outpost of "Judeo-Christian" heritage in the midst of a despotic, misogynist Arab world. In celebrating Israel and the West as feminist havens, these writers ignore the egregious problems still facing Palestinian women and men colonized and dispossessed by Israel, with Western support, and women and men of color and of low income in the West.

One explanation for these authors' rapid success was that they perfectly fit the image of "moderate Muslims" that US agencies wanted to promote in the early twenty-first century. For instance, in a 2007 report on US strategies vis-à-vis the Muslim world since 9/11, the Rand Corporation called on the United States to help develop and support networks of "moderate Muslims" to fight the "ideologically driven global jihadist movement," just as the United States had tried to fight the spread of communism during the Cold War by supporting selected networks and institutions around the world, including within the Soviet Bloc. One of the first steps in this process, the report pointed out, was to separate true moderates from those who only appeared to be moderate. To quote from the report, "The issue of women's rights is a major battleground in the war of ideas within Islam, and women's rights advocates operate in very adverse environments. Promotion of gender equality is a critical component of any project to empower moderate Muslims."[74] However, as it turned out, support for neoliberal and neoconservative agendas was taken to be a far more reliable indicator of one's moderation in the early twenty-first century.

DEFINING THE GOOD MUSLIM FEMINIST

Let us turn our attention back briefly to the Bangladeshi writer Taslima Nasreen, who often appeared on the same lists as Manji and Hirsi Ali—but, significantly, not always. For example, in response to worldwide protests following the 2005 decision of the Danish newspaper *Jyllands-Posten* to publish twelve cartoons under the headline "The Face of Muhammad," all three women were among the twelve signatories to a much-publicized statement in the French newspaper *Charlie Hebdo* warning against Islamic "totalitarianism."[75] Nasreen too antagonized both progressive and conservative activists, consistently failed to acknowledge the efforts of others, and minimized the contributions of Bangladesh's long-standing feminist movement.[76]

There are a number of possible explanations as to why Nasreen did not achieve the level of acclaim and popularity of Manji and Hirsi Ali in the West. Her rise to international fame preceded that of the others by a full decade, thus also preceding the Feminist Majority's campaign in Afghanistan, the attacks of 9/11, and the US fervor to save Muslim women. She wrote her major works in Bengali, and they were then translated into English. While the later cohort of Muslim escapees achieved fame by telling their stories of overcoming Islamic strictures, Nasreen did not write her personal story until several years after she had appeared on the global stage as a besieged writer.[77] Although she made several extended visits to the United States in her early years of exile, she did not make the United States her home until 2015. She lacks both the westernized fashion flair of Hirsi Ali (which warranted a 2007 *Vogue* profile) and the media presence of Manji.[78] Perhaps most significant, however, she has tended to be critical of *all* religions, while admitting that she has most experience with Islam. As she put it in her rejoinder to the controversial May 1994 interview with the Indian English daily the *Statesman:* "I hold the Koran, the Vedas, the Bible and all such religious texts determining the lives of their followers as 'out of place and out of time.' We have crossed that historical context in which these were written and therefore we should not be guided by their precepts; the question of revising thoroughly or otherwise is irrelevant. We have to move beyond these ancient texts if we want to progress. In order to respond to our spiritual needs, let humanism be our new faith."[79]

In addition, Nasreen spoke out against the US-led wars in Afghanistan and Iraq and the global war on terror, quickly distinguishing herself as the wrong kind of Muslim dissident: "There are three kinds of terrorism in the world. Private, group, and state. Among these, state terrorism is the most dangerous terrorism. The Bush administration is involved in state terrorism; you cannot eradicate terrorists by dropping bombs. In South Asia, religious terrorists have become much more active since the war on terrorism began, and it's because of the inhuman activities of Bush. In the Middle East, the hatred against the United States is increasing, too. More and more people are joining the fundamentalist organizations, and will continue to."[80] Finally, and this is related to the first explanation, she did not identify Christianity or Judaism as better for women than Islam, or the West or Israel as havens for women. She could not therefore be as easily promoted as a reasonable or "moderate" Muslim who openly embraced the supposedly obvious superiority of Israel and the West, as did so many of the memoirs by Muslim women that flooded the Western market in the aftermath of 9/11.

The implicit distinction on the part of US pundits, media, and policy makers between the right and wrong kind of Muslim woman was also manifest in a December 2002 *Washington Post* article by Robert Satloff, director for policy and strategic planning at the Washington Institute for Near East Policy. He criticized the State Department's decision to use scholar Asma Barlas as an official government speaker in a program meant to help the United States win the hearts and minds of Muslims. He did this on the grounds that her website was a "collection of blame-America-first tirades," citing such excerpts from her articles as "when we ask, 'Why do they hate us' I believe it is because we don't want to ask the question we should be asking: Why do we hate and oppress them."[81] Although Satloff conceded that speakers in this State Department program "should be independent, not government surrogates, and constructive critiques of U.S. policy should be tolerated," he pointed out that using someone like Barlas was "self-defeating" and ultimately only "lends succor to our enemies."[82] Barlas, perhaps best known for her work on nonpatriarchal interpretations of the Quran, responded, "The irony of this has never escaped me. For criticizing Muslim interpretive violence, I am courted as a moderate Muslim but, for criticizing the U.S.'s political violence, I am denounced as a militant anti-American. Where then is the space for Muslim-Americans like me to live in accordance with our religious and political principles and beliefs?"[83]

Barlas perfectly pinpoints the strategic nature of the search for and celebration of moderate Muslims, and in particular moderate Muslim women, by the US government, think tanks, the media, and sections of the public. The moderate Muslim has been fabricated in direct opposition to the terrorist or fundamentalist. According to this perspective, since the latter is generally a bearded man who is pious, lives in the past, and hates the United States, Israel, and their culture and policies, the moderate Muslim must be a woman who is not visibly religious but rather modern and Western (read: she doesn't veil), thinks critically about Islamic texts and traditions—or better still has renounced Islam—and loves the United States, Israel, and their culture and policies. Any attempt to situate one's understanding of Muslim women's oppression under religion-based law or government in the broader context of war, occupation, colonialism, or globalization is dismissed as unnecessarily nuanced and complicated—and certainly suspicious. In other words, there are good and bad Muslim feminists, and the Western mainstream media, feminists, and pundits have arrogated to themselves the authority to decide between them.[84]

Epilogue

THE JANUARY 2017 WOMEN'S MARCHES in Washington, DC, and other cities in the United States and around the world featured a poster of a woman wearing a US flag as a headscarf, making her immediately recognizable as a Muslim woman. Many appreciated the intent of artist Shepard Fairey and the march participants who carried the poster to send a message about a more inclusive United States and a broader definition of US feminism that now embraces Muslims. The model for the original decade-old photo by Ridwan Adhami was Munira Ahmed, a US woman from New York whose family had moved there from Bangladesh before she was born. Muslim women who attended the 2017 march reported feeling welcomed and included. Saira Toor, a member of the Muslim Women's Alliance in Chicago, recalled, "I was amazed by the outpouring of support and love. People saying, 'Thanks for being here,' like we were VIPs."[1]

At the same time this iconic image also raised concerns. Observers pointed out that the poster had altered the original photo to make the woman conform better to White standards of beauty and allure with lighter skin, more prominent cheekbones, and bright red lipstick; that the image reinforced the idea that all Muslim women wear headscarves; and that the image implied that the only good US Muslim was one who broadcast her patriotism—notably, it was the only image in the poster series to include the flag. Many also noted that such images of inclusivity coincided with anti-Muslim racism within the United States and US-government-sponsored wars and killings of Muslims overseas. As Chicago-based activist and political fashion blogger Hoda Katebi noted at the time, "How are we able to hold up signs of Muslim women wearing the flag and chant slogans of supposed solidarity while drones carrying the same flag killed our Muslim family in Yemen at

FIGURE 24. *Greater Than Fear*. Art by Shepard Fairey for Amplifier.org.

the exact same moment and we said nothing?"[2] Zainab Khan, a community organizer from Atlanta, later recalled, "I remember there were these posters of a Muslim woman in an American hijab flag. That is all I needed to know."[3] In the end we should not assume that the greater visibility of Muslim women in the United States—for example, at the Women's March, in Congress, in corporate fashion lines, and on TV and cinema screens—indicates that Muslim women no longer stoke a range of emotions from fear to pity and arrogance among non-Muslim Americans, any more than the 2008 election of its first Black president should be taken as evidence that the United States had resolved its anti-Black racism.

More serious problems further marred the relationship between the Women's March organizers and US Muslim women in the years that followed. The organization's decision to successively oust two Muslim women, Linda Sarsour and Zahra Billoo, from national leadership positions because of their criticism of Israeli policy vis-à-vis Palestinians, had a chilling effect on other Muslim women's participation in the march. Many US Muslim women now feel that they, and other women of color, were embraced so visibly in the 2017 Women's March only as a way to make this new twenty-first-century feminist movement appear more diverse than past women's rights campaigns. Asma Elhuni, a community organizer from Vermont who participated enthusiastically in the first marches, explained why she would no longer attend: "This country has a history of a type of feminism that leaves out certain women. Through the Women's March, this practice of valuing the experience of some women over others continues today." She added, "They need to know: leaving Palestinian women out, leaving Muslim women out, is not okay."[4] African American women, similarly, have complained about the organization's lack of interest in issues that matter to them, such as police brutality against Black men and women.[5]

The highly visible marches aside, the real expansion of the older, narrow notion of Western feminism is being pushed by emerging coalitions of feminists of color, including Muslim women, who are opposed to a wide range of injustices, including racism, Islamophobia, transphobia, homophobia, and economic exploitation. For instance, a 2017 poll by the Institute for Social Policy and Understanding (ISPU) found that 75 percent of US Muslim women support the Black Lives Matter (BLM) movement, in comparison to 77 percent of the general Black public, 60 percent of Muslim men, and 38 percent of the general White public.[6] US Muslims themselves, while just over 1 percent of the total US population, are the most ethnically diverse religious group. About a quarter are Black and just under a quarter are White, followed by lower percentages of Asian and Arab Muslims and even smaller percentages that identify as "mixed," Latino, or other. As the authors of the ISPU report point out, "This finding should further undercut the misguided tendency among some public officials and media portrayals to broad-brush

American Muslims."[7] Indeed, to ignore the diversity among Muslims—and their multiple identities and varied concerns—is to have learned nothing from history and to repeat the pitfalls of earlier eras.

Just days after the first Women's March, US president Donald Trump invoked Muslim women in issuing new restrictions on travel and immigration to the United States by the citizens of several Muslim-majority nations. The first iteration of what was immediately recognized as a "Muslim ban" justified the new restrictions on the grounds that they would keep out of the country "those who engage in acts of bigotry or hatred (including 'honor' killings, other forms of violence against women, or the persecution of those who practice religions different from their own)." There was no need to be explicit. In popular Western understanding, honor killings are linked almost exclusively to Islam. The need to protect Americans from Muslim forms of violence against women was cited twice in the January draft. Not only does such targeting of Muslims continue alongside wars and sanctions against Muslim-majority countries, but it presents violence against women as utterly alien to US realities, with the implication that there is no need to fund improved services for US women survivors of violence, as US feminists of all backgrounds have long demanded.[8]

Born in the Little Bangladesh neighborhood of Kensington, Brooklyn, to parents from neighboring villages in the southeastern port district of Chittagong (or Chattogram) in Bangladesh, Shahana Hanif is representative of the new generation of Muslim feminist activists in the West. Like the many reformers and activists we have encountered in this book, Hanif's politics and activism are informed by a variety of concerns and experiences, as well as, of course, the larger political context in which she has come of age. Growing up in New York, Hanif and her two younger sisters spoke Bengali at home, sang Bengali and Hindi/Urdu songs at private parties and public events, and took Quranic lessons at the local mosque after attending their local public school. Being diagnosed with lupus when she was in high school, Hanif recalls, was the "catalyst to my politicization." Her desire to "to deep dive into the politics of surviving as immigrant, faith-based, working-class, disabled, [and] lower-income" led her to major in women's and gender studies at Brooklyn College. She went on to work for an organization focused on affordable housing for working-class Asian communities and as a community liaison in city government. Her activism is fueled by her "commitment to a Bangladeshi-Muslim social justice framework in the New York diaspora." Hanif speaks with excitement of meetings at which "women tenant leaders share their feminist dreams, talk about gender equality within Islam and Bangladesh, and bring to light the myth that is the American Dream and anti-immigrant rhetoric."[9]

New York–based law professor, social-justice lawyer, human rights activist, and filmmaker Chaumtoli Huq, who moved from Bangladesh to the United States as a young child, made national headlines in 2014 when she was arrested while allegedly obstructing the sidewalk at a New York City rally in support of Gaza. Upon learning that she and her husband have different last names, one of the arresting police officers informed her, "In America, wives take the names of their husbands."[10] Huq works on labor rights in both the United States and Bangladesh, for example, on the connections between the garment industry in both countries.

Thahitun Mariam spent the first six years of her life in rural Bangladesh before moving to the Bronx. Today a poet, writer, and community activist working in the New York City mayor's office, she is as passionate about creating spaces for Bangladeshi immigrant women to learn about and organize around their rights (in the face of Immigration and Customs Enforcement raids, for example) and forge new connections as she is about working with other groups to help Bronx residents access groceries and services during the COVID-19 lockdown and rallying the Bangladeshi community in New York to support the BLM movement in its fight against police brutality. In interviews she has spoken about the inspiration she draws from the long history of feminist and nationalist activism in Bangladesh in her decision to support US liberation movements such as BLM.[11] Mariam reflected on these connections when Naripokkho's Shireen Huq recently visited New York: "Her visit reminds us that our feminist work here is deeply rooted back to our motherland.... There is power in our narratives, being tied between diaspora and homeland, and being intentionally intergenerational. Our future, our past and our present are inevitably intertwined."[12]

Hanif, Huq, and Mariam pose a sharp contrast to such Muslim or ex-Muslim celebrities such as Irshad Manji and Ayaan Hirsi Ali. Like them, these activists recognize the consequences of male dominance within their communities. Unlike them, they do not see male dominance as the only problem nor as a uniquely Muslim problem, and they do not see themselves as exceptional or iconic. Their objective is not to reform or reject an abstract Islam so much as it is to empower immigrant men and women of low income and "limited English proficiency" to navigate life in New York. They work

FIGURE 25. *Left to right:* Shahana Hanif, Chaumtoli Huq, Shireen
Huq, and Thahitun Mariam, in front of the Malcolm Shabazz Mosque
in Harlem, New York, September 2018. Courtesy of the Bangladeshi
Feminist Collective, New York.

as hard to reach out to the politically conservative "uncles" (male community elders) as they do to collaborate with progressive organizations all over
the city and country. Today these three women are part of an organization
called Naari Shongothok (Bangladeshi Feminist Collective), which has been
particularly active in protesting anti-immigrant policies such as the Muslim
ban and family separations at the US-Mexico border—neither of which, it
is worth noting, directly affects Bangladeshis. It is this politics of compas-
sion and solidarity that characterizes the best of feminist organizing today,
Muslim and otherwise.

NOTES

INTRODUCTION

1. E. Kaplan, *Rocking around the Clock*, 137–38.

CHAPTER ONE

1. Ibn Battuta, *Travels in Asia*, 268.

2. Tolmacheva, "Women's Travel"; Ibn Battuta, *Travels in Asia*, 192–93.

3. Ibn Battuta, *Travels in Asia*, 243–44; Dunn, *Adventures of Ibn Battuta*, 234–35; Kruk, "Ibn Battuta"; Tolmacheva, "Concubines on the Road."

4. Ibn Battuta, *Travels in Asia*, 268; R. Chakravarti, "Indic Mercantile Networks," 214–15.

5. Ibn Battuta, *Travels in Asia*, 268–69; Waines, "Ibn Baṭṭūṭah"; Dunn, *Adventures of Ibn Battuta*.

6. Phillips, "Mahuan's Account"; Huan, *Ying-Yai Sheng-Lan*, 159–64; Levathes, *When China Ruled;* T. Sen, "Chinese Maritime Networks"; A. Forbes, "Ma Huan."

7. Subrahmanyam, *Europe's India*, 17; Subrahmanyam, *Empires*, 26–27.

8. Barbosa, *Book of Duarte Barbosa*, 2:3; Prange, *Monsoon Islam*, 1, 93.

9. Boxer, *Joao de Barros;* Subrahmanyam, *Portuguese Empire in Asia*, 53.

10. Harrison, "Five Portuguese Historians," 165.

11. Tarafdar, *Husain Shahi Bengal*, 31.

12. A. Karim, *Social History*, 190.

13. Barbosa, *Book of Duarte Barbosa*, 2:xxvi, 2:147–48.

14. Cortesão, introd. to Pires, *Suma Oriental*, xxiii; Pires, *Suma Oriental*, 88, 92–93, 142–43; Tarafdar, *Trade, Technology and Society*.

15. Flores, "Floating Franks," 33; *Voyage dans les Deltas*, xx.

16. L. Ahmed, "Western Ethnocentrism"; Alloula, *Colonial Harem;* Yegenoglu, *Colonial Fantasies;* Lewis, *Rethinking Orientalism;* Booth, *Harem Histories.*

17. *Voyage dans les Deltas,* 326, 319–22; Subrahmanyam, *Portuguese Empire in Asia,* 75–77, 265–66.

18. Subrahmanyam, *Improvising Empire,* 96–127.

19. Tarafdar, *Husain Shahi Bengal,* 344.

20. Campos, *History of the Portuguese,* 193–94; R. Harvey, *Clive,* 18–22.

21. Raychaudhuri, *Bengal under Akbar;* Prakash, "Dutch East India Company."

22. Foster, *Letters Received,* 4:315.

23. Subrahmanyam, "Taking Stock," 72–74; A. Chakravarti, *Empire of Apostles,* 26–28.

24. Matar, *Europe through Arab Eyes,* 56–57, 61, 86.

25. Stowasser, *Women in the Qur'an,* 67–82; Abboud, *Mary in the Qur'an.*

26. Kozlowski, "Private Lives," 473.

27. Fazl, *Akbar Nama,* 3:37; Flores, "Floating Franks," 40; Flores, *Unwanted Neighbors,* xi, 21–22.

28. Subrahmanyam, "Taking Stock," 85–87; Flores, "Floating Franks."

29. Jasanoff, *Edge of Empire,* 23.

30. Fisher, *Visions of Mughal India,* 59.

31. Purchas, *Hakluytus Posthumus,* 4:361; MacLean and Matar, *Britain,* 77, 195.

32. Lal, *Empress,* 13, 118.

33. Foster, *Embassy,* 90–93, 109, 111, 114–15, 118, 188; Findly, *Nur Jahan,* 139.

34. Lal, *Empress,* 123.

35. Findly, *Nur Jahan,* 150; MacLean and Matar, *Britain,* 74–75.

36. Foster, *Early Travels in India,* 203; Foster, *Letters Received,* 2:213.

37. Findly, *Nur Jahan,* 156.

38. Foster, *Embassy,* 281, 215; Terry, *Voyage to East,* 407; Findly, "Capture."

39. Foster, *Embassy,* 436–37.

40. Foster, *Letters Received,* 5:329.

41. Foster, *Early Travels in India,* 118.

42. Foster, *Embassy,* 321.

43. Pelsaert, *Jahangir's India,* 64–66.

44. Moreland, introd. to Pelsaert, *Jahangir's India,* xii; Lal, *Domesticity and Power,* 39–42.

45. Heeres, *Part Borne,* 61.

46. Bernier, *Travels,* 267.

47. Teltscher, *India Inscribed,* 42–43.

48. Peirce, *Imperial Harem;* Lal, *Domesticity and Power.*

49. Boxer, *Iberian Expansion Overseas,* 41–44; Bailey, "Mughal Princess"; Ronald Morgan, *Spanish American Saints,* 119–42.

50. A. Beveridge, introd. to G. Begum, *History of Humayun,* 7, 69, 71–72, 75; Lal, *Domesticity and Power,* 31, ch. 3; Balabanlilar, "Gulbadan Begam."

51. Foster, *Embassy,* 483–84; Fisher, "Seeing England Firsthand," 143–54; Robertson, "Stranger Bride," 52; A. Sen, "Traveling Companions"; A. Sen, "Sailing to India."

52. Wheeler, *Early Travels in India,* 72–73; A. Sen, "Sailing to India"; Lal, *Empress,* 61–62.

53. Foster, *English Factories in India,* xxvi.

54. Foster, *English Factories in India,* 16, 155, 168, 184, 327.

55. Fisher, "Seeing England Firsthand," 151, 154–55.

56. Sayers, *Song of Roland;* Kahf, *Western Representations.*

57. Raychaudhuri, *Bengal under Akbar,* 49–52.

58. Lal, *Empress,* 65–72, 92–93.

59. Pires, *Suma Oriental,* 90.

60. Eaton, *Rise of Islam;* P. Hasan, *Sultans and Mosques;* Van Schendel, *History of Bangladesh.*

61. Eaton, *Rise of Islam,* 278, 308; Husain, *Social Life of Women,* 9, 56; T. Stewart, "In Search of Equivalence"; Uddin, *Constructing Bangladesh,* 32–36; Irani, "Sacred Biography," 283–86; *Banglapedia,* s.v. "Saduktikarnamrita," by Shahanara Husain, accessed 5 August 2019, http://en.banglapedia.org/index.php?title= Saduktikarnamrita.

62. Rafiuddin Ahmed, *Bengal Muslims;* Chatterji, "Bengali Muslim."

63. A. Karim, *Murshid Quli Khan,* 29–30; Asher and Talbot, *India before Europe,* 250–52.

64. Calkins, "Formation"; J. Sarkar, *History of Bengal,* 408–17.

65. Travers, "Eighteenth Century"; Datta, *Society.*

66. Colley, *Ordeal of Elizabeth Marsh,* 177.

67. Scott and Park, *Poetical Works,* 57–64; Arnold, "Hunger in the Garden"; Watt, *British Orientalisms,* 129–30.

68. *Maharashta Purana,* xxi; Begum and Huq, *Ami Nari,* 10.

69. N. Sinha, *Economic History of Bengal,* 1:184–85; Hameeda Hossain, "Alienation of Weavers," 325.

70. Begum and Huq, *Ami Nari,* 20.

71. Begum and Huq, *Ami Nari,* 18; M. Khan, *Muslim Heritage of Bengal,* 73–79.

72. Abdul Khan, *Transition in Bengal,* 70, 71n2, 72.

73. Abdul Khan, *Transition in Bengal,* 224; Asher, *Architecture of Mughal India,* 330–31.

74. *Oxford Dictionary of National Biography,* s.v. "Munni Begam (1723?–1813)," by P. J. Marshall, accessed 15 October 2015, www.oxforddnb.com.

75. A. Ali, "Munny Begum," 150.

CHAPTER TWO

1. Parker, *Early Modern Tales,* 85; MacLean, *Rise of Oriental Travel,* 88; Andrea, "Western Responses," 277.

2. Foster, *Embassy,* 42; Foster, *English Factories in India,* 20n1; Foster, *Letters Received,* 1:300.

3. Vitkus, *Three Turk Plays*, 41, 256; Matar, "Representation of Muslim Women," 52.

4. *A New Dictionary of the Terms Ancient and Modern of the Canting Crew*, s.v. "Turk," by B. E. Gent, 1699, https://archive.org/details/newdictionaryoft00begeuoft; *Oxford English Dictionary*, s.v. "Turk," accessed 17 November 2015, www.oed.com.

5. Hunt, "Women in Ottoman"; Hunt, *Eighteenth-Century Europe*, 4, 89, 296.

6. Sprint, *Bride-Woman's Counsellor*, 30, 40; Apetrei, *Women, Feminism and Religion*, 8; Teltscher, *India Inscribed*, 37.

7. De Groot, "Oriental Feminotopias," 82.

8. Zonana, "Sultan and the Slave," 600; *Oxford English Dictionary*, s.v. "seraglio, n.," accessed 2 March 2016, www.oed.com.

9. Kabbani, *Imperial Fictions*; Melman, *Women's Orients*; Lowe, *Critical Terrains*; Grosrichard, *Sultan's Court*; Euben, *Journeys*, ch. 5; Yeazell, *Harems of the Mind*, 59; De Groot, "Oriental Feminotopias," 83n5.

10. Shklar, "Montesquieu."

11. Yapp, "Turkish Mirror," 147.

12. Astell, *Serious Proposal*, 47–48; Rogers, *Feminism*; Smith, *Reason's Disciples*; Perry, *Celebrated Mary Astell*; Broad, *Philosophy of Mary Astell*; Sowaal and Weiss, *Feminist Interpretations*.

13. Astell, *Christian Religion*, 296; Perry, *Celebrated Mary Astell*, 61; Andrea, "Western Responses," 281n14.

14. Andrea, "Western Responses," 280–81.

15. Montagu, preface to *Letters*.

16. Hill, "Refuge from Men," 107, 109, 120.

17. Chudleigh, *Ladies Defence*; M. Ferguson, *First Feminists*; Kelly, "Early Feminist Theory," 17.

18. Kugler, *Errant Plagiary*, 49.

19. Chapone, *Hardships*, 45–46; Broad, "Great Championess," 98, 83; Glover, "Further Reflections upon Marriage"; Tucker, *Women, Family, and Gender*; Hunt, *Eighteenth-Century Europe*, 66–69; *Oxford Dictionary of National Biography*, s.v. "Chapone [Capon; née Kirkham], Sarah," by Thomas Keymer, accessed 20 November 2015, www.oxforddnb.com.

20. Blackstone, *Commentaries*, bk. 1, ch. 15, p. 430.

21. Freeman, "Legal Basis," 209; Isenberg, *Sex and Citizenship*; Vickery, "Don't Marry a Christian"; Stretton and Kesselring, *Married Women*; Shephard, *Accounting for Oneself*.

22. Andrea, *Women and Islam*, ch. 4, pp. 78–104, 105, 111, 114–17.

23. Ballaster, introd. to Manley, *New Atalantis*, v.

24. Fernea, "Early Ethnographer," 329; Grundy, introd. to Grundy, *Lady Mary Wortley Montagu*, xviii, n. 5; Heffernan, "Feminism"; Still, "Hospitable Harems"; Makdisi and Nussbaum, *Arabian Nights*; Montagu, *Turkish Embassy Letters*, 158, 281.

25. Montagu, *Turkish Embassy Letters*, 104, 148–49; Fernea, "Early Ethnographer," 332.

26. Pope, *Correspondence*, 1:369; Cahill, *Intelligent Souls*, 5–6; Garcia, *English Enlightenment*, 61; Montagu, *Turkish Embassy Letters*, 104; Halsband, *Complete Letters*, 1:363, 1:375; Grundy, *Lady Mary Wortley Montagu*, 88–89.

27. Halsband, *Complete Letters*, 1:328; Still, "Hospitable Harems," 99; Aravamudan, "Lady Mary Wortley Montagu," 76–79.

28. Montagu, *Turkish Embassy Letters*, 115–16; Halsband, *Complete Letters*, 1:329; Andrea, "Western Responses," 279–80; Still, "Hospitable Harems," 91–93; Hunt, *Eighteenth-Century Europe*, 59–60.

29. Pope, *Correspondence*, 1:368; Bohls, "Aesthetics and Orientalism"; Halsband, *Complete Letters*, 1:406.

30. Halsband, *Complete Letters*, 1:315.

31. Halsband, *Complete Letters*, 1:314.

32. Pratt, *Imperial Eyes*, 166–67; Nussbaum, *Torrid Zones*, ch. 6.

33. Aravamudan, "Lady Mary Wortley Montagu," 70, 81.

34. Halsband, *Complete Letters*, 1:314.

35. Lowe, *Critical Terrains;* Yegenoglu, *Colonial Fantasies;* Aravamudan, "Lady Mary Wortley Montagu," 83; Still, "Hospitable Harems"; Kietzman, "Montagu's *Turkish Embassy Letters.*"

36. Halsband, *Complete Letters*, 1:330; Heffernan, "Feminism," 213.

37. Secor, "Orientalism, Gender and Class"; Garcia, *English Enlightenment*, ch. 2.

38. Meek, *Social Science;* Rendall, "Scottish Orientalism," 43.

39. Mander, "No Woman," 113n9.

40. A. Ferguson, *History of Civil Society*, 176–78.

41. Nussbaum, *Torrid Zones*, 8–9.

42. Rendall, "Grand Causes," 156.

43. Millar, *Origin of the Distinction*, 103.

44. B. Taylor, "Feminists versus Gallants," 130; Sebastiani, *Scottish Enlightenment*, 140; O'Brien, *Women and Enlightenment*, 88.

45. Moran, "Savage and the Civil," 9.

46. A. F. M. Kadir, "Early Muslim Visitors"; Fisher, *Counterflows to Colonialism;* Fisher, "From India to England," 157; P. Chatterjee, *Black Hole of Empire*, 67.

47. Digby, "Eighteenth-Century Narrative."

48. I'tesamuddin, *Wonders of Vilayet*, 54; Visram, *Asians in Britain*.

49. P. Chatterjee, *Black Hole of Empire*, 68.

50. Haq, "Translator's Introduction"; G. Khan, *Indian Muslim Perceptions*, 72; P. Chatterjee, *Black Hole of Empire*, 68; Banerjee-Dube, *History of Modern India*, 48.

51. I'tesamuddin, *Wonders of Vilayet*, 53–54.

52. I'tesamuddin, *Wonders of Vilayet*, 137–38, 141, 13, 16, 125–37, 145; P. Chatterjee, *Black Hole of Empire*, 70.

53. I'tesamuddin, *Wonders of Vilayet*, 13, 16, 125–37, 145; P. Chatterjee, *Black Hole of Empire*, 70.

54. G. Khan, *Indian Muslim Perceptions*, 73; I'tesamuddin, *Wonders of Vilayet*, 11, 124; P. Chatterjee, *Black Hole of Empire*, 67.

55. I'tesamuddin, *Wonders of Vilayet,* 26; Raychaudhuri, *Europe Reconsidered,* ix; Chakrabarty, *Provincializing Europe;* S. Sen, *Travels to Europe,* 52–53.

56. Gaughan, *Incumberances.*

57. Stevenson, *Victorian Women Travel Writers,* 9; Fisher, *Travels of Dean Mahomet,* 138.

58. Smart, "Letter from a Lady."

59. Kindersley, *Letters,* 72–79.

60. Dyson, *Various Universe,* 124–25; Midgley, *Feminism and Empire,* 67–68; Barros and Smith, *Anthology,* 176; Gregg, *Empire and Identity,* 193.

61. "Letters from the Island."

62. Kindersley, *Letters,* 171–78.

63. Kindersley, *Letters,* 189, 193, 244; Dyson, *Various Universe,* 125; Gregg, *Empire and Identity,* 199.

64. Kindersley, *Letters,* 102–3, 220, 222, 225.

65. Thomas, *Essay on the Character,* 65–71, 219–27; Lee, "Sex in Translation."

66. Colley, *Ordeal of Elizabeth Marsh,* ch. 5.

67. Hoeveler, "Female Captivity Narrative"; Colley, *Ordeal of Elizabeth Marsh.*

68. Colley, *Ordeal of Elizabeth Marsh,* 160.

69. Colley, *Ordeal of Elizabeth Marsh,* 172–75.

70. Gleig, *Memoirs of the Life,* 1:293.

71. Colley, *Ordeal of Elizabeth Marsh,* 178, 183, 186–87.

72. Colley, *Ordeal of Elizabeth Marsh,* ch. 4, pp. 154–55, 160, 172–73, 197, 213–33.

73. Bage, *Mount Henneth,* 1:239.

74. Bage, *Fair Syrian,* 2:38, 2:59, 2:74.

75. Matar, *Turks, Moors, and Englishmen,* 104.

76. Bage, *Fair Syrian,* 2:31–32.

77. B. Joseph, *East India Company,* 76–77; Hoeveler, "Female Captivity Narrative," 68; Watt, *British Orientalisms,* 76–77, 107–12.

78. Robinson, *Edmund Burke,* 109; Clark, *Scandal,* 103; Reynolds, "Phebe Gibbes."

79. "Abigail Adams"; *Trial of Warren Hastings,* 1; O'Quinn, *Staging Governance,* 116–17; Reynolds, "Phebe Gibbes"; Jasanoff, *Liberty's Exiles,* 139.

80. Clark, *Scandal,* 96.

81. Colley, "Gendering the Globe," 138.

82. Marshall, *Impeachment of Warren Hastings,* 134; *Trial of Warren Hastings,* title page, 78; P. Chatterjee, *Black Hole of Empire,* 59; Clark, *Scandal,* ch. 4; O'Quinn, *Staging Governance,* 221; Reynolds, "Phebe Gibbes," 153, 172n52, 176; Colley, "Gendering the Globe," 138–39; Suleri, *Rhetoric of English India,* 56–64.

83. A. Ali, "Munny Begum"; Clark, *Scandal,* ch. 4; *Oxford Dictionary of National Biography,* s.v. "Munni Begam (1723?–1813)," by P. J. Marshall, accessed 15 October 2015, www.oxforddnb.com.

84. Marshall, *Bengal,* 101.

85. Marshall, *Impeachment of Warren Hastings,* ch. 6; Fisher, "Women and the Feminine"; Barnett, "Embattled Begams."

86. A. Ali, "Munny Begum," 149.

87. *Works of the Right.*

88. Burke, *Right Honourable Edmund Burke,* 9:435, 10:33, 10:194–99; *Trial of Warren Hastings,* 58.

89. Burke, *Reflections,* 69; Wollstonecraft, *Rights of Men,* 67–68; Clark, *Scandal,* 107–9.

90. T. Metcalf, *Ideologies of the Raj;* Dirks, *Scandal of Empire.*

91. *Oxford Dictionary,* s.v. "Munni Begam."

92. A. Ali, "Munny Begum," 151.

93. Nugent, *Journal,* 175–79.

94. Franklin, "Radically Feminizing India," 155; B. Joseph, *East India Company,* 88–90; Grundy, "Barbarous Character," 79.

95. Gordon, *Romantic Outlaws,* 153, 170.

96. Yeo, *Mary Wollstonecraft;* Offen, "Mary Wollstonecraft," 6; Stansell, *Feminist Promise,* xiv; R. Strachey, *Cause,* 12; Botting, "Wollstonecraft in Europe," 506.

97. Isenberg, *Fallen Founder,* 80–81.

98. Burr, "Aaron Burr Jr."; Burr, *Complicated Lives,* 84–85.

99. Midgley, *Feminism and Empire,* 15–16.

100. Hill, "Links Between"; Gunther-Canada, "Cultivating Virtue."

101. Rousseau, *Emile,* 365.

102. C. Macaulay, *Letters on Education,* 213, 220.

103. Wollstonecraft, *Rights of Woman,* 114, 36, 114, 12, 93, 242.

104. Moran, "Savage and the Civil," 8; Looser, *British Women Writers,* 85–86; B. Taylor, "Feminists versus Gallants," 130.

105. Wollstonecraft, *Rights of Woman,* 11, 72, 74, 31–32; B. Taylor, "Feminists versus Gallants," 126.

106. Wollstonecraft, *Rights of Woman,* 72, 75; B. Taylor, "Feminists versus Gallants," 126–27, 139–40.

107. Wollstonecraft, *Rights of Woman,* 15, 40.

108. Wollstonecraft, *Rights of Woman,* 90; Nussbaum, *Torrid Zones,* 92.

109. Wollstonecraft, *Rights of Woman,* 55–56, 160.

110. Wollstonecraft, *Rights of Woman,* 28.

111. M. Ferguson, "Mary Wollstonecraft," 82, 86–87; Curthoys, "Mary Wollstonecraft Revisited," 39.

112. Midgley, *Feminism and Empire,* 42–43.

113. M. Ferguson, "Mary Wollstonecraft," 84–86; Mellor, "Sex, Violence, and Slavery"; Howard, "Wollstonecraft's Thoughts."

114. Zonana, "Sultan and the Slave"; Nussbaum, *Torrid Zones,* 1–2; S. Makdisi, *William Blake,* 209; Watt, "Blessings of Freedom," 59.

115. Wollstonecraft, *Rights of Woman,* 93.

116. Wollstonecraft, *Rights of Woman,* 218–19; B. Taylor, "Religious Foundations," 99–101; Cahill, *Intelligent Souls.*

117. S. Makdisi, *William Blake,* ch. 5; Watt, "Blessings of Freedom"; Yeazell, *Harems of the Mind,* 78; Zonana, "Sultan and the Slave."

118. Randall, *Letter to the Women*, 4, 13, 69; Midgley, *Feminism and Empire*, 19–20.

119. Garcia, "Transports of Lascar Specters."

120. C. Stewart, preface to Abu Taleb Khan, *Travels*, 1:vii; Minault, "Impressions of Europe," 2.

121. S. Sen, *Travels to Europe*, 26; Chambers, *Britain through Muslim Eyes*, 33.

122. Abu Taleb Khan, *Travels*, 1:21; Fisher, "From India to England," 167.

123. Abu Taleb Khan, *Travels*, 1:80, 1:134, 1:192; S. Sen, *Travels to Europe*, 31.

124. Abu Taleb Khan, *Travels*, 2:32–33.

125. Leask, "Travelling the Other Way," 232; Abu Taleb Khan, *Travels*, 2:47, 2:51; Chambers, *Britain through Muslim Eyes*, 33–34.

126. Abu Taleb Khan, *Travels*, 2:61; Leask, "Travelling the Other Way," 230–31.

127. Fisher, "Representing 'His' Women," 223–24.

128. Abu Talib Khan, "Vindication," 101; Fisher, "Representing 'His' Women," 231–32; Digby, "Eighteenth-Century Narrative," 54.

129. Abu Taleb Khan, *Travels*, 2:401–6; Abu Taleb Khan, "Vindication," 101; I. Chatterjee, introd. to I. Chatterjee, *Unfamiliar Relations*, 14; B. Mukhopadhyay, "Writing Home, Writing Travel," 296.

130. S. Sen, *Travels to Europe*, 49.

131. Abu Taleb Khan, *Travels*, 2:404–7.

132. Abu Taleb Khan, *Travels*, 1:262.

133. Tavakoli-Targhi, "Imagining Western Women," 78.

134. Fisher, "Representing 'His' Women," 226–27, 229.

135. Abu Taleb Khan, *Travels*, 1:292.

136. Abu Taleb Khan, *Travels*, 1:191–92; Narain, "Indians' Travel Narratives."

137. Fisher, "Representing 'His' Women," 230.

138. Fisher, "Representing 'His' Women," 226n49.

CHAPTER THREE

1. Carey, *Enquiry into the Obligations*, 11, 69–70, 75; Robert, *American Women in Mission*, 4–5.

2. White, *From Little London*, 59–60.

3. Carey and Chaplin, *Memoir of William Carey*, 93, 105; White, *From Little London*, 60.

4. Montgomery, *Western Women*, 11–12.

5. Viswanathan, *Masks of Conquest*, 23–24; Kopf, *British Orientalism*, 47; Abu Kamal, *Bengali Press*, 9; Harlow and Carter, *Imperialism and Orientalism*, 67; Uddin, *Constructing Bangladesh*, 48–51; Sengupta, *Pedagogy For Religion*, 12–13; Banerjee-Dube, *History of Modern India*, 81–89.

6. Roebuck, *Annals of the College*, xx, 114.

7. Abu Kamal, *Bengali Press,* 9–10; A. Ghosh, *Power in Print,* 73; Uddin, *Constructing Bangladesh,* 51–52; White, *From Little London,* 61.

8. Johnston, *Missionary Writing and Empire,* 80–81.

9. Carey, *Enquiry into the Obligations,* 49–54, 62.

10. Carey and Chaplin, *Memoir of William Carey,* 69; Kopf, *British Orientalism,* 103; Powell, *Muslims and Missionaries,* 79–81.

11. Carey and Chaplin, *Memoir of William Carey,* 124–25.

12. Uddin, *Constructing Bangladesh,* 52.

13. Rafiuddin Ahmed, *Bengal Muslims,* 97–98; A. Ghosh, *Power in Print,* ch. 7.

14. Jones, *Socio-religious Reform Movements,* 22–23; Hourani, *Arab Peoples,* 257–58; Rafiuddin Ahmed, *Bengal Muslims,* 40; Iqbal, *Bengal Delta,* ch. 4.

15. Banerjee-Dube, *History of Modern India,* 59–61; Iqbal, *Bengal Delta,* 68–69.

16. Begum and Ahmed, "Beliefs and Rituals," 53, 68–95.

17. Carey and Chaplin, *Memoir of William Carey,* 254; Rafiuddin Ahmed, *Bengal Muslims,* 54, 58–60.

18. Rafiuddin Ahmed, *Bengal Muslims,* 88–89.

19. Anisuzzaman, *Muslim Manas,* 117; Rafiuddin Ahmed, *Bengal Muslims,* 75, 78, 84–87.

20. Dil, *Two Traditions,* 64; Anisuzzaman, *Muslim Manas,* 152; Amin, *World of Muslim Women,* 48–49.

21. Salomon, "Baul Songs"; Knight, *Contradictory Lives.*

22. Rendall, "Scottish Orientalism."

23. James Mill, *History of British India,* 1:ix, xi; J.S. Mill, *Autobiography,* 26.

24. Knowles, "Conjecturing Rudeness," 46.

25. Ball, introd. to James Mill, *James Mill,* xii–xxviii; Ryan, *On Politics,* 2:697.

26. Ryan, *On Politics,* 2:697.

27. Inden, "Orientalist Constructions of India," 418; S. Makdisi, *Romantic Imperialism,* 114–15; Dirks, *Castes of Mind,* 32.

28. James Mill, *History of British India,* 1:383; Pitts, *Turn to Empire,* 129–30; Knowles, "Conjecturing Rudeness," 51.

29. James Mill, *History of British India,* 1:383–86, 5:513.

30. James Mill, *History of British India,* 1:132, 2:456–57.

31. James Mill, *History of British India,* 2:453–54, 1:393–94.

32. James Mill, *History of British India,* 1:385.

33. Knowles, "Conjecturing Rudeness," 41; Pitts, *Turn to Empire,* 106.

34. Reeves, *John Stuart Mill,* 35; James Mill, *James Mill,* 27.

35. Thompson, *Appeal of One Half;* Midgley, *Feminism and Empire,* 22–23.

36. Banerjee-Dube, *History of Modern India,* 94.

37. Banerjee-Dube, *History of Modern India,* 93.

38. Mani, *Contentious Traditions,* 1; M. Sinha, *Specters of Mother India,* 152.

39. R. Roy, *English Works.*

40. Kopf, *Brahmo Samaj.*

41. R. Roy, *English Works,* 2:329; Mani, *Contentious Traditions,* 58.

42. Mani, *Contentious Traditions.*

43. Bates, *Subalterns and Raj,* 49–50.

44. T. Macaulay, "Minute on Indian Education"; Banerjee-Dube, *History of Modern India,* 91–92.

45. Trevelyan, *Life and Letters,* 1:300; Skuy, "Indian Penal Code."

46. Midgley, *Feminism and Empire,* 65.

47. W. Ward, "Burning of Women"; Mani, *Contentious Traditions,* 140–42.

48. Midgley, *Feminism and Empire,* 27, 71.

49. Midgley, *Feminism and Empire,* 73–75.

50. Spivak, "Three Women's Texts"; Midgley, *Feminism and Empire,* 86, 90–91; Zaeske, *Signatures of Citizenship,* 7–8.

51. G. Forbes, "Pure Heathen," WS6–8; Jayawardena, *White Woman's Other Burden,* 27; Midgley, *Feminism and Empire,* 73–75; Aparna Basu, "Century and Half's Journey," 183.

52. Richter, *History of Missions,* 329.

53. Storrow, *Eastern Lily Gathered,* 2, 28–29; Johnston, *Missionary Writing and Empire,* 85–86; Dandekar, "Translation."

54. Arnold, *Science, Technology and Medicine,* 4.

55. G. Murshid, *Reluctant Debutante,* 71–72.

56. Zastoupil, *Rammohun Roy,* 28, 102.

57. Le Breton, *Memoirs,* 230–31; Midgley, *Feminism and Empire,* 90.

58. U. Chakravarti, "Whatever Happened"; Tharu, "Tracing Savitri's Pedigree."

59. Pratt, *Imperial Eyes,* 167.

60. Fakrul Alam, "Englishwoman's Quest," 23–24; Dyson, *Various Universe,* 124–26; Winchester, introd. to Fay, *Original Letters from India,* xi, viii, xii.

61. Fay, *Original Letters from India,* 202–3; Fakrul Alam, "Englishwoman's Quest," 42–43.

62. P. Chatterjee, *Black Hole of Empire,* 124; Dalrymple, introd. to Parkes, *Begums,* v–xix; William Dalrymple, "Lady of the Raj," *Guardian,* 9 June 2007, www .theguardian.com/books/2007/jun/09/featuresreviews.guardianreview35.

63. Stepan, *Idea of Race;* Cooper and Stoler, "Between Metropole and Colony"; Mills and Ghose, introd. to Mills and Ghose, *Wanderings of a Pilgrim,* 4; D. Ghosh, *Sex and Family,* 9–10.

64. Dalrymple, introd. to Parkes, *Begums,* vi.

65. Mills and Ghose, introd. to Mills and Ghose, *Wanderings of a Pilgrim,* 4.

66. Mills and Ghose, introd. to Mills and Ghose, *Wanderings of a Pilgrim,* 3, 70–73.

67. Parkes, *Wanderings of a Pilgrim,* 1:60, 1:378–89.

68. Parkes, *Wanderings of a Pilgrim,* 1:381, 2:57.

69. Parkes, *Wanderings of a Pilgrim,* 2:420 (emphasis added); Mills and Ghose, introd. to Mills and Ghose, *Wanderings of a Pilgrim,* 14.

70. Parkes, *Wanderings of a Pilgrim,* 2:7–9.

71. Parkes, *Wanderings of a Pilgrim,* 1:194, 2:9, 2:292–93.

72. Parkes, *Wanderings of a Pilgrim,* 1:387, 2:216, 1:451.

73. Parkes, *Wanderings of a Pilgrim,* 1:162, 1:184, 2:191.

74. Green, *Islam and the Army*, 71.
75. Mackenzie, *Life in the Mission*, 1:193, 1:229.
76. Mackenzie, *Life in the Mission*, 1:243–44.
77. Mackenzie, *Life in the Mission*, 1:254.
78. Urquhart, *Spirit of the East*, 2:381; M. Taylor, "David Urquhart."
79. Mackenzie, *Life in the Mission*, 1:253–54.
80. Mackenzie, *Life in the Mission*, 1:207.

CHAPTER FOUR

1. Offen, "Defining Feminism," 126–27.
2. Brougham, *Letter to the Queen*, 1.
3. Vickery, "Golden Age"; Davidoff and Hall, *Family Fortunes;* Steinbach, "Separate Spheres."
4. Ruskin, *Sesame and Lilies*, 146–50.
5. Poovey, *Uneven Developments*, 52; Hall, "Of Gender and Empire," 51.
6. B. Taylor, *New Jerusalem*, xiii; Schwarzkopf, *Chartist Movement*.
7. British and Foreign Anti-slavery Society, *Proceedings*, 25, 37–38, 594; Midgley, *Women against Slavery*, 158–60.
8. Kozlowski, "Muslim Women"; Agarwal, *Field of One's Own*, 227–30; Esposito, *Muslim Family Law*, 35–36; F. Khan, "Tafwid al-Talaq."
9. Caine, *English Feminism*, 67; Atkinson, *Criminal Conversation*, 1–23.
10. Perkins, *Honourable Mrs. Norton*, 104, 129–33.
11. Caine, *English Feminism*, 66; Poovey, *Uneven Developments*, 51–88.
12. Norton, *English Laws*, 166.
13. Caine, *English Feminism*, 68.
14. Botting and Kronewitter, "Westernization and Women's Rights," 469.
15. T. Metcalf, *Ideologies of the Raj*, 44.
16. J.S. Mill, *Writings on India*, 165.
17. J.S. Mill, *Autobiography*, 40.
18. J.S. Mill, *Autobiography*, 28, 40, 78; Reeves, *John Stuart Mill*, 41, 43–44.
19. J. Jacobs, *Harriet Taylor Mill*, 65.
20. S. Mill, *Enfranchisement of Women*, 3–4.
21. Robson, "Harriet Hardy Taylor Mill," 502.
22. R. Strachey, *Cause*, 69, 102–3; Hirsch, *Barbara Leigh Smith Bodichon*.
23. J.S. Mill, "Admission of Women"; Kent, *Sex and Suffrage*, 187–88.
24. Reeves, *John Stuart Mill*, 1; Ryan, *On Politics*, 2:726.
25. J.S. Mill, *Subjection of Women*, 133, 219, 220.
26. Ryan, *On Politics*, 2:726–27.
27. Revividus, "On the Condition," 217; Camlot, "Character."
28. J. Jacobs, *Harriet Taylor Mill*, 44, 47–48.
29. J.S. Mill, *Subjection of Women*, 163, 174, 217; Robinson-Dunn, *Harem*, 116.

30. J. S. Mill, *Subjection of Women,* 217, 191n1; Botting and Kronewitter, "Westernization and Women's Rights," 472.

31. J. S. Mill, *Collected Works;* Reeves, *John Stuart Mill,* 426.

32. Boyd-Kinnear, "Social Position of Women," 355; Grewal, *Home and Harem,* 64.

33. J. S. Mill, *Principles of Political Economy,* bk. 5, ch. 11, para. 15.

34. J. S. Mill, *Memorandum of the Improvements,* 47, 94; Habibi, "Moral Dimensions," 131.

35. Ryan, *On Politics,* 2:860.

36. Habibi, "Moral Dimensions," 132.

37. Ryan, *On Politics,* 2:860–61; J. S. Mill, *Principles of Political Economy,* bk. 2, ch. 9, para. 3.

38. Alavi, *Sepoys and the Company,* 35–37; K. Roy, *Brown Warriors.*

39. Orme, *Military Transactions,* 5.

40. T. Macaulay, *Essay on Lord Clive,* 39; M. Sinha, *Colonial Masculinity,* 15.

41. A. Salam, *Physical Education in India,* dedication page, 16–18; M. Sinha, *Colonial Masculinity,* 16.

42. G. Murshid, *Reluctant Debutante,* 70–71.

43. Collet, preface to Keshub Sen, *Sen's English Visit,* v.

44. Keshub Sen, *Sen's English Visit,* 465.

45. *Oxford Dictionary of National Biography,* s.v. "Sen, Keshub Chunder (1838–1884)," by Tapan Raychaudhuri, accessed 21 May 2016, www.oxforddnb.com; Keshub Sen, *Sen's English Visit,* 481–82.

46. Keshub Sen, *Sen's English Visit,* 132–34, 467–76.

47. Butler, *Personal Reminiscences,* 42; Walkowitz, *Prostitution and Victorian Society;* Midgley, *Women against Slavery,* 172.

48. Butler, *Revival and Extension,* 5; Burton, *Burdens of History;* Levine, *Prostitution, Race and Politics.*

49. Scherer, "Annette Akroyd Beveridge," 220–21.

50. Kopf, *Brahmo Samaj,* 35.

51. L. Beveridge, *India Called Them,* 87–88.

52. Ramusack, "Cultural Missionaries," 312–13; Jayawardena, *White Woman's Other Burden,* 72; S. Sen, *Travels to Europe,* 141; G. Murshid, *Reluctant Debutante,* app. 3, pp. 241–49; Bannerji, "Attired in Virtue."

53. L. Beveridge, *India Called Them,* 349–51.

54. Ramusack, "Cultural Missionaries"; M. Sinha, "Chathams, Pitts, and Gladstones"; Sharpe, *Allegories of Empire,* 90–91; Ware, *Beyond the Pale,* pt. 3.

55. Said, *Orientalism;* Cohn, *Colonialism.*

56. Waterfield, *Memorandum on the Census,* 5, 16, 19.

57. Banerjee-Dube, *History of Modern India,* 155.

58. Rafiuddin Ahmed, *Bengal Muslims,* 134–36.

59. Rafiuddin Ahmed, *Bengal Muslims,* 11.

60. T. Murshid, *Sacred and the Secular,* 46.

61. Rafiuddin Ahmed, *Bengal Muslims,* 139; Sengupta, *Pedagogy for Religion,* 133.

62. R. Chatterjee, *Queens' Daughters;* Mitra, *Indian Sex Life,* ch. 2.

63. Mitra, *Indian Sex Life,* ch. 2.

64. Ahmad, "Sayyid Aḥmad Khān," 65–66.

65. Lelyveld, *Aligarh's First Generation.*

66. S. A. Khan, *Indian Revolt,* 20.

67. Graham, *Life and Work,* 323–24.

68. Aftab, "Negotiating with Patriarchy," 80.

69. Graham, *Life and Work,* 324–25.

70. U. Banu, *Islam in Bangladesh,* 43–47.

71. Amin, *World of Muslim Women,* 141.

72. Bradley-Birt, *Twelve Men of Bengal,* 111–38.

73. Cromer, *Modern Egypt,* 2:134, 2:155–56; Tignor, "Lord Cromer on Islam"; L. Ahmed, *Women and Gender,* 152–53.

74. Cromer, *Modern Egypt,* 2:157, 2:538–39; L. Ahmed, *Women and Gender,* 153.

75. Minault, *Secluded Scholars,* 51; Hasanat, *Nawab Faizunnesa's Rupjalal,* 26.

76. S. Sen, *Travels to Europe,* 22, 24, 137.

77. Burton, *Heart of the Empire,* 52.

78. Chaudhuri, "Finding an Archive"; S. Sen, *Travels to Europe;* K. Das, *Bengali Lady in England;* Mandal, introd. to K. Das, *Bengali Lady in England,* xv–xvi; G. Murshid, *Reluctant Debutante,* 73–75; G. Murshid, *Rassundori Thekey Rokeya,* 97.

79. Chaudhuri, "Finding an Archive," 140, 144; Fisher, foreword to K. Das, *Bengali Lady in England,* xii.

80. K. Das, *Bengali Lady in England,* 10.

81. K. Das, *Bengali Lady in England,* 11; S. Sen, *Travels to Europe,* 144–45.

82. Chaudhuri, "Finding an Archive," 145–46.

83. Chaudhuri, "Finding an Archive," 151, 144.

84. K. Das, *Bengali Lady in England,* 10.

85. G. Murshid, *Reluctant Debutante,* 86–87.

86. Chaudhuri, "Krishnobhabini Das's *Englande Bangamohila,*" 202, 208.

87. S. A. Ali, *Memoirs and Other Writings;* Powell, "Islamic Modernism"; Bayly, "Representing Copts and Muhammadans," 158–203.

88. S. A. Ali, *Memoirs and Other Writings,* 25.

89. *Oxford Dictionary of National Biography,* s.v. "Fawcett, Dame Millicent Garrett (1847–1929)," by Janet Howarth, accessed 31 August 2015, www.oxforddnb.com; Rubinstein, *Different World,* 36.

90. Shanley, *Law in Victorian England.*

91. S. A. Ali, *Memoirs and Other Writings,* 25–26.

92. Powell, "Islamic Modernism," 286.

93. Ramusack, "Cultural Missionaries"; Jayawardena, *White Woman's Other Burden.*

94. Powell, "Islamic Modernism," 289.

95. E. A. Manning, "Women in India," *Times* (London), 21 December 1878, 6.

96. Burton, *Heart of the Empire,* 57; Burton, "Institutionalizing Imperial Reform."

97. Burton, *Heart of the Empire*, 60–61.

98. S. A. Ali, *Memoirs and Other Writings*, 31.

99. Powell, "Islamic Modernism," 289–90.

100. Powell, "Islamic Modernism," 290.

101. Banerji, *Indian Pathfinder;* Chakrabarty, "Sasipada Banerjee"; Guha, "Labour History."

102. Banerji, *Indian Pathfinder*, 34.

103. Powell, "Islamic Modernism," 291.

104. S. A. Ali, *Mahommedans of India;* Powell, "Islamic Modernism," 290.

105. S. A. Ali, "Real Status of Women," 390, 396, 399.

106. S. A. Ali, "Real Status of Women," 388, 397–98.

107. S. A. Ali, *Life and Teachings*, vii, 365.

108. Sommer and Zwemer, *Our Moslem Sisters*, 9, 298.

CHAPTER FIVE

1. Karlekar, *Voices from Within*, 11.

2. G. Murshid, *Reluctant Debutante*, 232–36; Krishna Sen, "Lessons in Self-Fashioning, 177–78.

3. Krishna Sen, "Lessons in Self-Fashioning," 177–78.

4. G. Murshid, *Rassundori Thekey Rokeya*, 90–96; Chanda and Bagchi, *Shaping the Discourse*, xxix.

5. Ray, *Bamabodhini Patrika*, 26–27; Chanda and Bagchi, *Shaping the Discourse*, 2–3.

6. Krishna Sen, "Lessons in Self-Fashioning," 180.

7. S. Chakraborty, "European Nurses and Governesses."

8. Hasanat, *Nawab Faizunnesa's* Rupjalal, 6–7, 43–45.

9. Shahjahan, *Táj-ul Ikbál Tárikh Bhopal*, 194; Lambert-Hurley, *Muslim Women*, 23; Amin, *World of Muslim Women;* Hasanat, *Nawab Faizunnesa's* Rupjalal, 5–6; R. Chakraborty, "Muslim Women's Education," 83; M. Khan, *Muslim Heritage of Bengal*, 141–47; Azim and Hasan, "Construction of Gender."

10. Hasanat, *Nawab Faizunnesa's* Rupjalal, 43.

11. Amin, *World of Muslim Women*, 14; Hasanat, *Nawab Faizunnesa's* Rupjalal, 4–5; Lambert-Hurley, *Muslim Women*, 4.

12. L. Strachey, *Queen Victoria*, 357–59.

13. Hasanat, *Nawab Faizunnesa's* Rupjalal, 30–32; Azim, "Getting to Know You."

14. Hasanat, *Nawab Faizunnesa's* Rupjalal, 45–46.

15. Amin, *World of Muslim Women*, 216–17; Hasanat, *Nawab Faizunnesa's* Rupjalal, 123–24.

16. B. Metcalf, *Perfecting Women;* Pernau, "Motherhood and Female Identity."

17. Logan, *Indian Ladies' Magazine.*

18. Anisuzzaman, *Muslim Manas,* 418–22; M. Alam, *Rokeya Sakhawat Hossain,* 60; Hossein, *God Gives, Man Robs,* 5; Ray, *Early Feminists,* 17; Akhtar and Bhowmik, *Women in Concert,* 2.

19. M. Hasan, "Muslim Bengal Writes Back," 6.

20. Ray, *Early Feminists,* 17–18.

21. M. Alam, *Rokeya Sakhawat Hossain,* 74–77.

22. Amin, *World of Muslim Women,* 14.

23. Anisuzzaman, *Muslim Manas,* 6.

24. M. Alam, *Rokeya Sakhawat Hossain,* 74–76; Amin, *World of Muslim Women,* 219, 233; Ray, *Early Feminists,* 18.

25. S. Sarkar, *Swadeshi Movement,* 426–29.

26. Amin, *World of Muslim Women,* 45.

27. Bhuiyan, *Begum Rokeya,* 39.

28. S. Mahmud, *Rokeya Jiboni,* 39; Amin, *World of Muslim Women,* 155.

29. Bhuiyan, *Begum Rokeya,* 65.

30. Ray, *Early Feminists,* 20; Ray, "Voice of Protest," 432.

31. Roushan Jahan, "Rokeya."

32. Zaidi, *Muslim Womanhood in Revolution,* 121–25; Hasina Hossain, "Rokeya Sakhawat Hossain," 127; Saber, "Khujista Akhtar Banu."

33. Southard, "Bengal Women's Education League"; Y. Hossain, "Begum's Dream"; Southard, "Colonial Politics"; Bagchi, "Towards Ladyland"; Bagchi, "Two Lives."

34. R. Hossain, *Strijatir abonoti,* 3; M. Sarkar, *Visible Histories,* 122; Amin, *World of Muslim Women,* 132; Ray, *Early Feminists,* 22–23.

35. Azim and Hasan, "Construction of Gender," 35.

36. R. Hossain, "Alonkar na badge," 245; M. Sarkar, *Visible Histories,* 119; Akhtar and Bhowmik, *Women in Concert,* xxxiv.

37. P. Chatterjee, "Nationalist Resolution"; Devji, "Politics of Space."

38. Roushan Jahan, "Rokeya," 50.

39. Roushan Jahan, "Rokeya," 49; Amin, *World of Muslim Women,* 205.

40. Devee, *Autobiography,* 21.

41. Quayum, *Essential Rokeya,* 36.

42. Quayum, *Essential Rokeya,* 36, xxv, 132.

43. T. Sarkar, *Words to Win.*

44. Amin, *World of Muslim Women,* 224; Quayum, *Essential Rokeya,* 37.

45. R. Hossain, *Motichur,* 169; Bagchi, "Two Lives," 55; M. Hasan, "Muslim Bengal Writes Back," 9–10.

46. M. Hasan, "Muslim Bengal Writes Back," 8–9.

47. Corelli, *Murder of Delicia,* 174.

48. R. Hossain, *Motichur,* 169; M. Hasan, "Muslim Bengal Writes Back," 9–10.

49. Quayum, *Essential Rokeya,* 37, 169–70.

50. Quayum, *Essential Rokeya,* 129, 131; Minault, "Shaikh Abdullah."

51. Anisuzzaman, *Muslim Manas,* 419.

52. R. Hossain, *Sultana's Dream,* 7; Quayum, *Essential Rokeya,* 39–40.

53. Quayum, *Essential Rokeya,* 51–57; M. Hasan, "Commemorating Rokeya Sakhawat Hossain," 52.

54. Quayum, *Essential Rokeya,* 61–74, 72.

55. M. Jha, *Katherine Mayo and India,* 82–83; M. Sinha, "Reading *Mother India,*" 11.

56. Hasina Hossain, "Rokeya Sakhawat Hossain," 206–7.

57. Quayum, *Essential Rokeya,* 130.

58. S. Sarkar, *Swadeshi Movement,* 17; Mamoon, *Bengal Partition.*

59. S. Sarkar, *Swadeshi Movement,* 28–29.

60. Woolf, *Three Guineas,* 109; Black, *Virginia Woolf as Feminist;* M. Sinha, "Imperial Crucible"; J. Makdisi, "War and Peace"; Snaith, "Race, Empire, and Ireland."

61. Sufia Ahmed, *Muslim Community in Bengal,* 215–16; T. Sarkar, *Hindu Wife, Hindu Nation,* ch. 5; T. Sarkar, "Birth of a Goddess."

62. Akhtar and Bhowmik, *Women in Concert,* 60.

63. Akhtar and Bhowmik, *Women in Concert,* 60, 61–62.

64. Akhtar and Bhowmik, *Women in Concert,* 65–70; S. Mukhopadhyay, "Open Sesame."

65. Akhtar and Bhowmik, *Women in Concert,* 67, 72, 77, 86, 81.

66. Akhtar and Bhowmik, *Women in Concert,* 73–74, 86.

67. Amin, *World of Muslim Women,* 132; S. Zaman, *Kalantoray Nari,* 66–69.

68. Amin, *World of Muslim Women,* 226; Chatterji, *Bengal Divided;* S. Zaman, *Kalantoray Nari,* 68; Bose, *His Majesty's Opponent,* 126; Banglapedia, s.v. "Chowdhury, Ashrafuddin Ahmad," by Rana Razzaq, accessed 12 April 2020, http://en.banglapedia.org/index.php?title=Chowdhury,_Ashrafuddin_Ahmad; Kishwar Kamal Khan and Irshad Kamal Khan (Chaudhurani's grandchildren), electronic communication with the author, 12 May 2020.

69. Gupta, "Reformed Bengali Muslim Woman," 343.

70. Amin, *World of Muslim Women,* 226; S. Hossain, "Razia Khatun Choudhurani."

71. Minault, *Khilafat Movement;* Minault, "Purdah Politics."

72. Shaikh, *Footprints in Time;* Lambert-Hurley, *Elusive Lives;* Hameeda Hossain, interview with the author, Dhaka, 2 January 2018.

73. Akhtar and Bhowmik, *Women in Concert,* 267–68; Amin, *World of Muslim Women,* 159.

74. Uday Sankar Das, "Nazrul's Sojourns in Chittagong," *Dhaka Tribune,* 4 March 2014; Akhtar and Bhowmik, *Women in Concert,* 268–69.

75. Amin, *World of Muslim Women,* 158–60, 168–69; Akhtar and Bhowmik, *Women in Concert,* 268–69; M. Mahmud, *Begum Shamsunnahar Mahmud,* 72–73; R. Chakraborty, "Muslim Women's Education."

76. Chanda and Bagchi, *Shaping the Discourse,* 340–41.

77. I. Choudhury, *Anwara Bahar Choudhury.*

78. Jahangir, *Sufia Kamal;* M. Begum, *Sufia Kamal.*

79. K. Ahmed, *Social History,* 23; Begum and Huq, *Ami Nari,* 108–9.

80. Southard, "Colonial Politics," 417–18.
81. Quayum, *Essential Rokeya*, 129.
82. G. Forbes, *Women in Modern India*, 196–98; M. Sinha, "Refashioning Mother India," 635, 643n55.
83. Burton, *Burdens of History*.
84. M. Sinha, "Suffragism and Internationalism," 475.
85. S. Mahmud, "Women's Political Rights"; Chanda and Bagchi, *Shaping the Discourse*, 340–44.
86. Gupta, "Reformed Bengali Muslim Woman," 329; Akhtar, "East Bengal Women's Education," 114.
87. Gupta, "Reformed Bengali Muslim Woman," 340, 341.
88. *Saogat*.
89. Gupta, "Reformed Bengali Muslim Woman," 340.
90. Woodsmall, *Moslem Women*, 370; Weber, "Making Common Cause," 48, 66–68; M. Sinha, *Specters of Mother India*, 293n3.
91. Woodsmall, *Moslem Women*, 12; Sicherman and Green, *Notable American Women;* Weber, "Making Common Cause," 48, 56–57.
92. Woodsmall, *Moslem Women*, 40, 42.
93. Edib, *Inside India*, 60, 5–8, 25.
94. Edib, *Inside India*, 10; "Margaret Sanger"; M. Sinha, *Specters of Mother India*, 107.
95. Edib, *Inside India*, 10, 16, 28–29, 135–38; Wasti, "Indian Red Crescent Mission."
96. Aghavnie Yegheniann, "The Turkish Jeanne d'Arc: An Armenian Picture of Remarkable Halide Edib Hanoum," *New York Times*, 17 September 1922.
97. M. Mahmud, *Begum Shamsunnahar Mahmud*, 47–50.
98. Crabitès, "Woman in Islam"; Zaidi, *Muslim Womanhood in Revolution*, 15–16; Parkinson, "Creole in Cairo."
99. Zaidi, *Muslim Womanhood in Revolution*, 15–16, 125.
100. Rupp, *Worlds of Women*, 51; Van Voris, *Carrie Chapman Catt*, 57.
101. Sandell, *Women's Transnational Activism*, 34–36.
102. Burton, "Feminist Quest for Identity"; Sneider, *Suffragists;* Hoganson, "As Badly Off"; Sandell, *Women's Transnational Activism*, 37.
103. Feinberg, "Pioneering Dutch Feminist"; Weber, "Making Common Cause."
104. Van Voris, *Carrie Chapman Catt*, 105.
105. Rupp, *Worlds of Women*, 58.
106. Weber, "Unveiling Scheherezade," 130; Weber, "Making Common Cause," 31.
107. Bosch, "Colonial Dimensions."
108. Bosch, "Colonial Dimensions," 14, 26.
109. A. Jacobs, *Reisbrieven*, 2:451, cited in Bosch, "Colonial Dimensions," 25.
110. A. Jacobs, *Reisbrieven*, 2:451.
111. Rupp, *Worlds of Women*, 55, 75.
112. Rupp, "Challenging Imperialism."

113. Photo with detailed caption of "Mrs. Iqbalunnisa Hussain, B.A." *Jus Suffragii,* April 1935, 59; "India," *Jus Suffragii,* February 1936, 38.

114. "Resolutions Adopted by the XII Congress of the Alliance, Istanbul: 18–24 April 1935," *Jus Suffragii,* May 1935, 74; Jayawardena, *Feminism and Nationalism;* Weber, "Making Common Cause."

115. Woodsmall, *Moslem Women,* 370–71.

116. Nour Hamada and Avra S. Theordoropoulos, "The Oriental Women's Congress in Damascus," *Jus Suffragii,* September 1930, 189–90; Weber, "Making Common Cause," 101–2; Mukherjee, "All-Asian Women's Conference"; Nijhawan, "International Feminism."

117. Weber, "Making Common Cause," 146, 162–63; Freedman, *Essential Feminist Reader,* 217–19.

118. Schreiber and Mathieson, *Journey towards Freedom,* v–vi.

119. Schreiber and Mathieson, *Journey towards Freedom,* 36.

120. Chanda and Bagchi, *Shaping the Discourse,* 69–73.

121. S. Zaman, *Pothe Chole Jete Jete,* 95–96.

122. Ikramullah, *From Purdah to Parliament.*

123. Cooper, *Sharecropping;* Custers, "Women's Role"; S. Das, "Marginal Communities."

CHAPTER SIX

1. M. Mahmud, *Begum Shamsunnahar Mahmud,* 111–12, 139.

2. "Move to Partition."

3. Menon and Bhasin, *Borders and Boundaries;* Butalia, *Other Side of Silence;* Dutta, "Voices"; Guhathakurta, "Uprooted and Divided"; T. Sarkar, foreword to Chakravartty, *Coming Out of Partition,* vii–x.

4. T. Hashmi, *Pakistan;* Anisuzzaman, *Creativity, Reality, and Identity;* Feldman, "Feminist Interruptions"; Ahmed Kamal, *State against the Nation,* 13; Siddiqi, "Left Behind"; Ananya Kabir, "Utopias Eroded and Recalled."

5. M. Begum, *Nirbachito Begum,* 53–54.

6. Umar, *Emergence of Bangladesh,* 1:14–35.

7. Stock, *Memoirs of Dacca University;* Clarke, *Taking What Comes.*

8. Stock, *Memoirs of Dacca University,* 45, 117–18, 92–94, 138.

9. Umar, *Emergence of Bangladesh,* 1:180–81.

10. Umar, *Emergence of Bangladesh,* 1:190–229; Sufia Ahmed, interview with Iftekhar Iqbal, 23 October 2009, in "Bengali Cultural Heritage"; Sufia Ibrahim Ahmed, interview with the author, Dhaka, 2 December 2018.

11. K. Hasan, "Foreign Policy"; Rotter, "South Asia"; Jalal, *Struggle for Pakistan,* 88.

12. Rotter, "Christians, Muslims, and Hindus," 596.

13. Medhurst, "Eisenhower."

14. "The Moslem World," *Time,* 13 August 1951, 30; Kumar, *Islamophobia.*

15. Rotter, "Christians, Muslims, and Hindus," 607.

16. Roosevelt, *Awakening East,* xiii, xvi; Lash, *Eleanor,* 192–93.

17. Michael James, "Islam Rights Told to Mrs. Roosevelt," *New York Times,* 22 February 1952; Ansari, "Polygamy."

18. Roosevelt, *Awakening East,* 68–69, 73–75.

19. Roosevelt, *Awakening East,* 67, 85.

20. S. Zaman, *Pothe Chole Jete Jete,* 72.

21. "Muslim Prime Ministers"; Prashad, *Darker Nations;* Aydin, *Muslim World,* 180–84.

22. "Governor-General Opens."

23. M. Mahmud, *Begum Shamsunnahar Mahmud,* 117.

24. S. Mahmud, *Amar Dekha Turashko.*

25. S. Mahmud, *Amar Dekha Turashko.*

26. M. Mahmud, *Begum Shamsunnahar Mahmud,* 140.

27. "Papers of the Committee."

28. Parveen, *Shamsun Nahar Mahmud,* 130, 133.

29. M. Mahmud, *Begum Shamsunnahar Mahmud,* 153–54; Robert T. Howard, "Women's Leader from Pakistan Likes Questions of Small Children, She Says during Oxford Visit," *Hamilton Journal,* 27 October 1956.

30. "Service Bureau Sponsors Talk by Pakistan Leader," *Hartford Courant,* 11 September 1956; Jessie A. Arndt, "Pakistan Women Push Ahead," *Christian Science Monitor,* 12 November 1956.

31. Arndt, "Pakistan Women Push Ahead."

32. Dillon Graham, "Figure over $10 Million in Estimate," *Daily Argus-Leader,* 15 March 1955.

33. "Lake Preston Woman Given Foreign Job," *Daily Argus-Leader,* 21 October 1954; Ida B. Alseth, "'People Are Everywhere': Argus-Leader Correspondent Writes of Life in Pakistan," *Daily Argus-Leader,* 12 December 1954.

34. Ida B. Alseth, "Argus-Leader Writer Finds East Pakistan Interest in Political Affairs Is High," *Daily Argus-Leader,* 9 January 1955.

35. Akhtar, "East Bengal Women's Education," 114.

36. M. Begum, *Nirbachito Begum;* S. Hashmi, "Zero Plus Zero Plus Zero."

37. Nasiruddin, "Illustrated Weekly for Women"; Akhtar, "East Bengal Women's Education," 115–16.

38. Ida B. Alseth, "S.D. Woman Finds Pakistan Is Land of Fun with Philanthropy and Squalor Side by Side," *Daily Argus-Leader,* 23 January 1955.

39. Woodsmall, *New East,* i.

40. Woodsmall, *New East,* 118, 127.

41. H. Reid, "Review of *Women.*"

42. Laville, *Cold War Women;* Wilford, *Mighty Wurlitzer;* Van Voris, *Committee of Correspondence.*

43. Ikramullah, *From Purdah to Parliament;* Wilford, *Mighty Wurlitzer,* ch. 7.

44. "Canadian Girl Greets Royalty as Secretary to Pakistan PM," *Ottawa Journal,* 19 January 1955.

45. "Moslem Premier of Pakistan Brings Home a Second Wife," *St. Louis Post-Dispatch,* 7 April 1955.

46. "Pakistani Wives Revolt against Evil of Polygamy," *Medford Mail Tribune,* 20 December 1954.

47. Nurmila, *Everyday Life;* Ansari, "Polygamy," 1426–27; "Karachi Women Call for End of Polygamy," *Bridgeport Post,* 13 April 1955; Chipp, "Role of Women Elites," 170; Nelson, *Doria Shafik Egyptian Feminist,* 221.

48. *Pakistan Times* (Lahore), 6 December 1954, cited in Abbott, "Pakistan's New Marriage Law," 26.

49. "Wives Fight Polygamy in Pakistan," *Eugene Guard,* 19 December 1954; Ansari, "Polygamy," 1449.

50. M. Begum, *Nirbachito Begum,* 2243–44.

51. "Abida Sultana on Polygamy," *Dawn,* 21 April 1955, quoted in Chipp, "Role of Women Elites," 170–71.

52. "Mohammed Ali Favors American Way," *Times Record* (Troy, NY), 23 November 1955.

53. Coulson, "Reform of Family Law," 136, 152; M. Begum, *Nirbachito Begum,* 353–54; Akhtar, "East Bengal Women's Education," 116; Ansari, "Polygamy," 1449.

54. "Pakistan Envoy Poses Protocol Problem for US," *Lethbridge Herald,* 6 October 1955.

55. "An Anguished Pakistani: Mohammed Ali," *New York Times,* 23 November 1962; "Mohammed Ali Favors."

56. Elaine Engst and Blaine Friedlander, "Cornell Rewind: The Influence of Eleanor Roosevelt," *Cornell Chronicle,* 11 December 2014.

57. Elias, *Stir It Up.*

58. "Broader Education for Women Urged," *New York Times,* 30 October 1954.

59. Hood, "Modern Pakistani Dress"; "OSU Professor Helps Establish Three Home Economics Colleges in Pakistan," *Wichita Falls Times,* 24 October 1969.

60. Elise Emery, "Look Who's Cooking with Solar Heat in Dacca," *Independent* (Long Beach, CA), 5 July 1961.

61. "Moslem Women Report: Harems Out of Fashion in Modern Pakistan," *Arizona Daily Star,* 10 August 1960.

62. "Teacher from East Pakistan Speaks before Mexia Lions," *Mexia Daily News,* 28 December 1960.

63. Vantoch, *Jet Sex,* 124; Virdee, "International Airlines."

64. Shireen Huq, interview with the author, Dhaka, 30 December 2017; "Home Away from Home."

65. Rathore, *Pakistan Student,* 17, 19, 34–35, 42.

66. Rathore, *Pakistan Student,* 19–21.

67. S. Zaman, *Pothe Chole Jete Jete,* 136–39; Rahnuma Ahmed, "Women's Movement in Bangladesh," 47; Kabeer, "Subordination and Struggle"; Saleque Khan,

"Performing the (Imagi)Nation"; Anisuzzaman, "Claiming and Disclaiming"; Christiansen, "Beyond Liberation"; Rahman, "Urban Dance in Bangladesh."

68. A. Majeed Khan, "Rural Pilot Family Planning," 11.

69. Akhter Khan, *Akhter Hameed Khan,* 1:89.

70. Kabeer, *Reversed Realities,* 1–2.

71. Akhter Khan, *Akhter Hameed Khan,* 64–65.

72. Stossel, *Sarge;* Juliane Heyman, "How an Aspenite met Sargent Shriver and Joined the Peace Corps." *Aspen Times* (CO), 12 August 2010. www.aspentimes.com /news/how-an-aspenite-met-sargent-shriver-and-joined-the-peace-corps/.

73. "Dean Rusk's Directive."

74. Dean, "Masculinity as Ideology," 55–57; Stossel, *Sarge,* ch. 15.

75. Dean, "Masculinity as Ideology," 58–60; Stossel, *Sarge,* ch. 15.

76. "Speech of Senator."

77. Latham, *Modernization as Ideology,* 115–17.

78. Latham, *Modernization as Ideology,* 122–23.

79. Thomas F. Brady, "Peace Corpsmen Crack the Bengali Barrier," *New York Times,* 29 September 1963.

80. McCarthy, "Bengali Village Women."

81. Florence McCarthy, electronic communication with the author, 9 May 2020.

82. Alberta Rosiak, "An Interview with Akhtar Hameed Khan," *East Pakistan Peace Corps Newsletter,* June 1964.

83. T. Ali, "Technologies of Peasant Production," 450.

84. "Tahrunessa Ahmed Abdullah: Women's Development," *Daily Star* (Dhaka), 5 February 2016.

85. Abdullah, *Village Women.*

86. McCarthy, "Bengali Village Women," 2, 167–68.

87. Akhtar, "East Bengal Women's Education," 115.

88. M. Begum, *Nirbachito Begum,* 1008.

89. Raper, *Rural Development in Action,* 178.

90. B. Harvey, *Fifties,* 47.

91. Coontz, *Strange Stirring,* xxi; Stansell, *Feminist Promise,* 183, 192–96.

92. Friedan, *Feminine Mystique,* 15; Horowitz, *Betty Friedan;* Coontz, *Strange Stirring.*

93. *American Women;* Stansell, *Feminist Promise,* 198–203.

94. Sklar, "How and Why"; "Women in the Movement."

95. Peterson, "Working Women."

96. Rossi, "Equality between the Sexes"; Brick, *Age of Contradiction,* 50.

97. S. Reid, "Cold War."

98. Kadnikova, "Women's International Democratic Federation," 33–34, 36, 55–59.

99. "Gagarin Stresses Joint Space Plans" *New York Times,* 17 October 1963.

100. T. Kaplan, "Socialist Origins"; C. Chatterjee, *Celebrating Women.*

101. Chaudhri, "Pakistan's Relations."

102. S. Kamal, *Sufia Kamal Rochonasongroho,* 521–22.

103. S. Kamal, *Sufia Kamal Rochonasongroho,* 524–26.

104. S. Kamal, *Sufia Kamal Rochonasongroho,* 524–26.

105. S. Kamal, *Sufia Kamal Rochonasongroho,* 526–27.

106. S. Kamal, *Sufia Kamal Rochonasongroho,* 532.

107. S. Kamal, *Sufia Kamal Rochonasongroho,* 550–53.

108. S. Kamal, *Sufia Kamal Rochonasongroho,* 521–56.

109. Fraser, "Convention on the Elimination," 92.

110. Aline Mosby, "Women Need Equal Rights in 'Advanced' Nations, Too," *San Bernardino County Sun,* 21 May 1967; "Aline Mosby, 76, a U.P.I. Correspondent," *New York Times,* 19 August 1998.

CHAPTER SEVEN

1. Judy Klemesrud, "International Women's Year World Conference Opening in Mexico," *New York Times,* 19 June 1975; Klemesrud, "Scrappy, Unofficial Women's Parley Sets Pace," *New York Times,* 29 June 1975; Rounaq Jahan, "International Women's Year Conference," 38, 40; Rounaq Jahan, "Sustaining Advocacy," 208.

2. Mohanty, "Under Western Eyes."

3. "Non-Aligned Movement"; Prashad, *Darker Nations.*

4. "Bengali Wives Raped in War Are Said to Face Ostracism," *New York Times,* 18 January 1972; "200,000 Wives Rejected," *Ithaca Journal,* 18 January 1972.

5. Jill Tweedie, "The Rape of Bangladesh," *Guardian,* 6 March 1972; J.D. Smithard and International Planned Parenthood Federation, "Letter, 'Woman's Guardian,'" *Guardian,* 5 April 1972; Jill Tweedie, "Poste Wrestante," *Guardian,* 5 June 1972; "Abortionists Plan Bangladesh Mission," *Orlando Evening Star,* 10 February 1972.

6. Germaine Greer, "The Rape of the Bengali Women," *Sunday Times* (London), 9 April 1972.

7. Bunch, "Out Now"; Bunch, *Passionate Politics,* 1–23.

8. Lauré and Goldman, "Women of Bangladesh"; Pogrebin, "Spell Ms."

9. Rich, "Anti-feminist Woman."

10. Daly, *Beyond God the Father,* 114–16.

11. Daly, *Gyn/Ecology,* 112–33; P. Jha, "Making a Point."

12. Brownmiller, *Against Our Will,* 15 (emphasis added).

13. Brownmiller, *Against Our Will,* 86.

14. Roushan Jahan, "Men in Seclusion."

15. Lauré and Goldman, "Women of Bangladesh," 88.

16. Omran, *Family Planning,* 191.

17. Sydney H. Schanberg, "Population Huge in East Pakistan," *New York Times,* 12 April 1970; Connelly, *Fatal Misconception,* 11, 185.

18. Robert Trumbull, "Dacca Raising the Status of Women While Aiding Rape Victims," *New York Times,* 12 May 1972; Lauré and Goldman, "Women of Bangla-

desh"; Jane E. Brody, "Physicians throughout the World Are Studying New, Simple Technique for Terminating Pregnancies," *New York Times,* 20 December 1973; D'Costa, *Nationbuilding;* Murphy, *Seizing the Means,* ch. 4.

19. Lauré and Goldman, "Women of Bangladesh"; Pogrebin, "Spell Ms."

20. "Is Supercoil Foiled?"; Borman, "Harvey Karman"; Lee Edwards, "Gosnell"; Tunc, "Harvey Karman."

21. *First Five-Year Plan,* 538; Sattar, "Demographic Features of Bangladesh," 15; Amin and Hossain, "Women's Reproductive Rights," 1325–26; Mookherjee, "Available Motherhood"; Murphy, *Seizing the Means,* 150.

22. Ravenholt, "World Population Crisis," 40; Mookherjee, "Available Motherhood," 345–46; Murphy, *Seizing the Means,* 164–69.

23. "Self Help."

24. Murphy, *Seizing the Means,* 172.

25. Walter Schwarz, "Nation Fights for Survival," *Guardian,* 19 August 1974; Nan Robertson, "Parley Gives Bucharest a Taste of Overpopulation," *New York Times,* 24 August 1974; Associated Press, "Population Parley Dilutes Statement to Curb Increase," *Minneapolis Tribune,* 30 August 1974; Finkle and Crane, "Politics of Bucharest."

26. Stienstra, *Women's Movements,* 119; Tinker, "Challenging Wisdom," 70–72; Fraser, "Seizing Opportunities," 164–66; Olcott, *International Women's Year,* 38.

27. Kabeer, *Reversed Realities;* Kongar, Olmsted, and Shehabuddin, "Gender and Economics," 10.

28. Oriana Fallaci, "The Shah of Iran: An Interview with Mohammad Reza Pahlevi," *New Republic,* 30 November 1973.

29. Garavini, "Completing Decolonization"; U. Makdisi, *Faith Misplaced,* ch. 7.

30. "Arabs' New Oil Squeeze," 110.

31. Betty Friedan, "Friedan Talk in Iran," 1974, Audio Collection of Betty Friedan, 1963–2007: A Finding Aid, series 2, Speeches, 1974–99 T-125.28, Arthur and Elizabeth Schlesinger Library on the History of Women in America, Radcliffe Institute for Advanced Study, Harvard University, accessed January 2021, https://hollisarchives.lib.harvard.edu/repositories/8/resources/6083; Hennessee, *Betty Friedan,* 198–205; Afkhami, "Women's Human Rights"; Friedan, *Life So Far,* 283–85.

32. Friedan, "Coming Out," 98–100, 103–4.

33. Friedan, "Coming Out," 104; Hennessee, *Betty Friedan,* 203.

34. Tabari, "Veiled Iranian Women"; Sullivan, "Eluding the Feminist"; Naghibi, *Rethinking Global Sisterhood,* ch. 3.

35. Tinker and Jaquette, "UN Decade for Women"; M. Chen, "Engendering World Conferences"; Popa, "Translating Equality," 63; Ghodsee, "Socialist Mass Women's Organizations"; Olcott, *International Women's Year,* ch. 2; Gasiorowski, "1953 Coup D'etat."

36. Bass, *Blood Telegram;* Raghavan, *Global History.*

37. "Special Actions Group Meeting"; Jack Anderson, "Texts of Secret Docu-

ments on Top-Level U.S. Discussions of Indian-Pakistani War," *New York Times,* 6 January 1972.

38. Khushwant Singh, "Bangladesh, after the First Year: Will It Ever Be a Workable Country?," *New York Times,* 21 January 1973.

39. Benjamin Welles, "Bangladesh Gets U.S. Recognition, Promise of Help," *New York Times,* 5 April 1972.

40. Roushan Jahan, "Men in Seclusion," 93; M. Begum, *Nirbachito Begum,* 721–22; A. Banu, "Feminism in Bangladesh."

41. Ghodsee, "Socialist Mass Women's Organizations."

42. Olcott, *International Women's Year,* 196–98.

43. Bier, *Revolutionary Womanhood,* 162.

44. *Second Afro-Asian Women's Conference,* 70, 72–73, 29, 49.

45. M. Begum, *Nirbachito Begum,* 727–28.

46. Judy Klemesrud, "U.S. Group Assails Women's Parley," *New York Times,* 22 June 1975.

47. Kathleen Teltsch, "The Selling of Women's Year 1975," *New York Times,* 4 June 1975; Friedan, "Scary Doings."

48. Papanek, "Work of Women," 217, 225.

49. Whitaker, "Women of the World"; "Lecture Listed at Vassar College," *Poughkeepsie Journal,* 9 November 1975.

50. Whitaker, "Women of the World," 181.

51. Douglas Martin, "Flo Kennedy, Feminist, Civil Rights Advocate and Flamboyant Gadfly, Is Dead at 84," *New York Times,* 23 December 2000; Randolph, *Florynce "Flo" Kennedy,* 218.

52. El Saadawi, Mernissi, and Vajarathon, "Critical Look," 102–3.

53. Patterson and Gillam, "Out of Egypt," 32.

54. Robin Morgan, "Planetary Feminism," 27–29.

55. Esposito and Voll, *Makers of Contemporary Islam,* 54–57.

56. Maudoodi and Jameelah, *Correspondence,* 3–4; Esposito and Voll, *Makers of Contemporary Islam,* 54–67; Baker, *Convert.*

57. Maudoodi and Jameelah, *Correspondence,* 18, 14–15, 34; "Maryam Jameelah Papers."

58. Maudoodi and Jameelah, *Correspondence,* 35.

59. Maudoodi and Jameelah, *Correspondence,* 11, 46–49; Jameelah, *Muslim Woman Today,* 15–20.

60. Maudoodi and Jameelah, *Correspondence,* 62–63, 67; Baker, *Convert,* 6–10; Jameelah, *Why I Embraced Islam,* 9.

61. Jameelah, *Muslim Woman Today,* 5–6.

62. Jameelah, *Muslim Woman Today,* 8–9, 28–29; Esposito and Voll, *Makers of Contemporary Islam,* 67.

63. Jameelah, *Muslim Woman Today,* 30–32, 36.

64. Robin Morgan, *Word of a Woman;* Horowitz, *Betty Friedan;* Baxandall and Gordon, *Dear Sisters,* 184.

65. Judith Duffett, "WLM vs. Miss America," *Voice of the Women's Liberation Movement,* October 1968, 4; Dow, "Feminism," 131.

66. Roudakova and Ballard-Reisch, "Double Burden."

67. Jameelah, *Muslim Woman Today,* 27.

68. John Kifner, "Iran's Women Fought, Won and Dispersed," *New York Times,* 16 March 1979; Chan-Malik, *Being Muslim.*

69. Kelber, "Five Days in March" (emphasis added).

70. Jain, *Women,* 28.

71. Kassamali, "When Modernity Confronts," 52.

72. Morgan and Steinem, "International Crime"; Steinem, *Outrageous Acts,* 325.

73. Hubbard and Farnes, "Letter to the Editor"; Chase, "Hermaphrodites with Attitude," 204–5, 207.

74. El Saadawi, *Hidden Face of Eve.*

75. Patterson and Gillam, "Out of Egypt," 35.

76. El Saadawi, *Hidden Face of Eve,* xiv.

77. Patterson and Gillam, "Out of Egypt," 35–36.

78. Freedman, *Essential Feminist Reader,* 351–54.

79. Eugénie Rokhaya Aw, "Assault on Third World Culture," letter to the editor, *Forum '80,* 28 July 1980, 7, cited in Nicklen, "Rhetorics of Connection," 96.

80. Nnaemeka, "Female Circumcision."

81. Davis, *Angela Davis,* 120, 124–45.

82. Davis, *Angela Davis,* 120–22; Young, *Soul Power,* 201–3.

83. Davis, *Angela Davis,* 126–27.

84. D. Taylor, *Women.*

85. Davis, "Sex," 325, 328; McAlister, "Suffering Sisters," 242; S. Salem, "On Transnational Feminist Solidarity."

86. Davis, "Sex," 325–27.

87. Davis, "Sex," 329.

88. Gilliam, "Historic Gathering of Women"; Çağatay, Grown, and Santiago, "Nairobi Women's Conference," 404–6.

89. Hoffman, "Flo Kennedy"; O'Barr et al., "Reflections on Forum '85," 586–89, 603; Tifft, O'Reilly, and Vollers, "Triumphant Spirit of Nairobi"; Gilliam, "Historic Gathering of Women," 156–58, 160, 162.

90. O'Barr et al., "Reflections on Forum '85," 592.

91. Gilliam, "Historic Gathering of Women."

92. O'Barr et al., "Reflections on Forum '85," 593–97, 604.

93. Sen and Grown, *Alternative Visions,* 9, 20–21; "History"; Antrobus, "Third World Feminist Network," 164, 173n45.

94. Moghadam, *Globalizing Women,* 144.

95. Sharify-Funk, *Encountering the Transnational,* 96.

96. Rounaq Jahan, email communication with the author, 9 January 2020.

97. Hameeda Hossain, email communication with the author, 8 January 2020; "Who We Are."

98. O'Barr et al., "Reflections on Forum '85," 605.

99. N. Zaman, "National Policies for Women," 338.

100. Guhathakurta, "Gender Violence," 86; Kabeer, "Quest for National Identity," 126–28; Shehabuddin, *Reshaping the Holy,* 72–73.

101. Elson and Pearson, "Nimble Fingers"; Hossain, Jahan, and Sobhan, *No Better Option;* Siddiqi, "Miracle Worker or Womanmachine."

102. Feldman, "Exploring Theories of Patriarchy," 1097.

103. Alam and Matin, "Limiting the Women's Issue," 2, 4, 8.

104. "Farida Akhtar."

105. Akhter, *Depopulating Bangladesh,* 14–24; Hartmann, *Reproductive Rights and Wrongs,* 225–26; Connelly, *Fatal Misconception,* 349; N. Hossain, *Aid Lab,* 15–16.

106. Akhter, *Depopulating Bangladesh;* Hartmann, *Reproductive Rights and Wrongs,* 225–26; Connelly, *Fatal Misconception,* 349; N. Hossain, *Aid Lab,* 15–16.

107. "Text of the Convention"; Jain, *Women.*

108. "Short History."

109. S. S. Ali, *Conceptualising Islamic Law,* 83–90; "Short History"; "United Nations Treaty Collection."

110. Huda, "Women's Movement in Bangladesh," 142; Brandt and Kaplan, "Tension between Women's Rights."

111. Sonbol, "Muslim Countries' Reservations."

112. Najma Chowdhury, "Bangladesh"; D. Choudhury, "Women and Democracy," 570.

113. Najma Chowdhury, "Implementing Women's Rights," 225; Shehabuddin, *Reshaping the Holy,* 232.

114. Baldez, *Defying Convention.*

115. Kabeer, "Quest for National Identity," 139.

116. Huq, "My Body, My Life."

117. Salomyn and Huq, "Interview"; Azim, "Formulating an Agenda"; Azim, "Secularism."

CHAPTER EIGHT

1. Adrian Turpin, "I Had Never Come to a Western Country Before; It Is Good for My Writing," *Independent* (London), 7 November 1995, 6.

2. Taslima Nasrin, "Sentenced to Death," *New York Times,* 30 November 1993.

3. Roy Gutman, "Muslims Claim Rape a Serbian War Strategy," *Times Union* (Albany, NY), 9 August 1992.

4. Huntington, "Clash of Civilizations."

5. Meredith Tax, interview by Kate Weigand, transcript of video recording, Voices of Feminism Oral History Project, Sophia Smith Collection, 11–12 June 2004, www.smith.edu/libraries/libs/ssc/vof/transcripts/Tax.pdf, 6, 20.

6. Tax, interview, 86–87; Deen, *Crescent and the Pen,* 226–27.

7. Riaz, "Taslima Nasrin," 23.

8. Weaver, "Fugitive from Injustice."

9. Tax, "Taslima's Pilgrimage."

10. Eric Weiner, "Bangladeshi Writer Draws Death Threat," *Christian Science Monitor,* April 1994, www.csmonitor.com/1994/0401/01082.html; Tax, interview, 90; Deen, *Crescent and the Pen,* 143–44.

11. Weaver, "Fugitive from Injustice," 57–58; Siddiqi, "Taslima Nasreen and Others," 221.

12. Pamela Bone, "The Other Author Marked for Death—No Booker Prize, Just Persistence," *Age,* 7 March 1994, 13.

13. Cherry and Smith, "One Brave Woman."

14. Deen, *Crescent and the Pen,* 138.

15. Weaver, "Fugitive from Injustice," 59.

16. Weaver, "Fugitive from Injustice," 58.

17. Carolyne Wright, "Taslima Nasreen's Campaign Endangers Other Reformers," *Christian Science Monitor,* 18 August 1994, 19; Deen, *Crescent and the Pen,* 22.

18. Wright, "Diary."

19. Weaver, "Fugitive from Injustice," 60; Targett, "Holy Men."

20. Shabnam Nadiya, "Woman Alone," *Daily Star* (Dhaka), October 2008, https://shabnamnadiya.com/non-fiction/woman-alone/.

21. Riaz, "Taslima Nasrin," 24.

22. Wright, "Taslima Nasreen's Campaign."

23. Wright, "Diary."

24. Stiglmayer, *Mass Rape;* Huq, "My Body, My Life," 12; Hossain and Mohsin, *Of the Nation Born;* Nazneen, *Women's Movement in Bangladesh,* 8–10.

25. Shehabuddin, "Fatwa"; Nazneen, *Women's Movement in Bangladesh;* A. Banu, "Feminism in Bangladesh," 127–31.

26. Huq, "Bodies as Sites"; Shehabuddin, "Contesting the Illicit"; L. Karim, "Democratizing Bangladesh"; E. Chowdhury, *Transnationalism Reversed,* 100–107.

27. Hartmann, *Reproductive Rights and Wrongs,* 134; Shehabuddin, *Reshaping the Holy,* 132–38.

28. Kabeer, *Power to Choose;* Dannecker, *Between Conformity and Resistance;* Siddiqi, "Miracle Worker or Womanmachine"; Kabeer, "Globalization"; Azim, "Feminist Struggles in Bangladesh."

29. Cohen, "Road from Rio"; Susan Chira, "Women Campaign for New Plan to Curb the World's Population," *New York Times,* 13 April 1994.

30. Linden and Bloch, "Showdown in Cairo"; Bowen, "Cairo Population Conference"; Connelly, *Fatal Misconception,* 362–66.

31. Amin and Hossain, "Women's Reproductive Rights," 1319, 1337–38.

32. Amin and Hossain, "Women's Reproductive Rights."

33. Amin and Hossain, "Women's Reproductive Rights," 1340.

34. Buchanan, "Culture War."

35. Buchanan, *Death of the West,* 42.

36. Chesler, "Stop Coercing Women."

37. Hassan, "Backlash at Beijing"; Hassan, "Feminist Theology."
38. Cathleen Miller, *Champion of Choice.*
39. Gorman and Burke, "Clash of Wills"; Crossette, "UN Expert on Women."
40. "Address."
41. Ghodsee, "United Nations Decade."
42. S. Reid, "Cold War"; Griswold, "Russian Blonde in Space."
43. Abugideiri, "Renewed Woman"; "Muslim Women Bridging Culture Gap: Tugs of the Sacred and American Secularism," *New York Times,* 8 November 1993.
44. Webb, *Windows of Faith,* 210; Chishti, "Political-Social Movements."
45. Brooks, "Nasreen's Nose Ring."
46. Patt Morrison, "Trying to Save Women Buried Alive," *Los Angeles Times,* 21 October 1998.
47. Russo, "Feminist Majority Foundation's Campaign."
48. Farrell and McDermott, "Claiming Afghan Women," 46–48.
49. Russo, "Feminist Majority Foundation's Campaign."
50. Mavis Nicholson Leno, "The Lost Women of Afghanistan," *Los Angeles Times,* 26 February 1999; Leno, "Readers Support Afghan Women," *Los Angeles Times,* 23 July 1999.
51. Fluri and Lehr, *Carpetbaggers of Kabul,* 7.
52. Brodsky, *With All Our Strength,* 33–45.
53. Rostami-Povey, "Gender, Agency and Identity," 297–98.
54. Bick, *Walking the Precipice,* 39; Unveiling Afghanistan, "Shukria Haidar"; "Call for Action."
55. Cited in Fluri, "Feminist-Nation Building," 42.
56. Farrell and McDermott, "Claiming Afghan Women"; Fluri, "Feminist-Nation Building," 39–42; Sajjad, "Political-Social Movements."
57. Steven LeVine, "Unocal Quits Afghanistan Pipeline Project: It Cites Falling Oil Prices amid a Retreat from the Caspian Region," *New York Times,* 5 December 1998; "Victory!"; Hirschkind and Mahmood, "Politics of Counter-Insurgency."
58. Brodsky, *With All Our Strength,* 80–81; Farrell and McDermott, "Claiming Afghan Women," 39–40.
59. Kolhatkar, "'Saving' Afghan Women."
60. Brown, "Coalition of Hope."
61. E. Miller, "Open Letter."
62. Abu-Lughod, *Muslim Women.*
63. Shehabuddin, "Gender and the Figure."
64. Keith Bradsher, "Bangladesh Is Surviving to Export Another Day," *New York Times,* 14 December 2004; Siddiqi, "Bangladeshi Factory Workers."
65. Sabur, "Post Card from Shahabag," 10; Nusrat Chowdhury, *Paradoxes of the Popular,* 5.
66. Siddiqi, "Saving Muslim Women"; Holmes, "American Apparel"; T. Islam, "Those American Apparel Ads"; Tanjeem, "Social Media."
67. Dickey and Power, "Rocking the Casbah," 30.
68. Harris, "Response to Controversy"; "Dark Secrets"; Sam Harris and Salman

Rushdie, "Ayaan Hirsi Ali: Abandoned to Fanatics," *Los Angeles Times,* 9 October 2007; Johnson, "Unbeliever"; Barry Gewen, "Muslim Rebel Sisters: At Odds with Islam and Each Other," *New York Times,* 27 April 2008.

69. Manji, *Trouble with Islam,* 69, 74, 85, 102; El-Ariss, "Making of an Expert"; Podur, "Multifaceted Fraud"; Hirsi Ali, *Infidel,* 85; Gewen, "Muslim Rebel Sisters."

70. Hamid Dabashi, "Native Informers and the Making of the American Empire," *Al-Ahram Weekly,* 1 June 2006; Keshavarz, *Jasmine and Stars;* Donadey and Ahmed-Ghosh, "Why Americans Love"; Abu-Lughod, *Muslim Women;* Narayan, *Dislocating Cultures,* 43–80; Shehabuddin, "Gender and the Figure."

71. Podur, "Multifaceted Fraud"; Manji, *Trouble with Islam;* De Leeuw and Van Wichelen, "Please, Go Wake Up," 332.

72. Afzal-Khan, "Muslim Feminist Voices."

73. Fareena Alam, "Enemy of the Faith."

74. Rabasa et al., *Building Moderate Muslim Networks,* 35, 143.

75. "Writers' Statement on Cartoons."

76. Shakira Hussein, "Contrary Dissident," *Weekend Australian,* 27 January 2007, 10.

77. Nasrin, *Meyebala, My Bengali Childhood;* S.J. Ahmed, "'Non-dit' in the Zenana," 448.

78. Johnson, "Unbeliever."

79. Riaz, "Taslima Nasrin," 23.

80. Frey and Baldwin, "Interview with Taslima Nasrin," 213–14.

81. Robert Satloff, "Voices Who Speak for (and against) Us," *Washington Post,* 1 December 2002; Barlas, "Why Do They Hate."

82. Satloff, "Voices Who Speak."

83. Barlas, *"Believing Women" in Islam;* Barlas, *Islam, Muslims, and the US,* 34.

84. Mamdani, *Good Muslim, Bad Muslim;* Zine, "Between Orientalism and Fundamentalism," 37; Maira, "Muslim Citizens."

EPILOGUE

1. Parsons, "Muslim Activists."

2. Sadler, "Did Shepard Fairey Whitewash"; Edward Helmore, "Munira Ahmed: The Woman Who Became the Face of the Trump Resistance," *Guardian,* 23 January 2017, www.theguardian.com/us-news/2017/jan/23/womens-march-poster-munira-ahmed-shepard-fairey-interview; Katebi, "Keep Your American Flags"; Gökarıksel and Smith, "Intersectional Feminism."

3. Essa, "Why Many Muslim Women."

4. Essa, "Why Many Muslim Women."

5. Holloway, "Why This Black Girl."

6. Mogahed and Chouhoud, *American Muslim Poll 2017;* Mogahed and Mahmood, *American Muslim Poll 2019.*

7. Mogahed and Chouhoud, *American Muslim Poll 2017*, 8–9.

8. Khabeer, "Trump's Muslim Ban"; Abu-Lughod, *Muslim Women,* ch. 4; Razack, *Casting Out.*

9. Sharmin Hossain, *"Amader Golpo";* Carly Miller, "Shahana Hanif."

10. "Human Rights Lawyer."

11. Mariam, "In the Bronx"; Gandhi, "This Bangladeshi American Organizer"; Venugopal, "Wave of Leftist Bangladeshis."

12. Thahitun Mariam, "Naripokkho x naree o shongothok (bangladeshi feminist collective). this is a living testament to transnational feminist organizing work and relationships that go beyond borders," Facebook photo caption, 14 September 2018, www.facebook.com/photo?fbid=10156386627234927.

BIBLIOGRAPHY

Abbott, Freeland. "Pakistan's New Marriage Law: A Reflection of Qur'anic Interpretation." *Asian Survey* 1, no. 11 (1962): 26–32.

Abboud, Hosn. *Mary in the Qur'an: A Literary Reading.* New York: Routledge, 2013.

Abdullah, Tahrunnessa Ahmed. *Village Women as I Saw Them.* Bangladesh Academy for Rural Development, 1974.

"Abigail Adams to Cotton Tufts." *Adams Papers.* Massachusetts Historical Society. 20 February 1788. www.masshist.org/publications/apde2/view?id=ADMS-04 -08-02-0105.

Abugideiri, Hibba. "The Renewed Woman of American Islam: Shifting Lenses toward 'Gender Jihad?'" *Muslim World* 91, nos. 1–2 (2001): 1–18.

Abu-Lughod, Lila. *Do Muslim Women Need Saving?* Cambridge, MA: Harvard University Press, 2013.

———, ed. *Remaking Women: Feminism and Modernity in the Middle East.* Princeton: Princeton University Press, 1998.

Abu Taleb Khan, Mirza. *Travels of Mirza Abu Taleb Khan in Asia, Africa, and Europe, during the Years 1799, 1800, 1801, 1802, and 1803.* Translated by Charles Stewart. 2 vols. London: Longman, Hurst, Rees and Orme, 1810.

———. "Vindication of the Liberties of the Asiatic Women." In *Asiatic Annual Register, or A View of the History of Hindustan and of the Politics, Commerce and Literature of Asia, for the Year 1801,* 101–7. Miscellaneous Tracts. London: Debrett, Piccadilly/Cadell Jun./Davies, Strand, 1802.

"Address by Mohtarma Benazir Bhutto, Prime Minister of Islamic Republic of Pakistan, at the Fourth World Conference on Women." 4 September 1995. www.un .org/esa/gopher-data/conf/fwcw/conf/gov/950904202603.txt.

Afkhami, Mahnaz. "Women's Human Rights: From Global Declarations to Local Implementation." In *Women and Girls Rising: Progress and Resistance around the World,* edited by Ellen Chesler and Terry McGovern, 129–43. New York: Routledge, 2016.

Aftab, Tahera. *Inscribing South Asian Muslim Women.* Leiden: Brill, 2007.

———. "Negotiating with Patriarchy: South Asian Muslim Women and the Appeal to Sir Syed Ahmed Khan." *Women's History Review* 14 (2005): 75–97.

Afzal-Khan, Fawzia. "Here Are Voices of Muslim Feminists!" *Counterpunch,* 16 November 2001. www.counterpunch.org/2001/11/16/here-are-voices-of-muslim-feminists/.

Agarwal, Bina. *A Field of One's Own: Gender and Land Rights in South Asia.* Cambridge: Cambridge University Press, 1994.

Ahmad, Aziz. "Sayyid Aḥmad Khān, Jamal al-Din al-Afghani and Muslim India." *Studia Islamica* 13 (1960): 55–78.

Ahmed, Enver. *The Anatomy of Betrayal.* New Delhi: Rajhans, 1971.

Ahmed, Kamruddin. *The Social History of East Pakistan.* Dacca: Crescent Book Centre, 1967.

Ahmed, Leila. *A Border Passage: From Cairo to America.* Farrar, Straus, and Giroux, 1999.

———. "Western Ethnocentrism and Perceptions of the Harem." *Feminist Studies* 8 (1982): 521–34.

———. *Women and Gender in Islam: Historical Roots of a Modern Debate.* New Haven, CT: Yale University Press, 1992.

Ahmed, Rafiuddin. *The Bengal Muslims, 1871–1906.* New Delhi: Oxford University Press, 1982.

Ahmed, Rahnuma. "Women's Movement in Bangladesh and the Left's Understanding of the Women Question." *Journal of Social Studies* 30 (1985): 41–56.

Ahmed, Sufia. *Muslim Community in Bengal, 1884–1912.* 1974. Reprint, Dhaka: University Press Limited, 1996.

Ahmed, Syed Jamil. "The 'Non-dit' in the Zenana: Representation of Muslim Women in Islamic Canonical Texts, the Neo-colonial Imagination and a Feminist Response from Bangladesh." *Inter-Asia Cultural Studies* 7, no. 3 (2006): 431–55.

Ahmed, Tahrunnesa. *Women's Education Programme.* Comilla: Pakistan Academy of Rural Development, 1965.

Akhimie, Patricia, and Bernadette Andrea, eds. *Travel and Travail: Early Modern Women, English Drama, and the Wider World.* Lincoln: University of Nebraska Press, 2019.

Akhtar, Shaheen, and Moushumi Bhowmik, eds. *Women in Concert: An Anthology of Bengali Muslim Women's Writings (1904–1938).* Translated by Stree. Kolkata: Stree, 2008.

Akhtar, Shaheen, Suraiya Begum, Meghna Guhathakurta, Hameeda Hossain, and Sultana Kamal, eds. *Rising from the Ashes: Women's Narratives of 1971.* Dhaka: Ain o Salish Kendra, 2013.

Akhtar, Shirin. "East Bengal Women's Education, Literature, and Journalism: From the Late Nineteenth Century through the 1960s." In *Women's Activism: Global Perspectives from the 1890s to the Present,* edited by Francisca de Haan, Margaret Allen, June Purvis, and Krassimira Daskalova, 106–20. New York: Routledge, 2012.

Akhter, Farida. *Depopulating Bangladesh: Essays on the Politics of Fertility.* Dhaka: Narigrantha Probortona, 1992.

Alam, Fakrul. "An Englishwoman's Quest for Independence in Eighteenth-Century Calcutta: Eliza Fay's Original Letters from India." In *Infinite Variety: Women in Society and Literature,* edited by Firdous Azim and Niaz Zaman, 22–44. Dhaka: University Press Limited, 1994.

Alam, Fareena. "Enemy of the Faith." *New Statesman,* 24 July 2006. www .newstatesman.com/node/164844.

Alam, M. Shamsul. *Rokeya Sakhawat Hossain: Jibon o Sahityokormo* [Life and literary work]. 1989. Reprint, Dhaka: Bangla Academy, 2009.

Alam, S. M. Shamsul. "Women in the Era of Modernity and Islamic Fundamentalism: The Case of Taslima Nasrin of Bangladesh." *Signs* 23, no. 2 (1998): 429–61.

Alam, Sultana, and Nilufar Matin. "Limiting the Women's Issue in Bangladesh: The Western and Bangladesh Legacy." *Comparative Studies of South Asia, Africa and the Middle East* 4, no. 2 (1984): 1–10.

Alavi, Seema. *The Sepoys and the Company: Tradition and Transition in Northern India, 1770–1830.* New Delhi: Oxford University Press, 1995.

Alexander, Claire, Joya Chatterji, and Annu Jalais. *The Bengal Diaspora: Rethinking Muslim Migration.* New York: Routledge, 2018.

Alexander, M. Jacqui, and Chandra T. Mohanty, eds. *Feminist Genealogies, Colonial Legacies, Democratic Futures.* New York: Routledge, 1997.

Ali, A. F. M. Abdul. "Munny Begum: The 'Mother of the Company.'" *Bengal: Past and Present* 29 (1925): 148–54.

Ali, Shaheen Sardar. *Conceptualising Islamic Law, CEDAW and Women's Human Rights in Plural Legal Settings: A Comparative Analysis of Application of CEDAW in Bangladesh, India and Pakistan.* New Delhi: UNIFEM, South Asia Regional Office, 2006.

Ali, Syed Ameer. *Life and Teachings of Mohammed, or The Spirit of Islam.* London: Allen, 1891.

———. *The Mahommedans of India: A Lecture Delivered to the "London Association in Aid of Social Progress in India."* London: National Indian Association, 1872.

———. *Memoirs and Other Writings of Syed Ameer Ali.* Edited by Syed Razi Wasti. Lahore: People's, 1968.

———. "The Real Status of Women in Islam." *Nineteenth Century,* September 1891, 387–99.

Ali, Tariq Omar. "Technologies of Peasant Production and Reproduction: The Postcolonial State and Cold War Empire in Comilla, East Pakistan, 1960–70." *South Asia* 42, no. 3 (2019): 435–51.

Allen, Rosamund, ed. *Eastward Bound: Travel and Travellers, 1050–1550.* Manchester: Manchester University Press, 2004.

Alloula, Malek. *The Colonial Harem.* Minneapolis: University of Minnesota Press, 1986.

American Women: Report of the President's Commission on the Status of Women (1963). Washington, DC: Government Printing Office.

Amin, Sajeda, and Sara Hossain. "Women's Reproductive Rights and the Politics of Fundamentalism: A View from Bangladesh." *American University Law Review* 44, no. 4 (1995): 1319–43.

Amin, Sonia. *The World of Muslim Women in Colonial Bengal, 1876–1939.* Leiden: Brill, 1996.

Amireh, Amal, and Lisa Suhair Majaj, eds. *Going Global: The Transnational Reception of Third World Women Writers.* Shrewsbury, MA: Garland, 2000.

Amos, Valerie, and Pratibha Parmar. "Challenging Imperial Feminism." *Feminist Review* 17 (1984): 3–19.

Amrith, Sunil S. *Crossing the Bay of Bengal: The Furies of Nature and the Fortunes of Migrants.* Cambridge, MA: Harvard University Press, 2013.

Andrea, Bernadette. "Islam, Women, and Western Responses: The Contemporary Relevance of Early Modern Investigations." *Women's Studies* 38 (2009): 273–92.

———. *Women and Islam in Early Modern English Literature.* Cambridge: Cambridge University Press, 2008.

Anisuzzaman. "Claiming and Disclaiming a Cultural Icon: Tagore in East Pakistan and Bangladesh." *University of Toronto Quarterly* 77, no. 4 (2008): 1058–69.

———. *Creativity, Reality, and Identity.* Dhaka: International Centre for Bengal Studies, 1993.

———. *Muslim Manas o Bangla Shahityo, 1757–1918* [The Muslim mind and Bengali literature, 1757–1918]. Dhaka: Lekhak Shangho Prokashoni, 1964.

Ansari, Sarah. "Polygamy, Purdah and Political Representation: Engendering Citizenship in 1950s Pakistan." *Modern Asian Studies* 43 (2009): 1421–61.

Antrobus, Peggy. "DAWN, the Third World Feminist Network: Upturning Hierarchies." In *The Oxford Handbook of Transnational Feminist Movements,* edited by Rawwida Baksh and Wendy Harcourt, 159–87. New York: Oxford University Press, 2015.

Apetrei, Sarah. *Women, Feminism and Religion in Early Enlightenment England.* Cambridge: Cambridge University Press, 2010.

"The Arabs' New Oil Squeeze: Dimouts, Slowdowns, Chills." *Time,* 19 November 1973.

Aravamudan, Srinivas. "Lady Mary Wortley Montagu in the *Hammam:* Masquerade, Womanliness, and Levantinization." *English Literary History* 62 (Spring 1995): 69–104.

Arjana, Sophia. *Muslims in the Western Imagination.* New York: Oxford University Press, 2015.

Armstrong, Elisabeth. "Before Bandung: The Anti-imperialist Women's Movement in Asia and the Women's International Democratic Federation." *Signs* 41, no. 2 (2016): 305–31.

Arnold, David. "Hunger in the Garden of Plenty: The Bengal Famine of 1770." In *Dreadful Visitations: Confronting Natural Catastrophe in the Age of Enlightenment,* edited by Alessa Johns, 81–111. New York: Routledge, 1999.

———. *Science, Technology and Medicine in Colonial India.* Cambridge: Cambridge University Press, 2000.

Asher, Catherine. *Architecture of Mughal India*. Cambridge: Cambridge University Press, 1992.

Asher, Catherine, and Cynthia Talbot. *India before Europe*. Cambridge: Cambridge University Press, 2006.

Astell, Mary. *The Christian Religion, as Profess'd by a Daughter of the Church of England*. London: Wilkin, 1705.

———. *A Serious Proposal to the Ladies for the Advancement of Their True and Greatest Interest, in Two Parts, by a Lover of Her Sex*. London: Wilkin, 1697.

Atkinson, Diane. *The Criminal Conversation of Mrs. Norton*. Chicago: Chicago Review, 2013.

Aydin, Cemil. *The Idea of the Muslim World*. Cambridge, MA: Harvard University Press, 2017.

Azim, Firdous. "Feminist Struggles in Bangladesh." *Feminist Review* 80 (2005): 194–97.

———. "Formulating an Agenda for the Women's Movement." *Inter-Asia Cultural Studies* 2, no. 3 (2001): 389–94.

———. "Getting to Know You, or The Formation of Inter-Asian Identities." *Inter-Asia Cultural Studies* 11, no. 2 (2010): 165–73.

———. "Secularism and the Women's Movement in Bangladesh." In *Feminist Subversion and Complicity: Governmentalities and Gender Knowledge in South Asia*, edited by Maitrayee Mukhopadhyay. Zubaan, 2016.

Azim, Firdous, and Perween Hasan. "Construction of Gender in the Late Nineteenth and Early Twentieth Century in Muslim Bengal: The Writings of Nawab Faizunnessa Chaudhurani and Rokeya Sakhawat Hossain." In Fernandes, *Routledge Handbook of Gender,* 28–40.

Badran, Margot. *Feminism in Islam: Secular and Religious Convergences*. Oxford: Oneworld, 2009.

Bagchi, Barnita. "Towards Ladyland: Rokeya Sakhawat Hossain and the Movement for Women's Education in Bengal, c. 1900–c. 1932." *Paedagogica Historica* 45, no. 6 (2009): 743–55.

———. "Two Lives: Voices, Resources, and Networks in the History of Female Education in Bengal and South Asia." *Women's History Review* 19 (2010): 51–69.

Bagchi, Jasodhara, and Subhoranjan Dasgupta, eds. *The Trauma and the Triumph: Gender and Partition in Eastern India*. 2 vols. Kolkata: Stree, 2003.

Bage, Robert. *The Fair Syrian*. 2 vols. Dublin: Gilbert, 1787.

———. *Mount Henneth*. 2 vols. London: Lowndes, 1782.

Bailey, Gauvin. "A Mughal Princess in Baroque New Spain: Catarina de San Juan (1606–1688), the China Poblana." *Anales Del Instituto de Investigaciones Estéticas* 71 (1997): 37–73.

Baker, Deborah. *The Convert: A Tale of Exile and Extremism*. Minneapolis: Graywolf, 2011.

Balabanlilar, Lisa. *The Emperor Jahangir: Power and Kingship in Mughal India*. London: Tauris, 2020.

———. "Gulbadan Begam." In Fleet et al., *Encyclopaedia of Islam III*.

Baldez, Lisa. *Defying Convention: US Resistance to the UN Treaty on Women's Rights.* Cambridge University Press, 2014.

Ball, Terence. Introduction to James Mill, *James Mill,* xi–xxviii.

Ballaster, Rosalind. Introduction to Manley, *New Atalantis,* v–xxi.

Banerjee-Dube, Ishita. *A History of Modern India.* Cambridge: Cambridge University Press, 2015.

Banerji, Albion Rajkumar. *An Indian Pathfinder: Being the Memoirs of Sevabrata Sasipada Banerji.* Kemp Hall, 1934.

Bannerji, Himani. "Attired in Virtue: The Discourse on Shame *(lojja)* and Clothing of the *Bhadramahila* in Colonial Bengal." In Ray, *Seams of History,* 67–106.

Banu, Ayesha. "Feminism in Bangladesh: 1971–2000." PhD diss., University of Dhaka, 2015.

Banu, U. A. *Islam in Bangladesh.* Leiden: Brill, 1992.

Barbosa, Duarte. *The Book of Duarte Barbosa.* Translated by Mansel Longworth Dames. 2 vols. 1581. Reprint, Hakluyt Society, 1921.

Barlas, Asma. *"Believing Women" in Islam: Unreading Patriarchal Interpretations of the Qur'an.* Austin: University of Texas Press, 2002.

———. *Islam, Muslims, and the US: Essays on Religion and Politics.* New Delhi: Global Media, 2004.

———. "Why Do They Hate Us?" *Ithaca College Quarterly* 4 (2001). www.ithaca.edu/icq/2001v4/reflections/wt5.htm.

Barnett, Richard B. "Embattled Begams: Women as Power Brokers in Early Modern India." In Hambly, *Medieval Islamic World,* 521–36.

Barros, Carolyn A., and Johanna M. Smith, ed. *An Anthology: Life-Writings by British Women, 1660–1815.* Northeastern University Press, 2000.

Bass, Gary. *The Blood Telegram: Nixon, Kissinger, and a Forgotten Genocide.* Knopf, 2013.

Basu, Amrita, ed. *The Challenge of Local Feminisms: Women's Movements in Global Perspective.* Boulder, CO: Westview, 1995.

———. *Women, Political Parties and Social Movements in South Asia.* UNRISD, 2005.

———, ed. *Women's Movements in the Global Era: The Power of Local Feminisms.* Boulder, CO: Westview, 2010.

Basu, Aparna. "A Century and Half's Journey: Women's Education in India, 1850s to 2000." In Ray, *Women of India,* 183–207.

Bates, Crispin. *Subalterns and Raj: South Asia since 1600.* New York: Routledge, 2007.

Baxandall, Rosalyn Fraad, and Linda Gordon, eds. *Dear Sisters: Dispatches from the Women's Liberation Movement.* Basic Books, 2001.

Bayly, C. A. "Representing Copts and Muhammadans: Empire, Nation, and Community in Egypt and India, 1880–1914." In *Modernity and Culture: From the Mediterranean to the Indian Ocean,* edited by Leila T. Fawaz and C. A. Bayly, 158–203. New York: Columbia University Press, 2002.

Begum, Maleka, ed. *Nirbachito Begum: Ordhoshatabdir Somajchitro, 1947–2000*

[Selections from Begum: A half century of social portraits, 1947–2000]. 3 vols. Pathak Somabesh, 2006.

———. *Sufia Kamal*. Prothoma, 2014.

Begum, Gulbadan. *The History of Humayun (Humayun-nama)*. Translated by Annette S. Beveridge. London: Royal Asiatic Society, 1902.

Begum, Maleka, and Syed Azizul Huq. *Ami Nari: Tinsho Bochhorer (18–20 Shatak) Bangali Narir Itihash* [I am woman: Three hundred years (18th to 20th c.) of Bengali women's history]. Dhaka: University Press Limited, 2001.

Begum, Suraiya, and Hasina Ahmed. "Beliefs and Rituals in a Shrine in Bangladesh." *Journal of Social Studies* 53 (1991): 68–95.

"Bengali Cultural Heritage: Visualizing Oral Histories Using Digital Tools." Tufts University. Accessed 23 April 2018. https://corpora.tufts.edu/catalog/tufts:33.

Bennett, Clinton. "Henry Martyn." In *Mission Legacies: Biographical Studies of Leaders of the Modern Missionary Movement,* edited by Gerald H. Anderson, Robert T. Coote, Norman A. Horner, and James M. Phillips, 264–70. Maryknoll, NY: Orbis Books, 1994.

Bernier, François. *Travels in the Mogul Empire, A.D. 1656–1668.* Translated by Archibald Constable and revised by Vincent A. Smith. London: Milford/Oxford University Press, 1916.

Beveridge, Annette S. Introduction to *The History of Humayun (Humayun-nama).* By Gulbadan Begum. Translated by Annette S. Beveridge, 1–79. Royal Asiatic Society, 1902.

Beveridge, Lord. *India Called Them.* Allen and Unwin, 1947.

Bhuiyan, Harunur Rashid, ed. *Begum Rokeya: Rachonashamogro* [Begum Rokeya: Collected works]. Dhaka: Hashi Prokashoni, 2004.

Bick, Barbara. *Walking the Precipice: Witness to the Rise of the Taliban in Afghanistan.* New York: Feminist Press at City University of New York, 2015.

Bier, Laura. *Revolutionary Womanhood: Feminisms, Modernity, and the State in Nasser's Egypt.* Palo Alto: Stanford University Press, 2011.

Black, Naomi. *Virginia Woolf as Feminist.* Ithaca, NY: Cornell University Press, 2004.

Blackstone, William. *Commentaries on the Laws of England.* Yale Law School. Accessed 13 January 2016. http://avalon.law.yale.edu/18th_century/blackstone_bk1ch15.asp.

Bloch, Ruth. "The Origins of Feminism and the Limits of Enlightenment." *Modern Intellectual History* 3 (2006): 473–94.

Bodman, Herbert, and Nayereh Tohidi, eds. *Women in Muslim Societies: Diversity within Unity.* Boulder, CO: Rienner, 1998.

Bohls, Elizabeth. "Aesthetics and Orientalism in Lady Mary Wortley Montagu's Letters." *Studies in Eighteenth-Century Culture* 23 (1994): 179–205.

Booth, Marilyn, ed. *Harem Histories: Envisioning Places and Living Spaces.* Durham, NC: Duke University Press, 2010.

Borman, Nancy. "Harvey Karman: Savior or Charlatan?" *Majority Report* 3 (January 1974): 6.

Bosch, Mineke. "Colonial Dimensions of Dutch Women's Suffrage: Aletta Jacobs's Travel Letters from Africa and Asia, 1911–1912." *Journal of Women's History* 11 (1999): 8–44.

Bose, Sugata. *His Majesty's Opponent: Subhas Chandra Bose and India's Struggle against Empire.* Cambridge, MA: Harvard University Press, 2012.

Boserup, Ester. *Women's Role in Economic Development.* Allen and Unwin, 1970.

Botting, Eileen. "Wollstonecraft in Europe, 1792–1904: A Revisionist Reception History." *History of European Ideas* 39 (2013): 503–27.

Botting, Eileen Hunt, and Sean Kronewitter. "Westernization and Women's Rights: Non-Western European Responses to Mill's *Subjection of Women*, 1869–1908." *Political Theory* 40 (2012): 466–96.

Bowen, Donna Lee. "Islam, Abortion and the 1994 Cairo Population Conference." *International Journal of Middle East Studies* 29, no. 2 (1997): 161–84.

Boxer, Charles R. *Joao de Barros: Portuguese Humanist and Historian of Asia.* Xavier Centre of Historical Research, Concept, 1980.

———. *Women in Iberian Expansion Overseas, 1415–1815.* New York: Oxford University Press, 1975.

Boyd-Kinnear, John. "The Social Position of Women." In Butler, *Woman's Work,* 331–69.

Bradley-Birt, Francis Bradley. *Twelve Men of Bengal in the Nineteenth Century.* 4th ed. Lahiri, 1910.

Brandt, Michele, and Jeffrey A. Kaplan. "The Tension between Women's Rights and Religious Rights: Reservations to CEDAW by Egypt, Bangladesh and Tunisia." *Journal of Law and Religion* 12, no. 1 (1995): 105–42.

Brick, Howard. *Age of Contradiction: American Thought and Culture in the 1960s.* Ithaca, NY: Cornell University Press, 2000.

British and Foreign Anti-slavery Society. *Proceedings of the General Anti-slavery Convention: Called by the Committee of the British and Foreign Anti-slavery Society, and Held in London, from Friday, June 12th, to Tuesday, June 23rd, 1840.* London: British and Foreign Anti-slavery Society, 1841.

Broad, Jacqueline. "'A Great Championess for Her Sex': Sarah Chapone on Liberty as Nondomination and Self-Mastery." *Monist* 98, no. 1 (2015): 77–88.

———. *The Philosophy of Mary Astell.* Oxford University Press, 2015.

Brodsky, Anne E. *With All Our Strength: The Revolutionary Association of the Women of Afghanistan.* New York: Routledge, 2003.

Brooks, Geraldine. "What Does the Koran Say about Nasreen's Nose Ring?" *New York Times Magazine,* 7 December 1997, 76–79.

Brougham, Lord. *Letter to the Queen on the State of the Monarchy by a Friend of the People.* London: Jones, 1840.

Brown, Janelle. "A Coalition of Hope: How the International Feminist Community Mobilized around the Plight of Afghan Women." *Ms.* 12 (Spring 2002): 65–76.

Brownmiller, Susan. *Against Our Will: Men, Women, and Rape.* New York: Simon and Schuster, 1975.

Brumberg, Joan. "Zenanas and Girlless Villages: The Ethnology of American Evangelical Women, 1870–1910." *Journal of American History* 69, no. 2 (1982): 347–71.

Buchanan, Patrick J. "The Culture War Coming to Cairo." Patrick J. Buchanan's official website. 29 August 1994. http://buchanan.org/blog/the-culture-war-coming-to-cairo-161.

———. *The Death of the West: How Dying Populations and Immigrant Invasions Imperil Our Country and Civilization*. St. Martin's Griffin, 2002.

Buckle, Edmund. *Memoir of the Services of the Bengal Artillery, from the Formation of the Corps to the Present Time, with Some Account of Its Internal Organization*. Edited by John William Kaye. London: Allen, 1852.

Bulbeck, Chilla. *Re-orienting Western Feminisms*. Cambridge: Cambridge University Press, 1997.

Bunch, Charlotte. "Out Now!" *Furies* 1, no. 5 (1972): 12–13. Rainbow History Project Digital Collections. Accessed 2 January 2020. https://archives.rainbowhistory.org/files/original/211a5a060ecb2eda02536f0d3740c45d.pdf.

———. *Passionate Politics: Feminist Theory in Action: Essays, 1968–1986*. New York: St. Martin's Press, 1987.

Burke, Edmund. *Reflections on the Revolution in France*. 1790. Reprint, London: Dent and Sons, 1951.

———. *The Works of the Right Honourable Edmund Burke*. 12 vols. London: Nimmo, 1887.

Burr, Sherri. "Aaron Burr Jr. and John Pierre Burr: A Founding Father and His Abolitionist Son." *Princeton and Slavery*. Accessed 15 November 2020. https://slavery.princeton.edu/stories/john-pierre-burr.

———. *Complicated Lives: Free Blacks in Virginia, 1619–1865*. Durham, NC: Carolina Academic Press, 2019.

Burton, Antoinette. *At the Heart of the Empire: Indians and the Colonial Encounter in Late-Victorian Britain*. Berkeley: University of California Press, 1998.

———. *Burdens of History: British Feminists, Indian Women, and Imperial Culture*. Chapel Hill: University of North Carolina Press, 1994.

———. "The Feminist Quest for Identity: British Imperial Suffragism and 'Global Sisterhood,' 1900–1915." *Journal of Women's History* 3 (1991): 46–81.

———. "Institutionalizing Imperial Reform: *The Indian Magazine* and Late-Victorian Colonial Politics." In *Negotiating India in the Nineteenth-Century Media*, edited by David Finkelstein and Douglas M. Peers, 23–50. Macmillan, 2000.

Butalia, Urvashi. *The Other Side of Silence: Voices from the Partition of India*. Durham, NC: Duke University Press, 2000.

Butler, Josephine. *Personal Reminiscences of a Great Crusade*. 1896. Reprint, London: Marshall and Son, 1910. https://archive.org/details/personalreminisc00butliala/mode/2up.

———. *The Revival and Extension of the Abolitionist Cause: A Letter to the Members of the Ladies' National Association*. Winchester, England: Doswell, 1887.

———, ed. *Woman's Work and Women's Culture: A Series of Essays*. 1869. Reprint, Cambridge: Cambridge University Press, 2010.

Çağatay, Nilüfer, Caren Grown, and Aida Santiago. "The Nairobi Women's Conference: Toward a Global Feminism?" *Feminist Studies* 12, no. 2 (1986): 401–12.

Cahill, Samara Anne. *Intelligent Souls? Feminist Orientalism in Eighteenth-Century English Literature*. Lewisburg, PA: Bucknell University Press, 2019.

Caine, Barbara. *English Feminism, 1780–1980*. 1997. Reprint, New York: Oxford University Press, 2004.

Calkins, Philip B. "The Formation of a Regionally Oriented Ruling Group in Bengal, 1700–1740." *Journal of Asian Studies* 29, no. 4 (1970): 799–806.

"Call for Action by the Women on the Road for Afghanistan." Women on the Road for Afghanistan. 28 June 2000. http://worfa.free.fr/call_for_action.htm.

Camlot, Jason Evan. "Character of the Periodical Press: John Stuart Mill and Junius Redivivus in the 1830s." *Victorian Periodicals Review* 32 (Summer 1999): 166–76.

Campos, Joachim Joseph A. *History of the Portuguese in Bengal*. London: Butterworth, 1919.

Carey, Eustace, and Jeremiah Chaplin. *Memoir of William Carey, D. D., Late Missionary to Bengal: Professor of Oriental Languages in the College of Fort William, Calcutta*. Hartford: Canfield and Robins, 1837.

Carey, William. *An Enquiry into the Obligations of Christians to Use Means for the Conversion of the Heathens*. Leicester: Ireland, 1792.

Chakrabarty, Dipesh. *Provincializing Europe: Postcolonial Thought and Historical Difference*. Princeton: Princeton University Press, 2000.

———. "Sasipada Banerjee: A Study in the Nature of the First Contact of the Bengali Bhadralok with the Working Classes of Bengal." *Indian Historical Review* 3 (1976): 339–64.

Chakraborty, Rachana. "Beginnings of Muslim Women's Education in Colonial Bengal." *History Research* 1, no. 1 (2011): 75–88.

Chakraborty, Satyasikha. "European Nurses and Governesses in Indian Princely Households: 'Uplifting That Impenetrable Veil'?" *Journal of Colonialism and Colonial History* 19, no. 1 (2018). https://muse.jhu.edu/article/689962.

Chakravarti, Ananya. *The Empire of Apostles: Religion,* Accommodatio, *and the Imagination of Empire in Early Modern Brazil and India*. New York: Oxford University Press, 2018.

Chakravarti, Ranabir. "Indic Mercantile Networks and the Indian Ocean World: A Millennial Overview (c. 500–1500 CE)." In *Early Global Interconnectivity across the Indian Ocean World*. Vol. 1, *Commercial Structures and Exchanges,* edited by Angela Schottenhammer, 191–224. New York: Palgrave Macmillan, 2019.

Chakravarti, Uma. "Whatever Happened to the Vedic *Dasi?* Orientalism, Nationalism and a Script for the Past." In Sangari and Vaid, *Recasting Women,* 27–87.

Chakravartty, Gargi, ed. *Coming Out of Partition: Refugee Women of Bengal*. New Delhi: Srishti, 2005.

Chambers, Claire. *Britain through Muslim Eyes: Literary Representations, 1780–1988*. New York: Palgrave Macmillan, 2015.

Chanda, Ipshita, and Jayeeta Bagchi, eds. *Shaping the Discourse: Women's Writings in Bengali Periodicals, 1865–1947*. Kolkata: Stree, 2014.

Chan-Malik, Sylvia. *Being Muslim: A Cultural History of Women of Color in American Islam*. New York: New York University Press, 2018.

Chapone, Sarah. *The Hardships of the English Laws in Relation to Wives: With an Explanation of the Original Curse of Subjection Passed upon the Woman; In an Humble Address to the Legislature*. London: Roberts, 1735.

Chase, Cheryl. "Hermaphrodites with Attitude: Mapping the Emergence of Intersex Political Activism." *GLQ: A Journal of Lesbian and Gay Studies* 4, no. 2 (1998): 189–211.

Chatterjee, Choi. *Celebrating Women: Gender, Festival Culture, and Bolshevik Ideology, 1910–1939*. Pittsburgh: University of Pittsburgh Press, 2002.

Chatterjee, Indrani. Introduction to *Unfamiliar Relations: Family and History in South Asia*, edited by Indrani Chatterjee, 3–45. New Brunswick, NJ: Rutgers University Press, 2004.

Chatterjee, Kumkum. *The Cultures of History in Early Modern India: Persianization and Mughal Culture in Bengal*. New York: Oxford University Press, 2009.

Chatterjee, Partha. *The Black Hole of Empire: History of a Global Practice of Power*. Princeton: Princeton University Press, 2012.

———. "The Nationalist Resolution of the Women's Question." In Sangari and Vaid, *Recasting Women*, 233–53.

Chatterjee, Ratnabali. *The Queens' Daughters: Prostitutes as an Outcast Group in Colonial India*. Bergen: Chr. Michelsen Institute Department of Social Science and Development, 1992.

Chatterjee, Sunil Kumar. *William Carey and Serampore*. Calcutta: Ghosh, 1984.

Chatterji, Joya. *Bengal Divided: Hindu Communalism and Partition, 1932–1947*. Cambridge: Cambridge University Press, 2002.

———. "The Bengali Muslim: A Contradiction in Terms? An Overview of the Debate on Bengali Muslim Identity." *Comparative Studies of South Asia, Africa and the Middle East* 16, no. 2 (1996): 16–24.

Chaudhri, Mohammed A. "Pakistan's Relations with the Soviet Union." *Asian Survey* 6, no. 9 (1966): 492–500.

Chaudhuri, Nupur. "Finding an Archive in Krishnobhabini Das's *Englande Bangamohila*." In Chaudhuri, Katz, and Perry, *Contesting Archives*, 135–55.

———. "Krishnobhabini Das's *Englande Bangamohila*: An Archive of Early Thoughts on Bengali Women's Nationalism and Feminism." *Journal of Women's History* 20, no. 1 (2008): 197–216.

Chaudhuri, Nupur, Sherry J. Katz, and Mary Elizabeth Perry, eds. *Contesting Archives: Finding Women in the Sources*. Champaign: University of Illinois Press, 2010.

Chaudhuri, Nupur, and Margaret Strobel, eds. *Western Women and Imperialism*. Bloomington: Indiana University Press, 1992.

Chen, Jeng-Guo S. "Gendering India: Effeminacy and the Scottish Enlightenment's Debates over Virtue and Luxury." *Eighteenth Century: Theory and Interpretation* 51, nos. 1–2 (2010): 193–210.

Chen, Martha Alter. "Engendering World Conferences: The International Women's

Movement and the United Nations." *Third World Quarterly* 16, no. 3 (1995): 477–93.

Cherry, Matt, and Warren Allen Smith. "One Brave Woman vs. Religious Fundamentalism." *Free Inquiry* 19, no. 1 (1998): 34–37.

Chesler, Ellen. "Stop Coercing Women." *New York Times Magazine*, 9 February 1994: 31, 33.

Chipp, Sylvia A. "The Role of Women Elites in a Modernizing Country: The All Pakistan Women's Association." PhD diss., Syracuse University, 1970.

Chishti, Maliha. "Political-Social Movements: Feminist; United States." In Joseph, *Encyclopedia of Women*, 2:597–99.

Choudhury, Cyra Akila. "National and Transnational Security Regimes: South Asia." In *Encyclopedia of Women and Islamic Cultures, 2010–2020*, edited by Suad Joseph, 332–50. Vol. 4. Leiden: Brill, 2021.

Choudhury, Dilara. "Women and Democracy: A Bangladesh Perspective." *Round Table* 89, no. 357 (2000): 563–76.

Choudhury, Iqbal Bahar, dir. *Anwara Bahar Choudhury: A Documentary*. FABC, 2015.

Chowdhury, Elora Halim. *Transnationalism Reversed: Women Organizing against Gendered Violence in Bangladesh*. Albany: State University of New York Press, 2011.

Chowdhury, Najma. "Bangladesh: Gender Issues and Politics in a Patriarchy." In *Women and Politics Worldwide*, edited by Barbara J. Nelson and Najma Chowdhury, 94–113. New Haven, CT: Yale University Press, 1994.

———. "The Politics of Implementing Women's Rights in Bangladesh." In *Globalization, Gender, and Religion: The Politics of Women's Rights in Catholic and Muslim Contexts*, edited by Janet H. Bayes and Nayereh Tohidi, 203–30. New York: Palgrave, 2001.

Chowdhury, Nusrat. *Paradoxes of the Popular: Crowd Politics in Bangladesh*. Palo Alto: Stanford University Press, 2019.

Christiansen, Samantha. "Beyond Liberation: Students, Space, and the State in East Pakistan/Bangladesh, 1952–1990." PhD diss., Northeastern University, 2012.

Chudleigh, Mary. *The Ladies Defence*. Penn Libraries. Accessed 15 December 2020. https://digital.library.upenn.edu/women/chudleigh/defence/defence.html.

Citino, Nathan. *Envisioning the Arab Future: Modernization in US-Arab Relations, 1945–1967*. Cambridge: Cambridge University Press, 2017.

Clark, Anna. *Scandal: The Sexual Politics of the British Constitution*. Princeton: Princeton University Press, 2003.

Clarke, Basil. *Taking What Comes: A Biography of A. G. Stock (Dinah)*. Chandigarh: Punjab University, 1999.

Cohen, Susan A. "The Road from Rio to Cairo: Toward a Common Agenda." *International Family Planning Perspectives* 19, no. 2 (1993): 61–66.

Cohn, Bernard S. *Colonialism and Its Forms of Knowledge: The British in India*. Princeton: Princeton University Press, 1996.

Collet, Sophia Dobson. Preface to Keshub Sen, *Sen's English Visit*, v–vii.

Colley, Linda. "Gendering the Globe: The Political and Imperial Thought of Philip Francis." *Past and Present* 209 (2010): 117–48.

———. *The Ordeal of Elizabeth Marsh: A Woman in World History.* New York: Pantheon Books, 2007.

"Conference of Muslim Prime Ministers Proposed." *Pakistan Affairs* 5, no. 17 (1952): 2.

Connelly, Matthew J. *Fatal Misconception: The Struggle to Control World Population.* Cambridge, MA: Harvard University Press, 2008.

cooke, miriam. "The Muslimwoman." *Contemporary Islam* 1, no. 2 (2007): 139–54.

Coontz, Stephanie. *A Strange Stirring: "The Feminine Mystique" and American Women at the Dawn of the 1960s.* New York: Basic Books, 2011.

Cooper, Adrienne. *Sharecropping and Sharecroppers' Struggles in Bengal, 1930–1950.* Calcutta: K.P. Bagchi & Co., 1988.

Cooper, Frederick, and Ann Laura Stoler. "Between Metropole and Colony: Rethinking a Research Agenda." In Cooper and Stoler, *Tensions of Empire*, 1–56.

———, eds. *Tensions of Empire: Colonial Cultures in a Bourgeois World.* Berkeley: University of California Press, 1997.

Corelli, Marie. *The Murder of Delicia.* Philadelphia: Lippincott, 1896.

Cortesão, Armando. Introduction to Pires, *Suma Oriental*, xiii–xcvi.

Coulson, Noel J. "Reform of Family Law in Pakistan." *Studia Islamica* 7 (1957): 133–55.

Crabitès, Pierre. "Woman in Islam." *American Bar Association Journal* 17, no. 10 (1931): 677–80.

Crenshaw, Kimberlé. "Mapping the Margins: Intersectionality, Identity Politics, and Violence against Women of Color." *Stanford Law Review* 43, no. 6 (1991): 1241–99.

Cromer, Evelyn Baring, Earl of. *Modern Egypt.* 2 vols. London: Macmillan, 1908.

Crossette, Barbara. "A UN Expert on Women Who Refused to Be Silenced." PassBlue: Independent Coverage of the UN. 1 July 2013. www.passblue.com/2013/07/01/a-un-expert-on-women-who-refused-to-be-silenced/.

Curthoys, Ann. "Mary Wollstonecraft Revisited." *Humanities Research* 35 (2010): 29–48.

Custers, Peter. "Women's Role in Tebhaga Movement." *Economic and Political Weekly* 21, no. 43 (1986): WS97–104.

Dalrymple, William. *The Anarchy: The East India Company, Corporate Violence, and the Pillage of an Empire.* London: Bloomsbury, 2019.

———. Introduction to Parkes, *Begums*, v–xix.

Daly, Mary. *Beyond God the Father: Toward a Philosophy of Women's Liberation.* Boston: Beacon, 1973.

———. *Gyn/Ecology: The Metaethics of Radical Feminism.* 1978. Reprint, Boston: Beacon, 1990.

Dandekar, Deepra. "Translation and the Christian Conversion of Women in Colonial India: Rev. Sheshadri and Bāḷā Sundarābāī Ṭhākūr." *South Asia* 41, no. 2 (2018): 366–83.

Daniel, Norman. *Islam and the West: The Making of an Image.* London: Oneworld, 2009.

Dannecker, Petra. *Between Conformity and Resistance: Women Garment Workers in Bangladesh.* Dhaka: University Press Limited, 2002.

"Dark Secrets." *Economist,* 8 February 2007. www.economist.com/books-and-arts /2007/02/08/dark-secrets.

Das, Krishnabhabini. *A Bengali Lady in England.* 1885. Edited and translated by Somdatta Mandal. Reprint, Newcastle upon Tyne: Cambridge Scholars, 2015.

Das, Susnata. "Marginal Communities in Peasant Movement: The Sharecroppers' Struggle for 'Tebhaga' in North Bengal (1946–47)." *Proceedings of the Indian History Congress* 74 (2013): 640–51.

Datta, Rajat. *Society, Economy and the Market: Commercialization in Rural Bengal, c. 1760–1800.* New Delhi: Manohar, 2000.

Davidoff, Leonore, and Catherine Hall. *Family Fortunes: Men and Women of the English Middle Class, 1780–1850.* 3rd ed. New York: Routledge, 2019.

Davis, Angela. *Angela Davis: An Autobiography.* New York: Random House, 1974.

———. "Sex: Egypt." In D. Taylor, *Women,* 325–48.

D'Costa, Bina. *Nationbuilding, Gender and War Crimes in South Asia.* New York: Routledge, 2011.

Dean, Robert D. "Masculinity as Ideology: John F. Kennedy and the Domestic Politics of Foreign Policy." *Diplomatic History* 22 (1998): 29–62.

"Dean Rusk's Directive to All Embassies: Do Not Involve Peace Corps Volunteers." Peace Corps Worldwide. 3 February 2015. https://peacecorpsworldwide.org/dean -rusks-directive-to-all-embassies-do-not-involve-peace-corps-volunteers/.

Deen, Hanifa. *The Crescent and the Pen: The Strange Journey of Taslima Nasreen.* Westport, CT: Greenwood, 2006.

De Groot, Joanna. "Oriental Feminotopias? Montagu's and Montesquieu's 'Seraglios' Revisited.'" *Gender and History* 18 (April 2006): 66–86.

De Haan, Francisca. "Continuing Cold War Paradigms in Western Historiography of Transnational Women's Organisations: The Case of the Women's International Democratic Federation (WIDF)." *Women's History Review* 19 (2010): 547–73.

De Leeuw, Marc, and Sonja van Wichelen. "'Please, Go Wake Up!': Submission, Hirsi Ali and the 'War on Terror' in the Netherlands." *Feminist Media Studies* 5, no. 3 (2005): 325–40.

Devee, Sunity. The *Autobiography of an Indian Princess.* London: Murray, 1921.

Devji, Faisal. "Gender and the Politics of Space: The Movement for Women's Reform, 1857–1900." In *Forging Identities: Gender, Communities and the State in India,* edited by Zoya Hasan, 22–37. Boulder, CO: Westview, 1994.

———. *Muslim Zion: Pakistan as a Political Idea.* Cambridge, MA: Harvard University Press, 2013.

Dickey, Christopher, and Carla Power. "Rocking the Casbah." *Newsweek,* 20 December 2004, 30–31.

Digby, Simon. "An Eighteenth-Century Narrative of a Journey from Bengal to England: Munshi Ismail's *New History.*" In *Urdu and Muslim South Asia: Studies in*

Honor of Ralph Russell, edited by Christopher Shackle, 49–65. SOAS University of London, 1989.

Dil, Afia. *Two Traditions of the Bengal Language.* Islamabad: National Institute of Historical and Cultural Research, 1993.

Dirks, Nicholas. *Castes of Mind: Colonialism and the Making of Modern India.* Princeton: Princeton University Press, 2001.

———. *The Scandal of Empire: India and the Creation of Imperial Britain.* Cambridge, MA: Harvard University Press, 2006.

Documents of the Second Afro-Asian Women's Conference, 13–18 August, 1972, Ulan-Bator, Mongolia. Cairo: Permanent Secretariat of the Afro-Asian Peoples' Solidarity Organization, 1973.

Donadey, Anne, and Huma Ahmed-Ghosh. "Why Americans Love Azar Nafisi's *Reading Lolita in Tehran.*" *Signs* 33, no. 3 (2008): 623–46.

Dow, Bonnie J. "Feminism, Miss America, and Media Mythology." *Rhetoric and Public Affairs* 6, no. 1 (2003): 127–49.

Dryden, John. *Amboyna.* London: Herringman, 1673.

Dunn, Ross E. *The Adventures of Ibn Battuta.* Berkeley: University of California Press, 2012.

Dutta, Debjani. "Voices from the Other Side." In Bagchi and Dasgupta, *Trauma and the Triumph,* 2:162–65.

Dyson, Ketaki Kushari. *A Various Universe: A Study of the Journals and Memoirs of British Men and Women in the Indian Subcontinent, 1765–1856.* Oxford University Press, 1978.

Eaton, Richard. *The Rise of Islam and the Bengal Frontier, 1204–1760.* Berkeley: University of California Press, 1993.

Edib, Halidé. *Inside India.* New Delhi: Oxford University Press, 2002.

Edwards, Lee. "Gosnell and the Super Coil." *American Spectator,* April 2013. https://spectator.org/55739_gosnell-and-super-coil/.

Eisenstein, Hester. *Feminism Seduced: How Global Elites Use Women's Labor and Ideas to Exploit the World.* New York: Routledge, 2009.

El-Ariss, Tarek. "The Making of an Expert: The Case of Irshad Manji." *Muslim World* 97 (January 2007): 93–110.

Elias, Megan J. *Stir It Up: Home Economics in American Culture.* Philadelphia: University of Pennsylvania Press, 2010.

El Saadawi, Nawal. *The Hidden Face of Eve: Women in the Arab World.* Translated by Sherif Hetata. London: Zed Books, 1980.

El Saadawi, Nawal, Fatima Mernissi, and Mallica Vajarathon. "A Critical Look at the Wellesley Conference." *Quest: A Feminist Quarterly* 4 (Winter 1978): 101–8.

Elson, Diane, and Ruth Pearson. "'Nimble Fingers Make Cheap Workers': An Analysis of Women's Employment in Third World Export Manufacturing." *Feminist Review* 7 (1981): 87–107.

Enloe, Cynthia. *Bananas, Beaches, and Bases: Making Feminist Sense of International Politics.* Berkeley: University of California Press, 1989.

———. *The Curious Feminist: Searching for Women in a New Age of Empire.* Berkeley: University of California Press, 2004.

Esposito, John L. *Women in Muslim Family Law.* With Natana J. DeLong-Bas. Syracuse: Syracuse University Press, 2001.

Esposito, John L., and John O. Voll. *Makers of Contemporary Islam.* New York: Oxford University Press, 2001.

Essa, Azad. "Why Many Muslim Women in the US Are Skipping the Women's March This Year." Middle East Eye. 17 January 2020. www.middleeasteye.net /news/why-many-muslim-women-are-skipping-womens-march-year.

Euben, Roxanne L. *Journeys to the Other Shore: Muslim and Western Travelers in Search of Knowledge.* Princeton: Princeton University Press, 2006.

"Farida Akhtar: Founder of UBINIG." *Seedling,* 9 July 2002. www.grain.org/article /entries/336-farida-akhtar-founder-of-ubinig.

Farrell, Amy, and Patrice McDermott. "Claiming Afghan Women: The Challenge of Human Rights Discourse for Transnational Feminism." In Hesford and Kozol, *Just Advocacy?,* 33–55.

Fay, Eliza. *Original Letters from India.* New York: New York Review of Books, 2010.

Fazl, Abul. *The Akbar Nama of Abu'l Fazl.* Translated by Henry Beveridge. 3 vols. Reprint, Calcutta: Asiatic Society, 2000.

Feinberg, Harriet. "A Pioneering Dutch Feminist Views Egypt: Aletta Jacobs's Travel Letters." *Feminist Issues* 10 (Fall 1990): 65–78.

Feldman, Shelley. "Exploring Theories of Patriarchy: A Perspective from Contemporary Bangladesh." *Signs* 26, no. 4 (2001): 1097–127.

———. "Feminist Interruptions: The Silence of East Bengal in the Story of Partition." *Interventions* 1, no. 2 (1999): 167–82.

Ferguson, Adam. *An Essay on the History of Civil Society.* Edinburgh: Millar and Cadell, 1767.

Ferguson, Moira, ed. *First Feminists: British Women Writers, 1578–1799.* Bloomington: Indiana University Press, 1985.

———. "Mary Wollstonecraft and the Problematic of Slavery." *Feminist Review* 42 (1992): 82–102.

Fernandes, Leela, ed. *Routledge Handbook of Gender in South Asia.* New York: Routledge, 2014.

———. *Transnational Feminism in the United States: Knowledge, Ethics, Power.* New York: New York University Press, 2013.

———. "Unsettling 'Third Wave Feminism': Feminist Waves, Intersectionality, and Identity Politics in Retrospective." In Hewitt, *No Permanent Waves,* 98–118.

Fernea, Elizabeth Warnock. "An Early Ethnographer of Middle Eastern Women: Lady Mary Wortley Montagu (1689–1762)." *Journal of Near Eastern Studies* 40 (October 1981): 329–38.

Ferree, Myra Marx, and Aili Mari Tripp, eds. *Global Feminism: Transnational Women's Activism, Organizing, and Human Rights.* New York: New York University Press, 2006.

Findly, Ellison B. "The Capture of Maryam-uz-Zamani's Ship: Mughal Women and European Traders." *Journal of the American Oriental Society* 108 (1988): 227–38.

———. *Nur Jahan: Empress of Mughal India*. New York: Oxford University Press, 1993.

Finkle, Jason L., and Barbara B. Crane. "The Politics of Bucharest: Population, Development, and the New International Economic Order." *Population and Development Review* 1, no. 1 (1975): 87–114.

First Five-Year Plan. Dacca: Government of Bangladesh, 1973.

Fisher, Michael H. *Counterflows to Colonialism: Indian Travellers and Settlers in Britain, 1600–1857*. New Delhi: Permanent Black, 2004.

———. Foreword to K. Das, *Bengali Lady in England*, xi–xii.

———. "From India to England and Back: Early Indian Travel Narratives for Indian Readers." *Huntington Library Quarterly* 70 (March 2007): 153–72.

———. "Representing 'His' Women: Mirza Abu Talib Khan's 1801 'Vindication of the Liberties of Asiatic Women.'" *Indian Economic and Social History Review* 37 (2000): 215–37.

———. "Seeing England Firsthand: Women and Men from Imperial India, 1614–1769." In *Europe Observed: Multiple Gazes in Early Modern Encounters*, edited by Kumkum Chatterjee and Clement Hawes, 143–71. Lewisburg, PA: Bucknell University Press, 2008.

———, ed. *The Travels of Dean Mahomet: An Eighteenth-Century Journey through India*. Berkeley: University of California Press, 1997.

———, ed. *Visions of Mughal India: An Anthology of European Travel Writing*. London: Tauris, 2007.

———. "Women and the Feminine in the Court and High Culture of Awadh, 1722–1856." In Hambly, *Medieval Islamic World*, 488–519.

Fleet, Kate, Gudrun Krämer, Denis Matringe, John Nawas, and Everett Rowson, eds. *Encyclopaedia of Islam III*. Leiden: Brill, 2010.

Flores, Jorge. "Floating Franks: The Portuguese and Their Empire as Seen from Early Modern Asia." In *The Routledge History of Western Empires*, edited by Robert Aldrich and Kirsten McKenzie, 33–45. New York: Routledge, 2014.

———. *Unwanted Neighbors: The Mughals, the Portuguese, and Their Frontier Zones*. New York: Oxford University Press, 2018.

Fluri, Jennifer L. "Feminist-Nation Building in Afghanistan." *Feminist Review* 89 (2008): 34–54.

Fluri, Jennifer L., and Rachel Lehr. *The Carpetbaggers of Kabul and Other American-Afghan Entanglements*. Athens: University of Georgia Press, 2017.

Forbes, Andrew D. W. "Ma Huan." In *Encyclopaedia of Islam, Second Edition*, edited by P. Bearman, Th. Bianquis, C. E. Bosworth, E. van Donzel, and W. P. Heinrichs. Leiden: Brill, 2012.

Forbes, Geraldine. *Women in Modern India*. Cambridge: Cambridge University Press, 1999.

———. "In Search of the 'Pure Heathen': Missionary Women in Nineteenth Century India." *Economic and Political Weekly* 21, no. 17 (1986): WS2–8.

Foster, William, ed. *Early Travels in India, 1583–1619*. New York: Oxford University Press, 1921.

———, ed. *The Embassy of Sir Thomas Roe to the Court of the Great Mogul, 1615–1619*. London: Haklyut Society, 1899.

———. *The English Factories in India, 1618–1621*. Oxford: Clarendon, 1906.

———, ed. *Letters Received by the East India Company from Its Servants in the East*. 6 vols. London: Sampson Low, Martson, 1900.

———, ed. *The Voyage of Thomas Best to the East Indies, 1612–1614*. London: Hakluyt Society, 1934.

Franklin, Michael J. "Radically Feminizing India: Phebe Gibbes's *Hartly House, Calcutta* (1789) and Sydney Owenson's *The Missionary: An Indian Tale* (1811)." In Franklin, *Romantic Representations*, 154–79.

———, ed. *Romantic Representations of British India*. New York: Routledge, 2006.

Fraser, Arvonne. "The Convention on the Elimination of All Forms of Discrimination against Women (the Women's Convention)." In *Women, Politics, and the United Nations*, edited by Anne Winslow, 77–94. Westport, CT: Greenwood, 1995.

———. "Seizing Opportunities: USAID, WID, and CEDAW." In Fraser and Tinker, *Developing Power*, 164–75.

Fraser, Arvonne S., and Irene Tinker. *Developing Power: How Women Transformed International Development*. New York: Feminist Press at City University of New York, 2004.

Freedman, Estelle, ed. *The Essential Feminist Reader*. New York: Modern Library, 2007.

———. *No Turning Back: The History of Feminism and the Future of Women*. New York: Ballantine Books, 2003.

Freeman, Jo. "The Legal Basis of the Sexual Caste System." *Valparaiso University Law Review* 5 (1971): 203–36.

Frey, Hillary, and Ruth Baldwin. "An Interview with Taslima Nasrin." In *Nothing Sacred: Women Respond to Religious Fundamentalism and Terror*, edited by Betsy Reed, 209–14. New York: Thunder's Mouth/Nation Books, 2002.

Friedan, Betty. "Coming Out of the Veil." *Ladies' Home Journal*, June 1975, 98–104.

———. *The Feminine Mystique*. 1963. Reprint, Dell, 1983.

———. *It Changed My Life: Writings on the Women's Movement*. New York: Random House, 1976.

———. *Life So Far*. New York: Simon and Schuster, 2000.

———. "Scary Doings in Mexico City (1975)." In Friedan, *It Changed My Life*, 342–65.

Friedman, Elisabeth Jay. "Gendering the Agenda: The Impact of the Transnational Women's Rights Movement at the UN Conferences of the 1990s." *Women's Studies International Forum* 26, no. 4 (2003): 313–31.

Gandhi, Lakshmi. "This Bangladeshi American Organizer Is Rallying Her Community to Support Black Lives." *Supermajority News*, 5 June 2020. https://

supermajority.com/news/education-fund/this-bangladeshi-american-organizer
-is-rallying-her-community-to-support-black-lives/.

Garavini, Giuliano. "Completing Decolonization: The 1973 'Oil Shock' and the
Struggle for Economic Rights." *International History Review* 33, no. 3 (2011):
473–87.

Garcia, Humberto. *Islam and the English Enlightenment, 1670–1840*. Baltimore:
Johns Hopkins University Press, 2012.

———. "'To Strike Out a New Path': Lady Mary Wortley Montagu, Mary Astell,
and the Politics of the Imperial Harem." In *Under the Veil: Spirituality and Feminism in Post-Reformation Britain and Europe*, edited by Katherine M. Quinsey,
113–44. Newcatsle upon Tyne: Cambridge Scholars, 2012.

———. "The Transports of Lascar Specters: Dispossessed Indian Sailors in Women's
Romantic Poetry." *Eighteenth Century* 55 (Summer/Fall 2014): 255–72.

Gasiorowski, Mark J. "The 1953 Coup D'etat in Iran." *International Journal of
Middle East Studies* 19, no. 3 (1987): 261–86.

Gaughan, Joan Mickelson. *The Incumberances: British Women in India, 1615–1856*.
New York: Oxford University Press, 2013.

Ghodsee, Kristen. "Rethinking State Socialist Mass Women's Organizations:
The Committee of the Bulgarian Women's Movement and the United Nations
Decade for Women, 1975–1985." *Journal of Women's History* 24, no. 4 (2012):
49–73.

———. "Revisiting the United Nations Decade for Women." *Women's Studies International Forum* 33, no. 1 (2010): 3–12.

Ghose, Indira, ed. *Memsahibs Abroad*. New Delhi: Oxford University Press, 1998.

Ghosh, Anindita. *Power in Print: Popular Publishing and the Politics of Language
and Culture in a Colonial Society*. New Delhi: Oxford University Press, 2006.

Ghosh, Bishnupriya. "An Affair to Remember: Scripted Performances in the 'Nasreen Affair.'" In Amireh and Majaj, eds. *Going Global*, 39–83.

Ghosh, Durba. *Sex and Family in Colonial India*. Cambridge: Cambridge University Press, 2006.

Gibbes, Phebe. *Hartly House, Calcutta*. Edited by Michael Franklin. 1789. Reprint,
New Delhi: Oxford University Press, 2007.

Gill, Gillian. *We Two: Victoria and Albert, Rulers, Partners, Rivals*. New York: Ballantine, 2009.

Gilliam, Dorothy B. "A Historic Gathering of Women." *Ebony*, October 1985,
156–58, 160, 162.

Gleig, George Robert. *Memoirs of the Life of the Right Hon. Warren Hastings*. 3 vols.
London: Bentley, 1841.

Glenn, Evelyn Nakano. *Unequal Freedom: How Race and Gender Shaped American
Citizenship and Labor*. Cambridge, MA: Harvard University Press, 2002.

Glover, Susan Paterson. "Further Reflections upon Marriage: Mary Astell and Sarah
Chapone." In Sowaal and Weiss, *Feminist Interpretations*, 93–108.

Gökarıksel, Banu, and Sara Smith. "Intersectional Feminism beyond U.S. Flag

Hijab and Pussy Hats in Trump's America." *Gender, Place and Culture* 24, no. 5 (2017): 628–44.

Gordon, Charlotte. *Romantic Outlaws: The Extraordinary Lives of Mary Wollstonecraft and Her Daughter Mary Shelley*. New York: Random House, 2015.

Gorman, Christine, and Greg Burke. "Clash of Wills in Cairo." *Time* 144, no. 11 (1994): 56.

"Governor-General Opens All-Pakistan Women's Conference in Lahore." *Pakistan Affairs* 5, no. 17 (1952): 3–5.

Graham, George Farquar Irving. *The Life and Work of Syed Ahmed Khan*. Edinburgh: Blackwood and Sons, 1885.

Green, Nile. *Islam and the Army in Colonial India: Sepoy Religion in the Service of Empire*. Cambridge: Cambridge University Press, 2009.

Gregg, Stephen H. *Empire and Identity: An Eighteenth-Century Sourcebook*. New York: Palgrave Macmillan, 2005.

Grewal, Inderpal. *Home and Harem: Nation, Gender, Empire, and the Cultures of Travel*. Durham, NC: Duke University Press, 1996.

———. "Reading and Writing the South Asian Diaspora: Feminism and Nationalism in North America." In Women of South Asian Descent, *Our Feet Walk*, 226–36.

Grewal, Inderpal, and Caren Kaplan, eds. *Scattered Hegemonies: Postmodernity and Transnational Feminist Practices*. Minneapolis: University of Minnesota Press, 1994.

Griswold, Robert. "'Russian Blonde in Space': Soviet Women in the American Imagination, 1950–1965." *Journal of Social History* 45, no. 4 (2012): 881–907.

Grosrichard, Alain. *The Sultan's Court: European Fantasies of the East*. New York: Verso, 1998.

Grundy, Isobel. "'The Barbarous Character We Give Them': White Women Travellers Report on Other Races." *Studies in Eighteenth-Century Culture* 22 (1993): 73–86.

———. Introduction to Grundy, *Lady Mary Wortley Montagu*, xvii–xxiv.

———. *Lady Mary Wortley Montagu*. New York: Penguin, 1997.

Guha, Ranajit Das. "A Labour History of Social Security and Mutual Assistance in India." *Economic and Political Weekly* 29, no. 11 (1994): 612–20.

Guhathakurta, Meghna. "Gender Violence in Bangladesh: The Role of the State." *Journal of Social Studies* (1985) 30: 57–76.

———. "Uprooted and Divided." In Bagchi and Dasgupta, *Trauma and the Triumph*, 1:98–112.

———. "Women Negotiating Change: The Structure and Transformation of Gendered Violence in Bangladesh." *Cultural Dynamics* 16, nos. 2–3 (2004): 193–211.

Gunther-Canada, Wendy. "Cultivating Virtue: Catharine Macaulay and Mary Wollstonecraft on Civic Education." *Women and Politics* 25 (2003): 47–70.

Gupta, Sarmistha Dutta. "*Saogat* and the Reformed Bengali Muslim Woman." *Indian Journal of Gender Studies* 16, no. 3 (2009): 329–58.

Habibi, Don. "The Moral Dimensions of J. S. Mill's Colonialism." *Journal of Social Philosophy* 30 (Spring 1999): 125–46.

Hall, Catherine. "Of Gender and Empire: Reflections on the Nineteenth Century." In Levine, *Gender and Empire,* 46–76.

Halsband, Robert. *The Complete Letters of Lady Mary Wortley Montagu.* 3 vols. Oxford: Clarendon, 1965.

Hambly, Gavin. *Women in the Medieval Islamic World: Power, Patronage, and Piety.* New York: St. Martin's Press, 1998.

Haq, Kaiser. "Translator's Introduction." In I'tesamuddin, *Wonders of Vilayet,* 7–15.

Harlow, Barbara, and Mia Carter, eds. *Imperialism and Orientalism: A Documentary Sourcebook.* Oxford: Blackwell, 1999.

Harris, Sam. "A Response to Controversy." Sam Harris's official website. 4 April 2013. https://samharris.org/response-to-controversy/.

Harrison, John Bennett. "Five Portuguese Historians." In *Historians of India, Pakistan and Ceylon,* edited by Cyril Henry Philips, 155–69. London: Oxford University Press, 1961.

Hartmann, Betsy. *Reproductive Rights and Wrongs.* Boston: South End, 1999.

Harvey, Brett. *The Fifties: A Women's Oral History.* New York: HarperCollins, 1993.

Harvey, Robert. *Clive: The Life and Death of a British Emperor.* New York: Dunne Books, 2000.

Hasan, K. Sarwar. "The Foreign Policy of Liaquat Ali Khan." *Pakistan Horizon* 61, nos. 1–2 (2008): 37–52.

Hasan, Md. Mahmudul. "Commemorating Rokeya Sakhawat Hossain and Contextualising Her Work in South Asian Muslim Feminism." *Asiatic* 7 (2013): 39–59.

———. "Muslim Bengal Writes Back: A Study of Rokeya's Encounter with and Representation of Europe." *Journal of Postcolonial Writing* 52 (2016): 1–13.

Hasan, Perween. *Sultans and Mosques: The Early Muslim Architecture of Bangladesh.* London: Tauris, 2007.

Hasanat, Fayeza. *Nawab Faizunnesa's Rupjalal.* Leiden: Brill, 2008.

Hashmi, Sohail H. "'Zero Plus Zero Plus Zero': Pakistan, the Baghdad Pact, and the Suez Crisis." *International History Review* 33, no. 3 (2011): 525–44.

Hashmi, Taj I. *Pakistan as a Peasant Utopia: The Communalization of Class Politics in East Bengal, 1920–1947.* Boulder, CO: Westview, 1992.

Hassan, Riffat. "Backlash at Beijing." Accessed 13 January 2021. http://riffathassan .info/wp-content/uploads/2014/09/Backlash_at_Beijing.pdf.

———. "Feminist Theology: The Challenges for Muslim Women." *Critique: Journal of Critical Studies of Iran and the Middle East* 5, no. 9 (1996): 53–65.

Hatem, Mervat. "In the Eye of the Storm: Islamic Societies and Muslim Women in Globalization Discourses." *Comparative Studies of South Asia, Africa and the Middle East* 26, no. 1 (2006): 22–35.

———. "Through Each Other's Eyes: Egyptian, Levantine-Egyptian, and European Women's Images of Themselves and of Each Other (1862–1920)." *Women's Studies International Forum* 12, no. 2 (1989): 183–98.

Heeres, Jan Ernst. *The Part Borne by the Dutch in the Discovery of Australia, 1606–1765*. London: Luzac, 1899.

Heffernan, Teresa. "Feminism against the East/West Divide: Lady Mary's 'Turkish Embassy Letters.'" *Eighteenth-Century Studies* 33 (2000): 201–15.

Hemmings, Clare. *Why Stories Matter: The Political Grammar of Feminist Theory*. Durham, NC: Duke University Press, 2011.

Hennessee, Judith A. *Betty Friedan: Her Life*. New York: Random House, 1999.

Hennessy, Rosemary. *Materialist Feminism and the Politics of Discourse*. New York: Routledge, 1993.

Herr, Ranjoo Seodu. "Reclaiming Third World Feminism, or Why Transnational Feminism Needs Third World Feminism." *Meridians: Feminism, Race, Transnationalism* 12, no. 1 (2014): 1–30.

Hesford, Wendy S., and Wendy Kozol, eds. *Just Advocacy? Women's Human Rights, Transnational Feminisms, and the Politics of Representation*. New Brunswick, NJ: Rutgers University Press, 2005.

Hewitt, Nancy A. *No Permanent Waves: Recasting Histories of U.S. Feminism*. New Brunswick, NJ: Rutgers University Press, 2010.

Hill, Bridget. "The Links between Mary Wollstonecraft and Catharine Macaulay: New Evidence." *Women's History Review* 4 (1995): 177–91.

———. "A Refuge from Men: The Idea of a Protestant Nunnery." *Past and Present* 117 (1987): 107–30.

Hirsch, Pam. *Barbara Leigh Smith Bodichon: Feminist, Artist and Rebel*. New York: Random House, 2010.

Hirschkind, Charles, and Saba Mahmood. "Feminism, the Taliban, and Politics of Counter-Insurgency." *Anthropological Quarterly* 75, no. 2 (2002): 339–54.

Hirsi Ali, Ayaan. *Infidel*. New York: Free Press, 2008.

"History." Development Alternatives with Women for a New Era. Accessed 25 November 2020. https://dawnnet.org/about/history/.

History of the Trial of Warren Hastings, Esq. London: Debrett, 1796.

Hoeveler, Diane. "Female Captivity Narrative: Blood, Water, and Orientalism." In Hoeveler and Cass, *Interrogating Orientalism*, 46–71.

Hoeveler, Diane, and Jeffrey Cass, eds. *Interrogating Orientalism: Contextual Approaches and Pedagogical Practices*. Columbus: Ohio State University Press, 2006.

Hoffman, Merle. "Flo Kennedy and Irene Davall: Forever Activists." *On the Issues* 5 (1985). www.ontheissuesmagazine.com/1985vol5/mh_vol5_1985.php.

Hoganson, Kristin. "'As Badly Off as the Filipinos': U.S. Women's Suffragists and the Imperial Issue at the Turn of the Twentieth Century." *Journal of Women's History* 13 (2001): 9–33.

Holloway, S. T. "Why This Black Girl Will Not Be Returning to the Women's March." HuffPost. 19 January 2018. www.huffpost.com/entry/why-this-black-girl-will-not-be-returning-to-the-womens-march_n_5a3c1216e4b0b0e5a7a0bd4b.

Holmes, Sally. "American Apparel Releases Controversial New Ad." *ELLE*, 6 March 2014. www.elle.com/news/culture/american-apparel-bangladesh-ad.

"A Home Away from Home?" *Exhibits*. Duke University Libraries. Accessed 9 May 2020. https://exhibits.library.duke.edu/exhibits/show/dukeintlstudents/-a-home -away-from-home.

Hood, Maude Pye. "Modern Pakistani Dress with Traditional Influence." *Journal of Home Economics* 51 (November 1959): 336–39.

Horowitz, Daniel. *Betty Friedan and the Making of "The Feminine Mystique": The American Left, the Cold War, and Modern Feminism*. Amherst: University of Massachusetts Press, 1998.

Hossain, Hameeda. "The Alienation of Weavers: Impact of the Conflict between the Revenue and Commercial Interests of the East India Company, 1750–1800." *Indian Economic and Social History Review* 16, no. 3 (1979): 323–45.

Hossain, Hameeda, Roushan Jahan, and Salma Sobhan. *No Better Option? Industrial Women Workers in Bangladesh*. Dhaka: University Press Limited, 1990.

Hossain, Hameeda, and Amena Mohsin, eds. *Of the Nation Born: The Bangladesh Papers*. New Delhi: Zubaan, 2016.

Hossain, Hasina Yasmin. "Rokeya Sakhawat Hossain, 1880–1932: The Status of Muslim Women in Bengal." PhD diss., University of London, 1996.

Hossain, Naomi. *The Aid Lab: Understanding Bangladesh's Unexpected Success*. New York: Oxford University Press, 2017.

Hossain, Rokeya Sakhawat. "Alonkar na badge of slavery" [Jewelry or badge of slavery]. In M. Alam, *Rokeya Sakhawat Hossain*, 240–49.

———. *Motichur: Sultana's Dream and Other Writings of Rokeya Sakhawat Hossain*. New York: Oxford University Press, 2015.

———. *Strijatir abonoti* [The degradation of women]. Dhaka: Narigrantha Prabartana, 2002.

———. *Sultana's Dream: A Feminist Utopia and Selections from the Secluded Ones*. New York: Feminist Press, 1988.

Hossain, Selina. "Razia Khatun Choudhurani." In Hossain and Masuduzzaman, *Gender Bishwakosh,* 2:425–26.

Hossain, Selina, and Masuduzzaman, eds. *Gender bishwakosh* [Encyclopedia of gender]. 2 vols. Dhaka: Mowla Brothers, 2006.

Hossain, Sharmin. *"Amader Golpo:* Meet Shahana Hanif, Bangladeshi Visionary." *Medium,* 18 February 2016. https://medium.com/@bangladeshistry/amader -golpo-meet-shahana-hanif-bangladeshi-visionary-6ef1b5899f1a.

Hossain, Yasmin. "The Begum's Dream: Rokeya Sakhawat Hossain and the Broadening of Muslim Women's Aspirations in Bengal." *South Asia Research* 12, no. 1 (1992): 1–19.

Hossein, Roquiah Sakhawat. *God Gives, Man Robs and Other Writings*. Dhaka: Narigrantha Prabartana, 2002.

Hourani, Albert. *A History of the Arab Peoples*. New York: Warner Books, 1992.

Howard, Carol. "Wollstonecraft's Thoughts on Slavery and Corruption." *Eighteenth Century* 45 (2004): 61–86.

Huan, Ma. *Ying-Yai Sheng-Lan: The Overall Survey of the Ocean's Shores*. 1433. Translated by J. V. G. Mills. Cambridge: Hakluyt Society/Cambridge University Press, 1970.

Hubbard, Ruth, and Patricia Farnes. "Letter to the Editor." *Ms.*, April 1980, 9–10.

Huda, Sigma. "Women's Movement in Bangladesh." *Asian Women* 5 (1997): 133–43.

"Human Rights Lawyer Sues NYPD after Arrest for Blocking Sidewalk." NBC News. 31 August 2014. www.nbcnews.com/news/asian-america/human-rights-lawyer-sues-nypd-after-arrest-blocking-sidewalk-n198211.

Hunt, Margaret R. *Women in Eighteenth-Century Europe*. New York: Routledge, 2014.

———. "Women in Ottoman and Western European Law Courts: Were Western Women Really the Luckiest Women in the World?" In *Structures and Subjectivities: Attending to Early Modern Women*, edited by Joan E. Hartman and Adele Seeff, 176–99. Newark: University of Delaware Press, 2007.

Huntington, Samuel P. "The Clash of Civilizations?" *Foreign Affairs* 72, no. 3 (1993): 22–49.

Huq, Shireen. "Bodies as Sites of Struggle: Naripokkho and the Movement for Women's Rights in Bangladesh." *Bangladesh Development Studies* 29, nos. 3–4 (2003): 47–65.

———. "My Body, My Life, Whose Rights? Bangladeshi Women's Struggle for a Fair Deal." *Contemporary South Asia* 20, no. 1 (2012): 11–18.

Husain, Shahanara. *The Social Life of Women in Early Medieval Bengal*. Dhaka: Asiatic Society of Bangladesh, 1985.

Ibn Battuta. *Travels in Asia and Africa, 1325–1354*. Translated and edited by H. A. R. Gibb. London: Broadway House, 1929.

Ikramullah, Shaista S. *From Purdah to Parliament*. London: Cresset, 1963.

Inden, Ronald. "Orientalist Constructions of India." *Modern Asian Studies* 20, no. 3 (1986): 401–46.

Iqbal, Iftekhar. *The Bengal Delta: Ecology, State and Social Change, 1840–1943*. New York: Palgrave Macmillan, 2010.

Irani, Ayesha. "Sacred Biography, Translation, and Conversion: The Nabīvaṃśa of Saiyad Sultān and the Making of Bengali Islam, 1600–Present." PhD diss., University of Pennsylvania, 2011.

Isenberg, Nancy. *Fallen Founder: The Life of Aaron Burr*. New York: Viking Penguin, 2007.

———. *Sex and Citizenship in Antebellum America*. Chapel Hill: University of North Carolina Press, 1998.

Islam, Mahmuda. "Women's Organisations and Programmes for Women." In Women for Women, *Situation of Women*, 352–78.

Islam, Naheed. "In the Belly of the Multicultural Beast I Am Named South Asian." In Women of South Asian Descent, *Our Feet Walk*, 242–45.

Islam, Tanwi Nandini, "Those American Apparel Ads Are Shilling Poverty, Not Porn." *ELLE*, 7 March 2014. www.elle.com/news/culture/response-to-american-apparel-bangladesh-ad.

"Is Supercoil Foiled?" *Philadelphia NOW Newsletter,* July 1973.

I'tesamuddin, Mirza Sheikh. *The Wonders of Vilayet: Being the Memoir, Originally in Persian, of a Visit to France and Britain in 1765.* Translated by Kaiser Haq. Leeds: Peepal Tree, 2002.

Jacobs, Aletta H. *Memories: My Life as an International Leader in Health, Suffrage, and Peace.* Edited by Harriet Feinberg. New York: Feminist Press at CUNY, 1996.

———. *Reisbrieven uit Afrika en Azië, benevens eenige brieven uit Zweden en Norwegen* [Travels letters from Africa and Asia]. 2 vols. Almelo, Netherlands: Hilarius, 1913.

Jacobs, Jo Ellen. *The Voice of Harriet Taylor Mill.* Bloomington: Indiana University Press, 2002.

Jahan, Rounaq. "The International Women's Year Conference and Tribune." *International Development Review* 17, no. 3 (1975): 36–40.

———. "Sustaining Advocacy for Women's Empowerment for Four Decades." *Journal of Women's History* 24, no. 4 (2012): 208–12.

Jahan, Roushan. "Men in Seclusion, Women in Public: Rokeya's Dream and Women's Struggles in Bangladesh." In Basu, *Challenge of Local Feminisms,* 87–109.

———. "Rokeya: An Introduction to Her Life." In Hossain, *Sultana's Dream,* 37–57.

Jahangir, Selim. *Sufia Kamal.* Dhaka: Bangladesh Shilpokola Academy, 1999.

Jain, Devaki. *Women, Development, and the UN: A Sixty-Year Quest for Equality and Justice.* Bloomington: Indiana University Press, 2005.

Jalal, Ayesha. *The Struggle for Pakistan: A Muslim Homeland and Global Politics.* Cambridge, MA: Belknap, 2014.

Jamal, Amina. *Jamaat-e-Islami Women in Pakistan: Vanguard of a New Modernity?* Syracuse: Syracuse University Press, 2013.

Jameelah, Maryam. *Islam and the Muslim Woman Today.* New Delhi: Crescent, 1976.

———. *Why I Embraced Islam.* Crescent, 1976.

Jasanoff, Maya. *Edge of Empire: Lives, Culture, and Conquest in the East, 1750–1850.* New York: Vintage Books, 2005.

———. *Liberty's Exiles: American Loyalists in the Revolutionary World.* New York: Knopf, 2011.

Jayawardena, Kumari. *Feminism and Nationalism in the Third World.* London: Zed Books, 1985.

———. *The White Woman's Other Burden: Western Women and South Asia during British Rule.* New York: Routledge, 1995.

Jha, Manoranjan. *Katherine Mayo and India.* New Delhi: People's, 1971.

Jha, Priya. "'Making a Point by Choice': Maternal Imperialism, Second Wave Feminisms, and Transnational Epistemologies." In *Women's Activism and "Second Wave" Feminism: Transnational Histories,* edited by Barbara Molony and Jennifer Nelson, 173–92. London: Bloomsbury, 2017.

Johnson, Rebecca. "The Unbeliever." *Vogue* 197, no. 2 (2007). https://archive.vogue.com/issue/20070201.

Johnston, Anna. *Missionary Writing and Empire, 1800–1860*. Cambridge: Cambridge University Press, 2003.

Jones, Kenneth W. *Socio-religious Reform Movements in British India*. Cambridge: Cambridge University Press, 1989.

Joseph, Betty. *Reading the East India Company, 1720–1840: Colonial Currencies of Gender*. Chicago: University of Chicago Press, 2004.

Joseph, Suad, ed. *Encyclopedia of Women and Islamic Cultures*. Vol. 2. Leiden: Brill, 2005.

Kabbani, Rana. *Imperial Fictions: Europe's Myths of Orient*. Bloomington: Indiana University Press, 1986.

Kabeer, Naila. "Globalization, Labor Standards, and Women's Rights: Dilemmas of Collective (In)Action in an Interdependent World." *Feminist Economics* 10, no. 1 (2004): 3–35.

———. *The Power to Choose: Bangladeshi Garment Workers in London and Dhaka*. New York: Verso, 2000.

———. "The Quest for National Identity: Women, Islam and the State of Bangladesh." In Kandiyoti, *Women, Islam and the State*, 115–43.

———. *Reversed Realities: Gender Hierarchies in Development Thought*. New York: Verso, 1994.

———. "Subordination and Struggle: Women in Bangladesh." *New Left Review* 1, no. 168 (1988): 95–121.

Kabir, Ananya J. "Utopias Eroded and Recalled: Intellectual Legacies of East Pakistan." *South Asia* 41, no. 4 (2018): 892–910.

Kadir, A. F. M. Abdul. "Early Muslim Visitors of Europe from India." *Proceedings and Transactions of the Sixth All-India Oriental Conference, Patna, 1930*, 83–96. Patna: Bihar and Orissa Research Society, 1933.

Kadnikova, Anna M. "The Women's International Democratic Federation World Congress of Women, Moscow, 1963: Women's Rights and World Politics during the Cold War." Master's thesis, Central European University, 2011.

Kahf, Mohja. *Western Representations of the Muslim Woman: From Termagant to Odalisque*. Austin: University of Texas Press, 1999.

Kamal, Abu Hena Mustafa. *The Bengali Press and Literary Writing, 1818–1831*. Dhaka: University Press Limited, 1977.

Kamal, Ahmed. *State against the Nation: The Decline of the Muslim League in Pre-Independence Bangladesh, 1947–54*. Dhaka: University Press Limited, 2009.

Kamal, Sufia. *Sufia Kamal Rochonasongroho* [Collected works of Sufia Kamal]. Edited by Sajed Kamal. Dhaka: Bangla Academy, 2002.

Kandiyoti, Deniz, ed. *Women, Islam and the State*. Philadelphia: Temple University Press, 1991.

Kaplan, E. Ann. *Rocking around the Clock: Music Television, Postmodernism, and Consumer Culture*. New York: Routledge, 1988.

Kaplan, Temma. "On the Socialist Origins of International Women's Day." *Feminist Studies* 11, no. 1 (1985): 163–71.

Karim, Abdul. *Murshid Quli Khan and His Times.* Dacca: Asiatic Society of Pakistan, 1963.

———. *Social History of the Muslims in Bengal (Down to AD 1538).* Dacca: Asiatic Society of Pakistan, 1959.

Karim, Lamia. "Democratizing Bangladesh: State, NGOs, and Militant Islam." *Cultural Dynamics* 16, nos. 2–3 (2004): 291–318.

———. *Microfinance and Its Discontents: Women in Debt in Bangladesh.* Minneapolis: University of Minnesota Press, 2011.

Karlekar, Malavika. *Voices from Within: Early Personal Narratives of Bengali Women.* New Delhi: Oxford University Press, 1991.

Kassamali, Noor J. "When Modernity Confronts Traditional Practices: Female Genital Cutting in Northeast Africa." In Bodman and Tohidi, *Women in Muslim Societies,* 39–62.

Katebi, Hoda. "Please Keep Your American Flags Off My Hijab." Hoda Katebi. 23 January 2017. https://hodakatebi.com/culture/please-keep-your-american-flags -off-my-hijab/.

Kelber, Mim. "Five Days in March." *Ms.,* June 1979, 90–96.

Kelly, Joan. "Early Feminist Theory and the 'Querelle des Femmes,' 1400–1789." *Signs* 8 (Autumn 1982): 4–28.

Kent, Susan Kingsley. *Sex and Suffrage in Britain, 1860–1914.* Princeton: Princeton University Press, 1987.

Keshavarz, Fatemeh. *Jasmine and Stars: Reading More Than Lolita in Tehran.* Chapel Hill: University of North Carolina Press, 2007.

Kettani, Houssain. "Muslim Population in Asia: 1950–2020." *International Journal of Environmental Science and Development* 1, no. 2 (2010): 143–53.

Khabeer, Suad Abdul. "Trump's Muslim Ban Is a Dangerous Distraction." *Al Jazeera,* 29 January 2017. www.aljazeera.com/indepth/opinion/2017/01/trump -muslim-ban-dangerous-distraction-170128144523073.html.

Khan, Abdul Majed. *The Transition in Bengal, 1756–1775: A Study of Saiyid Muhammad Reza Khan.* Cambridge: Cambridge University Press, 1969.

Khan, Akhter Hameed. *The Works of Akhter Hameed Khan.* Vol. 1. Comilla: Bangladesh Academy for Rural Development, 1983.

Khan, A. Majeed. "The Rural Pilot Family Planning Action Programme at Comilla." *Studies in Family Planning* 1 (April 1964): 9–11.

Khan, Fareeha. "Tafwid al-Talaq: Transferring the Right to Divorce to the Wife." *Muslim World* 99 (July 2009): 502–19.

Khan, Gulfishan. *Indian Muslim Perceptions of the West during the Eighteenth Century.* Karachi: Oxford University Press, 1998.

Khan, M. Mojlum. *The Muslim Heritage of Bengal.* Markfield, UK: Kube, 2013.

Khan, Saleque. "Performing the (Imagi)Nation: A Bangladesh Mise-en-Scène." PhD diss., New York University, 2007.

Khan, Syed Ahmed. *The Causes of the Indian Revolt.* 1873. Reprint, Karachi: Oxford University Press, 2000.

Khoja-Moolji, Shenila. *Forging the Ideal Educated Girl: The Production of Desirable Subjects in Muslim South Asia.* Berkeley: University of California Press, 2018.

Kibria, Nazli. *Muslims in Motion: Islam and National Identity in the Bangladeshi Diaspora.* New Brunswick, NJ: Rutgers University Press, 2011.

Kietzman, Mary Jo. "Montagu's *Turkish Embassy Letters* and Cultural Dislocation." *Studies in English Literature* 38 (1998): 537–51.

Kindersley, Jemima. *Letters from the Island of Teneriffe, Brazil, the Cape of Good Hope, and the East Indies.* London: Nourse, 1777.

Knight, Lisa I. *Contradictory Lives: Baul Women in India and Bangladesh.* New York: Oxford University Press, 2011.

Knott, Sarah, and Barbara Taylor, eds. *Women, Gender and Enlightenment.* New York: Palgrave MacMillan, 2005.

Knowles, Adam. "Conjecturing Rudeness: James Mill's Utilitarian Philosophy of History and the British Civilizing Mission." In *Civilizing Missions in Colonial and Postcolonial South Asia: From Improvement to Development,* edited by Carey A. Watt and Michael Mann, 37–64. London: Anthem, 2011.

Koikari, Mire. "'The World Is Our Campus': Michigan State University and Cold-War Home Economics in US-Occupied Okinawa, 1945–1972." *Gender and History* 24. no. 1 (2012): 74–92.

Kolhatkar, Sonali. "'Saving' Afghan Women." Revolutionary Association of the Women of Afghanistan. 9 May 2002. www.rawa.org/znet.htm.

Kongar, Ebru, Jennifer C. Olmsted, and Elora Shehabuddin. "Gender and Economics in Muslim Communities: A Critical Feminist and Postcolonial Analysis." *Feminist Economics* 20, no. 4 (2014): 1–32.

Kopf, David. *The Brahmo Samaj and the Shaping of the Modern Indian Mind.* Princeton: Princeton University Press, 1979.

———. *British Orientalism and the Bengal Renaissance: The Dynamics of Indian Modernization, 1773–1835.* Berkeley: University of California Press, 1969.

Kozlowski, Gregory C. "Muslim Women and the Control of Property in North India." *Indian Economic and Social History Review* 24 (1987): 163–80.

———. "Private Lives and Public Piety: Women and the Practice of Islam in Mughal India." In Hambly, *Medieval Islamic World,* 469–88.

Krey, August. C. *The First Crusade: The Accounts of Eyewitnesses and Participants.* Princeton: Princeton University Press, 1921.

Kruk, Remke. "Ibn Battuta: Travel, Family Life, and Chronology." *Al-Qantara* 16, no. 2 (1995): 369–84.

Kugler, Anne. *Errant Plagiary: The Life and Writing of Lady Sarah Cowper, 1644–1720.* Palo Alto: Stanford University Press, 2002.

Kumar, Deepa. *Islamophobia and the Politics of Empire.* Chicago: Haymarket Books, 2012.

Lal, Ruby. *Domesticity and Power in the Early Mughal World.* Cambridge: Cambridge University Press, 2005.

———. *Empress: The Astonishing Reign of Nur Jahan.* New York: Norton, 2018.

Lambert-Hurley, Siobhan. *Elusive Lives: Gender, Autobiography, and the Self in Muslim South Asia.* Palo Alto: Stanford University Press, 2018.

———. *Muslim Women, Reform and Princely Patronage: Nawab Sultan Jahan Begam of Bhopal.* New York: Routledge, 2006.

Lash, Joseph P. *Eleanor: The Years Alone.* New York: Norton, 2014.

Latham, Michael E. *Modernization as Ideology: American Social Science and "Nation Building" in the Kennedy Era.* Chapel Hill: University of North Carolina Press, 2000.

Lauré, Jason, and Joyce Goldman. "Women of Bangladesh." *Ms.* 1, no. 2 (1972): 84–89.

Laville, Helen. *Cold War Women: The International Activities of American Women's Organisations.* Manchester: Manchester University Press, 2002.

Leask, Nigel. "'Travelling the Other Way': The Travels of Mirza Abu Taleb Khan (1810) and Romantic Orientalism." In Franklin, *Romantic Representations,* 220–37.

Le Breton, Philip Hemery, ed. *Memoirs, Miscellanies and Letters of the Late Lucy Aikin.* London: Longman, Green Longman, Roberts and Green, 1864.

Lee, Natasha. "Sex in Translation: Antoine Léonard Thomas's *Essai Sur Les Femmes* and the Enlightenment Debate on Women." *Eighteenth-Century Studies* 47, no. 4 (2014): 389–405.

Lelyveld, David. *Aligarh's First Generation: Muslim Solidarity in British India.* Princeton: Princeton University Press, 1978.

"Letters from the Island of Teneriffe, Brazil, the Cape of Good Hope, and the East Indies." *London Review of English and Foreign Literature,* July 1777, 37–44.

Levathes, Louise. *When China Ruled the Seas: The Treasure Fleet of the Dragon Throne, 1405–1433.* New York: Oxford University Press, 1997.

Levine, Philippa, ed. *Gender and Empire.* New York: Oxford University Press, 2004.

———. *Prostitution, Race and Politics: Policing Venereal Disease in the British Empire.* New York: Routledge, 2003.

Lewis, Reina. *Rethinking Orientalism: Women, Travel, and the Ottoman Harem.* New Brunswick, NJ: Rutgers University Press, 2004.

Linden Eugene, and Hannah Bloch. "Showdown in Cairo." *Time,* 5 September 1994, 52–53.

Logan, Deborah Anna. *The Indian Ladies' Magazine: Raj and Swaraj.* New York: Routledge, 2016.

Loomba, Ania, and Jonathan Burton, eds. *Race in Early Modern England: A Documentary Companion.* New York: Palgrave Macmillan, 2007.

Looser, Devoney. *British Women Writers and the Writing of History, 1670–1820.* Baltimore: Johns Hopkins Press, 2000.

Lorde, Audre, *Sister Outsider: Essays and Speeches.* Berkeley: Ten Speed, 1984.

Lowe, Lisa. *Critical Terrains: French and British Orientalisms.* Ithaca, NY: Cornell University Press, 1994.

———. *The Intimacies of Four Continents.* Durham, NC: Duke University Press, 2015.

Macaulay, Catharine. *Letters on Education with Observations on Religious and Metaphysical Subjects.* 1790. Reprint, Cambridge: Cambridge University Press, 2014.

Macaulay, Thomas Babington. *Essay on Lord Clive.* 1830. Reprint, London: Harrap, 1910.

———. "Minute on Indian Education." In *Speeches: With His Minute on Indian Education,* edited by Thomas Babington Macaulay, 356–61. New York: Oxford University Press, 1935.

Mack, Phyllis. "The History of Women in Early Modern Britain. A Review Article." *Comparative Studies in Society and History* 28 (1986): 715–22.

Mackenzie, Helen [Mrs. Colin]. *Life in the Mission, the Camp, and the Zenana, or Six Years in India.* 3 vols. London: Bentley, 1853.

MacLean, Gerald. *The Rise of Oriental Travel: English Visitors to the Ottoman Empire, 1580–1720.* New York: Palgrave Macmillan, 2004.

MacLean, Gerald, and Nabil Matar. *Britain and the Islamic World, 1558–1713.* New York: Oxford University Press, 2011.

The Maharashta Purana: An Eighteenth Century Bengali Historical Text. Translated by Edward C. Dimock and Pratul Chandra Gupta. Honolulu: East-West Center Press, 1965.

Mahmud, Moshfeka. *Begum Shamsunnahar Mahmud, Ekti Pramanyo Jiboni* [Begum Shamsun Nahar Mahmud: An authoritative biography]. Dhaka: Bulbul, 2001.

Mahmud, Shamsunnahar. *Amar Dekha Turashko* [Turkey through my eyes]. Calcutta: Presidency Library, 1955.

———. *Rokeya Jiboni* [The life of Rokeya]. 1937. Reprint, Calcutta: Bulbul, 1987.

———. "Women's Political Rights." *Saogat* 11, no. 9 (1935): 469–73.

Maira, Sunaina. "'Good' and 'Bad' Muslim Citizens: Feminists, Terrorists, and U.S. Orientalisms." *Feminist Studies* 35, no. 3 (2009): 631–56.

Makdisi, Jean Said. "War and Peace: Reflections of a Feminist." *Feminist Review* 88 (2008): 99–110.

Makdisi, Saree. *Romantic Imperialism: Universal Empire and the Culture of Modernity.* Cambridge: Cambridge University Press, 1998.

———. *William Blake and the Impossible History of the 1790s.* Chicago: University of Chicago Press, 2003.

Makdisi, Saree, and Felicity Nussbaum, eds. *The Arabian Nights in Historical Context: Between East and West.* New York: Oxford University Press, 2009.

Makdisi, Ussama. *Faith Misplaced.* New York: PublicAffairs, 2011.

Mamdani, Mahmood. *Good Muslim, Bad Muslim: America, the Cold War and the Roots of Terror.* New York: Pantheon, 2004.

Mamoon, Muntassir. *Bengal Partition 1905 and East Bengal.* Translated by Rana Razzaque. Dhaka: Dhaka International Centre for Bengal Studies, 2008.

Mandal, Somdatta. Introduction to K. Das, *Bengali Lady in England,* xiii–xxvi.

Mander, Jenny. "No Woman Is an Island: The Female Figure in French Enlightenment Anthropology." In Knott and Taylor, *Women, Gender and Enlightenment*, 97–116.

Mani, Lata. *Contentious Traditions: The Debate on Sati in Colonial India*. Berkeley: University of California Press, 1998.

Manji, Irshad. *The Trouble with Islam: A Muslim's Call for Reform in Her Faith*. New York: St. Martin's Press, 2004.

Manley, Delarivier [Mrs. Mary de la Rivière]. *Almyna, or The Arabian Vow. A Tragedy: As It Is Acted at the Theatre Royal in the Hay-Market, by Her Majesty's Servants . . . Humbly Inscrib'd to the Right Honourable the Countess of Sandwich*. London : Turner, 1707.

———. *New Atalantis*. 1709. Edited by Rosalind Ballaster. New York: Routledge, 1991.

"Margaret Sanger and Edith How-Martyn: An Intimate Correspondence." Margaret Sanger Papers Project. Accessed 28 April 2020. www.nyu.edu/projects/sanger /articles/ms_and_edith_how_martyn.php.

Mariam, Thahitun. "In the Bronx, Bangladeshi Immigrant Women Convene to Know Their Rights, and Seek Community." Medium. 11 July 2018. https:// medium.com/@thahitun.mariam/in-the-bronx-bangladeshi-immigrant-women -convene-to-know-their-rights-and-seek-community-c701f4fc36b9.

Marshall, Peter James. *Bengal: The British Bridgehead*. Cambridge: Cambridge University Press, 1988.

———. *The Impeachment of Warren Hastings*. New York: Oxford University Press, 1965.

"Maryam Jameelah Papers, 1945–2005." *Archives and Manuscripts*. New York Public Library. Accessed 28 May 2017. http://archives.nypl.org/mss/1545#overview.

Massad, Joseph. *Islam in Liberalism*. Chicago: University of Chicago Press, 2015.

Matar, Nabil. *Europe through Arab Eyes, 1578–1727*. New York: Columbia University Press, 2008.

———, ed. and trans. *In the Lands of the Christians: Arabic Travel Writing in the Seventeenth Century*. New York: Routledge, 2003.

———. "The Representation of Muslim Women in Renaissance England." *Muslim World* 86 (1996): 50–61.

———. *Turks, Moors, and Englishmen in the Age of Discovery*. New York: Columbia University Press, 2000.

Maudoodi, Maulana, and Maryam Jameelah. *Correspondence between Maulana Maudoodi and Maryam Jameelah*. New Delhi: Markazi Maktaba Islam, 1986.

McAlister, Melani. "Suffering Sisters? American Feminists, Global Visions, and the Problem of Female Genital Surgeries." In *Americanism: New Perspectives on the History of an Ideal*, edited by Michael Kazin and Joseph A. McCartin, 242–62. Chapel Hill: University of North Carolina Press, 2006.

McCarthy, Florence E. "Bengali Village Women: Mediators between Tradition and Development." Master's thesis, Michigan State University, 1967.

McClintock, Anne. *Imperial Leather: Race, Gender, and Sexuality in the Colonial Contest*. New York: Routledge, 1995.

McMahon, Robert J. *The Cold War on the Periphery: The United States, India, and Pakistan.* New York: Columbia University Press, 1994.

Medhurst, Martin J. "Eisenhower and the Crusade for Freedom: The Rhetorical Origins of a Cold War Campaign." *Presidential Studies Quarterly* 27, no. 4 (1997): 654–55.

Meek, Ronald L. *Social Science and the Ignoble Savage.* Cambridge: Cambridge University Press, 1976.

Mellor, Anne K. "Sex, Violence, and Slavery: Blake and Wollstonecraft." *Huntington Library Quarterly* 58 (1995): 345–70.

Melman, Billie. *Women's Orients: English Women and the Middle East, 1718–1918.* Ann Arbor: University of Michigan Press, 1992.

Menon, Ritu, and Kamla Bhasin. *Borders and Boundaries: Women in India's Partition.* New Delhi: Kali for Women, 1998.

Metcalf, Barbara D. *Perfecting Women: Maulana Ashraf 'Ali Thanawi's Bihishti Zewar.* Berkeley: University of California Press, 1992.

Metcalf, Barbara D., and Thomas R. Metcalf. *A Concise History of India.* Cambridge: Cambridge University Press, 2002.

Metcalf, Thomas R. *Ideologies of the Raj.* Cambridge: Cambridge University Press, 1994.

Midgley, Clare. *Feminism and Empire: Women Activists in Imperial Britain, 1790–1865.* New York: Routledge, 2007.

———. *Gender and Imperialism.* Manchester: Manchester University Press, 1998.

———. *Women against Slavery: The British Campaigns, 1780–1870.* New York: Routledge, 1992.

Mill, James. *The History of British India.* 6 vols. 3rd ed. 1817. Reprint, London: Baldwin, Cradock, and Joy, 1826.

———. *James Mill: Political Writings.* Edited by Terence Ball. Cambridge: Cambridge University Press, 1992.

Mill, John Stuart. "The Admission of Women to the Electoral Franchise." 20 May 1867. In *The Collected Works of John Stuart Mill.* Vol. 28, *Public and Parliamentary Speeches.* Pt. 1, *November 1850–November 1868,* edited by John M. Robson and Bruce L. Kinzer. London: Routledge and Kegan Paul, 1988.

———. *Autobiography.* 1873. Reprint, New York: Penguin Books, 1989.

———. *The Collected Works of John Stuart Mill.* Vol. 17, *The Later Letters of John Stuart Mill 1849–1873.* Pt. 4. Edited by Francis E. Mineka and Dwight N. Lindley. New York: Routledge/Kegan Paul, 1972. http://oll.libertyfund.org/titles/252.

———. *Memorandum of the Improvements in the Administration of India during the Last Thirty Years.* London: Allen, 1858.

———. *On Liberty and the Subjection of Women.* 1869. Reprint, New York: Penguin Classics, 2006.

———. *Principles of Political Economy with Some of Their Applications to Social Philosophy.* 1909. 7th ed. Reprint, London: Longmans, Green, 1848.

———. *Writings on India.* Toronto: University of Toronto Press, 1990.

Mill, Mrs. Stuart [Harriet Hardy Taylor Mill]. *The Enfranchisement of Women*. 1851. Reprint, London: Trübner, 1868.

Millar, John. *The Origin of the Distinction of Ranks, or An Inquiry into the Circumstances Which Give Rise to Influence and Authority in the Different Members of Society*. Edited by Aaron Garrett. Indianapolis: Liberty Fund, 2006.

Miller, Carly. "Shahana Hanif Is the New Face of Kensington." Bklyner. 5 October 2016. https://bklyner.com/activist-shahana-hanif-muslim-womanhood-disability-justice-growing-kensington-ditmas-park/.

Miller, Cathleen. *Champion of Choice: The Life and Legacy of Women's Advocate Nafis Sadik*. Lincoln: University of Nebraska Press, 2013.

Miller, Elizabeth. "An Open Letter to the Editors of *Ms*. Magazine." 20 April 2002. www.rawa.org/tours/elizabeth_miller_letter.htm.

Mills, Sara. *Discourses of Difference: An Analysis of Women's Travel Writing and Colonialism*. New York: Routledge, 1991.

Mills, Sara, and Indira Ghose. Introduction to Mills and Ghose, *Wanderings of a Pilgrim*, 1–18.

——, eds. *Wanderings of a Pilgrim in Search of the Picturesque*. By Fanny Parkes. 1850. Reprint, Manchester: Manchester University Press, 2001.

Minault, Gail. "Impressions of Europe from Mirza Abu Taleb Khan's *The Travels of Taleb in Foreign Lands*, 1810." Islamfiche. 2004. https://docs.google.com/document/d/1VLlv6XNeJIVjMaF4QpaUewjges73NAImIjEHUl5QSs8/edit.

——. *The Khilafat Movement: Religious Symbolism and Political Mobilization in India*. New York: Columbia University Press, 1982.

——. "Purdah Politics: The Role of Muslim Women in Indian Nationalism, 1911–1924." In *Separate Worlds: Studies of Purdah in South Asia*, edited by Hanna Papanek and Gail Minault, 245–61. New Delhi: Chanakya, 1982.

——. *Secluded Scholars: Women's Education and Muslim Social Reform in Colonial India*. New Delhi: Oxford University Press, 1998.

——. "Shaikh Abdullah, Begam Abdullah and *Sharif* Education for Girls at Aligarh." In *Modernization and Social Change among Muslims in India*, edited by Imtiaz Ahmad, 207–36. New Delhi: Manohar 1983.

Minh-Ha, Trinh T. *Woman, Native, Other*. Bloomington: Indiana University Press, 1989.

"Minute by the Hon'ble T. B. Macaulay, Dated the 2nd February 1835." Columbia University. Accessed 20 May 2020. www.columbia.edu/itc/mealac/pritchett/00generallinks/macaulay/txt_minute_education_1835.html.

"Minutes of Washington Special Actions Group Meeting." Office of the Historian. 6 December 1971. https://history.state.gov/historicaldocuments/frus1969-76v11/d235.

Mir-Hosseini, Ziba. "Beyond 'Islam' vs 'Feminism.'" *IDS Bulletin* 42, no. 1 (2011): 67–77.

Mitra, Durba. *Indian Sex Life: Sexuality and the Colonial Origins of Modern Social Thought*. Princeton: Princeton University Press, 2020.

Mogahed, Dalia, and Youssef Chouhoud. *American Muslim Poll 2017: Muslims at the Crossroads.* Washington, DC: Institute for Social Policy and Understanding, 2017.

Mogahed, Dalia, and Azka Mahmood. *American Muslim Poll 2019: Predicting and Preventing Islamophobia.* Washington, DC: Institute for Social Policy and Understanding, 2019.

Moghadam, Valentine M. *Globalizing Women: Transnational Feminist Networks.* Baltimore: Johns Hopkins University Press, 2005.

Mohanty, Chandra T. "Defining Genealogies: Feminist Reflections on Being South Asian in North America." In Women of South Asian Descent, *Our Feet Walk,* 351–58.

———. *Feminism without Borders: Decolonizing Theory, Practicing Solidarity.* Durham, NC: Duke University Press, 2003.

———. "Under Western Eyes: Feminist Scholarship and Colonial Discourses." *Boundary 2* 12 (1984): 333–58.

Mohanty, Chandra T., Ann Russo, and Lourdes Torres, eds. *Third World Women and the Politics of Feminism.* Bloomington: Indiana University Press, 1991.

Montagu, Mary Wortley. Preface to *Letters of the Right Honourable Lady M--y W---y M----e,* v–xi. 4 vols. 2nd ed. London: Becket and DeHondt, 1763–67.

———. *The Turkish Embassy Letters.* Edited by Teresa Heffernan and Daniel O'Quinn. Peterborough, Canada: Broadview, 2012.

Montesquieu, Charles de. *Montesquieu: The Spirit of the Laws.* 1748. Edited by Anne M. Cohler, Basia Carolyn Miller, and Harold Samuel Stone. Cambridge: Cambridge University Press, 1989.

———. *Persian Letters.* 1721. Edited by Andrew Kahn. Translated by Margaret Mauldon. New York: Oxford University Press, 2008.

Montgomery, Helen Barrett. *Western Women in Eastern Lands.* New York: Macmillan, 1910.

Mookherjee, Nayanika. "Available Motherhood: Legal Technologies, 'State of Exception' and the Dekinning of 'War-Babies' in Bangladesh." *Childhood* 14, no. 3 (2007): 339–54.

———. *The Spectral Wound: Sexual Violence, Public Memories, and the Bangladesh War of 1971.* Durham, NC: Duke University Press, 2015.

Moraga, Cherríe, and Gloria Anzaldúa, eds. *This Bridge Called My Back: Writings by Radical Women of Color.* 4th ed. Albany: State University of New York Press, 2015.

Moran, Mary Catherine. "Between the Savage and the Civil: Dr. John Gregory's Natural History of Femininity." In Knott and Taylor, *Women, Gender and Enlightenment,* 8–29.

Moreland, William Harrison. Introduction to Pelsaert, *Jahangir's India,* ix–xvi.

Morgan, Robin, ed. "Planetary Feminism: The Politics of the 21st Century." In Morgan, *Sisterhood Is Global,* 1–37.

———. *Sisterhood Is Global: The International Women's Movement Anthology.* New York: Anchor Doubleday, 1984.

————. *The Word of a Woman: Feminist Dispatches, 1968–1992.* New York: Norton, 1994.

Morgan, Robin, and Gloria Steinem. "The International Crime of Genital Mutilation." *Ms.* 8, no. 9 (1980): 65–67, 98.

Morgan, Ronald J. *Spanish American Saints and the Rhetoric of Identity, 1600–1810.* Tucson: University of Arizona Press, 2002.

"Move to Partition Punjab and Bengal: Text of Mr. Jinnah's Speech, 4 May 1947." National Archives. Accessed 19 November 2019. www.nationalarchives.gov.uk /wp-content/uploads/2014/03/fo371-635331.jpg.

Mukherjee, Sumita. "The All-Asian Women's Conference 1931: Indian Women and Their Leadership of a Pan-Asian Feminist Organisation." *Women's History Review* 26, no. 3 (2017): 363–81.

Mukhopadhyay, Bhaskar. "Writing Home, Writing Travel: The Poetics and Politics of Dwelling in Bengali Modernity." *Comparative Studies in Society and History* 44 (April 2002): 293–318.

Mukhopadhyay, Subhas. "Open Sesame." In *Crossing Boundaries,* edited by Geeti Sen, 92–99. Hyderabad: Orient Longman, 1997.

Mumtaz, Khawar, and Farida Shaheed. *Women of Pakistan: Two Steps Forward, One Step Back.* London: Zed Books, 1987.

Murphy, Michelle. *Seizing the Means of Reproduction: Entanglements of Health, Feminism, and Technoscience.* Durham, NC: Duke University Press, 2012.

Murshid, Ghulam. *Rassundori Thekey Rokeya: Nari Progotir Eksho Bochhor* [From Rassundari to Rokeya: A century of women's progress]. 1993. Reprint, Dhaka: Aboshor 2013.

————. *Reluctant Debutante: Response of Bengali Women to Modernization, 1849– 1905.* Rajshahi: Sahitya Samad/Rajshahi University, 1983.

Murshid, Tazeen M. *The Sacred and the Secular: Bengal Muslim Discourses, 1871– 1977.* Dhaka: University Press Limited, 1995.

Nader, Laura. "Orientalism, Occidentalism and the Control of Women." *Cultural Dynamics* 2, no. 3 (1989): 323–55.

Naghibi, Nima. *Rethinking Global Sisterhood: Western Feminism and Iran.* Minneapolis: University of Minnesota Press, 2007.

Naples, Nancy A., and Manisha Desai, eds. *Women's Activism and Globalization: Linking Local Struggles and Global Politics.* New York: Routledge, 2002.

Narain, Mona. "Eighteenth-Century Indians' Travel Narratives and Cross-Cultural Encounters with the West." *Literature Compass* 9 (2012): 151–65.

Narayan, Uma. *Dislocating Cultures: Identities, Traditions, and Third World Feminism.* New York: Routledge, 1997.

Nasiruddin, Mohammed. "An Illustrated Weekly for Women and the Establishment of the Begum Club." In Begum, *Nirbachito Begum,* 2693–707.

Nasrin, Taslima. *Meyebala, My Bengali Childhood: A Memoir of Growing Up Female in a Muslim World.* Translated by Gopa Majumdar. Hanover, NH: Steerforth, 2002.

Nazneen, Sohela. *The Women's Movement in Bangladesh: A Short History and Current Debates.* Bonn: Stiftung, 2017.

Nazneen, Sohela, and Maheen Sultan. "Struggling for Survival and Autonomy: Impact of NGO-ization on Women's Organizations in Bangladesh." *Development* 52, no. 2 (2009): 193–99.

Nechtman, Tillman W. *Nabobs: Empire and Identity in Eighteenth-Century Britain.* Cambridge: Cambridge University Press, 2013.

Nelson, Cynthia. *Doria Shafik Egyptian Feminist: A Woman Apart.* Cairo: American University in Cairo Press, 1996.

Netton, Richard. "The Mysteries of Islam." In *Exoticism in the Enlightenment,* edited by George Sebastian Rousseau and Roy Porter, 23–45. Manchester: Manchester University Press, 1989.

Nicholson, Helen. "Women on the Third Crusade." *Journal of Medieval History* 23 (1997): 335–49.

Nicklen, Challen. "Rhetorics of Connection in the United Nations Conferences on Women, 1975–1995." PhD diss., Pennsylvania State University, 2008.

Nijhawan, Shobna. "International Feminism from an Asian Center: The All-Asian Women's Conference (Lahore, 1931) as a Transnational Feminist Moment." *Journal of Women's History* 29, no. 3 (2017): 12–36.

Nnaemeka, Obioma. "If Female Circumcision Did Not Exist, Western Feminism Would Invent It." In *Eye to Eye: Women Practising Development across Cultures,* edited by Susan Perry and Celeste Schenck, 171–89. London: Zed Books, 2001.

"Non-Aligned Movement 4th Summit, 1973, Algiers." Research and Information System for Developing Countries. Accessed 4 January 20201. http://ris.org.in/others/NAM-RIS-Web/NAM%20Declaration%20%26%20Docs/NAM%20Summit-4-Sep%205-9-1973-FinalDocument-AlgiersDeclaration-min.pdf.

Noonan, John T., Jr. "The Bribery of Warren Hastings: The Setting of a Standard for Integrity in Administration." *Hofstra Law Review* 10 (1982): 1073–120.

Norton, Caroline. *English Laws for Women in the Nineteenth Century.* London: printed for private circulation, 1854. https://archive.org/details/cu31924021877802.

Nugent, Maria. *A Journal from the Year 1811 till the Year 1815, Including a Voyage to and Residence in India.* London: Boone, 1839.

Nurmila, Nina. *Women, Islam and Everyday Life: Renegotiating Polygamy in Indonesia.* New York: Routledge, 2009.

Nussbaum, Felicity. *Torrid Zones: Maternity, Sexuality and Empire in Eighteenth-Century English Narratives.* Baltimore: Johns Hopkins University Press, 1995.

O'Barr, Jean F., Irene Tinker, Tami Hultman, Rudo Gaidzanwa, Beverly Guy-Sheftall, Helen Callaway, Amrita Basu, and Alison Bernstein. "Reflections on Forum '85 in Nairobi, Kenya: Voices from the International Women's Studies Community." *Signs* 11, no. 3 (1986): 584–608.

O'Brien, Karen. *Women and Enlightenment in Eighteenth-Century Britain.* Cambridge: Cambridge University Press, 2009.

Offen, Karen. "Defining Feminism: A Comparative Historical Approach." *Signs* 14 (1988): 119–57.

———, ed. *Globalizing Feminisms*. New York: Routledge, 2009.

———. "Was Mary Wollstonecraft a Feminist? A Comparative Re-reading of *A Vindication of the Rights of Woman, 1792–1992*." In Offen, *Globalizing Feminisms*, 5–17.

Olcott, Jocelyn. *International Women's Year: The Greatest Consciousness-Raising Event in History*. New York: Oxford University Press, 2017.

Omran, Abdel R. *Family Planning in the Legacy of Islam*. New York: Routledge, 1992.

Ong, Aihwa. "Colonialism and Modernity: Feminist Representations of Women in Non-Western Societies." *Inscriptions: Journal for the Critique of Colonial Discourse* 3–4 (1988): 79–93.

O'Quinn, Daniel. *Staging Governance: Theatrical Imperialism in London, 1770–1800*. Baltimore: Johns Hopkins University Press, 2005.

Orme, Richard. *History of the Military Transactions of the British Nation in Indostan, from the Year 1745*. Madras: Pharoah, 1861–62.

Paget, Karen M. *Patriotic Betrayal: The Inside Story of the CIA's Secret Campaign to Enroll American Students in the Crusade against Communism*. New Haven, CT: Yale University Press, 2015.

Papanek, Hanna. "The Work of Women: Postscript from Mexico City." *Signs* 1, no. 1 (1975): 215–26.

"Papers of the Committee of Correspondence." *Archives Unbound*. Sophia Smith Collection, Smith College. Accessed 7 January 2017. https://libraries.smith.edu/research-tools/smith-digital-collections/sophia-smith-collection-womens-history.

Parker, Kenneth, ed. *Early Modern Tales of Orient: A Critical Anthology*. New York: Routledge, 1999.

Parkes, Fanny. *Begums, Thugs, and White Mughals: The Journals of Fanny Parkes*. Edited by William Dalrymple. London: Eland, 2002.

———. *Wanderings of a Pilgrim in Search of the Picturesque, during Four-and-Twenty Years in the East; With Revelations of Life in the Zenana*. 2 vols. London: Pelham Richardson, 1850.

Parkinson, Brian. "A Creole in Cairo: Judge Pierre Crabitès' Thoughts on the Middle East." *Louisiana History* 49, no. 3 (2008): 315–34.

Parsons, Monique. "What These Muslim Activists Found at the Women's March." Religion and Politics. 5 February 2019. https://religionandpolitics.org/2019/02/05/what-these-muslim-activists-found-at-the-womens-march/.

Parveen, Shahida. *Shamsun Nahar Mahmud o Shamokalin Narishomajer Agrogoti* [Shamsun Nahar Mahmud and contemporary women's advancement]. Dhaka: Bangla Academy, 2012.

Patterson, Tiffany R., and Angela M. Gillam. "Out of Egypt: A Talk with Nawal El Saadawi." In *Women, Work, and Gender Relations in Developing Countries,* edited by Parvin Ghorayshi and Claire Bélanger, 31–39. Westport, CT: Greenwood, 1996.

Pavarala, Vinod. "Cultures of Corruption and the Corruption of Culture: The East India Company and the Hastings Impeachment." In *Corrupt Histories,* edited by Emmanuel Kreike and William C. Jordan, 291–336. Rochester, NY: University of Rochester Press, 2005.

Peirce, Leslie. *The Imperial Harem: Women and Sovereignty in the Ottoman Empire.* New York: Oxford University Press, 1993.

Pelsaert, Francisco. *Jahangir's India: The Remonstrantie of Francisco Pelsaert.* Translated by William Harrison Moreland and Pieter Geyl. Cambridge: Heffer and Sons, 1925.

Perkins, Jane Grey. *The Life of the Honourable Mrs. Norton.* New York: Holt, 1909.

Pernau, Margaret. "Motherhood and Female Identity: Religious Advice Literature for Women in German Catholicism and Indian Islam." In *Family and Gender: Changing Values in Germany and India,* edited by Margrit Pernau, Imtiaz Ahmed, and Helmut Reifeld, 140–61. New Delhi: Sage, 2003.

Perry, Ruth. *The Celebrated Mary Astell: An Early English Feminist.* Chicago: University of Chicago Press, 1986.

———. "The Veil of Chastity: Mary Astell's Feminism." In *Sexuality in Eighteenth-Century Britain,* edited by Paul-Gabriel Boucé, 141–58. Manchester: Manchester University Press, 1982.

Peterson, Esther. "Working Women." *Daedalus* 93, no. 2 (1964): 671–99.

Phillips, George. "Mahuan's Account of the Kingdom of Bengala (Bengal)." *Journal of the Royal Asiatic Society of Great Britain and Ireland,* July 1895, 523–35.

Pires, Tomé. *Suma Oriental of Tomé Pires and the Book of Francisco Rodrigues.* Edited and translated by Armando Cortesão. 1515. Reprint, London: Hakluyt Society, 1944.

Pitts, Jennifer. *A Turn to Empire: The Rise of Imperial Liberalism in Britain and France.* Princeton: Princeton University Press, 2005.

Podur, Justin. "A Multifaceted Fraud." Anti-Empire Project. 5 December 2003. https://podur.org/2003/12/05/a-multifaceted-fraud-reviewing-irshad-manjis-trouble-with-islam/.

Pogrebin, Abigail. "How Do You Spell Ms." *New York Magazine,* November 2011. http://nymag.com/news/features/ms-magazine-2011-11/index2.html.

Poovey, Mary. *Uneven Developments: The Ideological Work of Gender in Mid-Victorian England.* Chicago: University of Chicago Press, 1988.

Popa, Raluca Maria. "Translating Equality between Women and Men across Cold War Divides." In *Gender Politics and Everyday Life in State Socialist East and Central Europe,* edited by Jill Massino and Shana Penn, 59–74. New York: Palgrave Macmillan, 2009.

Pope, Alexander. *The Correspondence of Alexander Pope.* Edited by George Sherburn. 5 vols. Oxford: Clarendon, 1956.

Powell, Avril A. "Islamic Modernism and Women's Status: The Influence of Syed Ameer Ali." In Powell and Lambert-Hurley, *Rhetoric and Reality,* 282–317.

———. *Muslims and Missionaries in Pre-mutiny India*. 1993. Reprint, London: Routledge, 2003.

Powell, Avril A., and Siobhan Lambert-Hurley, eds. *Rhetoric and Reality: Gender and the Colonial Experience in South Asia*. New York: Oxford University Press, 2006.

Prakash, Om. "The Dutch East India Company in Bengal: Trade Privileges and Problems, 1633–1712." *Indian Economic and Social History Review* 9, no. 3 (1972): 258–87.

Prange, Sebastian R. *Monsoon Islam: Trade and Faith on the Medieval Malabar Coast*. Cambridge: Cambridge University Press, 2018.

Prashad, Vijay. *The Darker Nations: A People's History of the Third World*. New Press, 2007.

Pratt, Mary Louise. *Imperial Eyes: Travel Writing and Transculturation*. London: Routledge, 1992.

Purchas, Samuel, ed. *Hakluytus Posthumus, or Purchas His Pilgrimes*. 20 vols. Glasgow: Maclehose and Sons, 1905–7.

Quayum, Mohammad A. *The Essential Rokeya*. Leiden: Brill, 2013.

Quraishi, Uzma. *Redefining the Immigrant South: Indian and Pakistani Immigration to Houston during the Cold War*. Chapel Hill: University of North Carolina Press, 2020.

Rabasa, Angel, Cheryl Benard, Lowell H. Schwartz, and Peter Sickle. *Building Moderate Muslim Networks*. Santa Monica, CA: RAND Center for Middle East Policy, 2007.

Raghavan, Srinath. *A Global History of the Creation of Bangladesh*. Cambridge, MA: Harvard University Press, 2013.

Rahman, Munjulika. "Urban Dance in Bangladesh: History, Identity, and the Nation." PhD diss., Northwestern University, 2013.

Ramusack, Barbara N. "Cultural Missionaries, Maternal Imperialists, Feminist Allies: British Women Activists in India, 1865–1945." *Women's Studies International Forum* 13 (1990): 309–21.

Randall, Anne Frances [Mary Darby Robinson]. *A Letter to the Women of England, on the Injustice of Mental Subordination*. London: Longman and Rees, 1799.

Randolph, Sherie M. *Florynce "Flo" Kennedy: The Life of a Black Feminist Radical*. Chapel Hill: University of North Carolina Press, 2015.

Raper, Arthur F. *Rural Development in Action: The Comprehensive Experiment at Comilla, East Pakistan*. Ithaca, NY: Cornell University Press, 1970.

Rathore, Naeem G. *The Pakistan Student*. New York: American Friends of the Middle East, 1957.

Ravenholt, Reimert T. "World Population Crisis and Resolution: Taking Contraceptives to the World's Poor Creation of USAID's Population/Family Planning Program, 1965–80." Accessed 8 August 2017. www.ravenholt.com.

Ray, Bharati, ed. *Bamabodhini Patrika, 1270–1329 BS*. Calcutta: Women's Studies Research Center, Calcutta University, 1994.

———. *Early Feminists of Colonial India: Sarala Devi Chaudhurani and Rokeya Sakhawat Hossain.* New Delhi: Oxford University Press, 2002.

———, ed. *From the Seams of History: Essays on Indian Women.* New Delhi: Oxford University Press, 1995.

———. "A Voice of Protest: The Writings of Rokeya Shakhawat Hossain (1880–1932)." in Ray, *Women of India,* 427–53.

———, ed. *Women of India: Colonial and Post-colonial Periods.* New Delhi: Sage, 2005.

Raychaudhuri, Tapan. *Bengal under Akbar and Jahangir: An Introductory Study in Social History.* 1953. Reprint, New Delhi: Munshiram Manoharlal, 1969.

———. *Europe Reconsidered: Perceptions of the West in Nineteenth-Century Bengal.* New York: Oxford University Press, 1988.

Razack, Sherene. *Casting Out: The Eviction of Muslims from Western Law and Politics.* University of Toronto Press, 2008.

Reeves, Richard. *John Stuart Mill: Victorian Firebrand.* London: Atlantic Books, 2007.

Reid, Helen Dwight. "Review of *Women and the New East,* by Ruth Frances Woodsmall." *World Affairs* 123, no. 4 (1960): 124.

Reid, Susan. "Cold War in the Kitchen: Gender and the De-Stalinization of Consumer Taste in the Soviet Union under Khrushchev." *Slavic Review* 61, no. 2 (2002): 223–24.

Rendall, Jane. "'The Grand Causes Which Combine to Carry Mankind Forward': Wollstonecraft, History and Revolution." *Women's Writing* 4 (1997): 155–72.

———. "Scottish Orientalism: From Robertson to James Mill." *Historical Journal* 25, no. 1 (1982): 43–69.

Revividus, Junius [William Bridges Adams]. "On the Condition of Women in England." *Monthly Repository* 7 (1833): 217–31.

Reynolds, Nicole. "Phebe Gibbes, Edmund Burke, and the Trials of Empire." *Eighteenth Century Fiction* 20 (Winter 2007–8): 151–76.

Riaz, Ali, ed. *(Re)reading Taslima Nasrin.* Dhaka: Shrabon Prokashani, 2009.

———. "Taslima Nasrin: Breaking the Structured Silence." *Bulletin of Concerned Asian Scholars* 27, no. 1 (1995): 21–27.

Rich, Adrienne. "The Anti-feminist Woman." *New York Review of Books,* 30 November 1972. www.nybooks.com/articles/1972/11/30/the-anti-feminist-woman/.

Richter, Julius. *A History of Missions in India.* Edinburgh: Oliphant, 1908.

Robert, Dana Lee. *American Women in Mission: A Social History of Their Thought and Practice.* Macon, GA: Mercer University Press, 1996.

Robertson, Karen. "A Stranger Bride: Mariam Khan and the East India Company." In Akhimie and Andrea, *Travel and Travail,* 41–63.

Robinson, Nicholas K. *Edmund Burke: A Life in Caricature.* New Haven, CT: Yale University Press, 1996.

Robinson-Dunn, Diane. *The Harem, Slavery and British Imperial Culture: Anglo-Muslim Relations in the Late Nineteenth Century.* New York: Palgrave, 2006.

Robson, Ann. "Harriet Hardy Taylor Mill." In *Victorian Britain: An Encyclopedia,* edited by Sally Mitchell, 502. New York: Routledge, 2011.

Roebuck, Thomas. *The Annals of the College of Fort William.* Calcutta: Hindoostanee, 1819.

Rogers, Katharine M. *Feminism in Eighteenth-Century England.* Champaign: University of Illinois Press, 1982.

Roosevelt, Eleanor. *India and the Awakening East.* New York: Harper and Brothers, 1953.

Rossi, Alice S. "Equality between the Sexes: An Immodest Proposal." *Daedalus* 93, no. 2 (1964): 607–8.

Rostami-Povey, Elaheh. "Gender, Agency and Identity, the Case of Afghan Women in Afghanistan, Pakistan and Iran." *Journal of Development Studies* 43, no. 2 (2007): 294–311.

Rotter, Andrew J. "Christians, Muslims, and Hindus: Religion and U.S.-South Asian Relations, 1947–1954." *Diplomatic History* 24, no. 4 (2000): 593–613.

———. "South Asia." In *The Oxford Handbook of the Cold War,* edited by Richard H. Immerman and Petra Goedde, 212–29. New York: Oxford University Press, 2013.

Roudakova, Natalia, and Deborah S. Ballard-Reisch. "Femininity and the Double Burden: Dialogues on the Socialization of Russian Daughters into Womanhood." *Anthropology of East Europe Review* 17, no. 1 (1999): 21–34.

Rousseau, Jean-Jacques. *Emile, or On Education.* Translated by Allan Bloom. New York: Basic Books, 1979.

Roy, Kaushik. *Brown Warriors of the Raj.* New Delhi: Manohar, 2008.

Roy, Raja Rammohun. *The English Works of Raja Rammohun Roy.* Edited by Jogendra Chunder Ghose. 3 vols. Calcutta: Srikanta Roy, 1901.

Rubinstein, David. *A Different World for Women: The Life of Millicent Garrett Fawcett.* New York: Harvester Wheatsheaf, 1991.

Rupp, Leila J. "Challenging Imperialism in International Women's Organizations, 1888–1945." *NWSA Journal* 8, no. 1 (1996): 8–27.

———. *Worlds of Women: The Making of an International Women's Movement.* Princeton: Princeton University Press, 1997.

Ruskin, John. *Sesame and Lilies.* Smith, Elder, 1865.

Russo, Ann. "The Feminist Majority Foundation's Campaign to Stop Gender Apartheid." *International Feminist Journal of Politics* 8, no. 4 (2006): 557–80.

Ryan, Alan. *On Politics: A History of Political Thought from Herodotus to the Present.* 2 vols. New York: Liveright, 2012.

Saber, Majeda. "Khujista Akhtar Banu." In Hossain and Masuduzzaman, *Gender Bishwakosh,* 2:438–39.

Sabur, Seuty. "Post Card from Shahabag." ISA e-Symposium for Sociology. March 2012. www.isa-sociology.org/uploads/files/EBul-Sabur-March2012.pdf.

Sadler, Amanda. "Did Shepard Fairey Whitewash the Muslim Women's March Poster?" Muslim Girl. Accessed 27 November 2020. http://muslimgirl.com/37055/shepard-fairey-tokenizing-muslim-woman/.

Said, Edward W. *Culture and Imperialism*. New York: Knopf, 1993.
———. *Orientalism*. New York: Pantheon Books, 1978.
Saikia, Yasmin. *Women, War, and the Making of Bangladesh: Remembering 1971*. Durham, NC: Duke University Press, 2011.
Sajjad, Tazreena. "Political-Social Movements: Community-Based; Afghanistan." In *Encyclopedia of Women and Islamic Cultures, 2010–2020*, edited by Suad Joseph. Vol. 5. Leiden: Brill, forthcoming.
Salam, Abdus. *Physical Education in India*. Calcutta: Newman, 1895.
Salem, Sara. "On Transnational Feminist Solidarity: The Case of Angela Davis in Egypt." *Signs* 43, no. 2 (2017): 245–67.
Salomon, Carol. "Baul Songs." In *Religions of India in Practice*, edited by Donald Lopez, 187–208. Princeton: Princeton University Press, 1995.
Salomyn, Shay, and Shireen Huq. "Interview: Women Move Forward in Bangladesh." *off our backs* 22, no. 3 (1992): 12–15.
Sandell, Marie. *The Rise of Women's Transnational Activism: Identity and Sisterhood between the World Wars*. London: Tauris, 2015.
Sangari, Kumkum, and Sudesh Vaid, eds. *Recasting Women: Essays in Indian Colonial History*. New Brunswick, NJ: Rutgers University Press, 1990.
Saogat 11, no. 9 (1935). Accessed 14 April 2020. http://crossasia-repository.ub.uni-heidelberg.de/2696/1/SAOGAT_VOL_11_NO_9.pdf.
Sarkar, Jadunath. *The History of Bengal*. Vol. 2, *The Muslim Period, 1200–1757*. Dacca: University of Dacca, 1948.
Sarkar, Mahua. *Visible Histories, Disappearing Women: Producing Muslim Womanhood in Late Colonial Bengal*. Durham, NC: Duke University Press, 2008.
Sarkar, Sumit. *The Swadeshi Movement in Bengal, 1903–1908*. New Delhi: People's, 1973.
Sarkar, Tanika. "Birth of a Goddess: 'Vande Mataram,' 'Anandamath,' and Hindu Nationhood." *Economic and Political Weekly* 41, no. 37 (2006): 3959–69.
———. Foreword to Chakravartty, *Coming Out of Partition*, vii–x.
———. *Hindu Wife, Hindu Nation: Community, Religion, and Cultural Nationalism*. Bloomington: Indiana University Press, 2002.
———. *Words to Win: The Making of "Amar Jiban": A Modern Autobiography*. New Delhi: Kali for Women, 1999.
Sattar, Ellen. "Demographic Features of Bangladesh with Reference to Women and Children." In Women for Women, *Situation of Women*, 1–34.
Sayers, Dorothy L. *The Song of Roland*. Harmondsworth: Penguin Books, 1957.
Scherer, Mary Alice. "Annette Akroyd Beveridge: Victorian Reformer, Oriental Scholar." PhD diss., Ohio State University, 1995.
Schreiber, Adele, and Margaret Mathieson. *Journey towards Freedom: Written for the Jubilee of the International Alliance of Women*. Copenhagen: International Alliance of Women, 1955.
Schwarzkopf, Jutta. *Women in the Chartist Movement*. New York: St. Martin's Press, 1991.

Scott, Joan W. *Gender and the Politics of History.* New York: Columbia University Press, 1999.

Scott, John, and Thomas Park. *The Poetical Works of John Scott.* London: Sharpe, 1808.

Sebastiani, Silvia. *The Scottish Enlightenment: Race, Gender, and the Limits of Progress.* New York: Palgrave Macmillan, 2013.

Secor, Anna. "Orientalism, Gender and Class in Lady Mary Wortley Montagu's *Turkish Embassy Letters: To Persons of Distinction, Men of Letters &C.*" *Ecumene* 6 (1999): 375–98.

"Self Help: A Revolution in Women's Health." Feminist Women's Health Center News. September 2002. www.fwhc.org/health/self.htm.

Sen, Amrita. "Sailing to India: Women, Travel, and Crisis in the Seventeenth Century." In Akhimie and Andrea, *Travel and Travail,* 64–80.

———. "Traveling Companions: Women, Trade, and the Early East India Company." *Genre* 48, no. 2 (2015): 193–214.

Sen, Gita, and Caren Grown. *Development, Crises and Alternative Visions: Third World Women's Perspectives.* New York: Monthly Review Press, 1987.

Sen, Keshub Chunder. *Keshub Chunder Sen's English Visit.* Edited by Sophia Dobson Collet. London: Strahan, 1871.

Sen, Krishna. "Lessons in Self-Fashioning: *Bamabodhini Patrika* and the Education of Women in Colonial Bengal." *Victorian Periodicals Review* 37 (2004): 176–91.

Sen, Simonti. *Travels to Europe: Self and Other in Bengali Travel Narratives, 1870–1910.* Hyderabad: Orient Longman, 2005.

Sen, Tansen. "The Formation of Chinese Maritime Networks to Southern Asia, 1200–1450." *Journal of the Economic and Social History of the Orient* 49, no. 4 (2006): 421–53.

Sengupta, Parna. *Pedagogy for Religion: Missionary Education and the Fashioning of Hindus and Muslims in Bengal.* Berkeley: University of California Press, 2011.

Shahjahan, Nawab. *The Táj-ul Ikbál Tárikh Bhopal, or The History of Bhopal.* Calcutta: Thacker, Spink, 1876.

Shaikh, Ghulam Fatima. *Footprints in Time: Reminiscences of a Sindhi Matriarch.* Translated by Rasheeda Husain. New Delhi: Oxford University Press, 2012.

Shanley, Mary Lyndon. *Feminism, Marriage, and the Law in Victorian England, 1850–1895.* Princeton: Princeton University Press, 1989.

Sharify-Funk, Meena. *Encountering the Transnational: Women, Islam and the Politics of Interpretation.* New York: Routledge, 2016.

Sharpe, Jenny. *Allegories of Empire: The Figure of Women in the Colonial Text.* Minneapolis: University of Minnesota Press, 1993.

Shehabuddin, Elora. "Contesting the Illicit: Gender and the Politics of Fatwas in Bangladesh." *Signs* 24, no. 4 (1999): 1011–44.

———. "Fatwa: An Overview." In Joseph, *Encyclopedia of Women,* 2:171–74.

———. "Gender and the Figure of the 'Moderate Muslim': Feminism in the 21st Century." In *The Question of Gender: Engagements with Joan W. Scott's Critical*

Feminism, edited by Judith Butler and Elizabeth Weed, 102–42. Bloomington: Indiana University Press, 2011.

———. *Reshaping the Holy: Democracy, Development, and Muslim Women in Bangladesh.* New York: Columbia University Press, 2008.

Shephard, Alexandra. *Accounting for Oneself: Worth, Status, and the Social Order in Early Modern England.* New York: Oxford University Press, 2015.

Shklar, Judith. "Montesquieu and the New Repubublicanism." In *Machiavelli and Republicanism,* edited by Gisela Bock, Quentin Skinner, and Maurizio Viroli, 265–79. Cambridge: Cambridge University Press, 1993.

"Short History of CEDAW Convention." UN Women. Accessed 25 November 2020. www.un.org/womenwatch/daw/cedaw/history.htm.

Sicherman, Barbara, and Carol Hurd Green. *Notable American Women: The Modern Period; A Biographical Dictionary.* Cambridge, MA: Harvard University Press, 1980.

Siddiqi, Dina M. "Do Bangladeshi Factory Workers Need Saving? Sisterhood in the Post-sweatshop Era." *Feminist Review* 91 (2009): 154–74.

———. "Left behind by the Nation: 'Stranded Pakistanis' in Bangladesh." *Sites* 10, no. 2 (2013): 150–83.

———. "Miracle Worker or Womanmachine? Tracking (Trans)National Realities in Bangladeshi Factories." *Economic and Political Weekly* 35, nos. 21–22 (2000): L11–17.

———. "Solidarity, Sexuality, and Saving Muslim Women in Neoliberal Times." *Women's Studies Quarterly* 42, nos. 3–4 (2014): 292–306.

———. "Taslima Nasreen and Others: The Contest over Gender in Bangladesh." In Bodman and Tohidi, *Women in Muslim Societies,* 205–28.

Sinha, Mrinalini. "'Chathams, Pitts, and Gladstones in Petticoats': The Politics of Gender and Race in the Ilbert Bill Controversy, 1883–1884." In Chaudhuri and Strobel, *Western Women and Imperialism,* 98–116.

———. *Colonial Masculinity: The "Manly Englishman" and the "Effeminate Bengali" in the Late Nineteenth Century.* Manchester: Manchester University Press, 1995.

———. "Nations in an Imperial Crucible." In Levine, *Gender and Empire,* 181–202.

———. "Reading *Mother India*: Empire, Nation, and the Female Voice." *Journal of Women's History* 6, no. 2 (1994): 6–44.

———. "Refashioning Mother India: Feminism and Nationalism in Late-Colonial India," *Feminist Studies* 26, no. 3 (2000): 623–44.

———. *Specters of Mother India: The Global Restructuring of an Empire.* Durham, NC: Duke University Press, 2006.

———. "Suffragism and Internationalism: The Enfranchisement of British and Indian Women under an Imperial State." *Indian Economic and Social History Review* 36, no 4 (1999): 461–84.

Sinha, Narendra Krishna. *The Economic History of Bengal: From Plassey to the Permanent Settlement.* 3rd ed. 3 vols. Calcutta: Mukhopadhyay, 1965–68.

Sinha, Pradip. *Calcutta in Urban History.* Calcutta: Mukhopadhyay, 1978.

Sklar, Kathryn Kish. "How and Why Did Women in SNCC (the Student Non-

Violent Coordinating Committee) Author a Pathbreaking Feminist Manifesto, 1964–1965?" *Women and Social Movements in the United States, 1600–2000.* Alexander Street. Accessed 24 November 2020. https://womhist.alexanderstreet.com /SNCC/intro.htm#eightyfour.

Sklar, Kathryn Kish, and James Brewer Stewart, eds. *Women's Rights and Transatlantic Antislavery in the Era of Emancipation.* New Haven, CT: Yale University Press, 2007.

Skuy, David. "Macaulay and the Indian Penal Code of 1862." *Modern Asian Studies* 32, no. 3 (1998): 513–57.

Smart, Jean. "Letter from a Lady in Madrass to Her Friends in London." In *Vestiges of Old Madras, 1640–1800,* edited by Henry Davison Love, 2:282–84. 4 vols. London: Murray, 1913.

Smith, Hilda L. *Reason's Disciples: Seventeenth-Century English Feminists.* Champaign: University of Illinois Press, 1982.

Smuckler, Ralph H. *A University Turns to the World.* East Lansing: Michigan State University Press, 2002.

Snaith, Anna. "Race, Empire, and Ireland." In *Virginia Woolf in Context,* edited by Bryony Randall and Jane Goldman, 206–18. Cambridge: Cambridge University Press, 2012.

Sneider, Allison L. *Suffragists in an Imperial Age: U.S. Expansion and the Woman Question, 1870–1929.* New York: Oxford University Press, 2008.

Sommer, Annie Van, and Samuel M. Zwemer, eds. *Our Moslem Sisters: A Cry of Need from Lands of Darkness.* New York: Revell, 1907.

Sonbol, Amira. "A Response to Muslim Countries' Reservations against Full Implementation of CEDAW." *Hawwa* 8, no. 3 (2010): 348–67.

Southard, Barbara. "Bengal Women's Education League: Pressure Group and Professional Association." *Modern Asian Studies* 18, no. 1 (1984): 55–88.

———. "Colonial Politics and Women's Rights: Woman Suffrage Campaigns in Bengal, British India in the 1920s." *Modern Asian Studies* 27, no. 2 (1993): 397–439.

Sowaal, Alice, and Penny A. Weiss, eds. *Feminist Interpretations of Mary Astell.* University Park, PA: Penn State University Press, 2016.

"Speech of Senator John F. Kennedy, Cow Palace, San Francisco, CA." American Presidency Project. 2 November 1960. www.presidency.ucsb.edu/ws/index.php ?pid=25928.

Spivak, Gayatri Chakravorty. "Three Women's Texts and a Critique of Imperialism." *Critical Inquiry* 12 (1985): 243–61.

Sprint, John. *The Bride-Woman's Counsellor: Being a Sermon Preached at a Wedding, May the 11th, 1699, at She[r]Bourn in Dorsetshire.* London: Bowyer, 1700.

Stansell, Christine. *The Feminist Promise: 1792 to the Present.* New York: Modern Library, 2010.

Steinbach, Susie. "Can We Still Use 'Separate Spheres'? British History 25 Years after Family Fortunes." *History Compass* 10, no. 11 (2012): 826–37.

Steinem, Gloria. *Outrageous Acts and Everyday Rebellions.* New York: Holt Paperbacks, 1995.

Stepan, Nancy. *The Idea of Race in Science: Great Britain, 1800–1960*. Hamden, CT: Archon Books, 1982.

Stephens, Julie. "Feminist Fictions: A Critique of the Category 'Non-Western Women' in Feminist Writings on Indian Women." In *Subaltern Studies VI,* edited by Ranajit Guha, 92–131. New York: Oxford University Press, 1989.

Stevenson, Catherine B. *Victorian Women Travel Writers in Africa*. Boston: Twayne, 1982.

Stewart, Charles. Preface to Abu Taleb Khan, *Travels,* 1:v–viii.

Stewart, Tony K. "In Search of Equivalence: Conceiving Muslim-Hindu Encounter through Translation Theory." *History of Religions* 40, no. 3 (2001): 260–87.

Stienstra, Deborah. *Women's Movements and International Organizations*. New York: St. Martin's Press, 1994.

Stiglmayer, Alexandra. *Mass Rape: The War against Women in Bosnia-Herzegovina.* Translated by Marion Faber. Lincoln: University of Nebraska Press, 1994.

Still, Judith. "Hospitable Harems? A European Woman and Oriental Spaces in the Enlightenment." *Paragraph* 32 (2009): 87–104.

Stock, A. Geraldine. *Memoirs of Dacca University, 1947–1951*. Dacca: Green Book House, 1973.

Storrow, Edward. *The Eastern Lily Gathered: A Memoir of Bala Shoondoree Tagore.* 2nd ed. London: Snow, 1856.

Stossel, Scott. *Sarge: The Life and Times of Sargent Shriver*. Washington, DC: Smithsonian Books, 2004.

Stowasser, Barbara. *Women in the Qur'an, Traditions, and Interpretations*. New York: Oxford University Press, 1994.

Strachey, Lytton. *Queen Victoria*. New York: Harcourt Brace, 1921.

Strachey, Ray. *The Cause: A Short History of the Women's Movement in Great Britain.* 1928. Reprint, Port Washington, NY: Kennikat, 1969.

Stretton, Tim, and Krista J. Kesselring, eds. *Married Women and the Law: Coverture in England and the Common Law World*. Montreal: McGill-Queen's University Press, 2013.

Subrahmanyam, Sanjay. *Empires between Islam and Christianity, 1500–1800*. Albany: State University of New York Press, 2019.

———. *Europe's India: Words, People, Empires, 1500–1800*. Cambridge, MA: Harvard University Press, 2017.

———. *Improvising Empire: Portuguese Trade and Settlement in the Bay of Bengal, 1500–1700*. New York: Oxford University Press, 1990.

———. *The Portuguese Empire in Asia, 1500–1700*. Hoboken, NJ: Wiley-Blackwell, 2012.

———. "Taking Stock of the Franks: South Asian Views of Europeans and Europe, 1500–1800." *Indian Economic and Social History Review* 42 (2005): 69–100.

Suleri, Sara. *The Rhetoric of English India*. Chicago: University of Chicago Press, 1992.

Sullivan, Zohreh T. "Eluding the Feminist, Overthrowing the Modem? Transformations in Twentieth-Century Iran." In Abu-Lughod, *Remaking Women,* 215–42.

Swarr, Amanda, and Richa Nagar, eds. *Critical Transnational Feminist Praxis.* Albany: State University of New York Press, 2010.

Tabari, Azar. "The Enigma of Veiled Iranian Women." *Feminist Review* 5 (1980): 19–31.

Tanjeem, Nafisa. "Social Media and Conformist Voluntarism in the Neoliberal Era: The Case of Rana Plaza Collapse in Savar, Bangladesh." In *Revealing Gender Inequalities and Perceptions in South Asian Countries,* edited by Nazmunnessa Mahtab, Sara Parker, Farah Kabir, Tania Haque, Aditi Sabur, and Abu Saleh Mohammad Sowad, 57–79. Hershey, PA: IGI Global, 2016.

Tarafdar, Momtazur Rahman. *Husain Shahi Bengal, 1494–1538 AD.* Dacca: Asiatic Society of Pakistan, 1965.

———. *Trade, Technology and Society in Medieval Bengal.* Dhaka: International Centre for Bengal Studies, 1995.

Targett, Simon. "She Who Makes Holy Men Fume." *Times Higher Education,* February 1995. www.timeshighereducation.com/news/she-who-makes-holy-men -fume/96825.article.

Tavakoli-Targhi, Mohamad. "Imagining Western Women: Orientalism and Auto-eroticism." *Radical America* 24 (1993): 73–87.

Tax, Meredith. "Taslima's Pilgrimage." *Nation,* 31 October 2002. www.thenation .com/article/taslimas-pilgrimage/.

Taylor, Barbara. "Enlightenment and the Uses of Woman." *History Workshop Journal* 74 (Autumn 2012): 79–87.

———. *Eve and the New Jerusalem.* London: Virago, 1983.

———. "Feminism and the Enlightenment, 1650–1850." *History Workshop Journal* 47 (Spring 1999): 261–72.

———. "Feminists versus Gallants: Manners and Morals in Enlightenment Britain." *Representations* 87 (2004): 125–48.

———. "The Religious Foundations of Mary Wollstonecraft's Feminism." In *The Cambridge Companion to Mary Wollstonecraft,* edited by Claudia Johnson, 99–118. Cambridge: Cambridge University Press, 2002.

Taylor, Debbie, ed. *Women: A World Report.* London: Methuen, 1985.

Taylor, Miles. "David Urquhart (1805–1877), Diplomatist and Writer." In *Oxford Dictionary of National Biography,* edited by David Cannadine. Oxford: Oxford University Press, 2004.

Teltscher, Kate. *India Inscribed: European and British Writing on India, 1600–1800.* New York: Oxford University Press, 1995.

Terry, Edward. *A Voyage to East: India.* London: T. W. for Martin and Allestrye, 1655.

"Text of the Convention." UN Women. Accessed 31 July 2017. www.un.org /womenwatch/daw/cedaw/cedaw.htm.

Tharu, Susie. "Tracing Savitri's Pedigree: Victorian Racism and the Image of the

Woman in Indo-Anglian Literature." In Sangari and Vaid, *Recasting Women,* 254–68.

Thomas, Antoine Léonard. *An Essay on the Character, the Manners, and the Understanding of Women, in Different Ages: Translated from the French of Mons. Thomas, by Mrs. Kindersley; With Two Original Essays.* London: Dodsley, 1781.

Thompson, William. *Appeal of One Half the Human Race, Women, against the Pretensions of the Other Half, Men, to Retain Them in Political, and Thence in Civil and Domestic, Slavery: In Reply to a Paragraph of Mr. Mill's Celebrated "Article on Government."* London: Longman, Hurst, Rees, Orme, Brown and Green, 1825.

Tifft, Susan, Jane O'Reilly, and Maryanne Vollers. "The Triumphant Spirit of Nairobi." *Time,* 5 August 1985, 38.

Tignor, Robert. "Lord Cromer on Islam." *Muslim World* 52, no. 3 (1962): 223–33.

Tinker, Irene. "Challenging Wisdom, Changing Policies: The Women in Development Movement." In Fraser and Tinker, *Developing Power,* 65–77.

Tinker, Irene, and Jane Jaquette. "UN Decade for Women: Its Impact and Legacy." *World Development* 15, no. 3 (1987): 419–27.

Tolmacheva, Marina A. "Concubines on the Road: Ibn Battuta's Slave Women." In *Concubines and Courtesans: Women and Slavery in Islamic History,* edited by Matthew S. Gordon and Kathryn A. Hain, 163–89. New York: Oxford University Press, 2017.

———. "Ibn Battuta on Women's Travel in the Dar al-Islam." In *Women and the Journey: The Female Travel Experience,* edited by Bonnie Frederick and Susan H. McLeod, 119–40. Pullman: Washington State University Press, 1993.

Tomaselli, Sylvana. "The Enlightenment Debate on Women." *History Workshop Journal* 20 (1985): 101–24.

Toor, Saadia. "Imperialist Feminism Redux." *Dialectical Anthropology* 36, no. 3 (2012): 147–60.

———. *The State of Islam: Culture and Cold War Politics in Pakistan.* London: Pluto, 2011.

Travers, Robert. "The Eighteenth Century in Indian History." *Eighteenth-Century Studies* 40 (Spring 2007): 492–508.

Trevelyan, G. Otto. *The Life and Letters of Lord Macaulay.* 2 vols. New York: Harper and Brothers, 1876.

Tsiang, Hiuen. *Si-Yu-Ki: Buddhist Records of the Western World.* Translated by Samuel Beal. London: Trübner, 1884.

Tucker, Judith E. *Women, Family, and Gender in Islamic Law.* Cambridge: Cambridge University Press, 2008.

Tunc, Tanfer E. "Harvey Karman and the Super Coil Fiasco." *European Journal of Contraception and Reproductive Health Care* 13, no. 1 (2008): 4–8.

Uddin, Sufia M. *Constructing Bangladesh: Religion, Ethnicity, and Language in an Islamic Nation.* Chapel Hill: University of North Carolina Press, 2006.

Umar, Badruddin. *The Emergence of Bangladesh: Class Struggles in East Pakistan (1947–1958).* 2 vols. Karachi: Oxford University Press, 2004–6.

"United Nations Treaty Collection." United Nations. Accessed 31 July 2017. https://

treaties.un.org/Pages/ViewDetails.aspx?src=TREATY&mtdsg_no=IV-8&
chapter=4&lang=en.

Unveiling Afghanistan. "Shukria Haidar: 'I Was Forced to Leave My Country.'"
HuffPost. 6 February 2014. www.huffingtonpost.com/unveiling-afghanistan
/shukria-haidar-i-was-forc_b_4703426.html.

Urquhart, David. *The Spirit of the East.* 2 vols. London: Colburn, 1839.

Van Schendel, Willem. *A History of Bangladesh.* Cambridge: Cambridge University
Press, 2009.

Vantoch, Victoria. *The Jet Sex: Airline Stewardesses and the Making of an American
Icon.* Philadelphia: University of Pennsylvania Press, 2013.

Van Voris, Jacqueline. *Carrie Chapman Catt: A Public Life.* New York: Feminist
Press, 1987.

———. *The Committee of Correspondence: Women with a World Vision.* Northamp-
ton: Sophia Smith Collection, Smith College, 1989.

Venugopal, Arun. "A Wave of Leftist Bangladeshis Lands in New York." Gothamist.
10 June 2020. https://gothamist.com/news/wave-leftist-bangladeshis-lands-new
-york.

Vickery, Amanda. "Don't Marry a Christian." *London Review of Books* 33, no. 17
(2011): 24–25.

———. "Golden Age to Separate Spheres? A Review of the Categories and Chronology of English Women's History." *Historical Journal* 36, no. 2 (1993): 383–414.

"Victory! Unocal Quits Afghanistan Pipeline Project." Feminist Majority Foundation. 7 December 1998. https://feminist.org/news/victory-unocal-quits
-afghanistan-pipeline-project/.

Virdee, Pippa. "Women and Pakistan International Airlines in Ayub Khan's Pakistan." *International History Review* 41, no. 6 (2019): 1341–66.

Visram, Rozina. *Asians in Britain: 400 Years of History.* London: Pluto, 2002.

Viswanathan, Gauri. *Masks of Conquest: Literary Study and British Rule in India.*
New York: Columbia University Press, 1989.

Visweswaran, Kamala. "Small Speeches, Subaltern Gender: Nationalist Ideology
and Its Historiography." In *Subaltern Studies IX: Writings on South Asian History and Society,* edited by Shahid Amin and Dipesh Chakrabarty, 126–64. New
Delhi: Oxford University Press, 1996.

Vitkus, Daniel. *Three Turk Plays from Early Modern England.* New York: Columbia
University Press, 2000.

Voyage dans les Deltas du Gange et de l'Irraouaddy: Relation Portugaise Anonyme.
Edited and translated by Genevieve Bouchon and Luis Filipe Thomaz. Centre
Cultural Portugais, 1988.

Waines, David. "Ibn Baṭṭūṭa." In Fleet et al., *Encyclopaedia of Islam III.*

Walkowitz, Judith R. *Prostitution and Victorian Society: Women, Class, and the
State.* Cambridge: Cambridge University Press, 1980.

Ward, Barbara E. *Women in the New Asia: The Changing Social Roles of Men and
Women in South and South-East Asia.* Paris: UNESCO, 1963.

Ward, William. "On the Burning of Women in India." *Missionary Register,* June 1813, 214–18. https://archive.org/details/1813CMSMissionaryRegister/.

Ware, Vron. *Beyond the Pale: White Women, Racism and History.* 1992. Reprint, New York: Verso, 2015.

Wasti, Syed Tanvir. "The Indian Red Crescent Mission to the Balkan Wars." *Middle Eastern Studies* 45, no. 3 (2009): 393–406.

Waterfield, Henry. *Memorandum on the Census of British India of 1871–72.* London: Eyre and Spottiswoode for H. M. Stationery Office, 1871.

Watt, James. "'The Blessings of Freedom': Britain, America, and 'the East' in the Fiction of Robert Bage." *Eighteenth Century Fiction* 22, no. 1 (2009): 49–70.

———. *British Orientalisms, 1759–1835.* Cambridge: Cambridge University Press, 2019.

Weaver, Mary Anne. "A Fugitive from Injustice." *New Yorker* 70, no. 28 (1994): 48–60.

Webb, Gisela. *Windows of Faith: Muslim Women Scholar-Activists in North America.* Syracuse: Syracuse University Press, 2000.

Weber, Charlotte. "Making Common Cause? Western and Middle Eastern Feminists in the International Women's Movement, 1911–1948." PhD diss., Ohio State University, 2003.

———. "Unveiling Scheherezade: Feminist Orientalism in the International Alliance of Women, 1911–1959." *Feminist Studies* 27 (2001): 125–57.

Wenner, Manfred W. "The Arab/Muslim Presence in Medieval Central Europe." *International Journal of Middle East Studies* 12 (1980): 59–79.

Wheeler, J. Talboys, ed. *Early Travels in India.* Calcutta: LePage, 1864.

Whitaker, Jennifer Seymour. "Women of the World: Report from Mexico City." *Foreign Affairs* 54, no. 1 (1975): 173–81.

White, Daniel E. *From Little London to Little Bengal: Religion, Print, and Modernity in Early British India, 1793–1835.* Baltimore: Johns Hopkins University Press, 2013.

"Who We Are." Asia Pacific Forum on Women, Law and Development. Accessed 4 May 2020. https://apwld.org/about-us/who-we-are/.

Wild, Antony. *The East India Company: Trade and Conquest from 1600.* Guilford, CT: Lyons, 1999.

Wilford, Hugh. *The Mighty Wurlitzer: How the CIA Played America.* Cambridge, MA: Harvard University Press, 2009.

Winchester, Simon. Introduction to Fay, *Original Letters from India,* vii–xii.

Wollstonecraft, Mary. *A Vindication of the Rights of Men.* 2nd ed. London: Johnson, 1790.

———. *A Vindication of the Rights of Woman.* Edited by Miriam Brody. 1792. Reprint, New York: Penguin Books, 2004.

Women for Women, ed. *The Situation of Women in Bangladesh.* Dacca: Women for Women/UNICEF, 1979.

"Women in the Movement." Position paper 24. 6–12 November 1964. https://womhist.alexanderstreet.com/SNCC/doc43.htm.

Women of South Asian Descent Collective, ed. *Our Feet Walk the Sky: Women of the South Asian Women Diaspora.* San Francisco: Aunt Lute Books, 1993.

Woodsmall, Ruth Frances. *Moslem Women Enter a New World.* New York: Round Table, 1936.

———. *Women and the New East.* Washington, DC: Middle East Institute, 1960.

Woolf, Virginia. *Three Guineas.* 1938. Reprint, New York: Harcourt, 1966.

Wright, Carolyne. "Diary: Taslima Nasreen Gets Them Going." *London Review of Books,* 8 September 1994. www.lrb.co.uk/the-paper/v16/n17/carolyne-wright /diary.

"Writers' Statement on Cartoons." BBC News. 1 March 2006. http://news.bbc.co .uk/2/hi/europe/4764730.stm.

Wu, Judy Tsu-Chun. "Rethinking Global Sisterhood." In Hewitt, *No Permanent Waves,* 193–220.

Yapp, Malcolm E. "Europe in the Turkish Mirror." *Past and Present* 137 (1992): 134–55.

Yeazell, Ruth Bernard. *Harems of the Mind: Passages of Western Art and Literature.* New Haven, CT: Yale University Press, 2000.

Yegenoglu, Meyda. *Colonial Fantasies: Towards a Feminist Reading of Orientalism.* Cambridge: Cambridge University Press, 1998.

Yeo, Eileen Janes, ed. *Mary Wollstonecraft and 200 Years of Feminisms.* London: Rivers Oram, 1997.

Young, Cynthia A. *Soul Power: Culture, Radicalism, and the Making of a U.S. Third World Left.* Durham, NC: Duke University Press, 2006.

Zaeske, Susan. *Signatures of Citizenship: Petitioning, Antislavery, and Women's Political Identity.* Chapel Hill: University of North Carolina Press, 2003.

Zaidi, Syed M. H. *The Muslim Womanhood in Revolution.* Calcutta: Zaidi, 1937.

Zakaria, Rafia. "Sex and the Muslim Feminist." *New Republic,* 13 November 2015. https://newrepublic.com/article/123590/sex-and-the-muslim-feminist.

Zaman, Niaz. "National Policies for Women." In Women for Women, *Situation of Women,* 332–51.

Zaman, Selina Bahar. *Kalantoray Nari* [Women beyond time]. Dhaka: Narikendro, 2005.

———. *Pothe Chole Jete Jete* [An autobiography]. Dhaka: Sahityo Prokashoni, 2006.

Zastoupil, Lynn. *Rammohun Roy and the Making of Victorian Britain.* New York: Palgrave Macmillan, 2010.

Zia, Afiya S. *Faith and Feminism in Pakistan: Religious Agency or Secular Autonomy?* Eastbourne, East Sussex: Sussex Academic Press, 2018.

Zine, Jasmin. "Between Orientalism and Fundamentalism: Muslim Women and Feminist Engagement." In *(En)Gendering the War on Terror: War Stories and Camouflaged Politics,* edited by Krista Hunt and Kim Rygiel, 27–49. Farnham: Ashgate, 2006.

Zonana, Joyce. "The Sultan and the Slave: Feminist Orientalism and the Structure of 'Jane Eyre.'" *Signs* 18 (1993): 592–617.

INDEX

Note: page numbers in *italics* refer to figures.

Abdullah, Shaikh, 141
Abdullah, Tahrunnessa Ahmed, 196–97
Abercrombie, Alexander, 114
Abida Sultan (princess of Bhopal), 185
Aborodhbashini (Hossain), 134
abortion: Bangladesh law on, and mass
  rapes of 1971, 211–12; permissibility in
  Hanafi Islam, 212; and population control in Bangladesh, 212–13; supercoil
  method, 213
abortion in US: menstrual regulation (MR)
  and, 213–14; women's reluctance to use
  self-help methods, 214
Abu Taleb, Mirza: acceptance into high
  society, 65; anticipation of Bengali feminist arguments, 69; background of, 64;
  on British ignorance about India, 65;
  on Indian influences in Britain, 65; on
  Indian women's seclusion, as practical
  necessity, 67; observations on British
  culture, 65–66; on rights and freedoms
  of Muslim women, 66–69; on stadial theory, 66; *Travels*, 65, 66, 68–69;
  "Vindication of the Liberties of Asiatic Women," 66–68; visit to Britain,
  7, 64–66
"The Accession of the Queen of India"
  (*Punch* cartoon), 106, *107*
acid attacks, media focus on, 259–60
Adam, William, 83, 98

Adams, Abigail, 54
Adams, Dolly, 240
Adams, William Bridges. *See* Revividus,
  Junius
An Address to Mussulmuns (Serampore
  Mission), 73
Afghanistan, feminist groups in, 270–71
Afghanistan, Taliban government in:
  Afghan women's groups' views on US
  removal of, 271; existence of women's
  problems prior to, 270; as product of US
  policies, 272
Afghanistan, US feminists' commitment
  to save women in, 268–73; Afghan
  women's criticism of, 272–73; alli-
  ances with Islamist groups, 273; failure
  to consider larger political frame, 273;
  failure to recognize Afghan women's
  groups, 271–72; misinformation spread
  by, 272; organizations participating
  in, 269; publicizing of, 268–69, 271; as
  strategy to energize feminist movement,
  269; Taliban's easing of restrictions in
  response to, 270
Afkhami, Mahnaz, 217–18
Afro-Asian Women's Conference, first
  (Cairo, 1961), 221
Afro-Asian Women's Conference, Second
  (Ulan Bator, 1972), 221–22
Afzal-Khan, Fawzia, 278

371

"Ardhangi" (Hossain), 139
Arndt, Jessie, 178–79
Armenian Genocide, 158
Ashby, Margery Corbett, 158
Ashraf (princess of Iran), 217
Ashrafunnessa Khatun, 196
Ashurst, William Henry, 98
Asia Foundation, 183
Asia Pacific Forum on Women, Law and
    Development (Kuala Lumpur, 1986),
    242–43
Asiatic Society, 72, 78
Association of African Women for
    Research and Development, 234
Astell, Mary, 4–5, 36–37
Ataturk, Mustafa Kemal, 149
Atif, Nadia, 240
Atwood, Margaret, 253
Auckland, Lord (governor-general of
    India), 89
Auclert, Hubertine, 96
Aurangzeb (Mughal emperor), 28
Aurobindo, Sri, 133
Aw, Engénie Rokhaya, 235
Awami League, 258
Ayub Khan, Muhammad, 186, 202–3
Azim, Firdous, 248

Babbu Begum, 32
Babri Masjid, razing of, 251, 253
Babur (Mughal emperor), 19
Babur-nama, translation of, 111
Bage, Robert, 53
Bahadur, Kaliprasanna Ghose, 109
Bahadur Shah (Mughal emperor), British
    exile to Rangoon, 107
Bahar, Habibullah, 151–52
Bahar Choudhury, Anwara, 151–52
Bahu Begum, 56
Baiza Bai, 92
Baker, Ella, 199
Bamabodhini Patrika (periodical), 128–29
Bamabodhini Sabha, 128–29
"Bande Mataram" chant of anticolonial
    movement, 145
Banerji, Sasipada, 118, 123–24
Bangiya Nari Samaj (Bengali Women's

Society): Hossain's address at (1927),
    138–39, 141, 143, 153; Hossain's involve-
    ment with, 137
Bangladesh: anti-US sentiment in, 220;
    and CEDAW, 246–47; commitment to
    peace and human rights, 208; demands
    of women's organizations in, 246–47;
    feminists' agenda in, 208, 258–61; femi-
    nists' opposition to islamization, 250;
    First Five-Year Plan of 1973, 213; found-
    ing constitution of, 219; government's
    response to UN Decade for Women,
    243; Islamization, feminist opposi-
    tion to, 247–49, 250; as laboratory for
    women-centered advancement, 7; media
    portrayals of, 260; military dictator-
    ships in, 243; of 1970s–80s, Western
    view of as Third World rather than
    Muslim country, 207–8; and Non-
    Aligned Movement, 208; Planned Par-
    enthood aid to, 209, 212; politics of late
    20th century, women in, 251; return of
    democratic government, 251, 258–59;
    Soviet bloc allegiance of, 219; Soviet
    support for independence of, 219; ten-
    sion between demands of Western and
    Arab state donors, 243; turn to cloth-
    ing manufacture, in 1980s, 243–44,
    245; war of independence (1971), 171;
    Western view on, in light of Islamist
    rise, 250–51, 258; women in, portrayal as
    victims of Islam rather than corporate
    world order, 274–75; women's groups
    in, holistic agenda of, 248; women's
    groups in 21st century, 273–75; women's
    manufacturing jobs, emphasis on, 274;
    women's programs, and Western conde-
    scension, 244–45; women's programs,
    as donor-driven, 244, 245, 248; writers
    receiving fatwas and threats, 255
Bangladesh, mass rapes of 1971 in: and
    abortion laws, relaxation of, 211–12;
    calls for war-crimes tribunal on, 259;
    debate on, 267; and image of Bangla-
    deshi women as vulnerable, 211; as part
    of universal oppression of women, in
    feminists' analysis, 209–11; results of

birth control. *See* contraception

Black American feminists, opposition to US, 225

Black Lives Matter (BLM): support for, by race, 285; US Muslims' support for, 285

Blackstone, William, 38

Blackwood's Magazine, 87

BMP. *See* Bangladesh Mahila Parishad

Bodichon, Barbara, 100, 102

Bogra, Mohammad Ali, 183–84, 186

Bone, Pamela, 255

Book of Duarte Barbosa (1518), 14–15

Book of Travels (Ibn Battuta). *See Rihla* (Ibn Battuta)

Bose, "Netaji" Subhas Chandra, 148, 152

Boserup, Ester, 215

Boston Female Society for Missionary Purposes, 70

Boswell, James, 43

Boyd-Kinnear, John, 105

BRAC, 256

Brahmo Samaj (Brahmo Sabha), 80, 109, 124, 128, 130

Bread and Roses, 252

The Bride-Woman's Counsellor (Sprint), 35, 37

Britain: Ameer Ali in, 122–25, 160; early feminists on necessity of purging Eastern traits from, 63–64; first Indian woman to visit, 24–25; Ihtishamuddin in, 7, 43–45; Indians' travel to, in 19th century, 109; Indian students in, 123; Indian travel to, at end of 18th century, 43–44; Indian women's travel to, in 19th century, 118–21; literary production after loss of American colonies, 53; loss of India and Pakistan, 171; shift in focus from North Africa to India, 51

British civilizing mission: Hastings trial as justification of, 57; increase of, after First War of Indian Independence (1857), 93–94; Indian reformers' support for, 80–81; Mill on, 105–6; and sati, efforts to end, 79–81; and Western education, introduction of, 81

British East India Company: classes for employees of, 72; discouraging of Englishwomen's travel to India, 25, 46;

dissolution of, 101, 106; founding of, 20; loss of monopoly over Indian trade, 71; Mill on accomplishments of, 105–6; noninterference in local religion as initial policy, 70; takeover of Bengal, 17, 29, 31, 44, 52; turn from East Indies to India, 20; turnover of Indian rule to British Crown, 87, 96, 101, 106

British merchants, trade with Bengal, 18

British racism in India: belief in Muslim backwardness, 126; British unwillingness to be subject to Indian judges, 111–12; denigration of Indian masculinity, 107–8; hardening of, after Great Revolt of 1857, 107–8; racist superiority, development of, 101; views of Hindu *vs.* Muslim men, 78, 108

British rule in India: annexation of Oudh (Awadh), 93; and characterization of Muslims as invaders, 85–87; and economic changes of 19th century, 74–75; elite class of Indians educated to support, 81; first governor-general, 32; and "greatest happiness for greatest number" principle, 81; Ihtishamuddin on, 46; as improvement over Muslim rule, 124; influence of Mill's *History of British India* on, 77, 78; late-18th century debates on, 53; missionaries' legitimization of, 71; and public education, 71, 81; racist superiority, development of, 101; taxation, Parkes on, 93; turnover to British Crown, 87, 96, 101, 106. *See also* First War of Indian Independence (1857)

British women: campaign against sati, 82, 83; early travel in India, 46–52; encounters with Muslim women, in 18th century, 46–52; sense of superiority over Indian women, 83; tacit acceptance of their roles, 83; writings about travel in India, 87

British women's campaign for legal rights, 96–104; and antislavery movement, 98–99; and child custody laws, 99–100; coverture and, 96–97; divorce rights, 100; married women's control of property, 100; Mill and, 102–4, *103*

Brito, António de, 16
Brontë, Charlotte, 83
Brougham, Lord, 97
Brown, Rita Mae, 209
Brownmiller, Susan, 211
Bruce, Margaret, 206
Buchanan, Patrick J., 263–64
Bulbul (journal), 151
Bulbul Academy of Fine Arts, 152
Bunch, Charlotte, 209
Burke, Edmund: and Hastings trial, 11, 54, 56–57; *Reflections on the Revolution in France*, 57, 58
Burr, Aaron, 58
Bush, George W., 272, 273
Butler, Josephine, 105, 110
Bykovsky, Valery, 201

Caldicott, Helen, 272–73
cannula, 212, 213
Carey, Dorothy, 70
Carey, William: Christian missionary work in India, 70–72; and Muslims, effort to convert, 72–73; on Muslim women's participation in Hindu rituals, 74–75; supporters of, 70; teaching of classes at Fort William College, Calcutta, 71–72
Carpenter, Mary, 109, 123–24
Carter, James E. "Jimmy," 247
Castro, Fidel, 223
Catt, Carrie Chapman, 160–61
The Cause (Strachey), 58, 155
The Causes of the Indian Revolt (Ahmed), 115
CEDAW. See Convention on the Elimination of All Forms of Discrimination against Women
census of 1871–72, 112–14
Cervantes, Miguel de, 34
Chaffin, Ann, 83
change in Muslim world: ignoring of, by West, 277–78; long history of women advocating for, 278–79; necessity of US intervention for, as distorted view, 277
Channing, Henry, 125
Channing, William Ellery, 85
Chapone, Sarah, 37–38
Charlie Hebdo, 280

Charter Act of 1813, 70–72
Chatterjee, Bankim Chandra, 114
Chattopadhyay, Kamaladevi, 158
Chaudhurani, Faizunnesa, 130–32
Chaudhurani, Razia Khatun, 147–49, *148*
Chaudhury, Abdur Rab, 212
Chaudhury, Ashrafuddin Ahmed, 148–49
Chaudhury, Suniti, 153
Cheraman Perumal, 14–15
Chesler, Ellen, 264
Chhayanaut, *191, 192*
child marriage: debate on, in British India, 80; feminist activism against, 162, 163, 164; Kindersley on, 49; Mayo's *Mother India* on, 143; outlawing of, in British India, 81, 113; Parkes on, 91
La China Poblana, 23
Choudhury, Anwara Bahar, 174
Choudhury, Munier, 170–71
Christians, South Asian Muslim views on, in 16th century, 18–19
Christian Science Monitor, 178–79
Chudleigh, Lady Mary, 37
Chung, Connie, 260
Church Missionary Society, 83
CIA, overthrow of Mosaddegh in Iran, 219
Çiller, Tansu, 265
civil rights movement, as inspiration to US feminists, 199–200
"clash of civilizations" narrative of late 20th century, 252
climate and sexual desire, stadial theory on, 42–43
Clinton, William J. "Bill," 271
Clive, Robert: and British takeover of Bengal, 29, 31, 44; and Portuguese language in Bengal, 17; and successor to Mir Jafar, dispute over, 32, 56
Cold War: and Muslim difference, downplaying of, 178–79; and Pakistan's allegiance, struggle for, 171–74; US and Soviet wooing of Third World, 176–77; and US Committee of Correspondence, 183; and US-Soviet competition at women's world conferences, 266
Cold War, end of: and dominance of US liberal feminism, 266; and Islam as new US rival, 266–67

Development, Crises and Alternative Visions (DAWN), 241
Development Alternatives with Women for a New Era (DAWN), 241, *241*
Devi, Jnandanandini (Gyandanondini Debi), 118
Devi, Rajkumari, 118
Dey, Kalicharan, 130
Dhumketu (journal), 146
Diderot, Denis, 42
Dimashqiya, Julia, 164
divorce rights in Britain: activism to obtain, 96; and Custody of Infants Act of 1839, 98–100; Matrimonial Causes Act of 1857 and, 100
divorce rights under Muslim law, 40, 79, 99; Ali's defense of, 121–22, 125; critics of, 114; *vs.* polygamy, 185; women's education on, 75
"Drain Inspector's Report" (Gandhi), 143
Dudu Miyan, 74
Dumont, Jean, 40
Dutch Indies, women's rights in, 160
Dutch merchants, trade with Bengal, 17–18
Dutt, Aru, 86
Dutt, Kalpana, 153
Dutt, Toru, 86–87

eastern Bengal: concept of "West" (*poshchim*) in, 7; topography of, 6; as understudied, 6–7; various political divisions of, 6. *See also* Bangladesh; Bengal; Pakistan, East
Eastern bloc feminists: organizational development, 220–23; refusal to separate women's issues from issues of racism, imperialism, and Zionism, 119, 221–22, 223–27; rejection of Western feminism, 219, 220–21
The Eastern Lily Gathered (Storrow), 84
East India Association, 109
East Pakistan Mahila Parishad, 220
East Pakistan Peace Corps Newsletter, 195–96
East Pakistan Youth League, 171
Eden, Emily, 89
Eden, Fanny, 89

Eden College, 166
Edib, Halidé, 155, 156, 157–58, 176
education, public, British introduction of, 71, 81
education for Muslim women: British advocates for, 115–16; early students and instructors, 150–53; Muslim women college instructors, 151; schools and colleges for, 150–53, 155. *See also* education for women in zenanas
education for women: debate on, in 19th-century Bengal, 75; in 18th-century Bengal, 31; Hossain on, 135–36, 138–39, 141–42; Islamic reform movements of early 19th century and, 75; James Mill on, 78; J. S. Mill on, 104; Macaulay on, 59; Wollstonecraft on, 59, 73
education for women in Bangladesh: feminists' focus on, in late 20th century, 260; lack of books for, 260–61
education for women in India: advocates for Indian forms of, 109–10, 111; British advocates for, 110–11; British efforts to establish schools, 129–30; as focus of women missionaries, 83–84; Indian advocates for, 109–10; Muslim rejection of schools outside the home, 115–16, 117–18; Parkes on, 93; schools, 135–36; through private tutors, 129–30; women advocates for, 129, 144
education for women in zenanas, 152; advocates for, 109, 150–53; education materials aimed at, 128–29; by tutors, 129–30; women missionaries' focus on, 70, 83–84
education in India, Western-style: Bengali Muslims' lack of access to, 113; and denigration of Sanskrit and Arabic learning, 81; and elite class of Indians educated to support British rule, 81; Indian elite's interest in, 81; motives for introducing, 81
education in India, Western-style, Muslim advocates for, 115–18; prioritization of education for boys, 115–16; rejection of education for women outside the home, 115–16, 117–18; schools founded by, 115,

116; turn to advocacy of education for women, 117

Egypt: British rule in, and women's education, 117; feminists' resentment of White Western feminists' condescension, 237–38; and Non-Aligned Movement, 175; and Suez Canal crisis, 177, 180

Egyptian Feminist Union, 163

L'Egyptienne (journal), 163

Eisenhower, Dwight D., 172–73, 177

ekushey protests, 171–72, 176

Elbaz, Shahida, 237

elections in Bengal, dominance of Hindus and, 153

Elhuni, Asma, 285

Elizabeth I (queen of England), 20

El Saadawi, Nawal, 225–27, 234

Emecheta, Buchi, and *Women: A World Report*, 237

Emmons, Mary Eugénie Beauharnais, 59

The Enfranchisement of Women (Taylor), 102

Enlightenment, European, interest in women's status in West *vs.* East, 33–36

Enquiry into the Obligations of Christians to Use Means for the Conversion of the Heathens (Carey), 70, 72

Ensler, Eve, 270

"Equality between the Sexes" (Rossi), 200

Ershad, Hussain M., 243, 247–48, 251

Essai sur les femmes (Thomas), Kindersley translation of, 49–51

Estado da Índia: delegation to Bengal (1521), 16; and Mughal Empire, initial contact with, 19

Europeans' first visits to South Asia, 14

evidence, Islamic rules of, 78

Eviota, Elizabeth Uy, *242*

factories in Bangladesh, horrific accidents in, 261

factory labor by women in Bangladesh, 274–75; and, Western accusations of exploitation, 274–75; garment industry and, 243–44, 245; Western labor standards as threat to, 261

Fairey, Shepard, 283, *284*

Fallaci, Oriana, 216, 218

Family Planning Commission (Pakistan), 265

Farah Diba (empress of Iran), 216, 218

Faraizi movement, 73

Fawcett, Henry, 122

Fawcett, Millicent Garrett, 122, 160

Fay, Anthony, 88

Fay, Eliza, 87–89, 95

Faysal (king of Saudi Arabia), 217

Fazilatunnesa Begum, 165–66, *166*

Feit, Ronnie, 223

Feldman, Shelley, 244

The Female Captive (Marsh), 51–52

female circumcision: activists' association with corrective surgery for genital ambiguities, 233–34; depiction as Muslim-only practice, 233; El Saadawi on, 234; international debate on, 234; Third World feminists' resentment of Western feminists' approach to, 234–35, 237–38; as topic at women's world conference (Nairobi, 1985), 240; Western feminists' obsession with, 233

The Feminine Mystique (Friedan), 198, 218

feminism: accomplishments of 1980s, 1; history of, 2; indigenous origins in many cultures, 2; introduction of term, 96; ongoing need for, 10. *See also* Western feminism

Feminist Majority Foundation (FMF): domestic US focus of first decade, 269; purchase of *Ms.* magazine, 273

Feminist Majority Foundation Campaign to Stop Gender Apartheid in Afghanistan, 5, 268–69, 270–73; Afghan women's criticism of, 272–73; alliances with Islamist groups, 273; failure to recognize Afghan women's groups, 271–72; misinformation spread by, 272; publicizing of, 268–69, 271; as strategy to energize feminist movement, 269; Taliban's easing of restrictions in response to, 270

feminist movement in Bengal: "first wave" arguments for political participation, 144; and movement to create Pakistan,

Hanafi school of Sunni law, on divorce and child custody rights, 99

Hanif, Shanana, 286–87, *288*

Hanson, Doris, 188

Hardships of the English Laws in Relation to Wives (Chapone), 37–38

harems and seraglios: in British fiction, 53; comparison of British marriage laws to, 104, 105; early descriptions of, *12, 15, 16, 22–23, 25, 48–49, 50*; 18th century playwrights challenging stereotype of, 38–39; as evidence of women's oppression, in Western view, 60; growth of, under Akbar, 24; Hossain's "Sultana's Dream" on, 132; implications of 1871 census and, 114–15; origin of term, 35; political ties created by, 24; as prison-like, as Western misunderstanding, 35; and risk of fire, 49; women of, as standard of vapid womanhood in Wollstonecraft, 59–61, 62. *See also* zenana (*antahpur*; women's quarters)

Harris, Sam, 276

Hartly House, Calcutta (Gibbes), 58

Harvey, Alexander, 98

Hasan Khan, Muhammad, 94

Hasina, Sheikh, 251, 258

Hassan, Riffat, 264

Hastings, Warren, 32, 43, 52, 65

Hastings, Warren, impeachment trial of, 53–57, *55*; acquittal, 57; British ideas about Muslim women and, 11, 56–57; charges in, 54–56; circumstances leading to, 29–30; in fiction, 58; Francis and, 28; as justification for British civilizing mission, 57; Munni Begum as focus of, 11, 54–56; public interest in, 54

Hawkins, William, 20, 22, 24

Hayden, Casey, 200

Hélie-Lucas, Marie-Aimée, *242*

Heyzer, Noeleen, *241*

al-Hibri, Azizah, 268

The Hidden Face of Eve (El Saadawi), 225, 234

Hill, Aaron, 40

Hindu Nationalist movement, razing of Babri Masjid, 251, 253

Hindus: characteristics *vs.* Muslims, Mill on, 78; characteristics *vs.* Muslims, Muslims on, 108; traditional, and overseas travel as pollution, 119

Hirsch, Lolly, 214

Hirsi Ali, Ayaan: *The Caged Virgin*, 278; celebration of, as face of modern Muslim feminism, 276, 277; criticisms of, 278–79; as "moderate Muslim" promoted by US, 279–80; monolithic view of Muslim women, 279; on Muslim oppression of women and anti-Semitism, 277; rejection of Muslim women with different opinions, 278; US Muslim feminists more representative than, 287

history, stadial theory of. *See* stadial theory of history

History of British India (Mill), 76–79, 85, 101

"The Holy Land" (Catt), 160

Hood, Maude Pye, 187

hooks, bell, 211

Hoskens, Fran, 234

Hossain, Hameeda, 149–50, *222, 241, 241,* 253, 254

Hossain, Kamal, 254

Hossain, Mir Mosharraf, 117, 134

Hossain, Rokeya Sakhawat, 132–43, *136*; on achievement of Heaven, as reason for women's education, 141; address to Bangiya Nari Samaj (1927), 138–39, 141, 143, 153; background and education, 132–33, 134–35; children, 135; on colonial rule, 142; criticisms of religion, 137; on equality of men and women in Islamic scriptures, 140; essays by, 137–38, 140, 141, 142, 143, 144; family of, 132–34, *133,* 135; feminist writings, 137; on hijab, 69; husband's support for her education, 135; influence of, 146, 257; intertwining of nationalist and women's causes, 143; Kamal and, 152, 204; languages mastered by, 134; Mahmud and, 135, 150, 151, 168; marriage, 135; and Mayo's *Mother India,* 142–43; on missionaries, 142; *Motichur,* 134; on Muslim advances in women's education, 140–41; on Muslim women failing to vote, 153; Nasreen on,

Hossain, Rokeya Sakhawat *(continued)*
257; *Padmarag*, 135, 139; publication of
sister's poems, 134; and purdah, 134, 139;
reflections on colonial context, 7; school
started by, curriculum in, 138; stories by,
142; "Sultana's Dream," 132; translation
of *Murder of Delicia*, 139–40; and wom-
en's education, support for, 135–36, 138,
141–42; on women's education, limitations of, 138–39; and women's organizations, work with, 136–38; on women's
rights, as universally violated, 137–38,
139–40, 143
Hossain, Sara, 254
Hossain, Sufia N., 152–153, 155. *See also*
Kamal, Begum Sufia
Hossain, Syed Nehal, 152
Hossain, Syed Sakhawat, 135
Hossein, Mrs. R. S. *See* Hossain, Rokeya
Sakhawat
How-Martyn, Edith, 157
Huda, Kulsum Siddiqua, *177*
Huda, Sigma, 246, 256
human nature, universal, in stadial theory
of development, 42–43
human societies, stadial theory of develop-
ment, 42–43
Humayun-nama (Gulbadan), 24, 111, 112
Hunter, W. W., 75
Huntington, Samuel, 252
Huq, Abul Kasem Fazlul, 151
Huq, Chaumtoli, 287, *288*
Huq, Nazara, 169
Huq, Shireen, *288*; on acid attacks and
media, 259; and mass rapes of 1971, 259;
and Naripokkho, 248; on racism in
America, 189; translation of Ahmed's
Village Women as I Saw Them, 196; visit
to New York, 287
Hussain, Iqbalunnisa, 162, 163–64
Hutcheson, Francis, 79
Huyghen van Linschoten, Jan, *17*

IAW (IAWSEC). *See* International Alli-
ance of Women for Equal Citizenship
Ibn Battuta, Abu Abdallah, 27. *See also*
Rihla (Ibn Battuta)
Ibrahim, Sufia, 171, 176, *177*

ICPD. *See* UN International Confer-
ence on Population and Development
(ICPD) (Cairo, 1994)
Ihtishamuddin, Mirza Shaikh: background
of, 44, 45; visit to Britain, 7, 43–45; *The
Wonders of Vilayet*, 44–46.
Ihtisham-ul-Haq, Maulana, 185–86
Ikramullah, Shaistra Suhrawardy, 166, 183
Ilbert Bill (1883), opposition to, 111–12
Imam, Jahanara, 251, 257
"Imandar Nekbibir Kechcha" (Garibul-
lah), 75–76
India: increasing interactions with Britain
over 19th century, 96; independence,
171; judges' jurisdiction over Europeans,
Ilbert Bill on, 111–12; of 19th century,
British views on, 76–79; and Soviet-
brokered talks with Pakistan (1966),
203; spread of Islam in, 14–15. *See also*
British rule in India; Pakistan, creation
of
Indian Ladies' Magazine, 132
Indian Law Commission, 81
Indian Magazine and Review, 123
Indian National Congress: antipartition
rallies, 145; Bengal chapter, 148; motives
for creation of, 112
Indian nationalist movement, British
efforts to undermine, 143
Indian Penal Code of 1860, 81–82, 113
Indians: travel by, in 17th century, 23–24;
travel to Britain in 19th century, 109
Indian students in Britain: and dress, 123;
NIA and, 123
Indian women: dress, change with British contact, 111; emulation of British
women, in 19th century, 118, 119; travel
in 17th–18th centuries, 23–25; travel
to Britain, in 19th century, 118–21. *See
also* education for women in India;
Mughal court, women of; Muslim
women in India; women's political
equality in India; women's suffrage in
India
Indian women, British views on: British
women's invocation of, in debate over
women's rights, 96, 104; as product of
Muslim culture, 84; in 17th century,

25–26; stadial theory of development and, 42–43, 77, 78, 82, 85

Indonesia, and Non-Aligned Movement, 175

Institute for Social Policy and Understanding (ISPU), 285–86

International Abortion and Training Centre, 212

International Alliance of Women for Equal Citizenship (IAWSEC): accomplishments of, 164; Asian groups and individuals joining, 162, 163–64; goals of, 160; international congresses held by, 160; international congress in Budapest (1913), 161–62; international congress in Istanbul (1935), 162–64; outreach to non-Western women, 160–62; renaming of IWSA as, 159; tension between sisterhood and impulse to save oppressed non-Western women, 160–61, 162–63, 164. *See also Jus Suffragii* (journal)

"The International Crime of Genital Mutilation" (Morgan and Steinem), 233–34

international development establishment, focus on women's education in late 20th century, 260

international feminism: alliances in early 20th century, 159–65; coalitions formed in 1980s, 240–42; post–Cold War, 261–68; UN support for, 207

International Monetary Fund, and Bangladeshi economic policy, 243

International PEN, 253, 254

International Planned Parenthood Federation: aid to Bangladesh, 209, 212; and Bangladesh abortions, 212–13

International Woman Suffrage Alliance (IWSA), 159

International Women's Day celebration (Moscow, 1967), 202–4

International Women's Day celebration (Tehran, 1979), 232

Intersex Society of North America, 233–34

Iqbal, Muhammad, 157–58

Iran: and Arab oil embargo, 217; feminists invited to (1974), 217–18; feminists' rejection of US feminists' condescen-

sion, 232–33; funding for women's causes, 218; hostage crisis, and US's negative views of Islam, 233; Pakistani opposition to US-British policy in, 172; Revolution, and US views on Iranian women, 232–33; under Shah, as modern Muslim society in US view, 216; Western view on, after revolution and hostage crisis, 251; women's retention of surname after marriage, 218

Iraq, and Arab oil embargo, 217

Isfahani, Mirza Abu Mohammad Tabrizi. *See* Abu Taleb, Mirza

Islam, Tanwi Nandini, 275

Islam: White Western feminists' negative views of, 232–33; and women's freedom, debate on, 224–25

Islam and the Muslim Woman Today (Jameelah), 227, 229–32

Islamic law, property rights of women in, 38, 40

Islamic reform movements of early 19th century, 73–76; Arab influence and, 73; Faraizi movement, 73; and *nasihat namas* (religious instruction manuals), 75; targeting of women's participation in Hindu practices, 74–75; Tariqah-i-Muhammadiya movement, 73; Wahhabis' influence on, 73–74; on women's status and education, 75

Ismail, Munshi, 44

ISPU. *See* Institute for Social Policy and Understanding

Israel: claimed anti-Semitism of Muslims as strategy to benefit, 279; Pakistani resentment of US-British support for, 172; praise for, as qualification for "moderate" Muslim status, 281, 282

IWSA. *See* International Woman Suffrage Alliance

Jacobs, Aletta, 160–61

Jahan, Rounaq: career of, 207; and DAWN, 241; on first UN Women's Conference (1975), 207; on overpopulation issue, 214–15; and Regional South and South East Asian Women in Development Conference, 242, *242*; at UN

Mariam, Thahitun, 287, *288*

marriage in Britain: activism for legal equality in, 96–97; and coverture laws, 38, 40, 96–97, 122; early feminists' views on, 36–38

marriage in Muslim culture: as contractual rather than sacramental, 84–85, 114, 224–25; and prostitution, 114. *See also* polygamy

Married Women's Property Acts (1870, 1874, 1882), 100, 122

Marsh, Elizabeth, 51–53

Martyrs' Day (Shaheed Dibosh), 170–71

Mary (mother of Jesus), Muslim views on, 19

Massinger, Philip, 34

Matin, Nilufar, 244

Matrimonial Causes Act of 1857, 100

Maududi, Abul Ala, 228–29

Mayo, Katherine, 142–43, 156, 157, 164, 211

McCarthy, Florence "Kiki," 194–96, *195*, 196–97, 245

Medha, Dipti, 153

media: and acid attacks, focus on, 259–60; celebration of modern Muslim feminism, 275–76; and "clash of civilizations" narrative, 252; and identification of "moderate" Muslims, 281–82; monolithic view of Muslim women, 279; narrative on Muslims following September 11th attacks, 251; narrative on Nasreen, 251, 252, 254, 255–56, 258; portrayals of Bangladesh, 260

medicine, Muslim women's preference for women doctors and, 181

Meena, 270, 271

Mehrez, Shahira, 238

Melbourne, Lord, 99–100

menstrual regulation (MR), 213–14

Mernissi, Fatima, 225–27, 241

Mid-Decade UN Conference for Women (Copenhagen, 1980), 234, 246

middle-class European womanhood, Muslim women as negative ideal of, 62

Mill, James, 76–79; on education in India, 102; *History of British India* (Mill), 76–79, 85, 101; Macaulay and, 81; and son's education, 101; and son's employment in East India Company, 101; and

stadial theory of development, 42–43; on women's rights, 78–79

Mill, John Stuart: on colonialism, as instrument of progress, 105–6; election to Parliament, 102; employment with East India Company, 101; familiarity with India, 100–101; and father, 76, 77, 101; Fawcett and, 122; on Indian women's competence in government roles, 104–5; marriage, 101–2; on marriage laws, oppressiveness of, 104; on women's education, 104; and women's rights activism, 102–4, *103*; writing habits, 101. *See also The Subjection of Women* (Mill)

Millar, John, 43

Les mille et une nuits (Galland), 39

Miller, Elizabeth, 273

Millett, Kate, 217–18, 232, 257

Milton, John, 61

Mir Jafar, 31–32, 44, 54–55, 56

Mir Saidu, 31–32

Miss American pageant (1968), protests at, 231

missionaries in Bengal, 70–73; accounts of conversions, 84; attacks on Muhammad by, 72–73; campaign to allow single women missionaries, 82, 83; emulation of trading companies, 70; focus on Muslim women, 126–27; government ban on missionary activity and, 70–71; increased activity after Great Revolt of 1857, 93–94; Indian women's oppression as focus of, 82, 83; and missionary wives, 70; and Muslims, effort to convert, 72–73; as primary Western influence in 19th century, 70; publications on zenana, 72; racialized condescension to Muslim women, 127; support for British gender roles, 82–83; types of Bengali used by, 72, 73; women missionaries focus on women's education, 70, 83–84

missionaries in India: British ban on, 70; and legitimization of British rule, 71; lifting of ban on, 71, 82

Missionary Register, 82

missionary societies for women, 70

Mitra, Ila, 220

Mitra, Peary Chand, 116

"moderate" Muslim, US promotion of, 279–80

Modern Egypt (Cromer), on Islamic women's education, 116–17

Mongol invasions, and Muslim decline, Ameer Ali on, 125

Monnuzaman Khanam, 31

Monserrate, Father (Jesuit priest), 24

Montagu, Mary Wortley: influence of, 88, 90; *Letters* about women in Ottoman Empire, 36–37, 39–41; reconsideration of views on Muslim women, 5; residence in Turkey, 39

Montesquieu, Charles de, 35–36

Monthly Extract (journal), 214

Morgan, Robin, 226–27, 233–34

Mosaddegh, Mohammad, 219

Mosby, Aline, 205–6

Moslem, Fauzia, 221

Moslem Women Enter a New World (Woodsmall), 157

Mossadegh, Mohammad, 172

Mother India (Mayo), 142–43

Mother's Day Massacre, 213

Motichur (Hossain), 134, 137

Mount Henneth (Bage), 53

MR. *See* menstrual regulation

Ms. magazine: article on Afghan women, 273; on feminism in Iran, 232–33; "The International Crime of Genital Mutilation" (Morgan and Steinem), 233–34; "Women of Bangladesh" article, 209–10, 212

Mubarak-ud-daulah, 32, 56

Mughal court, women of: European doctors' treatment of, 22–23; seclusion of, 21–22; travel in 17th–18th centuries, 25. *See also* Nur Jahan

Mughal Empire: British exile of last emperor, 107; conquest of Gujarat and Bengal, 19, 26; constraints of women's freedom in, 24; founding of, 19; *mahals* (palaces for ladies) in, 22; nobles, number of wives, 22; and rise of Islam in Bengal, 26–27; seclusion of highborn women, 21–22

Muhammad, Maulvi Maleh, 75

Muhammad, Tahir, 20

Muhammadan Anglo-Oriental College, 115

Muhammadan Literary and Scientific Society, 116

Mulka Humanee Begum (Mughal princess), 91

Mullick, Babu Taraknath, 114

Munni Begum: accounts of, 7; and British ideas about Muslim women, 56–57, 114; children of, 32; and Chowk mosque, commissioning of, 32; English surprise at strength of character, 32; and Hastings trial, 11, 32, 54–56, 55; interaction with British, 31; life after Hastings trial, 57; power and influence of, 32; return to power under British governor-general, 32, 56; rise to power, 31; son of, as nawab of Bengal, 32, 56; sons by Mir Jafar, 32

Murray, John, 99

Murray, Pauli, 201

Muslim Family Law Ordinance of 1961, 186, 230, 259

Muslim Lady Reclining (Renaldi), 67

Muslim League: establishment of, 126; women's wing, establishment of, 154

Muslim men: advocates for women's education, 117; limited engagement with colonial government, 108; as oppressive husbands, in Western view, 34–35, 37; views on women, Western beliefs about, 36, 39, 40, 48, 61, 63

"Muslim Narir Mukti" (Begum), 165

Muslim oppression of women: as dominant Western discourse, 277; history of idea, 4–5; as justification for invading Muslim lands, 4–5; modern Muslim feminists on, 276–77; as oversimplified view, 277

Muslims: diversity of, 9, 156, 175; views on Western feminists, 3. *See also* United States Muslims

Muslims in Bengal: British views on characteristics of, 112–13; census of 1871–72 on, 112–13; lack of access to Western education, 113; loss of wealth and status under British rule, 113

Muslims in India: characteristics *vs.* Hindus, Muslims on, 108; Mill on characteristics *vs.* Hindus, 78

Muslim societies, and global disparities of wealth and power, 2–3

Muslim traditionalists: concerns about importing of Western sexual license, 262–63; opposition to UN population control measures, 262–63

Muslim-Western relations: antagonistic, as not inevitable, 4; changes over time, effect on feminist views, 3–4

The Muslim Womanhood in Revolution (Zaidi), 158–59

Muslim women: early feminist views on, 36, 37–42; English women's encounters with (18th century), 46–52; as object of Western pity in late 20th century, 266–67; Western depictions of, in late 20th century, 251

Muslim women, feminism of: as distinct from Muslim identity, 2, 3; increased militancy, post–Cold War, 267; long history of, 2; and shadow of Western imperialism and racism, 9–10; Western views on good form of, 280–82

Muslim women, 17th–18th century Western views on: Abu Taleb's rebuttal of, 66–69; and limited first-hand information, 39–40; as negative ideal of middle-class European womanhood, 62; as oppressed compared to Western women, 33–36, 37–38, 60; playwrights challenging stereotype, 38–39; as soulless, in Muslim men's view, 36, 39, 40, 48, 61, 63

Muslim women, Western views on: impact on Muslim women's feminist struggle, 9; implications of 1871 census and, 114–15; as without rights, 2. *See also* Muslim oppression of women

Muslim women in Bengal: and anticolonial movement, 145, 166–67; anticolonial nationalism, 153; contact with women of other Muslim nations, useful ideas gleaned from, 175–76; early-20th century activism by, 126; in 18th century, education of, 31; in 18th century, expected submission of, 30–31; first to earn master's degree, 165; mounting

grievances of early 20th century, 144; nationalist-feminist writers of 20th century, 143–50; rejection of Western feminists as models, 149, 168, 197; support of swadeshi movement, 145–46, 150–53. *See also* publications by Muslim women

Muslim women in India: and All India Muslim Ladies' Conference, 136; divorce and child custody rights, 40, 99; prostitution, views on causes of, 114

Muslim Women's League, 267

Muslim women writers, *Saogat* (journal) as outlet for, 154–55

Muslim world, as term, 3

Mussalman (journal), 140

Mutual Defense Assistance Agreement of 1954, 186–87

Naari Shongothok, 288

Nabanoor (journal), 137, 145

Nabarawi, Saiza, 163

NACMW. *See* North American Council of Muslim Women

Nadiya, Shabnam, 257

Naidu, Sarojini, 157, 158

Najm-ud-daula: as son of Munni Begum, 32; and successor to Mir Jafar, dispute over, 31–32, 56

Narijati-Bishayak Prastab (Bahadur), 109

Naripokkho, 248, 259

nasihat namas (religious instruction manuals), women and, 75

Nasiruddin, Mohammad, 152, 154–55, 180

Nasreen, Taslima, 250–58; actions leading to public attention, 255; aggressiveness of, as potentially counterproductive, 256; appeal to women readers, 257–58; association with Salman Rushdie, 250, 254–55, 258; Bangladesh government republishing of *Statesman* interview, 258; condemnation of Islam and all religion, 253–54, 255, 256, 280–81; criticism of US policies, 281; departure from Bangladesh, 255; on exile in Germany, 250; failure to qualify as "moderate" Muslim in Western view, 281; global fame of, 254; government charge of offending religious sentiments, 254; inclusion on some lists of moderate Muslims, 280; Islamic groups' death sentence on, 250; larger political context of controversy over, 251–52, 258; letter-writing campaign in support of, as counterproductive, 254–55; *Lojja*, 250, 251, 253; media narrative on, 251, 252, 254, 255–56, 258; as medical doctor, 255–56; minimizing of Bangladesh's feminist movement, 280; *New York Times* interview, 250, 252; *Nirbachito Kolum*, 257; origins of hostility toward, 253–54; reasons for lesser fame in West, 280; refusal to support other women activists, 257; "Sentenced to Death," 250; *Statesman* interview, 253, 257; Tax's publicity agenda and, 252–53; on war on terror, 281; and Western view of Bangladesh, 250–51; women's movement's ambivalence about, 256

Nasrin, Taslima. *See* Nasreen, Taslima

Nasser, Gamal Abdel, 177

National Indian Association in Aid of Social Progress in India (NIA), 123

nationalist Bengali struggle: and Tagore birth celebration, 190–91, *191*; women in, 190–92

National Muslim University (Jamia Millia Islamia), New Delhi, 157

National Organization for Women (NOW), 201, 269

The Natural Claim of a Mother to the Custody of Her Children (Norton), 99

Nawab Faizunnesa Girls' School, 136

Naya Krishi Andolan (New Agriculture Movement), 245

Nazrul Islam, Kazi, 146, 150–51, 152

Negar. *See* Support of Women of Afghanistan

neoliberalism, and Bangladesh's turn to clothing manufacture, 243–44

New Agriculture Movement (Naya Krishi Andolan), 245

The New Atalantis (Manley), 39

New York Radical Women, 231

NGOs: in Eastern Europe, post–Cold War,

266; focus on women's education in late 20th century, 260; Islamists as threat to, 256; obstacles to women's work with, 256, 263

NIA. *See* National Indian Association in Aid of Social Progress in India

Nijera Kori (We Do It Ourselves), 256, 257

Nixon, Richard M., 201, 219–20

Nobi Bangsho (Sultan), 27

Non-Aligned Movement, 175, 208, 223

Noncooperation movement, Kamal and, 152

non-Western feminism: development in tandem with White Western feminism, 3, 4, 10; disagreements with Western feminism, 1–2. *See also* Eastern bloc feminists; Third World feminists

Noon, Firoz Khan, 174

Noon, Viqarunnessa, 174, *175*

Noor Jehan, 158

North American Council of Muslim Women (NACMW), 267

Northbrook, Lord, 116

Norton, Caroline Sheridan, 99–100

Norton, George, 99–100

NOW. *See* National Organization for Women

Nugent, Lady Maria Skinner, 57–58

Nur Jahan (Nur Mahal, Mughal empress): birth name of, 26; control over emperor, 20–21; control over trade, 21; first husband of, 25, 26; Hossain on, 142; seclusion of, 21–22; time in Bengal, 26

Nurjahan Begum, 180

"Nurse Nelly" (Hossain), 142

Nusrat Shah, 16

October War (1973), US support of Israel in, 216

off our backs (journal), 248

Oikyo Boddho Nari Shomaj (United Women's Forum), 248

Oriental Women's Congress (Damascus, 1930), 163

Original Letters from India (Fay), 88–89

Orme, Richard, 108

Ottoman Empire: dismemberment of, 128;

Ottoman Empire *(continued)*
  as representative of East for Europeans
  of 17th–18th centuries, 33
Oudh (Awadh), British annexation of, 93
*Our Moslem Sisters, a Cry of Need from
  Lands of Darkness* (1907), 126–27
"Our True Nature" (Rahman), 147
overpopulation: and development *vs.* contraception methods for stemming,
  214–15; feminist views on, 215; funding
  targeting, 215. *See also* Bangladesh, overpopulation in

Padmarag (Hossain), 135, 139
Pahlevi, Mohammad Reza (shah of Iran):
  Iran under, as modern Muslim society
  in US view, 216; meeting with Friedan,
  218; on polygyny, 216; reforms under,
  232; on women's liberation, 216, 218
Pakistan: Cold War allegiance of, 172–74;
  declining importance of Islam in status
  of women, 181; exchange students studying home economics in US, 188; factors shaping US policy on, 172–73; first
  cricket test match with India, 180–81;
  government suppression of Tagore, 191–
  92; Khan on ignorance and weakness
  of women in, 192–93; and leadership
  in Muslim world, 174–75; movement
  to create, 126, 166; Muslim world congresses hosted by, 175; Mutual Defense
  Assistance Agreement of 1954 with US,
  186–87; rush to establish higher education institutions, 188–89; and Soviet-
  brokered talks with India (1966), 203;
  turn toward Soviets (1965), 202–3;
  united (1947–71), groundwork for
  future feminism in, 6–7; and US foreign policy of 1940–50s, 172
Pakistan, creation of, 168; and Bengalis'
  separation by border, 169; and East–
  West tensions, 169–70, 171–72; Muslims remaining in India and Hindus in
  Pakistan, 169; Muslims' utopian dreams
  for, 169; and official language, conflict
  over (*bhasha andolon*), 170–72, 190; and
  population transfers, abuses of women
  in, 169; separation of two wings, 169

Pakistan, East: food crisis of 1947, 169–70;
  resentment against West Pakistan, 183;
  US aid in, 187; US-sponsored home economics college in, 187–88; and Western condescension, resentment of, 188;
  Western women visitors to, 179–83
Pakistan Academy for Rural Development
  (Comilla): Bengali women on staff of,
  196; Peace Corps volunteers in, 193–96,
  195; program for women, founding of,
  192–93; as success, in US view, 198;
  women's goals in, 197; and women vol-
  unteers as models, 196
Palestine, 160, 162, 63
Paley, Grace, 253
Palli Anganader Jemon Dekhechhi
  (Ahmed), 196–97
pan-Asian women's conference (Lahore,
  1931), 163
Panni, Sultana, 188–89
Papanek, Gustav, 223
Papanek, Hanna Kaiser, 223–24
Parishad, Mahila, 259
Parkes, Bessie Rayner, 102
Parkes, Charles Crawford, 89
Parkes, Fanny: criticism of Indian women's
  oppression, 91; criticism of British rule,
  93; and denaturalization of British culture, 95; empathy with Indian women,
  87, 91; enjoyment of India, 89; failure to
  question British rule, 88; on oppression
  of English women, 87, 91, 93; and outsider view of British culture, 92–93; on
  polygamy, 92; questioning of colonial
  power, 89; study of Urdu, 89; on widows,
  impositions on, 92; on women's education in India, 93; writings about travel in
  India, 87, 89–93; on zenanas, 90–91
Patterson, Tiffany, 226
Payam-e Zan (journal), 272
Peace Corps: effectiveness in winning
  hearts and minds, 194; filtering of
  applicants, 193; and Pakistan Academy
  for Rural Development program for
  women, 193–96, *195*; volunteers' lack of
  technical skills, 194; women in, critics
  of, 193; and women volunteers as models, 196

Pelsaert, Francisco, 22
Percy, Charles, 215
Pereira, Diogo, 16
Permanent Settlement of Land Revenues (1793), 74
Persian: as language of Indian court, 28; as language of Indian Muslim elite, 75, 130, 135; replacement by English as official language, 113
Persian Letters (Montesquieu), 35
Peterson, Esther, 199, 200
Philadelphia incident, 213
Physical Education in India (Salam), 108
Pires, Tomé, 15–16, 26–27
Pix, Mary, 38
Plackett, Kitty, 70
Planned Parenthood, and Afghanistan women, 269. *See also* International Planned Parenthood Federation
Plassey, Battle of, 29, 31
Policy Research for Development Alternative. *See* Unnayan Bikalper Nitinirdharoni Gobeshona (UBINIG)
polygamy: activism against, in East Pakistan, 183–86; Ameer Ali on, 125; defenders of, 185, 230; as diplomatic concern for UWS, 186; feminist activism against, 162, 163; as issue at IAW congress of 1935, 163; Montagu on, 40; and Muslim Family Law Ordinance of 1961, 186; Pakistani government commission on, 185–86; Pakistani women's views on, 183; Shah of Iran on, 216; as topic at women's world conference (Nairobi, 1985), 240; US misconceptions about, 188; Wollstonecraft on, 61
Pope, Alexander, 40–41
Popova, Nina, 203, 220
Portuguese: arrival in South Asia, 14, 16–17; attraction to wealth of India, 15, 16; in Bengal, 17th-century decline in, 28–29; early trade with Bengal, 16–17; limited government control over, 16–17; main settlement at Hooghly, Mughal attack on, 28–29; and Mughal court, first contact with, 19–20; Muslim complaints about, 18; trade dispute with Mughal empire, 21; views on Muslims, 14–15

Portuguese language, spread in Bengal, 17
Potts, Malcolm, 212
power relations, unequal: effect on emergence of feminism, 2, 4, 9; and travel restrictions, 8
Presidency College (Calcutta), 116
President's Commission on the Status of Women, 198, 199, 200
Prevost, Theodosia, 58–59
property rights of women: in Islamic law, 38, 40; and Married Women's Property Acts of 1870, 100; in West, coverture laws and, 38, 40, 96–97, 122
prostitution in India: and 1871 census, number of prostitutes identified in, 113; feminists' addressing of, 110; views on causes of, 113–14
publications by Muslim women, at turn of 20th century: *Bamabodhini Patrika* (periodical) and, 128–29; Chaudhurani's *Rupjalal*, 130, 131–32; earliest work by Bengali Muslim woman, 128; Hossain's "Sultana's Dream," 132; increase in, 128
public baths (hammam) in Muslim lands, Montagu on, 40–41
public sphere, women in, as goal of Western feminism in early 20th century, 161
Punch magazine, *103*, 106, *107*
Purchas, Samuel, 25
purdah (seclusion) of women: Abu Taleb on, 66; as claimed Muslim imposition, 124; debate on, in early 20th century, 159, 165; debate on, in East Pakistan of 1960s, 197; defenses of, 123; early reports on, 15; early-20th century women eschewing, 145; East Pakistani women's views on, 183; and education by tutors, 129–30; Eleanor Roosevelt on, 174; ending of, by Parsis in India, 138; Hossain and, 134; Jameelah on, 230; Mackenzie on, 94; Nazrul Islam on, 151; as obstacle to women's education, 116–18, 150; pleasant circumstances of, for elite families, 134; as secondary to larger issue of rights and freedoms, 165; Western women's obsession with ending, 181, 244; women's views on, as class-based,

purdah (seclusion) of women *(continued)*
197–98. *See also* harems and seraglios;
zenana *(antahpur;* women's quarters)

Quli Khan. *See* Khan, Kartalab (Murshid
Quli)
Qutb, Sayyid, 228

Rahim, Zeenath, 188
Rahimi (ship), 21
Rahimtoola, Begum Zubeida Habib, 203
Rahimunnesa, 31
Rahman, Masuda, 7, 146–47
Rahman, Sheikh Mujibur, 223, 243
Rahman, Ziaur, 243, 248, 251
Ramabai, Pandita, 119
Ramadan, Said, 228
Ramadan War, US support of Israel in,
216
Ramna Park, new year celebration in, 192
Rana Plaza, collapse of, 261, 274
"Rani Bhikarini" (Hossain), 143
rape: feminist activism against, 209–11;
wartime, recognition as crime against
humanity, 259. *See also* Bangladesh,
mass rapes of 1971
Rashid Khan, Abdur, 147
Rau, Dhanvanthi Rama, 162
Ravenholt, Reimert, 213
RAWA. *See* Jamiat-e-Enqilabi-e-Zanan-e-
Afghanistan
Razzaq, Abdul, 262–63
Reagan, Maureen, 239–40
Reagan, Ronald W., 244
"The Real Status of Women in Islam"
(Ameer Ali), 121, 124–25
regional feminist gatherings, in 1970s–80s,
242–43
Regional South and South East Asian
Women in Development Conference,
242, *242*
Rehman, Shafik, 255
Reichardt, Annie, 121, 124–25
religion: in Bengal, coexistence of, 27; Hos-
sain on, 137; Morgan on, 227; Nasreen
on, 253–54, 255, 256, 280–81
religious men of India, feminist criticisms
of, 146–47

religious movements, conservative, rise in
1980s, 239
Renaldi, Francesco, *67*
The Renegado (Massinger), 34
Revividus, Junius (William Bridges
Adams), 104
Revolutionary Association of the Women
of Afghanistan. *See* Jamiat-e-Enqilabi-e-
Zanan-e-Afghanistan (RAWA)
Reza Khan, Muhammad, 32, 56
Rich, Adrienne, 210
Richardson, David, 64, 66
Richter, Julius, 84
Rihla (Ibn Battuta): on Bengal econ-
omy and culture, 13–14; discussions of
women, 13; as first Western account of
Bengal, 7, 13; on harems, *12*; on objec-
tionable customs, 13; travels described
in, 13; on travel to Bengal to visit Shah
Jalal, 11–13
Risley, Herbert H., 144
Robinson, Jo Ann Gibson, 199
Robinson, Mary Darby, 63–64
Robinson, Ruby Doris Smith, 199
"Rocking the Casbah" (2004 *Newsweek*
article), 275–76
Roe, Thomas: as British representative in
Agra, 34; and British trade with India,
18; on Maryam Khan's return from Brit-
ain, 24–25; at Mughal court, 20–21; on
Nur Jahan, 21–22, 33; silk trade and, 25
Roosevelt, Eleanor: and President's Com-
mission on the Status of Women, 199;
on purdah, 174; and US-sponsored
home economics courses in Pakistan,
187; visit to Pakistan, 173–74, *175*
Roquiah Khatun. *See* Hossain, Rokeya
Sakhawat
Rosiak, Alberta, 195–96
Rossi, Alice S., 200–201
Rothman, Lorraine, 214
Rousseau, Jean-Jacques, 59
Roy, Rammohan: Adam and, 98; and
Brahmo Sabha (Brahmo Samaj), 80,
109; and Hindu College, 116; reform
efforts of, 80; and sati, efforts to elimi-
nate, 80–81; support for British dis-
placement of Muslim rule, 85–86

Shastri, Lal Bahadur, 203
Sheridan, Richard, 54, 56, 58
Shriver, Sargent, 193
Shuja ud-Daula, 56
Sidi Muhammad, 51–52
Signs (journal), 224
Sikandar Begam, 130
Singh, Karan, 214
Singh, Khushwant, 220
Sipilä, Helvi, 217–18
Siraj-ad-daula, 29, 31
Sirajganj Hosainpur Girls' High School, 145
Sisterhood Is Global (Morgan, ed.), 226–27
"Sisters Are Doing It for Themselves" (song), 1, 10
Slatter, Claire, *241*
slavery: British campaign against, 62; Wollstonecraft's familiarity with issue, 62
Smart, Jane, 46–47
Smith, Adam, 43
Smythe, Thomas, 21–22
SNCC. *See* Student Nonviolent Coordinating Committee
"The Social Position of Women" (Boyd-Kinnear), 105
Society for International Development, 207
South Asian Muslims: large number of, 5; 16th-century views on Christians, 18–19
South Asian Muslim women: international feminist alliances in early 20th century, 159–65; Western women's views on, in early 20th century, 159–61
Soviet Union, brokering of Pakistan and India talks (1966), 203
Soviet Union, efforts to win hearts and minds, 201; and competition for allegiance of developing world, 193–94; and first woman in space, 201–2, 204; women's equality and, 203, 204–5; wooing of Pakistan, 202–3
Soviet Women's Committee, *221*
Spirit of the Laws (Montesquieu), 35–36
Sprint, John, 35, 37
Stacey, George, 98
stadial theory of history, 42–43, 78; Abu Taleb on, 66; in Mill's *History of Brit-

ish India*, 77; missionaries and, 82; and Muslim responsibility for Indian decline, 85–87; and status of women, 42–43, 77, 78, 82, 85
Stanton, Elizabeth Cady, 98–99
Steele, Frances Webbe, 24–25
Steele, Richard, 24–25
Steinem, Gloria, 233–34
stewardesses, Pakistani, training in US, 189
Stock, Amy Geraldine "Dinah," 170–71
Storrow, Edward, 84, 114
Strachey, Rachel (Ray), 58, 155
"Strijatir Abonoti" (Hossain), 138, 142
Student Nonviolent Coordinating Committee (SNCC), and gender discrimination, 199–200
The Subjection of Women (Mill), 79, 100–101, 103–4, 118
Suez Canal crisis, 177, 180
"Sugrihini" (Hossain), 141–42
Suharto, 262
Suhrawardy, Hussain Shaheed, 136, 180
Suhrawardy, Obaidullah al-Obaidi, 136
Suhrawardy Girls' School, 136
Sukarno, 184
Sultan, Syed, 27
Sultan, Wafa, 277
"Sultana's Dream" (Hossain), 132, 141, 144
supercoil abortion method, 213
Support of Women of Afghanistan (Negar), 271
swadeshi movement (boycott of British goods), 128; feminists supporting, 145–46; leaders of, 134; rise of, 144
Swaraj (Self-Rule) Party, leaders of, 147–48
Swinton, Archibald, 44–45
Syed Nuruddin, 31
Syrian (Thomas) Christians, 18

Tagore, Rabindranath: Bengali nationalists' celebration of birthday, 190–91, *191*; and Sufia Hossain, 152
Tagore, Satyendranath, 118
Taheran Lessa (Taherannesa), Bibi, 129
Tanbih al-Nisa (Muhammad), 75
Tariqah-i-Muhammadiya movement, 73
Tax, Meredith, 252–53, 254, 255
Taylor, Harriet Hardy, 101–2, 104

"Waveland Memo," 200
Weaver, Mary Anne, 254, 255, 257
Webbe, Frances, 24–25
Wellesley, Marquess, 72
West: as concept in eastern Bengal, 7; as term, 3
Western feminism: and Bangladesh women's programs, condescension toward, 244–45; Buchanan on cultural effects of, 264; development in tandem with non-Western feminism, 3, 4, 10; disagreements with non-Western women, 1–2; early views on marriage, 36–38; early views on Muslim women, 36, 37–42; Eastern bloc feminists' rejection of, 219, 220–21; Egyptian feminists' resentment of condescension from, 237–38; and female circumcision, 233, 234–35, 237–38; feminists of color's expansion of issues addressed in, 285; and Islam, negative views of, 232–33; Jameelah's critique of, 230–32; limited impact of Muslim feminists' views on, 9–10; Muslim Bengali women's rejection as models, 149, 168, 197; Muslim critique of, 227, 230–32; Muslim feminists' resentment of condescension from, 268; Muslim feminists' views on, 3; Muslims' views on, 3; negative views of Islam, 232–33; obsession with female circumcision, 233; Third World feminists' critiques of, 219, 220–21, 223–27, 239; Third World feminists' resentment of condescension from, 232–33, 237–38, 240; turn to India in second half of 19th century, 110; views on Zionist women in Palestine, 160; and Western imperialism, 2; women in public sphere as goal of, 161
Western women visitors to East Pakistan, 179–83
Wheeler, Anna Doyle, 79
Whitaker, Jennifer, 224
White Western women, premature complacency of, 205–6
WIDF. *See* Women's International Democratic Federation
Wilberforce, William, 82

Winfrey, Oprah, 270
Withers, Robert, 40
WOI. *See* Women's Organization of Iran
Wollstonecraft, Mary: and all-female spaces, rejection of, 61; death of, 64; on Eastern traits in English society, necessity of purging, 63; English middle-class feminist ideology of, 42; and English virtues, defining in opposition to Eastern cultures, 63; familiarity with slavery issue, 62; and founding of Anglo-American feminism, 11; influence of, 88; Macaulay's influence on, 59; *Maria, or The Wrongs of Woman*, 53, 69; on oppressed Muslim women, 4–5; review of Gibbes's Hartly House, 58; on sexuality, as source of women's oppression, 60; *Vindication of the Rights of Men*, 58, 61–62. *See also* A Vindication of the Rights of Woman (Wollstonecraft)
Woman's Work and Women's Culture (Butler, ed.), 105
women, status in Muslim society: defenses of, 121–22, 123, 126; and stadial theory of development, 42–43, 77, 78, 82, 85
women and men, separate spheres for: antislavery and antisati movements antecedent to activism against, 98; comparison to harem seclusion, 105; economic consequences of, 97–98; efforts to spread across colonies, 98; as middle-class aspiration, 97
Women and the New East (Woodsmall), 181
"Women Are People Too" (Friedan), 199
Women: A World Report, 236–37
Women for Women, 248
women in Bengal: and 1871 census, number of prostitutes identified in, 113. *See also* Muslim women in Bengal
Women Living Under Muslim Laws, 241–42
"Women Need Equal Rights in 'Advanced' Nations, Too" (Mosby), 205–6
women "of the Book," as eligible to marry Muslim men, 19
Women's International Democratic Federation (WIDF), 201, 219, 220, 247

Women's Marches (January, 2017): aspects offensive to Muslim women, 285; causes of African American women's unhappiness with, 285; false embrace of Muslim women in, 285; poster of Muslim women with headscarf, 283, *284*; support for Muslim women at, 283

women's obligation to obey men, Western texts on (17th century), 35

Women's Organization of Iran (WOI), 217–19; and *gharbzadegi* (Westoxification), 218; government support of, 232; and poor women, 218–19; Western feminists hosted by, 217–18

women's place in Islam, Benazir Bhutto on, 265–66

women's political equality in India: activism for, 152–53; and limited female suffrage (1921), 153

women's rights: James Mill on, 78–79; as tool in US fight against global jihadism, 279–80

Women's Role in Economic Development (Boserup), 192, 215

women's suffrage in India: lag of English rights behind, 154; limited suffrage rights (1921), 153; Muslim men's opposition to, 153; political issues surrounding, 153–54

women's suffrage in Turkey, granting of, 162

Women's WORLD (Women's World Organization for Rights, Literature, and Development), 253

women visitors to India in early 20th century, 156–59

The Wonders of Vilayet (Ihtishamuddin), 44–46

Woodsmall, Ruth, 5, 156–57, 163, 181, 197

Woolf, Virginia, 145, 257

work by Bangladeshi women, feminists' focus on, in late 20th century, 261

World Bank, and Bangladeshi economic policy, 243, 245

World Conference on Human Rights (Vienna, 1993), 272

world conferences on women, UN-sponsored. *See under* UN Women's Conference

World Congress of Women (Moscow, 1987), 246–47

World Congress of Women (Moscow, 1963), 201–2

World Health Organization (WHO), and female circumcision, 233

World Population Conference (Bucharest, 1974), 214–15

Wortley, Edward, 39

Wright, Carolyne, 258

Yom Kippur War, US support of Israel in, 216

Yorkin, Peg, 268

YWCA, and Afghanistan women, focus on, 269

Zaidi, Syed M. H., 158–59

Zaman, Selina Bahar, 174, *175*, 190–91, *191*

al-Zamani, Maryam, 19, 21

zenana (*antahpur;* women's quarters): advocates for education in, 109, 150–53; Bamabodhini Sabha publications for, 128–29; education by tutors in, 129–30; education materials aimed at, 128–29; education of women in, 152; and fire, 49; missionaries' publications on, 72; as Muslim imposition, in some accounts, 124; and protection of women, 49–50; reports of British women on, 90–91, 93, 94–95; resistance to Christian influences, 84; violation of, as charge in Hastings trial, 54; women missionaries' focus on educating women in, 70, 83–84; women's zenana hospital, establishment of, 130. *See also* harems and seraglios

Zetkin, Clara, 202

Zheng Hu, 14

Zia, Khaleda, 251, 254, 258, 265

Zionist women in Palestine, Western feminists' views on, 160

uz-Zoha, Shams, 166

Founded in 1893,
UNIVERSITY OF CALIFORNIA PRESS
publishes bold, progressive books and journals
on topics in the arts, humanities, social sciences,
and natural sciences—with a focus on social
justice issues—that inspire thought and action
among readers worldwide.

The UC PRESS FOUNDATION
raises funds to uphold the press's vital role
as an independent, nonprofit publisher, and
receives philanthropic support from a wide
range of individuals and institutions—and from
committed readers like you. To learn more, visit
ucpress.edu/supportus.